William Foxwell Albright

WILLIAM FOXWELL ALBRIGHT
in his study at home, 1960's.

LEONA GLIDDEN RUNNING

DAVID NOEL FREEDMAN

WILLIAM FOXWELL
ALBRIGHT

A Twentieth-Century Genius

THE TWO CONTINENTS PUBLISHING GROUP, LTD.

MORGAN PRESS

Library of Congress Cataloging in Publication Data
Running, Leona Glidden, 1916-
William Foxwell Albright, a twentieth-century genius.
xi, 447p. ; 25cm. Includes index.
1. Albright, William Foxwell, 1891-1971.
I. Freedman, David Noel, 1922-   joint author.
II.   Title
BS1161.A39R86   950'.07'2024 [B]   75-11180
ISBN 0-8467-0071-9

Library of Congress Catalog Card Number 75-11180
ISBN 0-8467-0071-9

Printed in the United States of America
Production by Planned Production
Text Design by Ernst Reichl

The Two Continents Publishing Group, Ltd.
30 East 42 Street
New York 10017

Morgan Press

Contents

DEDICATED TO
the memory of
WILLIAM FOXWELL ALBRIGHT
one of the last of the "universals,"
a gentle soul as well as an erudite scholar,
Dean of Biblical Archaeology
in the twentieth century,

and to
RUTH NORTON ALBRIGHT
without whose half-century
of devotion and good sense
there would not have been any
Professor Albright, alive, famous,
and still productive in his many
scholarly fields up to the age of eighty.

Preface

On his fifty-eighth birthday, writing on behalf of a younger scholar whose stipends were in danger of being cut off, Professor William F. Albright called first-class scholars rarities that any nation ought to foster and not to neglect, deluded by the idea that they could be replaced or rendered unnecessary by mass production. He himself eminently exemplified this rare value in his own career.

The novelist Henry James, referring to the death of the poet Robert Browning, said: "We possess a great man most when we begin to look at him through the glass plate of death."[1] Some of us may wish to disagree with James's opinion. But we have no choice, and we can find great value in now seeing William Foxwell Albright and his lifework in the whole.

It was the author's privilege to be a graduate student of, and in the latter six years of his life to work closely as editorial assistant with, one of the greatest minds and personalities of the twentieth century—Professor Albright, world-recognized Dean of biblical archaeologists. This biography is a labor of love undertaken in grateful homage by a devoted disciple toward a revered teacher—yet at the same time a genuine attempt to present objectively the man as he really was, letting him speak for himself. His life, character, personality and career deserve to be understood far beyond the wide circle of his scholarly colleagues and his students, now recognized scholars in their own right.

William Albright's later life and especially his career are quite well known, but only the barest facts have been known about his childhood and family life in his earliest years. Those still available family members and friends, mostly now in their seventies and eighties, who were closest to him, have recorded their recollections, and the story will be unfolded often in their own words to supply the missing foundational period. This method follows in the earlier time Boswell's injunction not to "melt down" the materials. But from the beginning of Albright's archaeological career on, in the words of Leon Edel concerning Henry James, "the contemporary biographer is forced, by the mere dead weight of paper, by the mountains of letters and journals and newspapers [plus, in Albright's case, voluminous publications], to melt his materials or be smothered by them."[2] However, since Albright published non-technical condensed reports of his work for a wider audience than his professional colleagues, and since his work and his life cannot be separated, he can be allowed to tell the story in his own (published) words, to a great extent. It is impossible to relate Albright's life story without mention of his colleagues and other facets of Biblical archaeology. Thus his story becomes also, in miniature, the story of biblical archaeology in Albright's career span, though space forbids its full narration. What is presented is a representative sampling of the vast output of this amazingly productive scholar, chosen to reveal his thinking and ideas, as well as the main events and activities of his life.

The author wishes to make clear that this is not an "authorized," family-censored biography, but the kind anyone is free to write of a well-known public figure. Thirty honorary doctorates and six decade-folders of newspaper clippings filed in the Alumni Records office at The Johns Hopkins University are ample attestation of what a well-known person he was. No direct quotations have been made from his unpublished papers, but information from them has been used and sometimes they have been paraphrased.

Speaking in a class in History of the Second Millennium B.C. in his last year of teaching before retirement, Professor Albright remarked that a historian has no right, *as historian*, to make value judgments. As *didactic* writer and as *biographer*, yes, he does have that right. He expressed doubts about the biographical method of Lytton Strachey and André Maurois, who psychologically reconstructed the character and motives of the hero and his personality; he did not think that truly possible. "Biography becomes *history* only as the hero is an important figure affecting many lives, and the account is accurate," he stated. He did not believe that the *life* of men does not matter but only their *work*. And he tended to think, he added, that "it is important to find out about *Mrs.* Dickens in order to judge *Charles* Dickens!"

Grateful acknowledgement is here expressed to Professor Albright's family, his brothers, sisters and cousins, his many former students, colleagues, and friends, who assisted the author by interviews and letters, and who will often be named in connection with their contributions; also to Mrs. Elsie Leight, manager, and Mrs. Susan Tozer, assistant manager, in the Johns Hopkins Alumni Records Office, and to Mrs. Edna C. Goodall, in the Frieda C. Thies Manuscript Room at Johns Hopkins, all of whom have been most graciously helpful in the author's search for materials.

The author expresses appreciation also to the Research Committee of the American Philosophical Society for a grant that helped meet some of the expenses of traveling and gathering materials, and to the administration of Andrews University, Michigan, for a sabbatical leave of a term in 1972 for the purpose of collecting materials and beginning the writing. Lastly, a great amount of recognition is due the genial co-author, Professor David Noel Freedman, of the University of Michigan, whose contributions, wisdom and assistance in gathering materials, especially from fellow scholars; in critically reading the various drafts and making helpful suggestions; and in many other ways, have been indispensable. His decades of collaboration with Professor Albright make him an integral part of the Albright story.

Leona Glidden Running

William Foxwell Albright

1

Childhood and School Days

A slim seven-year-old boy with crippled left hand peered nearsightedly out through the patio gateway. The cobbled street of La Serena, the "city of flowers," a cathedral town in Chile several miles up around the bay from the port city, Coquimbo, seemed clear of black-robed figures and taunting children. The street urchins often called him *gringo* and *canuto* (Protestant) and sometimes threw stones at him. He had already been well spanked for shrinking back from going into the street on an errand for his parents. Now William had screwed up his courage. After another myopic squint into the world beyond the patio wall, he dashed out and accomplished his assignment.

Three years later as a tall ten-year-old in 1901 in the seaport town of Antofagasta, at the edge of the Atacama Desert far north in Chile, William had a more persuasive incentive than whippings to drive him into the stone-paved streets on errands. His parents had told him that if he would fetch the bread from the bakery, thus saving the cost of delivery, he could have that money and save it to buy something he greatly desired. What young William wished for more than anything else in the whole world was the two-volume *History of Babylonia and Assyria* recently published by Professor R. W. Rogers of Drew University! Thus was William Albright launched on his lifelong study and career.

Why was this North American boy in Chile? How had his left hand become crippled? What forces had shaped his mind up to the age of ten, that he should so covet, and then devour and absorb, a book on ancient history? Why did he fear that by the time he grew up there would be nothing left in Palestine to discover or to excavate? In his lifetime he would accomplish wonderful things in the Near East—the Bible Lands.

Years later William looked back on the striking contrasts of the world in which this sensitive boy had spent his childhood years— the contrast between the towering Andes to the east, which prevented his ever seeing a sunrise, and the vast, thundering Pacific rolling into the western distance. In many ways the climate was similar to that in which he would later live in Palestine, the rainy season alternating with the long dry one, with the rainless desert very near. In addition, there was a similar contrast in both lands between the lot of the Chilean *peon* and the Arab *fellah* on the one hand, and the urban, landowner and business class on the other. The presence of ethnic hostility—and, to this child of Methodist missionaries, religious hostility—was another characteristic of both his first homeland and his later beloved Palestine.

Who was William Albright? He was one of the last of the "universals," men gifted and competent in many fields who left a permanent impress on their own and following generations. And he was an outstanding example of a person who, in attempting to compensate for great physical handicaps, overcompensates and becomes a genius. As we shall see, his handicaps originated in his childhood and turned him into unusual channels of interest and activity. The result was the formation of a precocious historian and linguist who nevertheless had a deepseated inferiority complex and frequently despaired of ever accomplishing anything worthwhile (at the same time he was producing phenomenal accomplishments). Not long after he was launched in his career of research and teaching, he was acknowledged by scholars in many countries as one of the leading orientalists. Before his eighty years were half over he was a leader in a group of archaeologists in British-mandated Palestine who were bringing to the fore a new discipline, Biblical Archaeology. By careful archaeological excavations and historical and linguistic studies they were correlating secular with biblical materials, with the result that the higher-critical and artificial views of Julius Wellhausen and his school, dominant since the latter part of the nineteenth century, were in retreat. William Albright literally turned biblical studies around and gave them a new direction.

Always both a scientist and an idealistic humanist, in his later years Albright was the acknowledged "Dean of Biblical Archaeologists" and was surrounded by a loyal group of students who had caught inspiration as well as sound methodology from him and continued his work into ever-expanding horizons. He himself remained at the forefront in all his fields up to the very last. For sixty years he was well known in many circles, and many outstanding honors were heaped upon him. By his prolific writings he dominated his constellation of scholarly fields; in his books that reached a wider audience, translated into many languages and selling into the scores of thousands, and his lectures to school and church groups, his influence spread among ordinary people who were not scholars or specialists. It is an amazing and inspiring life.

In his later years William loved to assert the claim that his ancestors had been "Cornish pirates and Hessian soldiers." The truth is not quite so dramatic, however. His mother's line, the Foxwells, went back at least to 1716, to landowners in Cornwall, England. His great-grandfather was born in 1761 in Mullion parish on the fertile peninsula called "The Lizard," jutting farthest south into the English Channel not far east from Land's End. A Methodist lay preacher for more than half a century, largely self-taught, this William Foxwell played the violin and the flute, enjoyed such studies as astronomy, mathematics and botany, knew simple herbal medicine, taught himself Greek and Latin after he was thirty, and owned much land in Cornwall. His sixth child of nine, born in 1812, was named Thomas Harris Foxwell.

Thomas emigrated to America in 1843 and settled in Racine County, Wisconsin, where some of his brothers and sisters had already bought farms. After Thomas's first wife died in 1845, he tried to win one of her sisters back in Cornwall, but returned to America and did not find a wife until 1852. Then he married a young, beautiful school teacher, Frances Humphry, who with her family had come from Cornwall ten years earlier. Their children were the Aunt Katie, Aunt Mollie, Aunt Lottie, Uncle Stephen, and Aunt Ella of the lad in Chile. Their fourth daughter Zephine (a shortened form of Josephine, and her real name) Viola Foxwell, born August 31, 1861, became the mother of William.

In the late summer of 1863, shortly before Stephen Humphry Foxwell was born, Thomas and Frances sold their farm in Caledonia, Wisconsin, to a relative and moved with their four girls straight west to 360 acres they bought in Fayette County, Iowa—

beautiful hilly country in the northeastern corner of the state. Thomas's partner in a sawmill business in Wisconsin had taken all the funds and departed, leaving Thomas with all the debts. He hoped in Iowa to rebuild his financial situation. But seven years later he died of blood poisoning, leaving Frances with six children under sixteen. She rented the farm out for about nine years, until Stephen turned sixteen and was able to take over its management. As the sisters began teaching school they helped repay the debts, finally paying heirs of creditors who had died, until all were paid in full. Because of this stubborn Cornish Methodist honesty, college education was not possible, much as Zephine desired it; but women in those days could teach school without it.

The children grew up on practically adjoining farms with the large family of William Kincaid Allbright. (The tombstones in the Illyria cemetery show two l's in the Allbright name.) With his wife Anna he had moved ten years earlier, in 1853, to an eighty-acre farm, also in Illyria Township, Fayette County. He was an occasional preacher, son of a John Christian Allbright whose ancestors may possibly be traced back to immigrants from Germany a half-century before the American Revolutionary War. The tradition among Christian's descendants that his father, John Albright, was a Hessian soldier in that war, captured at the Battle of Trenton, seems to have been disproved by the findings of two women who, in researching their own Albright ancestries during the 1960's, met each other. Joining forces, they found their lines apparently converging with that of Professor Albright, and learned that Christian's father was a Berks County, Pennsylvania, boy whose grandfather Johannes Albrecht had immigrated in 1732 from near Bingen-on-the-Rhine, rather than John's being a mercenary Hessian soldier.

The survivors among William and Anna Allbright's twelve children were our William's Aunt Jane, Aunt Hannah, Uncle Philip, Aunt Emmeline, Uncle Albert, and Uncle Charles. The tenth child, born October 11, 1859, was Wilbur Finley, who became William's father. Professor Albright was never fully persuaded, himself, that he could be sure of anyone as being related, farther back than his great-grandfather Christian Allbright, the first to be buried (in 1880) in the Illyria cemetery.

Wilbur was graduated from Upper Iowa University in Fayette, then a Methodist school, with the A.B. degree in 1885. A Military

Department was organized in his senior year and its first roster of cadets lists Wilbur F. Allbright as lieutenant. After graduation Wilbur went to Garrett Biblical Institute near Chicago for graduate study, but, his finances coming to an end, he soon left. He was pastor of several churches in northeastern Iowa, and while serving at Monona received an honorary A.M. from UIU, such as was then awarded to persons "holding the Bachelor's degree of three years standing."

Wilbur and Zephine were married on November 9, 1887, by Wilbur's father in the log house on the Foxwell farm. Wilbur was tall, slim, straight-backed, with dark hair, dark complexion, hazel eyes, mustache and a small beard. Zephine was short, blue-eyed, with rather high round cheekbones, dark hair combed close to her head, and a very sweet face. They were earnest Christians and strict Methodists. And in the family lines of both, those who survived into adulthood, as the great majority did, lived to an advanced age.

Wilbur and Zephine continued in parish work in Iowa for a couple of years after their wedding. Then they applied to Bishop William Finley Taylor, of the Methodist Episcopal Mission Board, to go abroad as members of a self-supporting mission, as it seemed that they would not have any children and thus could undertake such work. Immediately, the Board appointed them to go to Chile, the Rev. Albright to be head of a boys' school in the copper-port town of Coquimbo on the fertile central coast, north of the middle of Chile's long coastline. First they were assigned to Valparaiso, some 300 miles farther south, for a few months of Spanish language study, but they began learning Spanish on the ship going down from New York—easy for both, as they already knew Latin.

Spanish was not all they learned on shipboard; Zephine learned that she was pregnant. Before the first-born arrived they left Valparaiso and located at the Coquimbo boys' college. There William Thomas Albright, named in Cornish fashion after his two grandfathers, was born on May 24, 1891. (It was about twenty years later that he took Foxwell for his middle name instead of Thomas, partly because an Iowa boy cousin turned him against his given name by teasingly calling him "Bill Tom." Wilbur's early pronouncement was: "He is not to be Willy nor Will, Billy nor Bill, but *William!*")

One can imagine the joy that this longed-for, unexpected, despaired-of child brought to his parents, isolated in a foreign mission field far from their families. However, a cloud soon came over their happiness. Zephine wrote home that she was worried about "poor little William." At between two and three years of age he had a severe case of typhoid fever, and his mother later thought that his eyes had been injured then.

The family lived in the boys' school and the father continued as its head for three years. Having early come to the conviction that he must be a preacher, he also preached during the second and third years as appointed pastor of the English congregation at Coquimbo. Not long after he began work in Chile he spoke Spanish so well that he was often taken for a native Chilean (his dark complexion and tan from much outdoor activity helping), although he was unusually tall for a native. His success in preaching soon made it necessary for him to build a church. The church building, still in use by the Methodist congregation, stands on a hillside at the corner of Melgarejo and Benavente Streets.

After their second son, Paul Foxwell Albright, was born August 8, 1893, in Coquimbo, Wilbur was received by the Methodist Episcopal Church in 1894 and transferred to its South American Conference. Then he was appointed as pastor of the Spanish church at La Serena, a cathedral town and provincial capital using Coquimbo as its port on Guayacán Bay. It is located in the area where there are frequent and often severe earthquakes. At first the family lived in an old Spanish townhouse, or "mansion," as Zephine called it, with the church on the main floor and the parsonage on the second floor. There was an enclosed patio in which little William could play, and Zephine was creative in teaching him. He had learned to read soon after the age of two, before the attack of typhoid fever. When Zephine was busy caring for his new little brother Paul, William became bored one day and did not know what to do. His mother, realizing that she needed to show some attention to him also, said, "Come, William, let's play some games."

She led him out into the patio, gathered some stones, and said, "Let's play 'David and Goliath.'" They played the biblical story dramatically with the stones. William was delighted. He wanted to play other stories, and later went on to dramatize battles of ancient history. He grew up spending much time reading in his father's library, which contained mainly history and theology volumes, and then going out and dramatizing what he had read with stones in the patio. As his brothers and sisters well remembered, he had one special stone that looked like a tortoise shell, which he called King Tortoise. He kept it for many decades as a talisman. This was the leader of the armies of Sennacherib and other military heroes whose battles William rehearsed and reconstructed with armies of stones in their Chilean patios. The other children had to be very careful not to step on his "armies" and disarrange them.

At La Serena Wilbur again had good success and soon needed to provide a larger church building. Their third son, Finley Raymond, was born on June 4, 1895, at the old Alameda Street parsonage. In November of that year Wilbur printed a sheet to send "To the Protestants and Foreigners in Chile," appealing for funds with which to build a new church. His eloquent appeal must have brought good results, and perhaps the furlough that the family enjoyed in 1896 gave Wilbur an opportunity to raise money in the Methodist churches of Iowa to help build the mission church in La Serena. The new church of adobe blocks was built in the worst part of the town, not because that was the only place where a Protestant preacher could buy property, but because Wilbur felt that section needed a church the most. On account of the undesirable surroundings, there was a walled-in patio connected with the parsonage. The church was dedicated early in 1899.

William turned five on May 24, while the family was on furlough in Iowa. During haying season that summer tragedy occurred while he was closely watching the machine putting hay up into the haymow on his Grandmother Foxwell's farm. The machine employed many pulleys. The nearsighted little boy, seeing something moving upward, caught hold of it with his left hand to bring it near and look at it. But it was the moving, taut rope of the pulley, and it burned the flesh and ligaments off the inner side of his fingers as it drew his hand up into a pulley.

The injured boy was taken by buggy about ten miles from the farm to the home of Zephine's oldest sister Catherine, "Aunt Katie" Richards. "Cousin Bessie" Richards Shaffer at the age of 89 recalled seeing little William laid out on her mother's dining-room table while a doctor was being fetched from West Union, four miles away, by buggy; they had no telephone. The doctor formed a tin mitten as a splint for the injured hand, to try to straighten it and to protect it as it healed. But the hand healed curled up and restricted, and for many years it was the cause of anxiety—he always feared it would catch in something and cause an accident. Not until many years had passed and he had an operation that somewhat straightened the tightly curled little finger was that anxiety relieved, though the hand was not made much more useful. He really felt himself crippled from the age of five.

A few months later the family returned to La Serena, and soon afterward, on May 13, 1897, Mary, the fourth child, was born at the Alameda Street parsonage before the new church and parsonage were built. One of Mary's first memories was the sight of William's crippled left hand and the metal form.

Thus barred by his nearsightedness and his useless left hand from active sports and games, William occupied his time by ever more voracious reading in his father's library, and by his solitary games with armies of stones. Also there was schooling of a more formal kind. His first school outside of home was Mrs. Hislop's, a primary school at La Serena conducted by a missionary's wife for a few foreign families.

Soon after the family moved into the parsonage connected with the newly built church on Calle Benavente in La Serena, the fifth child and second girl, Shirley Constance, was born on March 10, 1899. All the children seemed to resemble Zephine, with round high cheekbones; William and Mary especially resembled her in the lower part of the face, with close, even teeth. Shirley had her father's hazel eyes; the rest had their mother's big blue eyes. Mary and William resembled their father in being tall and slim.

Mary described her father as "a believer in the idea that children were born without sin, and sin came to them only through contact with the evil world. Therefore he wished to keep his babies absolutely from contact with the evil world. That's why we were shut up in patios. Everything was censored that we read; and that's why William was spanked so much—Father said that the first child had to be kept straight and disciplined so as to be sure that the rest would be good. He must be an example to the others. William was the one who was spanked." The mother admitted to Mary years later, "Your father didn't believe in sin except as you came in contact with evil forces, but *I believe in original sin!*" She had closer contact with her little imps.

Philip Ninde, the youngest, named for one of their bishops in Chile, was born on March 6, 1901, again at Coquimbo. The father had been appointed to the pastorate in Antofagasta, about 600 miles north, the main port city for shipments of copper and nitrates mined in the Atacama Desert between the coast and the Andes. Perhaps Zephine, nearly at the end of her final pregnancy, worked too hard packing to move. From La Serena they had to take the local train to Coquimbo, twelve kilometers south, to embark; the main north-south transportation was by ship.

By the time the family reached Coquimbo and before they could embark, it became obvious that the child would be born very soon. They found refuge in the home of fellow Methodist missionaries. Mary, nearly four, and Shirley, almost two, were put to sleep in the first church their father had built, as there was not enough room in the attached parsonage. Mary became terrified as dogs began barking in the night. She started to cry, and her father came and carried her into the room where her mother lay, saying, "I want to show you something." He turned back the covers. "This is your little brother!"

"No, he isn't! I don't have a little brother!"

The next morning young Fremont and Marian Harrington were furious because a baby had been born in their house and it wasn't theirs. They refused to play with Mary and Shirley. Mary said to them, "Well, you can have him, 'cause *we don't want him!*" She often jokingly told Philip that she gave him away the day he was born.

When mother and baby could travel, the family took ship and went up the coastline to Antofagasta, trading earthquake dangers for scarcity of water. The children afterward remembered the borax, copper and nitrate mines, and also the buying of water. It is hot, barren, dry country; no rain ever falls on the Atacama Desert, and little on the coast even in the winter, July and August. The first trees and shrubs in the plazas were planted in earth brought as ballast in ships from Europe. Water is now piped from the Andes, but at the turn of the century it was brought by muleback. The boys had to count the pails of water that were carried in from containers on burros' backs and poured into the rainbarrel. Learning to save water (the family from baby up to father used the same Saturday-night bathwater in succession) was good training for William and Mary, both of whom would later live in Palestine.

By this time William constantly taught Mary and the younger ones not only bookish things but all kinds of practical things. He showed her how to be meticulous and accurate about everything from cutting out pictures to washing between the tines of every fork, and gave her a love for mathematics. The microbe theory was known by this time to the family in Chile, and William frequently washed his hands. One time on a trip to the bakery he saw a live chicken hopping and pecking in the bread-trough, and came home so horrified about the microbes that he refused to eat any more bakery bread. His mother baked their bread from then on with the help of a young, half-orphaned half-Scottish girl, Winnie, who worked for them and lived with them to learn English ways.

Another helper was a Danish sailor, Karl Hansen, who jumped ship, was stranded, and whom Wilbur brought home to live with the family for a while. Karl taught William his first German, thereby giving him a lifelong Scandinavian accent in German.

By the time William at the age of ten could no longer bear to eat the bakery bread, he had saved enough money from running errands to send the necessary $5.00 to America for R. W. Rogers' *History of Babylonia and Assyria*. When the two volumes arrived, the parents decided, with very poor psychology but knowing they would not have much money to spend on Christmas gifts, that the coveted set of books made a nice Christmas present for William. It was held back from him until Christmas time, although he had earned it—a fact which he never forgot. Finally at Christmas he could begin to enjoy and absorb it. Fortunately this was no dull chronicle, but a lively, well-written, up-to-date account of the intrinsically fascinating decipherment of long-dead languages, explorations of long-unknown lands, and beginning of archaeological research in them. Their history followed, from earliest times to the end of the Neo-Babylonian Empire, written in a way that gripped the attention and enthralled the imagination of young William.

At Antofagasta William attended an English boys' school run by a Mr. Herbert, where, as Mary recalled, "he learned mainly meanness and came home to beat up his younger brothers and sisters as though that was the accepted thing to do." So the parents removed him from that school after two months and he continued studying at home. A history notebook in William's childish handwriting remained among his mother's cherished keepsakes. It contained paragraphs on historical topics from various Indian tribes of the U.S. and early discoveries by many nations, to Colonial history and economic data. The gray-covered notebook, tied with a black shoestring, formed part of a teaching method of oral recitation followed by written summaries.

William, after listening to many years of his father's sermons, carried into adulthood a strong ethical sense, a bent toward logical thinking and conservative, frugal living, and an interest in uplifting depressed or degraded groups, even though he would later have to free himself from some excessive narrowness.

Years later, as William looked back on these years, he recalled how much safer he had felt in the more cosmopolitan mining center and seaport of Antofagasta than in La Serena; but there in the north he became even more aware of persecution of minority persons in nearby Bolivia and Peru. A Protestant missionary's life was not worth much. His later great interest in the problems of minorities stemmed from this early period. He considered his mother's home school very successful, and appreciated the stylistic foundation gained from devouring *Don Quixote* and Shakespeare, Tennyson, Becquer, and much reading of all types of history. From polemic religious literature he found in the home library he developed a strong anti-Catholic attitude, reinforced by the persecutions carried on in those areas by an ignorant medieval Catholicism very different from that found today. His early evangelical religious ideas included a large element of antialcoholism and hygiene necessitated in missionary work because of the lack of understanding of health and sanitation in those areas at that time.

Poor health resulting from severe illnesses finally forced Wilbur Albright to take his family back to the States. He contracted typhoid fever and nearly died; later he had pneumonia in such a severe form that Mary and Finley were sent elsewhere to stay, because they were at the noisiest age. After thirteen years of mission service Wilbur returned to Iowa.

The old Allbright farm, after William Kincaid Allbright's death in 1897, was sold to Zephine's eldest sister Katie and her husband (a first cousin), Tom Richards. Wilbur and his family at first stayed at the home of his sister Emmeline, then made headquarters at Grandmother Frances Foxwell's farm where Wilbur and Zephine had been married. Aunt Mollie, Aunt Ella, and Uncle Stephen still lived there in the twelve-year-old second house, successor to the original log cabin, with their mother, the girls teaching school (Aunt Lottie had married).

Aunt Mollie took Finley and Mary along to her school. William and Paul continued studying with their mother; the rest were too young for classes. Shirley remained at home until seven, and felt too big when she finally started to go to school with younger classmates.

When their father was assigned to the church at Dumont and the family moved there, William attended school regularly, a loner, unable to see well enough to engage in sports. The next year the family moved to Rudd and spent an unhappy year in that pastorate. They were foreigners in their own country, so regarded by Mid-westerners and their children.

At the next parish, Plainfield, they spent two years and William attended high school. He then obtained his first glasses. Finally they had discovered that he could not see anything written on a blackboard. When studying at home, much of the work had been with books and talking, with no need to use a blackboard. Another family memory is that soon after they returned from Chile William's mother took him to the University at Dubuque to have his eyes tested and the doctor said, "Take books away from him!"

When the school year closed just as William turned fifteen, his father sent him to work on the farm of one of his church members for the summer. The next year the family moved to Fayette, where Upper Iowa University was located, and nearer Grandmother Fox-well. Later in life William would look back on his Cornish grand-mother's home as an oasis in the dreary life he led with his family during his teens, moving from one drab parsonage to another in dusty prairie towns. The unhappiness of those intellectually un-inspiring surroundings almost blotted out their memories from his mind.

Perhaps there was something about the set-up of the Methodist Church organization, or maybe some professional jealousy, not wanting to make room for a minister returned from the mission field, or perhaps some lack on Wilbur's part (being strong-willed and rather dogmatic and independent). In any case, Wilbur Albright was put into situations where he had to ride circuit on horseback in bitter winter weather, after having had those severe illnesses. He concluded that with a family to support he simply could not continue preaching. The only way he could see to make a living was to claim land then being offered by the government in the Dakotas, and settle it. He moved his family into a small house that he bought in Fayette, and took Paul with him to Stanley County in the middle of South Dakota, for the three required years of living on their claim. Finley became a "printer's devil" and worked on the local newspaper to help support the family. William also lived at home and with Finley helped with the garden and cows and a few chickens.

At first William attended the "Senior Academy" preparatory department in Upper Iowa University. Already at the age of sixteen he began teaching himself Hebrew on Sundays, using his father's old copy of William Rainey Harper's inductive textbook. The school, which was Methodist until 1928, occupied a fine large building on a hill to the east side of Fayette, with a Ladies' Hall to the right or south, and behind that a chapel and a small observatory. Today as a private college it has many large new buildings. Its symbol is the peacock, featured on murals and giving its name to the yearbook three years after William's graduation. His cousin Jessie said sixty years later, "We were all 'peacocks' "—that is, students of UIU.

In summers William worked on his Grandmother Foxwell's farm, a lovely place where he was treated like a beloved grandson and coddled by his two aunts and his uncle. The children all recalled them as very loving people. They paid William for his work, and he thus learned more about farm work. His mother took in a niece to go to college during the years they lived in Fayette; she paid about two dollars a week for board and room.

When William looked back on this time he thought it fortunate for his development that his parents had been extremely poor, earning usually no more than $400 cash in a year on which to support a family of eight. He had to do manual labor when out of school, and found his crippled hand becoming stronger and more useful—even for milking cows, though perhaps not to the cow's satisfaction, as he used to say. From fifteen on he worked on farms during the summer and became physically strong as well as knowledgeable about agriculture. He considered that having to work his way through college had benefited him by depriving poverty of any terror, and training him wholesomely for later life experiences. In spite of his characteristic pessimism, William always could put the most favorable construction on events once they had happened.

In the year 1909-10 William became a sophomore in college. Physics and math were his favorite subjects, along with biological sciences and finally history and philosophy of science. While his father and Paul were still in South Dakota, William neared the end of his college work as the youngest in the class. The 1912 yearbook missed out in its predictions of future success, calling another student the youngest and the most promising to become a genius and a great success. William had no social life. While he earned excellent grades, he told his mother each day that he had flunked. This worried her terribly, and foreshadowed the habitual pessimistic viewpoint of the later scholarly William, who would claim (like Ralph Waldo Emerson) that such an attitude spared him many disappointments and provided many happy surprises.

Their father found himself unable to move his family to Stanley County, South Dakota, because his land was without water. He sold it and returned with Paul, driving a hundred head of cattle (as Finley vividly recalled) from the railway station at Lima out to a farm he rented and to which he moved his family from Fayette in 1911. William continued in college for his senior year, living with Finley in the upstairs of their Fayette house, with an elderly couple renting the downstairs. Finley worked mornings and evenings at Mr. Payne's printing office and attended high school. Their mother would send food to them on the weekend; William cooked oatmeal for the two of them mornings. Finley earned nothing during a six months' apprenticeship, and then started at five cents an hour with no regular paydays.

Before the family moved from Fayette to Lima, Zephine noticed in the Methodist church on Sundays that a young student in the college came to meet William in the aisles and hung around cheerfully as if he wanted to make friends. His name was Sam Geiser, and the mother wished to encourage the friendship, but at first had little success. During his senior year when William was twenty, Sam finally got through to him. Sam was very outgoing and wanted to make William over in his image, so he began tutoring him socially. There came a tremendous change in William that year. They went to ballgames and he rooted until he couldn't speak aloud; they went to parties and he did everything the rest did. He enjoyed life socially for the first time.

A classmate, Lula Hurd, recalled decades later as widowed Mrs. Blunt "the way he looked when he came onto the campus with thick glasses, and the way he matured there and got to dressing better." His cousins also remembered that at first his clothes were "very crude," with sleeves and pantlegs never long enough for his Lincolnesque frame. As a language major, Lula was in William's Latin and Greek classes. In Latin class William habitually studied his Greek lesson, and when called on to recite, nudged Lula and whispered, "Where's the place?" She showed him and then he recited flawlessly. Mrs. Blunt also enthusiastically remembered Sam Geiser and knew that he had continued as a lifelong friend of William Albright.

Another special friend of his was Emerald Robbins, who used to come over to their upstairs living quarters in the Fayette house and study math with William. "But he had no friends among the coeds except finally Maud Adams," Finley said much later—or was it Maude Stevens?

About that time William and Sam and one or two others with their beloved religion teacher, Dr. Danny Parker, formed the "Genius Club." Finley hand-set their articles at the printing office, and later said he found only one spelling mistake in William's articles—to which he was happy to call his brother's attention.

William Albright's first published article was one on archaeology which he wrote for the Genius Club on "Recent Discoveries at Elephantine." It appeared in 1911 in the Upper Iowa Academician, a paper temporarily issued by the Genius Club and hand-set by Finley.

In his senior year William entered an oratorical competition for some literary prizes. He and Finley would go out to the river-bank just north of town, and William would practice his speech with Finley acting as coach and critic, making him project his soft voice. "I thought it quite an honor to be able to tell my older brother how his speech was coming on!" commented Finley years later. William did not win any prize, but the family had reason later to think of the speech he wrote and memorized and practiced with Finley in the woods by the river. The judges said William was crazy—what he had put forth in his oration would never happen; there would never be another war in Europe!

Decades later William looked back at the narrow cultural horizon of the small college but valued the good education he nevertheless secured there in mathematics, Greek and Latin. In other classes one could get by on mere bluff (so that he had time to do manual work to earn his way), but he had the sense to concentrate on the solid subjects in which standards were high and teaching of good quality. With the help of the small scholarship at the start, he completed college work in the minimum time, which probably he could not have done at a more prestigious (and expensive) school.

2

"W. T. Albright, Prin., Menno, S. D."

After graduation from college with his A.B. in June of 1912, William accepted a position as principal of a high school in Menno, a German-speaking town in the southeastern corner of South Dakota, straight west from Fayette. Now he began to show himself as a wonderful correspondent, writing regularly to his mother or his father and occasionally to one of the other children.

The weekly *Hutchinson* [County] *Herald* published by J. S. Headley, in its fragile old pages of the huge bound volume for 1912, which in April carried stories and pictures of the sinking of the *Titanic,* on September 19 reported that "the second week of school opened most auspiciously on the 16th, with a total enrollment of 160, distributed as follows: high school, W. T. Albright, principal, 27; grammar room, Ben Patton [Patten], 22; 2nd intermediate Georgia Headley, 33; 1st intermediate, Lulu Headley, 33; primary, Esther Detterman[n], 45." After a lapse of four years there was again a tenth-grade class (of four), and German was once more taught.

William had taken the train from Fayette to Menno, arriving on the morning of September 4 after staying overnight in a crowded hotel in Marion Junction in which he had to share a bed with a green young fellow from Chicago, as he described him. He was routed out after only five hours of sleep to catch the 5:30 freight train, which however did not come until 7:00, and he arrived in Menno by 8:00 A.M. Within two days he claimed to have walked his legs off getting acquainted with his associate teachers and with the town's business men—Russian or Volga-German settlers. The only Americans were Headley, the newspaper editor, whose daughters were teachers, Douglas the druggist, and the station agent.

William soon began to think in German. At Herr Fred Baumann's, where the teachers usually stayed, he found a place to room and board. He shared a room with Ben Patten on the second floor of the large house, which still stands on the edge of the little town three blocks west from the modern high school building, near the grain elevators by the railway line. The house at that time already had electricity and steam heat, oiled floors, rugs, palms, and a piano, everything in good German style. He paid $5 a week for the shared room and his meals. His landlady was a cheerful, busy German Hausfrau with three daughters, who kept a scrupulously clean house and served excellent food. Another boarder was an eighteen-year-old German-American girl, golden-haired Esther Dettermann, who taught the primary room. However, William warned his family not to tease him about her, for, as he mysteriously said, he had irrevocably left his heart elsewhere.

William's salary that year amounted to only $765, out of which he had a certain amount of necessary entertaining to do as principal. He worked hard to win from the tight-fisted school board a physics lab, some gym equipment, and a few new books for the library, for which the budget allowed only $28.40. He put $9 into three good magazines and added some others for which he himself paid. He started a literary society, but soon found it "flourishing like a dentist's chair," and had to suspend it. The boys would not participate, though he tried to teach them to debate, and the girls were too timid to speak before the smallest audience. The school's music consisted of German folk-songs, but his room had little talent. However, athletics went quite well, mainly boxing and football, supervised by Patten, himself, and Schumacher, the janitor. Also William began educating against liquor and discouraging smoking.

His college friend, Sam Geiser, was principal that year of the high school in Brandon, Iowa, with a school board that William soon recognized as more tractable than his own penurious one. Sam wrote him long, effervescent letters which William answered in kind, and the two gave each other moral support. At this point in his life, instead of feeling that he was becoming established, William wrote that he felt completely at sea and unable to plan ahead, but fortunate in recognizing danger signals for the future. He already was sure he would not be in Menno more than this one school year,

but where would he go and what would he do after that? He hoped
to be elastic enough to cast off last year's cloak and don a new and
larger one. With his characteristic lifelong ability to draw whatever
good was possible from a bad situation, he considered that at least
his knowledge of people was bound to become broader during this
year—painful as it might be. He lived in the present with no expectations, hoping to do somebody some good, and if he failed he
would try something different—perhaps go to another country as a
consul. With Spanish as his second mother-tongue he seriously considered applying for consular service in the Philippines, wavering
between that and remaining in what he called the healthful climate
of the West. The Indian summer at the end of October had brought
glorious air, though the brown earth was flat to the horizon.

William ordered stationery printed, greenish-blue paper with
return address "W. T. Albright, Prin., Menno, South Dakota." Using the new stationery in early November, William expressed surprise at hints that his family might move to Virginia, and delight
over his father's rapid improvement from malaria he had contracted
on his trip down the East Coast as far as Florida, looking for a farm
to buy. William wagered they would not stay in Virginia long—five
years at the most. (Finley and Shirley would still be managing the
farm more than sixty years later.) But William thought he would
visit them there at least before the long-planned voyage to the
moon—a statement which, read today, sounds strangely prophetic.
As for his work, he considered the results fair, the order scant, and
confessed himself not cut out for a disciplinarian. He had just performed his first thrashings and felt exceedingly cruel, though the
recipients needed them.

He wrote his mother that he disagreed with William James's
idea that the chief end of education was the "formation of good
habits"; he considered it to be their *re*forming over and over again.
He was determined not to fall into routine habits, for he thought
they were as inimical to originality as were road-ruts to one's ability
to travel freely. His idea of happiness was the steady, soft glow coming to one who impersonally seeks truth, rather than the rapture
over his own achievements felt by one who egoistically scales
heaven, only to fall—an unusually rhetorical letter.

Unable to visit his family for Christmas, William sent a small
gift to his mother and repaid a $20 debt to his father. He looked

forward to two weeks' restful and peaceful vacation for his nerves
and to heal his nose, abused in boxing practice. He attended several
of the varied religious services for the two-day German celebration
of Christmas and walked from five to ten miles a day, sometimes up
to thirty. Most of the rest of the vacation time he spent moving desks
in the schoolrooms. There had been no snow yet that month, but he
already looked forward to spring, with the river only five miles
away. He was reading also—Jules Henri Poincaré, the French math-
ematician and physicist; Robert Herrick, the American novelist;
and a book on *Qoheleth (Ecclesiastes)* by a brilliant German rabbi,
Ludwig Levy. He used Sam Geiser for his safety-valve for various
refutations and discussions of his reading, rather than his ultra-
conservative family.

In mid-January, as winter returned, William expounded to his
mother on his ideas of the kind of education needed. Every high
school ought to teach domestic science, mechanics, and agriculture.
He recognized that all the things he was teaching were far above the
average pupil's interests and needs. There should be both trade and
arts high schools as in Germany, but different; separated according
to the pupil's intellectual capacity rather than his family's financial
status. While William enthusiastically supported the humanities
and pure science, he recognized they were not for more than a small
percentage of students.

The postscript to this letter of January 12, 1913, reveals a landmark decision: he had decided to follow his mother's suggestion and
change his middle name from Thomas to Foxwell. That would let
him have his father's initials, which he desired, and if there was ever
any danger of confusion he would add "Jr."

William now expected to come to the East in late summer. With
another swing of his pendulum he expressed disgust with school
teaching, and anticipated nothing but rejections to his many applications for positions from Florida to Idaho, because he would not
consider any salary less than $900. If no position turned up before
the first of June, he might plan to go to school, either at Cornell
University at Ithaca, New York, or at Johns Hopkins in Baltimore,
Maryland.

On April 27 William wrote his father that though he wished to
spend the summer with the family, he did not consider it wise. He
rather expected to leave Canada [where he would find farm work]

in late August or September, stop at Menno and in Iowa, and come
to the Virginia farm for a couple of weeks. He perhaps would enter
Johns Hopkins at the beginning of October. Although he had applied for a fellowship of $500, he hardly expected to win it. He
thought he might be able to spend a year there if he could secure
some scholarships and prizes. He confessed to being sick of teaching,
exhausted from this difficult (though productive) job, with the
many kinds of work involved in it, the teachers' meetings he had to
preside over and speak in, the problem of discipline which he found
a strain, besides gaining a broken nose from it one time. This was
the casual way he mentioned to his family what had happened on
a memorable day only several weeks earlier, when in lieu of a well-
deserved punishment he had offered his pupil "Spouts" a fist-fight
in the schoolroom. They long remembered the terrific bleeding and
excitement.

Years later, however, as William looked back on this year as
school principal in the Volga German-Russian community, he recalled that an effort was made to dismiss him after the climactic fist-
fight between him and his biggest pupil, and that the effort failed,
in part because of his desperation, abandoning prudence and simply
shouting down the school board, and in part thanks to kind
Providence.

In writing to his father William referred again to his fellowship
application and explained that Prof. Paul Haupt, a German scholar,
chairman of the "Oriental Seminary," in which Assyriology was a
main feature, was already probably the greatest authority in the
world on the Gilgamesh Epic.

William had discovered as he studied this cuneiform epic that
dallalu probably meant "bat," the night-flying creature, and thereby
cleared up a perplexing problem. He wrote up his discovery in a
short article which he submitted to the German learned journal,
Orientalistische Literaturzeitung. As he told his family, he had sent
a duplicate proof of his accepted article with his application blank
to Prof. Haupt. (He had referred to this article already in the German letter he had written to Paul, which none of the family had
read.) In addition he had sent along with his application an article
on "A Babylonian Loan-word in Homeric Greek." (This was apparently never published; it does not appear in his lifetime bibliography, at least under this title.) He closed his letter with a favor-

able opinion of the family's life and prospects in Virginia, only about 150 miles south of Baltimore, so that he could visit them occasionally *if* he went to school there.

The proof of his article in English on "Dallalu," already accepted by the learned journal in Germany and published in its April 1913 issue, column 213, convinced Paul Haupt that there was a young fellow of real ability out in the Midwest, who had already taught himself Hebrew and Assyrian. He admitted him as a student in Johns Hopkins, also granting him a $500 fellowship, on the strength of that article. In his senior year in college, William had sent an article to the same journal in Germany, and kept the handwritten note in German that he received from Prof. Ferdinand Bork, the editor, saying he was returning his manuscript with many thanks because it was too comprehensive to appear in their space-short journal in the foreseeable future.

Looking back later, William commented that Providence had again come to his aid, in that he was able to send proofs of this article on *dallalu* along with his application to Prof. Paul Haupt. He remembered the tremendous delight he felt on receiving the fellowship.

The *dallalu* article was not his only published piece resulting from his months in Menno. In the June 21, 1913 issue of the *Scientific American* appeared as a letter to the editor his first article published in a nationwide American journal. It was on "The Origin of the Arch," and explained how it originated in Babylonia, where unburned brick was used and the structure needed to be made stable so the opposite walls would not fall in. The corbeled arch of the Aegean architects was strong enough because they had stone to use. William wrote it in response to an article on the history of the arch appearing in the *Scientific American* issue of May 24, his twenty-second birthday. Both his articles were well written, already in mature style.

In his closing paragraph on the arch he pointed out that "the correspondent quotes the chronology of Petrie and Breasted in the same breath, and they differ in the period under question by a thousand years! This leads him to an unfortunate inaccuracy in stating the relative ages of certain Egyptian arches. The dates given by Breasted are based on Eduard Meyer's researches, and are, in their broad outlines, accepted by nearly all Egyptologists. The

Babylonian dates are no less than 1,500 years too high, as conclusively proved by Father Scheil's discoveries (1911-1912). Accordingly, 3000 B.C. should be read instead of 4500 B.C." William Albright was launched already on a six-decade concern with ancient chronology.

Word of the granting of his scholarship did not reach William until the end of May. By coincidence, in its April 24 issue the Menno weekly paper had a news story about Professor Haupt's critical views on Beelzebub as "Father of Flies, Not Lies." It also quoted him as saying that there was "no biblical foundation for the story of the final day of judgment." The article, with a Philadelphia dateline, cited Haupt's address before the American Philosophical Society on interpretation of the biblical book of Zechariah. If William's parents had seen this news story they might have tried to dissuade him from studying under such a higher-critical professor. But William by this time was mentally and emotionally weaned away from them and much closer to his few intellectual college friends with whom he had been corresponding.

Early in May William wrote to Paul of the provincial judgments that plain American people pass on others, having no understanding of any who do not fit into their narrow pattern. He felt that there was hope for a church that would realize Christianity is more than adherence to a set dogma, though some dogma was necessary. He knew that the New Testament authors had used common everyday language, and referred to recent discoveries of Greek papyri that made this clear.

On his twenty-second birthday William wrote his father that he was beginning to feel middle age creeping up. He requested that his mail, which would be sent to Beach, be opened and word sent to him about anything important. He intended to leave his packed trunk in Menno and pick it up on his return from Canada, also to leave over $200 deposited in the bank there. He asked his father to write to the President of Johns Hopkins University for a list of the university fellows appointed for the coming year and see whether his name was included—he did not yet know whether his application had been accepted. He expected to send postcards to let his family know news of him during the summer, and added a triumphant postscript that he had been able to pay off all his debts except $100 he owed the Board of Education.

A week later, May 30, he tore up a card he had begun to write his father, for word reached him at that moment that Prof. Haupt had nominated him as Semitic fellow for the next school year at Johns Hopkins! He would therefore come to the Virginia farm earlier, in August. It was gratifying to find that his hard study had not been in vain. He had been granted $350 besides the $150 tuition, and thought he could win a prize or two that would add to the funds. He was conscious of the honor of his fellowship, as he mentioned when he wrote again on June 3; Haupt had never before given the fellowship to anyone who was not already enrolled in the Oriental Seminary. Now William dreamed of being able to skimp on his expenses and help Mary to attend Upper Iowa University the next year with $150, if his parents would assist her to try for the Garrison scholarship which had helped him start school there.

William took up his friend's idea and "rode the rods" during the summer in order to save money when traveling from one farming job to another in the wheat and oat fields of Kansas, Nebraska, and South Dakota. One shudders to think of him, with his nearsightedness and his crippled hand, trying to catch hold and climb on boxcars and get off safely; he could have been killed. Mary recalled, "My mother thought he was dreadfully dishonest. He said they all did it, and the railway expected them to do it. They drove them off whenever they found them, but they didn't arrest them. I was rather shocked about the whole thing because my mother was shocked— not about the hardships and the dangers for him, alone, but about the dishonesty of the whole thing!" Saying that her mother had very strict ideas about honesty and morals, Mary added, "My mother was a saint if there ever was one, and she didn't just preach it, she lived it."

In later years William Albright always spoke rather proudly of that summer of hoboing to find farm work. He considered it a reckless gesture he had made before settling into university studies— probably a silly waste of time from some viewpoints, but giving him toughness and an experience of hardship that later would be helpful to him as an archaeologist.

A final postcard from Fayette shortly before he started the train ride home told his mother of good visits with the relatives, all of whom spoke kindly of her.

He learned there was only a narrow-gauge railroad from Richmond to Beach, and no tickets could be bought ahead of time for the slow train that stopped at every woodpile. When he reached Beach he set out to find the farm, first going to the post office to inquire and leaving his suitcase for the mail carrier to bring the next day. As Mary remembered, he walked all the way and found the house during the night. "I don't know how he ever made it, because when we got up in the morning he was there, lying asleep on the old lounge. He said he found the door open, and he walked in and looked at the furniture and the dog—the dog didn't bark at him and he decided this was his family's furniture, so he just lay down and went to sleep!"

Shirley remembered differently—the rural mail carrier picked up him as well as his suitcase and brought him to the right farm in daylight. As Shirley explained, "Mary doesn't exaggerate; she just sees everything more vividly than other people do!"

The farmhouse dated back to the Civil War and was not then the large, attractive, modern home it is today. Rural electrification did not reach it until 1948, delayed by World War II. When William came there summers and for some school vacations, all the inside walls were whitewashed. The parents' bedroom combined with family room was on the first floor in place of the present dining room. Upstairs were two large bedrooms, one on each side of the two separate stairways in the middle of the house. At first the boys used the room on the east side, but then they moved to the larger west room and the two girls took the east room over the parents' room and beside the smaller of the two stairways. The bathroom and laundry-room addition at the rear was built much later.

The family discussed what to name their new farm. The mother, loving the violets that bordered the driveway into the yard and still thinking sometimes in Spanish, wanted to call it "Las Violetas Bordas." But the father named it Gladbrook Farm, the name it still bears. The brook on the farm is Stony Creek; it runs down to the Appomattox River which borders the farm.

William stayed with the family for a few weeks and they all enjoyed each other's company after the year's separation. Shirley claimed she stood in awe of William practically all her life. She recalled how William expressed his self-image and ambition: "One evening when Mother and I were in the kitchen and it was about dark, William appeared at the door and in a very mysterious tone said:

> " 'I am neither man nor woman,
> I am neither brute nor human—
> I'm a scholar!' "

The last line was delivered in a stage whisper. Mary remembered his great ambition in life, with its realistic counterpoint: "I'm going to be a scholar and live in an attic!" To him, scholarship and money were in two different categories, and he chose the former. After a visit of several weeks, he boarded the train for Baltimore to begin the process of becoming a scholar.

3

The Making of an Orientalist

The slim, fearful lad of the early years in Chile had grown up into a tall, wiry young man of twenty-two. He now had glasses for his very nearsighted eyes; his crippled left hand had strengthened with use and become more useful to him. His early and voracious reading of ancient history and then his self-taught Hebrew and Assyrian, as well as study of French, German, Latin and Greek, beyond the Spanish and English which he spoke as mother-tongues, and science and math in which he reveled, had laid a broad and solid foundation for his graduate study. His God-fearing, terrifyingly honest, hard-working parents, who yet highly appreciated intellectual abilities and pursuits, had laid the foundation for a sturdy character that would form the bedrock of the man the rest of his long life. And the past year as principal of a high school in a German-speaking prairie town had brought out other latent capabilities and sharpened his understanding of human nature and his appreciation of true values in education. He had been forced by circumstances beyond anyone's control to come to terms with poverty and hard work, without being ground down by them to the loss of his finer intellectual capabilities. He had won his needed scholarship to Johns Hopkins University, improved the condition of nerves and muscles by his "hoboing" summer, and was ready to throw himself with all zeal and delight into the new world that now opened before him.

At the beginning of October William arrived by train in Washington, where he remained a couple of days doing enjoyable sightseeing for the first time in the nation's capital. Then he continued to Baltimore less than fifty miles farther north. He found a good rooming house at Mrs. Roeder's, 1120 Linden Avenue, paying $2.00 a week for a room shared with a Carolina German, a fine Christian named Sean. Albright was to pay $4.00 for board each week at Mrs. Riceman's, 261 Hoffman Street, a few blocks to the east. Both places were within easy walking distance of the Hopkins buildings in downtown Baltimore. By the 7th of October William was able to write his mother that he was settled, had attended his first classes, and had good places to room and board. His postal address was Box 16 at the JHU branch post office.

While William's letters from Menno did not often mention his eyes as giving him trouble, nearly every letter from this time on for years mentions them in some way. He thought now that if it were not for his eyes he would get along well, but because of them he might not be able to accomplish anything; if that happened it would be the Lord's will, however, and he would not worry. The fellow appointed in Latin for that year had the same problem; people who accomplished something in fields like theirs usually had good eyesight. He had met the five instructors and three graduate students in his department, being impressed that the former out-numbered the latter. And he had discovered that there were also several in the small undergraduate college taking Hebrew. He found himself with many Jews and was learning to speak Modern Hebrew with one of his teachers, Dr. Aaron Ember. A second pro-fessor, Dr. William Rosenau, was the rabbi of the nearby Oheb Shalom synagogue. William joked to his mother that he did not ex-pect to become Judaized.

William's classes consisted of several hours a week each in He-brew, Assyrian, and elementary Arabic, plus a lecture or two in Indo-European Philology by Bloomfield. He rated the instructors all first-class and found himself learning speedily, although he thought Dr. Paul Haupt's class would resemble a nursery kinder-garten to a blind man who might stray into it, for he treated students and staff as infants. Haupt no longer had so many students nor was so popular as formerly (though he was brilliant and interesting) be-cause of his Teutonic and autocratic ways, William remarked. He was, however, kind to William and impartial, and had a strong "Dutch" sense of humor. To William's relief he found the intel-lectual competition with the other students not nearly so keen as he had anticipated, though of course the Jews were ahead in knowledge of Hebrew. He saw he would not have to overwork drastically to keep up and that he was, candidly, the best fitted among them for the fellowship that had been awarded him. To keep up his muscle tone he exercised daily with spring dumbbells as well as gym work.

Study of Hebrew, Arabic, and cuneiform is hard even on good eyes. After a month William had to give his eyes a rest, and felt he was not learning as rapidly as he would like. Sometimes on Sunday he attended the German Methodist church, thus keeping up his understanding of German. Trying out several different churches, he found he enjoyed the young men's Bible class at the nearby Baptist Church and the pastor's sermons at the Lutheran Church. He thought Dr. Haupt's affiliation with the Friends was like the lion and the lamb lying down together—the higher critic with the Quaker. He asked his mother to send his Spanish Bible to him, as his English one had fallen to pieces.

In one of his classes Dr. Haupt was in the process of reconstructing the Song of Deborah, which he called the Battle of Taanach. William suggested to his family that, to understand the results, they should write out the fifth chapter of Judges on different slips of colored cardboard and jumble them together in the kaleidoscope. While the result would be fine and symmetrical, he questioned whether it reproduced the original Hebrew text. He admired Haupt's ingenuity and philological acumen, but in his independent mind doubted that even Yahweh could rethink the thoughts of the original writer, involving also the history of that time. To this textual problem William would return several times in his long scholarly career.

William did not go home for Christmas as he had intended, but ate Christmas dinner also at Riceman's, with the family and seven other men. During that vacation he rested his eyes, except for reading Churchill's 1913 book *Inside of the Cup,* the first novel he had read in a long time. It had been sent him by Maude Stevens, his UIU girl of whom he had said practically nothing to his family. He thought the book implausible until he heard a sermon at the Eutaw Place Baptist Church which made him realize the connection between biblical criticism and the rising social movement. He knew that the biblical prophets were not merely religious preachers, as typical conservative orthodoxy held, but were great social reformers. He did not intend to endure any more such sermons; from now on, he wrote his mother, he would see biblical criticism as a necessary crusade. He had once more decided on the usefulness of education but renounced his own hopes of ever becoming a real scholar; he respected genuine scholarship more and more highly.

In mid-December instead of going to church one Sunday William took a long walk in Druid Hill Park to the west, and relaxed by feeding the peacocks, geese and squirrels. When he returned from his walk the other men insisted he had been out on a "tryst." In defense he replied that he might as well have been—most girls were peacocks and all were geese. Thus he was building up a reputation for misogyny, though he made exceptions of his own mother and Mary and Shirley; of them he said he thought more highly than of such outstanding women as Joan of Arc, Frances Willard, and Florence Nightingale.

Doubtless there was a reason for William's misogyny. Finley much later recalled that "he had no friends among the coeds [at UIU] except finally he had Maud Adams." Mary and Shirley remembered vaguely something about a friendship, stemming from his last year or so at UIU, that developed by mail, after he had gone to Virginia and to Johns Hopkins, into an engagement. They remembered the name Maude, but Mary could not remember the last name and the other two confused the name with Maud Adams, the actress whom William saw in "Peter Pan" and "Blue Bird."

"We didn't know anything about girls and William," Mary said, "until he had been at Johns Hopkins for a time. Then he wrote that he was engaged—which was rather a bolt out of the blue. We were very much interested and found out that this girl was one of his classmates at UIU and that he had kept up correspondence with her. They got engaged long-distance; I think she was from somewhere in the West. It was a very strange courtship. My mother said, 'I doubt whether he ever had a chance to hold hands with her!' It seems this girl had marriage on her mind right away, and he didn't see any opportunity of ever getting married, so far as money was concerned. He always expected to be a scholar and live in an attic! That didn't fit in with this girl's ideas, so after a time it rather faded out of the picture. We never saw her, as far as we knew. He seemed to be disgusted with this girl because she had no feeling for scholarship. She must have been a very poor choice for him, although I suppose she made some man a very good domestic wife. That was not what he needed, certainly, at that time." What he really needed would come somewhat later, at the right time; and she *would* be willing to wait, and to help him live as a scholar.

His classmate, Lula Hurd Blunt, at eighty-two well remembered Maude Imogen Stevens and the fact that she and William became engaged before he left UIU. "You would never have thought he was interested in girls," she said. "I remember her telling me he had asked her to marry him, and it was a shock to me. He must have been quite in love with her. Maude later married a man who farmed after teaching school several years." Maude indeed married a professor-turned-farmer, G. Barton Woodworth, a Mason, and lived many years on a farm near Appleton, Minnesota. They had no children. In later years when William Albright lectured at Minneapolis, Mrs. Blunt said, Maude and her husband went to hear him and spoke with him. She died on January 15, 1970, twenty months before William's similar death, and her husband died two months after William.

The engagement apparently was ended by Christmas time of William's first year at Johns Hopkins. The Churchill novel may have been her farewell gift as she let him know she would not wait for one already wedded to scholarship.

William's letter home dated May 18 brought a complete reversal from his depressed recent letters. It announced that his plans had changed and he would not be home by the close of the week, and when he came, probably the second of June, he would stay at home all summer. The reason? That afternoon Dr. Haupt had offered him the Rayner Fellowship for the following year, $400 plus the $150 tuition, or $50 more than the fellowship he had held his first year! The only strings attached were to pass his two minor exams that week. He repeated that he felt on the edge of a nervous breakdown, but if he and his eyes could hold out until he wrote his exams—and he was glad they were not oral—he would use the following week to recover and would be all right when he came home. He was still in doubt as to the wisdom of continuing school work, but the summer at home would make a difference in his health, and God had given him an opening that he should utilize to the best of his ability. He expressed shock at the offer of the fellowship, claiming he hadn't remotely anticipated it. He could not understand why he still felt so shaky and tired when he was walking nearly ten miles a day. But with this abrupt change in his fortunes he suddenly felt well and eager to return to the farm. He recognized that a little success can work wonders even in one's physical feelings.

Four days later Dr. Haupt let him know indirectly through Dr. Ember that his Assyrian exam came out fine. Dr. Frank Blake had already told him that he considered his paper in Ancient History unusually good. The Rayner Fellowship was now a sure thing, and William felt wonderful! He wrote his father that he would loaf until the first of June—that is, he would attend a few days of Congressional sessions—and pick up his final check and catch the train home. He felt the need to take back anything negative he had written about Dr. Haupt, for the situation had proved to be transitory, the pendulum had swung back, and he did not know which of the two was more astounded by his sudden rise! He looked forward to being home four restful months and wanted plenty of work to do on the farm, perhaps in place of a brother who might wish to go West and work for cash.

Some memories of William's sister Mary clear up a mystery concerning events of that spring. "One time Haupt decided he was going to give the scholarship William had to one of the young Jewish students, who seemed to be a very much more promising student. But then Haupt decided he ought to find out what these young men had been doing all year and what they had learned, so he gave an impromptu test. He came back into the room after the test and had completely reversed his former decision. 'Gentlemen,' he announced, 'Mr. *Albright* can read Assyrian!' William was the one who had done best on the test and showed that he had really been working all year, while the others had been mostly blowing their own horns. He got the scholarship for the second year, and after that it seemed there was never any doubt as to his continuing." She added, "Every summer at home he worked on a different language."

An old brown, leather-covered rocking chair stood beside the front, north window in the living room. William would sit there studying with the large window open at his left and the scent of the cinnamon vine wafting in. Shirley remembered William studying there mornings. "Mother and I would be out in the other part of the house doing the work. One summer when my Aunt Ella was visiting us, he held regular school. Aunt Ella and Mary studied with him every morning—German and math, especially algebra—and I studied one subject for part of the time. Mother needed my help and said Mary was the older and should study. That was before we went to Blackstone [a nearby boarding school]. I studied Latin under William. He would bring to the table his little cards with vocabulary words on them to learn; he did that every mealtime, with every language he was studying."

Mary would sit hidden in the woodbox behind the kitchen stove, to listen as William and his mother discussed various subjects. Or, William would turn the hand-power washing machine for his mother as they discussed academic topics. Mary was hungry to learn all she could, and was spared the heavier work because she was more frail than sturdy Shirley, who loved activity. Shirley described the two of them as a Mary-Martha pair. But sometimes Mary's hiding place was discovered and she was sent off to help with light household tasks and relieve Shirley.

One language William studied at home that summer after his first year at Hopkins was hieroglyphic Egyptian. He wanted to teach it to Mary also, as he had taught her so many subjects, but this time she balked. "I said, 'I don't *want* to learn Egyptian!' He said, 'But you will be the only woman in the world who knows it! Don't you want to be?' I answered, 'No, I *don't* want to be the only woman in the world who knows Egyptian!' So I refused."

Shirley considered William "an excellent teacher, but a hard teacher, too. One time in doing some writing in Latin, I used the Spanish word for 'money' instead of the Latin word, and he would give me no credit whatsoever. I thought at that time he was quite cruel, since I was only about fourteen years old. He was a very good teacher—he got it from Father, who was one of the best teachers I have ever known, and hard too. Mother had regular classes with all of us. Finley read the history of Chile in Spanish, and we studied Spanish, and English history, and then Mary and Mother together worked out Mary's mathematical problems."

Wilbur Albright had done quite a bit of surveying for people in South Dakota, and did some also in Virginia. No longer a Methodist preacher, his strict religious ideas became ever more solidified and unyielding. He was no more able to adapt to new times than he was able to adapt the agricultural methods that worked fine in the lush fields of Iowa to the worn-out red-clay soil of the Virginia farm. Shirley would later sum up her ideas of her parents: "Father was

very stern, strict, a God-fearing man who believed in the Ten Commandments. Mother was one of the best mothers to be found anywhere; she struggled against hardships to give us a real home. From
Father we got the example of an educated person; from Mother we
got more teaching and loving concern that we would amount to
something; from both, cultural and religious background. Mother
would rather see us dead than grow up to be wicked."

To this home William returned in the summer of 1914 to recuperate. Mary also remembered his morning study sessions in the
rocker and his vocabulary flash cards. "He would bring me those
cards, for me to hear his vocabulary, practically every day. Also he
entertained the rest of us with his stories. One summer he was reading Greek. He used to read it aloud to me, and I thought it was the
most beautiful thing I had ever heard. He had a great fondness for
trying to keep our wits at work. Almost every day he would come in
with a new game for us—something he had devised or had read
about. For instance, he would come in and toss a couple of rhyming
words at us: 'Now make a poem on those!' "

All the children remembered verbatim the result on one such
occasion. William had given out "door—floor, lung—tongue." The
youngest, Philip, immediately responded:

> "The man stuck out his tongue;
>   He was hanging from the door.
> No movement in his lung,
>   For his feet were off the floor!"

"That was the kind of mental gymnastics we were getting,"
Mary explained. She learned practically all her high school subjects
in home study, validated by examination at UIU later, William
having taught or helped teach her math, German, Latin, English,
and French—but not Egyptian!

William would tell his mother of discoveries he had made. It
interested Mary to learn what was and what was not a "discovery."
"They were always discussing ideas. One time my brother came
forth with some very radical ideas, and they horrified my mother.
She said, as mothers often do, 'You don't love me, if you can think
things like that!' He pursued her all over the house while she was
doing her work, saying, 'Mother, I *do* love you, you *know* I love

you!' " That must have been psychological blackmail to such a sensitive young thinker as William.

His mother received reassurance, however, though his father was not present to benefit from it also. Wilbur about this time became very much worried about William's theology, and this worried William. One time when his father was away from home, at family prayers the mother asked William to lead out in prayer. Mary recalled how relieved and happy her mother was on hearing her son's prayer. She exclaimed, "Oh, if Father could just have heard that, he'd never worry about him again!" Some of the phrases of the prayer concerned being like a child and depending on God for His guidance and help—the incident outstanding enough to have left a verbal memory in the mind of at least one of the children.

That summer the First World War broke out. When the family heard the news, William dashed upstairs to the boys' room, burrowed through his papers, and came down with the one he had prepared for an oratorical contest at UIU, and read it to the family —a precise prediction of what would happen if European politics continued the course they were on. America would not become involved for some time, but down on the Virginia farm there was much awareness of it all.

Years later, William recalled his interest in archaeology and ancient languages, dating from his early days in Chile, and his beginning at sixteen to spend Sundays surreptitiously studying Hebrew and other books he ordered mainly from Germany. His Methodist conscience smarted a little, since he had to earn money to help support his family. Once his mother, having heard from a younger child that William had picked up a book at the post office, warned him that bad men sent boys evil literature by mail; he thought perhaps she had not been entirely relieved to learn that the book he had brought home was a Hebrew grammar. By the end of his college years he had a good grasp of both Hebrew and Assyrian, along with ancient history. At Baltimore, the fellowships during the next three years had enabled him to concentrate on his studies —which would have meant the end of his eyesight except for the relief afforded by summer work on the farm in Virginia.

William returned to Baltimore in the last week of September for his second year, having a weary stopover in Richmond on the way. He went straight to Mrs. Roeder's place on Linden Avenue and secured a room a little larger than his former one and with better lighting, though it did not have gas heat. He arranged for board again at Mrs. Riceman's on Hoffman Street. Dr. Ember was pleased with what William had accomplished on his Egyptian during the summer.

Immediately, as though on cue, William's eyes began bothering him, but improved the next week, and he was glad he had returned a week early to get himself in shape, though it would have been good to stay home longer. The summer had been most beneficial to his health and his knowledge of Hebrew and other languages. He felt he would now make a much better impression on his department. He started catching up with French and German learned journals that had come during the summer before the war stopped their publication. What excited him most was Stephen Langdon's discovery, while working in the Ottoman Museum at Constantinople, of tablets containing the North-Sumerian Genesis, a different account than the South-Sumerian one on which the Assyrian stories were based. The northern version was similar to the biblical account.

He drew his first check on the new fellowship and everything was fine except for his eyes. He reported that it was good to have a certain status—people took notice if one did. He had heard from schoolmates at UIU and was afraid his Richards cousins had spread exaggerated stories about his success. Jean West in her note had sent greetings to his mother, and he had also received a congratulatory letter from a member of his senior class, Maude Stevens. He used to think she was a mighty nice girl, but it was a farce (covering his disappointment at the broken engagement, which must have been a blow to his pride). He commented that it was a good idea to have more than one hook baited if one expected to catch any fish. (The time had not yet come when he would be hooked!) He contrasted this obviously broken friendship with that with Sam Geiser, from whom he had just heard. He looked forward to visiting Sam at Christmas time, for Sam was now teaching in North Carolina, having graduated from UIU that spring. William told his mother she had never understood Sam, but said she had never really known him.

The Richards cousins had probably spread the word that Wil-

liam was now a *teacher* at Johns Hopkins, for the Rayner is a teaching fellowship, and William now had to teach four hours a week—
he had expected to teach seven hours, but there were only four students majoring in the department. In one letter he commented on
the singular effect of bluffing—though it may succeed for a time, it
often deceives the one practicing it and prevents him from making
genuine accomplishment. (He doubtless referred to the Jewish student who he had expected in the spring would obtain the scholarship instead of him, and who now was his Assyrian student.) William pessimistically expected that his own work would eventually
evaporate, but hoped it would not do so before the family was better established and all the children launched in life.

William was already set in his habit of expressing negative
thoughts and expectations—a lifelong pattern, in spite of phenomenal successes. And yet at the same time he had a characteristic
way of rationalizing any disappointment with what his students
later would term his "all-purpose religious philosophy of Providential guidance." He also had very great ambitions and expectations,
and at the same time considered them unattainable and so attempted to rationalize the expected disappointment. He knew how
good he was, but probably was a bit shocked at himself for lacking
humility, and disguised the whole thing in his Protestant self-
deprecation.

Dr. Haupt bragged about him quite a bit, now that he was a
Rayner Fellow. But in November William, who walked four miles
a day with a fellow boarder, in spite of the rains, enjoying discussions on the way, felt more certain all the time of his inability to
learn. He did not yet know that everyone who goes through the
discipline of this field—and other fields—has these ups and downs,
these moments of absolute despair—as any of his own later successful students can testify. They had an additional disadvantage: their
awe-stricken terror of his genius and fabulous erudition, with the
handicap of not possessing his photographic memory.

In March William presented a major paper in a meeting of the
Philological Association started by Haupt at Hopkins; this was an
unusual thing for a student to do. Also he read his first paper at the
Easter-week meeting of the American Oriental Society in New
York, at which time he became a member of that society. His paper
was on "the Home of Balaam," almost identical to the German

article he had sent off the year before. It was published in the *Journal of the American Oriental Society* in the fourth quarter of volume 35 for 1915, but was actually printed in December of 1917, the proofs being held up in passage from Leipzig by the World War. Years later he refused to allow it to be reprinted, having changed his ideas about it. Two others of his articles were read at that meeting by title only: "The Conclusion of Esarhaddon's Broken Prism" and "Some Unexplained Cuneiform Words," both of which appeared late in 1917 in the delayed section of Volume 35.

William spent the summer at home again, working on the farm to regain physical tone, and studying mornings in the rocker beside the north window. There is a picture in more than one family album of William in one of the summers on the farm, standing with others in sunshine, smiling, with his pet snake coiled up his left arm. Also in more than one collection are dignified photos of him with rather dark blond hair, and his Kaiser Wilhelm mustache (which was reddish-brown). At first he curled up the ends as the Kaiser did, but a later photo shows it with ends tapered to the sides, after the war broke out. With his dark suit and high-collared white shirt, a stick-pin in his dark tie, and his small oblong, gold-rimmed glasses, he looked like a young professor.

William's third year at Hopkins began the first week in October full-force, with Prof. Haupt expecting the students to be ready with reconstructions of the biblical text. He outlined for them his own summer discoveries. There were now six men studying in the Oriental Seminary. William was beginning work on his dissertation and cutting down on other work; however, he took Haupt's classes in Assyrian, Arabic and Hebrew, plus Ethiopic and Egyptian. His teaching involved two hours of Assyrian to a new man and an hour of Egyptian, if the student arrived. As for his dissertation, he had just made what seemed philologically a great discovery: that *Noah* meant "the full moon." (This is doubtless in the category of youthful discoveries he would wish in his mature years to have forgotten and obliterated.)

By mid-November William had made dozens of worthwhile observations. Looking back he saw that in the first year he felt almost that he was a terrible misfit, and the second year he started to find solid ground under his feet. Now, though aware of his lacks, he could see for the first time the possibility of growing into a real scholar. He even felt rather sure he could attain the Thayer Fellowship of the American Schools of Oriental Research for a year's study in Jerusalem, though he might not have the use of it until after the war (a rather prophetic observation).

After Christmas (not able to go home, but receiving a box of food by mail from his mother) and after passing his three-hour Arabic exam in January, William sent to Yale his application for the Thayer Fellowship. In mid-February he broke off his thirteen-hour days of work on his dissertation, which was about ready for Haupt's criticism, and began studying for the Thayer exams. He worked hard on inscriptions in Aramaic and Phoenician, on Syriac and Josephus, and on the map of Palestine, which he claimed he could transpose to the fourth dimension with his eyes shut.

He spent eighteen hours on three days, March 7-9, at Prof. Haupt's home in the Baltimore suburb of Roland Park, writing the terrifying exams. He wrote sixty long sheets in small hand on Syriac, Arabic, Hebrew, Greek, Latin, French and German; Old Testament Literature and Criticism, Geography, Archaeology, History, and Epigraphy (inscriptions). From memory he produced a map of Palestine and Syria which he was confident was quite nearly perfect. Paul Haupt had previously shown him a letter of recommendation he had written to try to get William into his department as an instructor. William feared the "eyes of Argus," the hundred-eyed monster, and characteristically refused to anticipate good fortune. After William had finished the exhausting exams, Haupt chatted with him, giving him paternal advice and assuring him that he would either obtain the instructorship for him or renew the Rayner with an extra amount so that William could count on $600 the next year in either case. Besides, he would recommend him for Phi Beta Kappa—an honor that William had not thought of himself. Since his undergraduate college did not grant this recognition, Haupt would make up for its lack.

Haupt showed him the letter he wrote with this recommendation, including phrases that caused William to blush, such as "promise of future distinction," "native command of English, German, and Spanish," and mention of the very comprehensive examination he had handled well. William reported this in a letter to his father, saying he was now feeling quite well (over the series of painful boils of the winter), though thin; he had escaped colds and grip. He asked whether he had told his father that he cut off his mustache about the latter part of January.

On April 15 William attended the Phi Beta Kappa banquet, which was included in the initiation fee, immediately after being admitted into the society. It did him much good. The best part, as the misogynist reported, was that there were almost no women in attendance, to put a restraint on everything. Prof. Smith of Hopkins gave a good address, substituting for Prof. John Dewey of Columbia who had tonsillitis. William added that he expected Sam to visit him at the end of May on his way from North Carolina west to marry Bess Teeple, a UIU classmate. William was up in arms over something Paul had written—about not getting much out of some lectures at the agricultural school in Ames, Iowa, because of "lacking capacity." If there was one thing William did not feel he and his brothers and sisters lacked, it was brains! He wanted to burn it into Paul's head that their cultivation did not depend upon attending college, but upon self-discipline.

William spent April 25 and 26 in Washington attending meetings of the American Oriental Society, having skipped the first day's meeting because of wanting first to get over another huge boil on the back of his neck. He was still working a dozen hours a day on his dissertation, but greatly enjoyed the two days off at the AOS sessions. His two papers, "Some Misinterpreted Passages in the Cuneiform Flood Tablet" and "The Eighth Campaign of Sargon" (which were published in Volume 36 of the *Journal of the American Oriental Society* later that year) provoked more discussion, all of it favorable to him, than any other papers; a stranger had told him he would have to haul the bouquets off in a cart! Haupt stated that William's discoveries were opening a new period in Assyrian lexical studies. Such eminent Assyriologists as Jastrow, Nies, Morgenstern and Chiera applauded his presentations, also the editor of the society's journal, Prof. James Montgomery of the University of Pennsylvania, the last active Director of the American School of Oriental Research in Jerusalem. In fact, he expressed the hope that William would soon be able to work in Palestine—a reference to the Thayer Fellowship for which he had written the three days of exams. William was keeping to himself some of his best discoveries, he confided to his mother in reporting his triumph at this meeting. His trip had cost him only $2.50, for he had roomed with his pupil and friend Snyder. By the time William had paid for his Ph.D. and entailed expenses he would have barely enough money to reach home. If about five o'clock on the morning of June 14 the family should see a thin, hollow-eyed and hollow-cheeked person approaching the house, they should know that it was not (yet) a ghost.

While longing to recuperate in the summer, William already looked beyond it and hoped to be able to help Mary attend school the year after the next. Not yet sure of an instructorship, as the university was retrenching, at least he could be sure of the Rayner, and he contrasted that $400 with the $1800 that Standard Oil would pay one of the men in Chemistry the next year. Now he revealed that he had received only the equivalent of thirty cents for his first article published, the one on *dallalu* in OLZ three years before! That was the family's misfortune, to have a son good not for chemistry but only for philology!

William Albright was awarded the Thayer Fellowship and later, when the war ended, he made excellent use of the study opportunity in Jerusalem; it established his archaeological career. But at this point all of that was hidden in the impenetrable future.

He completed and sent off some of the many papers he had been preparing during the spring, including those he had read at the AOS meeting. His dissertation, on "The Assyrian Deluge Epic," was finished in time and he passed his oral examination with flying colors. He received his doctorate in June, 1916. Before going home he was sure of the Rayner Fellowship for the third year, which would enable him to continue research and teaching. Also he had the pleasure of Sam's visit, as planned. Then with great relief *Doctor* William F. Albright took the train for Petersburg, Virginia, and home.

The summer of 1916 at the farm restored William's physical and mental strength for another year at Hopkins, now with the prestige of the doctor's title but with no secure position or income other than the Rayner Fellowship for the year.

4

Army Interlude

When William returned to Baltimore at the beginning of October, 1916, he found his former room ready for his arrival, and his trunk came the next morning. He met all the students, including a new one who made a good impression on him as a hard worker. He expected to teach two classes in Assyrian to three students and one in Arabic for missionaries from Malaysia. Prof. Haupt piled other work on him as well, so that he did not expect to have much time for his own research nor to study Avestan (Persian).

During the summer following his graduation, the University moved from the crowded, dirty, noisy downtown location into the new buildings on the spacious 176-acre Homewood Campus on North Charles Street. It was a time of jubilation, although owing to a construction flaw the first occupants of the new chemistry building, Remsen Hall, had to dodge falling ceiling tiles in terror for a while. William's department moved into several rooms on the upper of two ground floors in the new Gilman Hall on the highest part of the hill, its clock tower visible for miles around. William continued, however, to board and room at his old places downtown.

As William and Dr. Ember inventoried his material on comparisons between Egyptian and Semitic, the latter made clear how impressed he was with what William had added during the summer. But in spite of this, William felt pessimistic, owing partly to homesickness and partly to the contrast between his ambitions and reality. His financial situation this year would still be very limited, though Haupt would do what he could on his behalf. In a postscript to a letter home, William despaired of ever conquering his limitations and deficiencies; his life would be useless if it did not impel his siblings, who, he claimed, had greater talents, to accomplish the best possible.

In addition to his six hours of teaching William took twelve hours: two each with Ember in Egyptian and Coptic and with Rabbi Rosenau in medieval Jewish literature, five with Haupt, one reading Patristic Greek with Prof. Miller of the Classical Seminary, one hour on Elephantine papyri and the Targumim with Dr. Seidel, and one more hour with Ember reading the *Seances of Hariri*. His cards and slips of paper containing original observations kept piling up and filling drawers, with never time to organize them, though they provided material for many papers on Egyptian and cuneiform lexicography, mythology, etc. He felt that his short technical articles published thus far did not make much impression compared with the more expanded, less technical publications of the average beginning scholar.

Prof. Haupt presented three papers at the December 27-28 meeting of the Society of Biblical Literature and Exegesis which met at Haverford College in Pennsylvania. Dr. Albright probably did not attend this meeting, for he did not become a member until a year later. Doubtless he spent the vacation in Baltimore studying and writing, as in 1913 and 1915. However, he attended the April 10-11 meeting of the American Oriental Society in Boston, presenting a paper on "Gilgames and Engidu, Babylonian Genii of Fertility" which was later published in JAOS. He followed Haupt's lead in such technical cuneiform studies.

In May William wrote Mary a birthday letter full of advice concerning her education, apologizing for being such an absent-minded professor that he had not written earlier so that the letter would reach her on the 13th. He mentioned subjects on which she and the others should work, promising to help them during the summer.

In late September of 1917 William returned to Baltimore to continue teaching and research, now as a Johnston Scholar and an instructor in the Oriental Seminary. There were fewer men at his boarding house and in the university because of the draft; he did not expect to have much teaching to do. Prof. Haupt was not well. William wrote that he was happy there were no jingos at Mrs. Roeder's rooming house, so they could speak freely. His boarding house seemed desolate, with so many men away; he was glad there were no longer any coeds there. (Perhaps William found it easier to favor women's suffrage theoretically than to associate with women in social and classroom situations, except for his own family.)

Although he was not feeling well in November and needed new glasses, he worked on short and long articles, and had a visit of several days from his father. William's letter afterward contained comments revealing their relationship; he indicated that he refrained from writing of things that might be of interest, in order to avoid stirring up antagonism. With so many different possible viewpoints, dogmatism was both unwarranted and dangerous, and God was not subject to human orthodoxy of any stripe. Honest differences in opinions held should not grow into storms that shatter friendships and families. (His growing inability to tolerate his father's increasing dogmatism had never before been so clearly expressed.)

At the end of November William moved nearer the campus, to Chew's house at 2526 Maryland Avenue, a few blocks to the south, but he still boarded at Riceman's downtown on Hoffman Street.

When the government finally sent him his draft questionnaire, William filled it out and returned it. Neither he nor his family expected that he, with his poor eyes and crippled hand, would be drafted or involved in the war effort in any way. But while suffering from insomnia and feeling run-down, he learned that his draft questionnaire had placed him in first class. He wrote that he would soon have his physical examination, and naturally expected to flunk. In any case, he expected the war would soon be over, with revolution brewing in Germany and Austria. Only in a draw was there hope for a fair peace settlement, with the liberals in control everywhere instead of the present reactionaries. He had been converted into a supporter of President Wilson, who had fine intentions in spite of some serious blunders he had made.

When in mid-February William got two new pairs of glasses, one for distance and the other for reading, he hoped they would be better than the previous ones. Referring in a letter to the University man who was responsible for the poor former glasses, he added in Arabic "Curse of Allah!"—a bit of satisfying self-expression that his mother would not be able to decipher. The first part of his "Notes on Egypto-Semitic Etymology" had just appeared and Paul Haupt was bragging it up at every opportunity. William told his mother that now his fears that the Johnston Scholarship might not be renewed were dissipating, and he intended the following year to save in order to have one or two terms at a German university after the war ended, and if possible to go to Constantinople and copy some of the cuneiform tablets there. The Archaeological School in Jerusalem was to benefit from a $50,000 gift; as Thayer Fellow after the war, he might even be able to participate in excavations in Palestine! He closed his letter with remarks of Prof. Paton of Hartford Theological Seminary to Christians and Jews, to the effect that the millennium would not arrive when Jerusalem was given to the Jews; the feelings and rights of 200,000,000 Moslems needed to be considered, and England, which posed as defender of Islam against the tyranny of the Turks and the Germans, would surely be careful not to let things go too far concerning the new Zionist state.

William's expectation that the war would be over before either brother could see active service did not prove correct. Paul arrived in France on January 29, 1918. His letter in mid-February described winter wheat as two inches high; the shores of France looked beautiful as his transport approached. Now Paul wished he had let William teach him French. He was with Evacuation Hospital #3, and remained with it throughout his months in France, soon becoming a cook, usually located not far behind the battle lines in northeastern France.

Finley had written William in mid-March from Camp Lee, asking how his physical exam for the draft came out; he hoped William would not be drafted, but said, "Your eyes and hand would never get you exempted if the local board passed you, as some of the men down here are worse off than you are."

Before William went north to the April 2-4 meeting of the AOS at Yale, he wrote home saying he expected to return there between May 20 and June 10—it depended on when he might complete the papers which he had promised himself to send to publishers before he left Baltimore. In the middle of the letter he buried his good news—he had been reappointed to the Johnston Scholarship. Although he would have to save for his year's study overseas, which would be expensive even with his frugal habits, he still wanted to help one of his sisters attend school, and suggested that Mary might be able to work some and to borrow $100, and get her teacher's certificate at UIU.

William's trip to New Haven cost him only $20, as he roomed

with his good Methodist friend Snyder in a dollar room and Snyder was generous in hosting him at several meals (William had often tutored him free). It was an eventful trip, he wrote Finley, and proved how rapidly he was increasing in scholarly bone-headedness and absent-mindedness—and also in his scholastic reputation, which was on the rise, as was testified on all sides. But in view of his bad physical condition he considered his future extremely problematical. If he had health, he could be assured of a sufficient though modest income and could do some good with it, as he never expected to marry but might enjoy a reputation as the leading orientalist in his fields in America. These were his dreams; the reality, he expected, would be quite different.

It is a striking coincidence that he should say he never expected to marry in the very letter telling of this trip to Yale for the AOS meeting, where he presented fine, well-accepted papers on "The Mouth of the Rivers" and "Some Cruces in the Langdon Epic"— and where another visitor, unknown to him as yet, saw him for the first time. She was his future wife.

In the same letter he wrote that Chaplain Bloomhardt, his Hopkins classmate now in the Navy, had married, and Prof. Haupt had sent him a congratulatory message in Sumerian cuneiform. The censors would have a hard time deciphering that, although it was beautifully written!

Tonsillitis kept him in his room the week following his return from New Haven. The poison of it affected his eyes and heart and prevented sleep for several nights. In spite of headache most of the time at Yale, something new for him, the trip was very successful, he wrote his mother. His work had been praised by leading orientalists; Haupt lost no opportunity of singing his praises, claiming credit for having from the first predicted a brilliant career for him. He hated to be thrust forward at the beginning of his career; his health did not permit much work. Prof. Haupt wanted to make him his successor as chairman of the Oriental Seminary; he could not tell Haupt he did not want the position. However, he felt sure that the authorities of the university would save him that trouble. He wanted his mother to understand clearly that even if he attained distinction in his field, it did not carry salary with it—some great orientalists were receiving scandalously low stipends. He had not gone with Haupt, after all, but alone, and had become lost in a New

York subway station. He was growing so absent-minded that now he was always lost in any rushing crowd, and this made him hate to travel.

After some remarks about those who rely on a Bible vaguely and magically understood and must have an authoritarian church for their support, William told his mother not to worry about the Book, for it was standing their scholarly tests magnificently, nor about their religion, the only way to ultimate salvation for the human race. It was good for it to be constantly tested by competition with other faiths. Christianity, like other earthly things, went through stages of growth, decay, and rebirth; it would thrive better on the simple gospel of the Man from Nazareth. Preaching the gospel of love instead of hatred of Germans would be more useful. Human nature was, however, much the same everywhere. At least the President had sane ideas and the courage to speak them. A triumphant liberalism deserved to have, and would have, victory, he felt, and occasionally to clear the air was the only way to avoid either suffocation or explosion.

The letter reveals something of William's thinking and his broad understanding in religion and politics in the last year of the First World War. He also showed awareness of his characteristic reverse-psychology, his feeling that something unfortunate might follow all this good publicity he was receiving. It might draw upon him the *invidia deorum*—envy of the gods.

After a few peaceful weeks at home, in which William studied Ethiopic in the rocker beside the parlor window, a complete change upset his plans. In the last week of July, 1918, he was inducted into the limited service and sent from Richmond to Syracuse, New York, along with ten other limited-service men from Chesterfield. On the 28th he was with two hundred such men from Virginia on their way north. After twenty-six hours' traveling he arrived at Camp Syracuse in bad shape and promptly fainted during his medical examination. He felt better several hours later, but did not think they would release him—that was not the present policy. He spoke in his letter to his mother of the irony of fate and said he would have to struggle along until he was transferred, if that indeed happened.

He nearly fainted several more times in the next days and was transferred to the clerical department to interview men arriving and fill out cards about them. The men suffered from the cold nights in August until straw was issued to them. The food was poor and the clerical work hard on his eyes. Of the 148 pounds he weighed in Washington, he lost several soon after reaching Syracuse (and he was over six feet tall). The reveille sounded at 6:00 A.M., before sunrise, and taps not until 11:00 P.M. He asked his mother to send his forgotten carborundum razor strop and the fountain pen and filler from a box in the top tray of his trunk. He needed Finley's and Paul's addresses in France. He told his mother not to worry about his language—it was angelic compared with most of what he heard, and he would be cured permanently. At least he was happy not to hear any anti-German remarks; he now feared that the war would continue at least another two years. He and the other limited-service men, with all kinds of physical handicaps, were being driven around as though they were all sound. A philosophical attitude, he felt, was the only thing possible: to trust in God and do what was right.

He was philosophical rather than enthusiastic over his work, but still felt it was the most interesting he could get, and might give some insights into human nature. He had not met, and did not expect to meet, any humanists. At this point he thought his occupation inferior to hoboing. He still had a glimmer of hope that when his physical exam came he would be rejected and sent home; thus he did not send his resignation to the university until the end of August.

But when he had his physical examination, he was not rejected. Then uniforms were issued, and he sent his own clothing home. Being reassigned to a different mess-hall brought an improvement in food. He met one interesting fellow, a Greek interpreter. The clerks were kept busy every day except part of Sunday afternoon; thousands of men arrived daily from as far away as Florida and Alaska. After changing tents William found himself with other clerks in a more congenial situation than where he had been with ignorant and coarse young fellows. He was able to take a cold shower daily and to wash some clothing.

He took out $5000 insurance in his mother's name and had an allotment sent to his father to help with Mary's school expenses at UIU besides what he would be able to send her directly. He learned that because in the previous school year he had paid $500 to help Mary and Shirley at Blackstone, he would be allowed a $10 additional allotment beyond the $15. But somehow his name did not get onto the payroll list, and it was November before he received his first pay—$35 after three months in the service. By then he had spent only $9 since the end of July, mostly in contributions to the company fund.

The money changing hands in poker games in the tents disgusted him, as did also the outrageously high prices around the camp. He had to work on Sundays, if not in the office, then with a shovel, or on guard duty. When he was assigned to the two hours on, two hours off, he wrote Philip between turns on duty that he was probably the most nearsighted guard in the whole U.S. army. That may well have been true, and it was a tragedy for him to be thus torn from his beloved studies. Sometimes it seemed more than he could bear, but he would later be able to draw benefit from even this painful interruption of his career.

His long letter home written on September 1, his first free Sunday, is important for the development it reveals in his thinking. He could not understand why he was so shaky and easily exhausted, but it was good to have learned the fragility of his system so that he could care for himself better from now on. In these weeks, he said, he had had more time for undisturbed thinking than for years, and the gain had been spiritual as well as intellectual. With the knowledge he had stored in his mind, he could carry on a great deal of work, especially in etymology and comparative grammar, without need for books. He had a stock of data and working hypotheses ready to write up in papers and monographs. He was now convinced that he had been right to assume that he was not fitted for any occupation that could be termed practical. Clerical work, or work needing distance vision, was impossible, though he could do a great deal of study if he could control the conditions.

Another facet interesting to William was the announcement in that day's newspaper of censorship, excluding from the camps both pro-German and Socialistic reading material. The rights of mankind are defended with one hand and attacked with the other! His mother need not, however, worry about his ideas. He was eager to see *Junkertum* banished into the past and forgotten, and he was also aware that Socialism presented certain dangers. He would not carry on propaganda for it—he was only a scholar, he remarked in French. Nor was he spreading ideas of higher criticism there, where the men needed only the simple faith of the Nazarene, as everyone did. He emphasized that the philosophical and scientific investigation of the religious development of mankind was not connected with the individual's immediate soul needs. However, the theologian and the philosopher who would be the future guides in religious thought absolutely had to undertake or at least build upon such studies as his own. He was sure that God would lead him as long as he was searching for truth—even though His way might differ from that of orthodoxy. To close he quoted Alexandre Vinet in French—"The truth, without the search for truth, is only half the truth."

These last thoughts might well shine forth as the motif of William Albright's entire career. His self-understanding and philosophical foundations had become more profound and strong during those weeks of painful separation from his beloved work and the enforced idle night hours which he filled with needed rest and meditation.

A week later he began working in the K.P. corps, as potato-peeler, as he expected. Five men were in each of two shifts, alternating twenty-four-hour duty. It was dirty work and he had only one pair of pants, but his physical condition improved with more rest and better nutrition—his cook was good to his men and gave them food left over from the officers' meals. He began to feel better and gain weight. Three of the men in his shift were college-trained and one was even more nearsighted than he.

When Paul heard that William was in the army, he mentioned his surprise in a letter to Philip, whom he had expected to see in the army before William. He realized it was playing havoc with William's scholastic plans and ambitions; "He will have to stop digging into Assyrian manuscripts and dig into pots and pans awhile," he commented.

The influenza epidemic of 1918 reached Camp Syracuse in late September, but when William finally caught it, it was a light attack, with fever never above 100 degrees, for he had been fortified by his kitchen work with good food and rest. Now he looked back on the quiet hours earlier in the summer by the window studying Ethiopic, as some of his happiest. In a letter to his mother he mentioned that the German Reichstag was to convene the 15th of November; he felt that something was to be expected to happen soon.

Replying to a good letter from Chaplain Bloomhardt, who did not yet know that William was in the "military," William wrote a long letter expressing his thoughts about the origins of the Christian faith. He wished to avoid both rigid Unitarianism's limitation and credulous "faith's" sacrifice of history and reason. Genuine faith comprised idealistic faith in God and right, assurance that love and loyalty would not be deceived, and belief that man's destiny is character. Credulous over-literal beliefs were part of the romance of childhood and had to be put away when one reached maturity.

Rumors of a coming Armistice were beginning to fly on both sides of the Atlantic, as a change occurred in William's situation. By October 21 he had a new address—Pvt. W. F. Albright, Co. 5, Ordnance Prov. Bn., May's Landing, N.J. He explained to his mother that he had been made time checker for the government in the building construction at Belcoville run by the Be(thlehem) L(oading) Co(mpany). It was not hard work but long hours, ten each day, even Sundays, and meant finding scores of men and filling out blanks on their work and time. The workmen were housed in dormitories and fed in mess-halls, and the soldiers with William were treated the same. With insufficient food, William rapidly lost the weight he had gained. Two-thirds of the eight hundred limited-service men there were Italians; William thought he might at least learn some Italian while there. His longing to return to his beloved studies was sometimes almost impossible to bear. After moving three times in eight days he found himself with two Methodists among three roommates. He tried to fire up a quiet chap who was at the beginning of theological training in Boston. William claimed to have a nose always scenting out young and promising scholars, wanting to gather a few around him for the future apologetic and dogmatic struggle. He intended to read some Greek—the Gospel of John—with this young theology student if he remained there.

On the Saturday after Christmas William left the army, a free man. He wrote to Mary from the fine YMCA building at Camp Dix on Christmas Day that his name had been read among eight hundred being discharged, six days earlier. He would have been among the three hundred remaining for guard duty except that he had helped her and Shirley with expenses the previous year at Blackstone, and thus they were listed as his dependents! He again performed clerical work, helping prepare the discharges. It was one of the best camps, and he found army fare wonderful after the food at Belcoville. He could now say frankly that the days there were terrible. He considered his "escape" from such a "prison camp" worth much. But as a gain from his army life he would re-member the human associations, the opportunity to become ac-quainted with many nationalities and types of men.

William spent some days at the farm after his discharge, and then went to Baltimore. He was so thrilled to be back in his old haunts that he absent-mindedly dated his January 8 card to his mother 1918 instead of 1919. He was wild to get into his work and enjoying himself immensely. He credited his mother's nutritious meals for ten days or so with helping him gain so that he now weighed about 160 pounds.

At last he could slip back into his real life. William later looked back on this period as an interruption that, though very distasteful, turned out wholesome because of the improvement in his health (in spite of the bad food in the labor battalion) during his forced vacation from books and studies.

5

A Fateful Year

Overjoyed to resume his studies and teaching at Johns Hopkins after being released from what seemed a combination of prison and purgatory, Dr. William Albright forgot his good resolutions and plunged too voraciously into his work. Besides the predictable effect on his eyes, he suffered from neuralgia. But his happiness to be again with his studies and in familiar, loved places outweighed these drawbacks. He noticed a difference in nourishment as well as filling quality between the food at Mrs. Riceman's and his mother's home cooking, for he lost five pounds in about ten days. There were now some undergraduates eating there, and also several women, but they stayed in the background; only one was a graduate student. New men were at Hopkins as well as his old colleagues. William began again making discoveries, philological at first; he planned soon to resume comparative religious and mythological investigations.

In a letter to Philip he advised his youngest brother to seek always for what was real behind outward appearance, and to keep in mind that all advance has to break with what went before and thus gives pain to those still clinging to the past, who look on everything new as devil-inspired. William saved his big news for the last paragraph, tempering it as usual by cautious pessimism: he had recently learned that Prof. Montgomery and others expected him to go that summer to Palestine! His stipend would be $1000 rather than $800 for the Thayer Fellowship! But he did not feel his health was equal to it, nor was the higher stipend equal to the war-inflated expenses he would have to meet with no other source of income. In view of the condition of his eyes he did not think the experience

53

would be very profitable, but he was delaying replying negatively for a time.

Prof. James A. Montgomery, of the University of Pennsylvania and the Episcopal Divinity School in Philadelphia, was chairman of the executive committee for the School in Jerusalem. Prof. Albert T. Clay, chairman of the department of Semitics and in charge of the Babylonian Collection at Yale, whom William had met as treasurer and librarian of the American Oriental Society, had been appointed Annual Professor for the School in Jerusalem. He wrote William about going to Palestine. He himself was anxious to go on to Baghdad and explore along the Euphrates. Prof. William H. Worrell, of Hartford Seminary, was the Director of the School for 1918-20, and he and Clay were leaving in June. Worrell replied to a letter from William, glad that he had taken him into his confidence and hoping he would always feel he could discuss his aims and purposes with him frankly. He felt great sympathy for him in his financial difficulties, having had similar ones; there were very few orientalists who had not suffered in the same way. He said Dr. Albright could come on to Palestine whenever he was ready.

William decided to go across in September after spending the summer at home. Other Hopkins people were tentatively planning to go also. Prof. Haupt told William that he had been appointed Johnston Scholar for 1920-21, with $1200. His Thayer stipend of $1000 had to cover transportation to Jerusalem and return as well as living expenses there. William considered these prospects pretty good for an orientalist who paid little attention to remuneration.

To save his own clothing, William continued wearing his army uniform as long as he legally could do so, putting on civilian clothing for the first time on February 24, sixty days after his discharge. He wrote that he hoped Shirley and his mother would mend his clothing when he came home—he did not want to buy new clothes until after the year in Palestine, when he might return looking like a ragged hobo. Three years had passed since he last bought a suit— it was more important that the others should get a college education and not be too proud to finish at a higher age than usual. He did not want his parents to work hard in their old age, either. He considered that he would certainly not marry; it was absurd even to think of it, he added.

From April 23 to 25 William attended the AOS meeting in

Philadelphia. His name was third in the list of members attending, which also included a "Miss Norton." At the second session, held Thursday morning the 24th at the Law School, "Miss Ruth Norton, of Johns Hopkins University" read her paper on "The Life-Index in Hindu Fiction." The abstract, as printed in the JAOS Proceedings, gave the gist of it in her own words: "We may distinguish two leading categories of this motif, terming them active and passive. The active index is some object, bird or bee or inanimate object, on which the life of a man or demon depends; destruction of the index involves destruction of the owner. The passive index is merely some token, often a plant, which signifies to a friend the illness, danger, or death of the bestower by some change of condition. The two are often used to advantage in the same story. A further type, tho small in scope, is the faith token. Life-index motif is widely disseminated in Hindu folklore, yet almost totally absent in literature." Remarks on the paper followed its presentation, and William later referred to it as a very fine paper. He had not yet mentioned Ruth Norton in any letter to his family, however.

William presented his paper on "Menes and Naramsin" in the last session, held the next day at Dropsie College. He identified Mani of Magan, whom Naramsin of Akkad defeated, with Menes, of the First Dynasty in Egypt, and defended this identification and chronological system in a number of articles that provoked scholarly controversy in journals for several years—only to abandon it himself later, in a lifelong pattern of being willing to change his views when more evidence became available that contradicted them. Later he lowered his dating for the Akkad Dynasty of Mesopotamia (and thus also for Mani) about six hundred years below the dates he held for Menes. Two other papers by William were presented at this meeting by title only: "The Cuneiform Prototype of Hidr-Elias, and the Messianic Expectation," and "The Mesopotamian Origin of the Gnostic Sophia." Most of his time in Philadelphia he spent with Prof. Lutz and the Max Müller family, enjoying his visit immensely.

In May William rented a typewriter to use in preparing articles for publication, as he usually did, and worked before his east window. This made him conscious of the very warm weather, and he knew he must leave Baltimore before its hot, humid weather lowered his vitality too much. In a letter he typed to Philip he mentioned having attended the Jewish temple on Friday evening, hearing Hoffman that Sunday morning, and intending to hear Dr. Kirk in the evening—much church-going, which he ascribed to feminine influence. He confessed to being strongly under such influence this spring—nothing serious, but his mother would feel reassured to learn that it was the kind of girl she would approve: American of English extraction, Protestant and middle-class as to family; sixty-three inches tall and twenty-six years of age, with dark hair. She was a graduate student at Hopkins in folklore and linguistics, and naturally she had neither race nor class prejudice, or he would not have let the friendship develop.

This is the young man who considered marriage absolutely out of the question, and who had long ago decided to be a scholar and live in an attic.

When he wrote his mother two weeks later, delighted that Paul was again in the U.S., he scolded her a bit for being surprised at all his church-going, and said she also should know he had never called women uncongenial—he had to avoid them precisely because of his great vulnerability! Realizing his weakness and feeling sure he was unattractive as well as poor, he had remained aloof in self-defense! Misogyny, he asserted, was merely his armor to shield a heart that had known some severe trials; he could now reveal these facts for the first time, because he was now engaged to the girl he had described in the letter to Philip! He had not broken any resolve, but had avoided the young woman until ashamed of himself, and had then let her take the lead. He considered himself extremely lucky to win Ruth; he felt he did not deserve her. Among her many fine qualities were intellect, attractiveness, good upbringing, and vivaciousness; in other words, she was adorable. Having started work toward a doctorate in Germanic studies, she had lost some time by transferring to Hopkins for Sanskrit when the war caused complications about German study and prospects for teaching it, and thus she still had two more years' work. She had been appointed the following year's Sanskrit Fellow.

William wrote, however, that there was no idea of marriage for some years, but he did not intend to worry whether he might lose her; he would do the best he could, believing in God's guidance. There would be no hindrance to what he wished to do to help educate his sisters and brothers, for he would not marry until he had a large enough income, and thus did not need to divert money toward saving for his marriage. Someone working in research needed at least $2000 a year, and he had no idea he would attain that level until he was nearly forty, if then. Another field would be different, but he was doing what he had dreamed of since he was eleven years old, for which God had opened the way. He felt that Ruth was equally idealistic to have picked him out, as she had let him know she had done. He had thought of temporarily teaching in the field of Romance languages, but agreed with her opinion that it was better for him to accomplish all he could in his chosen field, rather than waste time merely working for a living in order to get married.

The long walks William had been enjoying in the springtime breezes and flowers had not been, this year, with his men friends. Ruth Norton—he had not even told his family her last name yet— had first seen the tall young Dr. Albright across the room at the AOS meeting at Easter time in 1918 in New Haven. A couple of days later she asked a friend, "Who is with So-and-so?" as he passed through the Yale library with a colleague whom she knew. "Oh, that's Albright, one of Haupt's doctors," was the reply.

That fall she transferred to Johns Hopkins while William was in the limited service, and was keenly disappointed not to find him at Hopkins. When he returned to Baltimore in January to begin teaching in the second semester, the librarian of the special sectional library introduced them to each other. He was still wearing his uniform to save his civilian clothing. He was shy, but she was not, and she could talk on folklore, linguistics, and almost every possible subject. When spring came they talked more and more often and began going to church services together at various places. As the days grew longer he would meet her after the evening meal, and they would walk out to the road west of the campus just above the Wyman Park gorge, sit down and talk, then walk some more. It took him a long time to get around to proposing, for he was bashful and felt he had nothing to offer. He finally proposed in the small, deep-set, partly-wooded park called "The Dell" running along Charles Street just south of the Art Museum to the south side of the campus. It did not take her long to say yes. The day was May 15, nine days before his twenty-eighth birthday and seventeen days before her twenty-seventh birthday. They became engaged with the mutual understanding not to think for a long while of setting the date for their wedding. He was to spend a year in Jerusalem, and she had two years' work yet to complete for her doctorate.

A tiny, peppery person with flashing dark eyes, she had intuitively recognized on first glimpsing William that she had seen her future husband, and he seemed to have a similar intuition after meeting her. She fell in love with the man—the first and only man she ever knew, as she said; all the rest were just people.

Ruth was descended from the Martins, a Protestant landowner family in Bally-na-Hinch, County Down, Ireland, about twenty miles south of Belfast, also from some ancestors in County Galway in the South, and from the Thornleys of Lancashire. Other ancestors were the Nortons from Yorkshire and the Bains from the McKay clan of northern Scotland. From several generations engaged in business, ranging from the dye works established by Martin and Thornley partners in 1830 in Port Richmond, now a part of Philadelphia, to the coal business in Philadelphia in which both her grandfathers were engaged, to a metal fabricating company in Columbus, Ohio, which her father took over and reconstructed financially during the war years, Ruth inherited management and executive ability as well as language aptitude and teaching ability.

After her graduation in 1914 from Lake Erie College in Painesville, Ohio, and in 1915 from the University of Wisconsin with a Master's degree in German, Ruth taught German and Latin for a couple of years at an Episcopal boarding school for girls at Sioux Falls, South Dakota. There she became interested in Hindu literature in English translation, and in Sanskrit, the ancient language of India. A friend of her father, a Greek professor at Ohio State University, helped her learn it and she received a scholarship for the University of Pennsylvania, intending to study German and Sanskrit toward a doctorate, but her German professor suddenly died. After first seeing William Albright at Easter time at Yale, she transferred in the fall to Hopkins; her Sanskrit professor at Pennsylvania, Franklin Edgerton, was a Hopkins graduate and helped her obtain a scholarship.

William, with his characteristic modesty, did not dream that any woman would have him because of his physical handicaps, his personality quirks, and his poor prospects for earning a good living. For such a wonderful, talented woman to think him desirable did him tremendous good, and his following letters home were filled with praise of her and rejoicing over his unexpected (and he thought undeserved) good fortune.

When he wrote his mother the day after his birthday, he confessed that he was not working very diligently. He would be able to accomplish more on typing ten or more papers after Ruth's departure. In the meantime, they were spending pleasant hours together. His published materials now amounted to almost two hundred pages; when editors published papers he had already sent them, the number would practically be doubled. It now looked likely that he would go to Palestine, and he really hoped to go; tutoring would not be a very pleasant way to try to make a living for a year. He wanted to get the year in Palestine over and resume his studies—not dreaming how that year would change the direction of his studies and his life.

He belatedly mentioned Ruth's last name in answer to his mother's assertion that he had forgotten to do so, commenting that Norton had no Germanic element. He mentioned how well educated and bright she was. In a cryptic manner which he said he left for his mother to figure out for herself, he described himself and Ruth as being as near alike religiously as would be possible for a Nonconformist like him with a *Weltanschauung* both Germanic and Oriental, and a woman like her with catholic background and a rather medieval slant of mind.

To his father William wrote that he would be full of his prize all summer, while separated from her. Possessed of all admirable qualities and quite good-looking, with a fine skin that needed no cosmetics, and having the best mind he had ever found in a woman, she was so sensible and liberal that she was never shocked by his ideas and research. Her faith in him was so great that she took the initiative and did not care that he would be ignored by the world, or worse. This made him still more idealistic, and in spite of his pessimism he really knew that in the longer view he would not disappoint her, no matter what difficulties might have to be surmounted.

William said little about his engagement during the summer, but later wrote explaining that this had been nothing but camouflage. On the first of September he said goodby to his family and took the train to Baltimore to spend more than a month living at the suburban home of his friend Snyder, now the Methodist pastor at Ellicott City, who wished to be tutored in Assyrian. Ruth returned early for her fall semester so that they could be together a few weeks before William went overseas. He had to get his passport and other papers in order as well as work on his dissertation manuscript, which Haupt wanted him to prepare for publication. He secured passage on the *Duca d'Aosta,* an Italian steamship scheduled to sail from New York about the last week of October.

Several days after he left for New York, William wrote his mother on the 23rd of October from the Hotel Chelsea that his sailing date had been postponed because of the longshoremen's strike. It was expensive to stay in a hotel while waiting, and he had found a clean and inexpensive room through the YMCA. He confessed that it was extremely difficult to part from Ruth—he had been quite cut up over it. They so enjoyed the month together in Baltimore, in spite of the fact that he was working hard on his dissertation and evenings were not mild enough for sitting on park benches. They visited Sam and Bess Geiser a few times, and after a Sunday dinner with them, Sam and Bess thoughtfully left them in privacy for a while. They appreciated that, having really no place in which to carry on their courtship. Ruth's health improved after the end of the hot weather, but William was concerned for her as she began a difficult year. She was to take much French instead of less popular German; Sanskrit did not hold out any hope for earning a living.

In William's field also, positions were nonexistent. Haupt had given him all kinds of good counsel and was trying to find a position to which William could come on his return from Palestine, but some chairs had been discontinued rather than new ones being endowed in orientalistics. William had thought his living assured for several years, with fellowships that would support his research and allow him to help Shirley and Philip a little with their education; he had even envisioned spending summers studying in Europe. But the picture had changed with his engagement and his discovery that Ruth had lost interest in a career of her own, with slim prospects for a teaching position anyway. She was now more interested in having a husband and children, and therefore William became more concerned about his future. As usual, he tried to be philosophical. He had warned Ruth they might have a seven-year wait. By that time his prospects would be either established, or ruined by complete loss of his eyesight.

One afternoon in the library at Columbia University William was overjoyed to run into his old friend Chaplain Paul Bloomhardt, who was at that moment reading one of William's articles. Bloomhardt invited him onto his ship, the *George Washington,* for a complete tour, dinner, and an overnight stay. William noted that the ship was berthed between the *Imperator* and the *Leviathan,* the two largest ships of that time. President Wilson and members of the Belgian royal family had traveled on Bloomhardt's ship, one of the largest of the war transports. Bloomhardt did not have the prescience to tell William that Eleanor and Franklin Roosevelt also made the trip to Europe and back on his ship with the Wilsons.

October ended and the strike was still on. William spent most of his time in the Oriental Room of the public library reading on Assyriology and Egyptology, becoming really homesick for the first time in his life, as he confessed in a letter. The discomforts of Oriental life and its vermin were to be borne while he was learning all he possibly could over there, but he would be happy to return home afterward. He had had more than enough of New York.

However, before he sailed William began to enjoy New York, as he found acquaintances and friends who entertained him a great deal. He was toasted at the monthly session of the Oriental Club, and spent an afternoon and evening with Dr. James Buchanan Nies in his Brooklyn apartment, inspecting his collections worth $100,-000, from all over the world, including Bolivia and Peru; among them were six thousand cuneiform tablets from the Near East. Buchanan's wife, who had recently passed away, left her fortune to him and gave $50,000 for the archaeological school in Jerusalem. Dr. Nies predicted a splendid career for William in oriental studies and said he would even back him with funds if necessary—which must have relieved William's worries considerably as he sailed into the unknown.

Ruth sent him four tremendous cumulative letters. She and Sam and Bess were becoming great friends. William looked forward to returning to that wonderful group after difficult months abroad; he was now seeing a brighter future ahead, in place of the past twelve hard and cruel years filled with contempt and failure, as he regarded them—counting his years from the beginning of his college work. (Others had a very different view of his accomplishments in those years.) He did, however, recognize God's goodness and how completely Ruth's love was transforming his life. He had never dreamed before of such a source of happiness and strength. He wrote his family that they would also be delighted with her, but warned them that she shared many of his ideas and viewpoints with which they did not agree. He had never thought such a congenial mate existed in the whole world, though he realized that, with both of them liking to talk and both having a rather short temper, adjustments would need to be made. In his unaccustomed optimistic outlook he now was sure that love, with the help of God, would be sufficient for all circumstances.

Just before he finally departed, William heard from Prof. Worrell, who had arrived in Jerusalem on October 7. He warned William that he was "sailing into a sea of uncertainties, political, financial, scientific and academic. Those at home cannot be made to understand the difficulties outside of snug and rather smug America. There has in fact been a war out here; and it is still going. But in all your fortunes I pledge you my aid. . . . you shall have a bunk in our house, if by that time we shall still have been able to keep one for you, and all my official and personal backing." He continued by giving William some advice: "In dealing with the British you should never try to force anything. We have to take what we can get. . . . There remains for us this year only work in Arabic, folk-lore, inscriptions and above-ground archaeology. There can be no excavations as we have no funds and the authorities are not willing." William could not, he said, be held accountable for any delay in arriving.

William sailed at last on November 8. The voyage took more than two weeks to cross the Atlantic and pass through the Mediterranean as far as Naples, because of the need to economize on coal. In Naples he secured a room at the Hotel Cavour for 8.00 lire, less than a dollar a day, and found the food cheaper than in America. He was aware of being cheated sometimes—he blamed it on both nearsightedness and kindheartedness—but even so his expenses were running less than in New York. He would know how to travel still more cheaply in Europe the next time, he wrote. His fare, with tax and tips, had cost $157; he could have saved $75 by going third-class, but he had promised Ruth he would not, and was glad he had not. Steerage on an Italian ship was just as he had always heard. The food was poor in second class but there was plenty and he could eat it with good appetite, avoiding only the peppers. He had good roommates in the six-berth cabin—two priests, two other Italians, and a young printer returning to Italy. With his languages he had no trouble on the ship nor in Naples, though he did find himself mixing Italian, French, and Spanish!

The day he landed, he walked about in Naples, losing and finding his way, enjoying the city and his use of Italian, which was adequate. But he wrote his mother he would be happy to land at Jaffa and see how much of his stipend was left for use during the year and the return voyage. He said candidly that he had so needed what Ruth was now giving him, and receiving from him—moral support. He had received twelve wonderful, cheering letters from her in his long wait in New York. He thought it a miracle that he had won such a splendid person; such idealism, to become attached to him in spite of lack of promise in his appearance and in his future, was hard to believe, but he did believe in it, and it made all the difference in his determination for his difficult life. He could now, he told his mother, much better appreciate *her* life's meaning and splendor, having found out how marvelous was a noble woman's love. He intended to persuade Ruth, if at all possible, to visit the farm for a week or two. She would easily adapt to the new experience, for Sam called her a perfect brick, and her tastes were simple, quite similar to his mother's, he assured her.

He described old-fashioned Naples, with its narrow streets, some of them stone steps or arched-over alleys, some paved with square stone slabs like those in South American cities. Being regularly swept, they were quite clean, and there were not as many beggars as he had expected. The girls and women looked better than he had anticipated, and included a surprising number of blondes. The ancient trams still ran all right. He would learn next day about getting passage to Palestine and then would visit the Museo Nazionale as well as go over to nearby Pompeii, destroyed in the eruption of Vesuvius in A.D. 79. If he had to wait some time, he would make use of the time as well as he could.

It turned out that he had to wait almost three weeks for passage from Naples, and he was sick with colds most of that rainy

period. He finally sailed on the *Sicilia* on December 12. It was a
five-day voyage to Alexandria, a very damp one but otherwise
pleasant—there was even snow falling as they entered the harbor!
The passengers were polyglot and he became acquainted with
Italians and French, Egyptians and Syrians, American missionaries,
Jewish merchants and scholars, Spanish monks and a Cypriot
Greek. He made use of almost all his languages and even then
sometimes felt helpless. With his knowledge of Talmud as well as
Hebrew, he made friends in both the hidebound, orthodox group
of Jews and the intelligent, liberal group. He and the Greek talked
a great deal in French; he was both envious and admiring as the
fellow recited classical Greek poetry. As for political discussions,
he listened rather than talked.

After clearing customs he took the train to Cairo 125 miles
southeast, arriving before the end of that Wednesday afternoon,
December 17. On Friday, the Moslem holy day, he wrote letters
and read Arabic newspapers in his hotel room, enjoying the warm
weather.

He found it would take a week to obtain the permit to go to
Palestine; strict British military control was over everything. He
had to have his picture taken, for his supply of photos was exhausted. One day he selected a guide from among those pestering
him. But when the man learned that William intended to spend
the day walking, he turned him over to another who claimed to
have iron legs. By the end of the day the guide asserted he was about
to drop. William himself was not tired and refused to believe him
—the man had used a stout walking stick the whole time. William
made him teach him colloquial Arabic as they went through the
Cairo Museum, William reading the Arabic names of the exhibits
(hardly the usual kind of tourist). At William's insistence they
went to a native restaurant for a meal of mutton stew, rice-cake,
and greens, the flat native bread substituting for forks and spoons.
Since the meat was already cut into pieces, no knives were needed.
William was able to overlook how dirty the place was, since he
expected it to be that way.

He then had Hassan take him through the bazaars, though he
did not buy anything (frustrating for a guide who expected his
commission on sales), and to El-Azhar, the Moslem university.
They quickly left when a crowd gathered, mistaking William for
one of the hated Englishmen. There had been a political demon-

stration and general strike the preceding day; the tension was great, and about twenty thousand English soldiers were in and around Cairo. The Egyptians had been promised independence in 1914 and did not know why it was now refused, not understanding shifts of policy with shifts of government in Western democracies or bureaucracies, as William explained in his letter.

Living expenses were higher in Cairo than in Naples. William's room faced the Esbekiah park; it was a large, airy room costing 25 piastres a day, or a little over $1.00, but food in the Middle East was no longer cheap. By eating in restaurants instead of at the hotel, he saved almost half on cost of food, spending 50-60 piastres daily for both room and food, or between $2 and $2.50. A standard restaurant with moderate prices was really cheaper than most inferior restaurants, but one had better like mutton! The only inexpensive things in Cairo were oranges, two cents apiece.

William now felt wonderfully well in Egypt, where it was sunny and dry and he had people to meet, Arabic to study, and a great museum to visit at length and repeatedly. He could ignore the guides' pestering and the matter of *bakhsheesh* or tips.

Dr. Georges S. Kukhi, a Christian Syrian from Egypt, Yale-educated and a Unitarian, whom William had met at AOS meetings, traveled with him in Egypt. Prof. James Henry Breasted of the University of Chicago, America's foremost Egyptologist, invited William for tea one Friday late in December and gave him letters of introduction to Dr. Clarence S. Fisher, then excavating at Memphis, and Sir William Wilcocks, who was involved with methods of irrigation in Egypt.

In writing to his father, William contrasted a saintly (also homely and ungrammatical) Holiness missionary he met in Cairo with his friend Kukhi, and remarked that Christianity had to find its way between the two extremes these men represented; emphasis in either direction instead of a balance meant catastrophe. The origin and historical development of dogmas had to be studied in order to understand their meaning. This was the study in which he was engaged, and surely nothing but good could come from investigating the long background of Christian theology in Western Asia.

On the 30th of December 1919, with permit in hand, William boarded the train for Palestine and a new period in his life, opening vistas down which he would not have been able to look even with normal-sighted eyes.

6

Exploring Palestine

On the last day of 1919, as if in a dream coming true, Dr. William Albright arrived by train in Jerusalem about 4:30 in the afternoon. From Cairo, with transfer to another train after crossing the Suez Canal at Qantarah, he had traveled with Sheikh Khalil ed-Danaf, a chief of the Mosque of Omar, who shared his supper with him— bread, cheese, pickled olives and water—and helped him along the way. The Sheikh's robes were blue and red, with a green turban, and his long white beard gave him a patriarchal look belied by his rolling, shrewd eyes. William felt he could be a fanatical foe as well as a polite and helpful friend. He also had as a traveling companion the young Rev. Herbert Danby from Oxford, arriving at the same time to live in Jerusalem, associated with St. George's Anglican Cathedral. It was quite a change to go from mild, sunny Cairo to Jerusalem winter at 2500-foot elevation, with evening temperatures about 40° or 50°.

William went for the first night to the Grand New Hotel, just inside the Jaffa Gate, in which the American School had been housed in its first years. He spent the evening with the Rev. Dr. John P. Peters, excavator of Nippur before William was born and lecturer in the School, who had arrived in November. On the following morning Dr. Peters took Dr. Albright to the American School of Archaeological Research, as it was then called. Since 1906 the School had been in a rented building in the new quarter on Abyssinian Street, just across from the Spanish Consulate-General, off Jaffa Road northwest of the Old City and north of the New Gate. It was a ten-minute walk from the School to the Jaffa Gate and the Citadel or "Tower of David."

66

In 1895 Prof. J. H. Thayer, President of the Society of Biblical Literature and Exegesis, called in his presidential address for the establishing of an "American School of Oriental Study and Research in Palestine." A committee was appointed to study the question, and its six members became the "founding fathers" of the School: Prof. Thayer (chairman), G. F. Moore, Rev. J. P. Peters, Profs. W. H. Ward, J. W. White, and T. F. Wright. Twenty-six universities and seminaries agreed to contribute $100 per year for the support of the School, and it opened in 1900 with Prof. C. C. Torrey of Yale as its first Director. The American Oriental Society was one of the sponsoring organizations of the School, along with the SBL and the Archaeological Institute of America; each organization appointed one of the Trustees governing the School.

The Archaeological Institute of America offered a fellowship named in honor of Prof. Thayer beginning in 1901. The School had to close when Turkey entered the World War in 1914, and the building was left in the hands of the German-Swiss caretaker, Mr. Stahel. From 1917 on until the end of the war the Red Cross used the building. Beginning in 1918 an Annual Professor was appointed to be associated with the Director, the latter sometimes holding office for a number of years for continuity while a different Annual Professor came yearly to share in giving lectures to the students while carrying on his research projects.

Prof. Worrell, the Director, and Prof. Clay, the Annual Professor, were together in England in July negotiating with the British School of Archaeology in Palestine to cooperate in carrying on their work. Articles of agreement were signed to avoid unnecessary duplication of effort and to share lecture halls, library and museum, while maintaining each School's identity. Prof. Clay then conferred in Paris with French scholars about including the French in the cooperative plan.

That New Year's Day of 1920, Albright had dinner with Worrell and an Arab friend. In the afternoon and evening Albright and Worrell went over the latter's collection of Coptic materials. Albright immediately made arrangements for rooming and boarding at the School with the Worrells and having his laundry done there, all for 45 Turkish piastres per day (abbreviated P.T. and worth about 25 to a dollar, 85 to the English pound), compared with daily expenses at the Grand New Hotel of about 80 P.T. per day with no heat. That same day he met another Fellow of the School who had recently arrived, Samuel Feigin, a Jewish student at Yale.

On Friday Albright found three long letters from Ruth waiting for him at the American Consulate and had a pleasant chat with Consul Glazebrooke. He also visited the cooperative library, which was then in the Public Works Building or Lord Bute House, and for which the American School was responsible. With Prof. Clay he visited scholars at the institutions of the Franciscans and the Dominicans, and later that day went with Prof. Worrell to visit the Valley of Tombs. Feigin arranged to read Sumerian with Albright on a regular daily schedule and in exchange to speak Modern Hebrew with him evenings.

On Sunday morning Albright went with Worrell to the service at the beautiful Cathedral of St. George. Later they visited the Tomb of Helena to the north of the Damascus Gate, buying candles for 5 piastres each to light their way inside.

Dr. Albright was beginning to be painfully aware of a personality clash between the Director and the Annual Professor. He talked that evening with Dr. Peters, who lived, as Clay did, in the Lord Bute House just inside the Jaffa Gate. The house was under negotiation for the joint British and American Schools.

During the next days Albright divided his time between stamping books in the library and otherwise helping there, and reading, aside from the two daily sessions with Feigin. A week after his arrival he heard Père Marie-Joseph Lagrange lecture on Zion and Golgotha, and met that great scholar and archaeologist, founder of the French School, the École Biblique, in Jerusalem.

He was surprised to find German spoken more commonly than English; Worrell lectured in it, and William found himself speaking German more than English also. The Jerusalem Jews spoke Hebrew and understood Yiddish and Ladino, which were really German and Spanish in Hebraized form. Others such as the Greeks, Armenians and Syrians spoke French. He found prices for food about fifty percent higher in Jerusalem than in America, because everything had to be imported from Egypt, Europe, Australia, or America.

Albright appreciated Worrell's scholarship in Ethiopic magic and in Arabic and Coptic, and wrote home that he was happy earlier disagreements had been settled and they were now excellent friends. The Director planned to return to the States at the end of his year, both because the stipend was too scanty in view of war-inflated prices, and because of the Annual Professor, who was his associate but who treated him domineeringly as a subordinate. William tried to stay neutral and keep on friendly terms with both.

On the 9th there was a meeting of Jerusalem scholars called by Prof. Clay (to whom William had suggested the idea) to form the Palestine Oriental Society. The Rev. Père Lagrange was elected president, Rev. Herbert Danby of St. George's Episcopal Cathedral as treasurer, and Dr. Nahum Slousch, a Sorbonne Professor of New Testament, as secretary. Directors included Col. Ronald Storrs, the Military Governor of Jerusalem; the School's neighbor, Eliezer Ben Yehudah, reviver of Hebrew as a modern language and editor of the new Hebrew dictionary; and Rev. Père Cré of the Mission-aires d'Afrique. Page 1 of *The Journal of the Palestine Oriental Society* (JPOS), Vol. 1, No. 1, published in the following October, listed those present at the formative meeting, including "Dr. W. F. Albright, Fellow and Instructor in Semitic Languages, John[s] Hopkins University, Baltimore; Fellow of the American School of Archaeological Research in Palestine."

On the following rainy Tuesday evening Albright heard a very orthodox lecture by Clay in the American School on Babylonian civilization in the time of Abraham, in which Clay nervously claimed that even Methuselah was a historical name. When Albright came late the next afternoon for his session with Feigin, Clay was there, weary and scowling, refusing to look William in the face, and acting very queerly. At a School faculty meeting next day, in which Albright was not included, Clay so insulted Worrell that Peters intervened, telling Clay his conduct was beneath contempt, and Clay went out slamming the door. Albright knew he had a narrow chalk-line to walk between these personalities.

Mud and rain kept him in his room on Sunday. Prof. Peters came to bid him goodby, for he and Clay were departing next day for Mesopotamia by way of the Suez Canal and ship to India, then by another ship back to Basra. He told Albright that Clay had sent a pseudo-apology to Worrell. The two separated in Mesopotamia less than two months later, however, Peters returning ahead of Clay.

When Albright and Feigin attended a Hebrew lecture on conditions in Russia, William was dismayed because he hardly understood a word of the Modern Hebrew. But the next evening he attended a lecture by Prof. Lifshitz on the development of Modern Hebrew, sat near the front, and this time understood much more, to his satisfaction. He described to his mother his system of study with Feigin: he would slowly read to Feigin an English sentence, which Feigin would repeat; William would then translate it into German, and Feigin would take it from German into Hebrew, which William would then repeat.

He said he had received no mail from anyone but Ruth, who weekly wrote twenty- to fifty-page cumulative letters that he welcomed. To his dismay Haupt and some other orientalists were foolishly predicting that in a few years Albright would be the leading orientalist in America. Though he had carefully not raised Ruth's hopes by any such nonsense, evidently Haupt had talked to her. It reminded him of "Dr. Danny's" foundationless talk in the Iowa days, that made him want to hide for embarrassment.

As for politics, William told his mother that the British were in an impossible situation, since they had made conflicting promises to Arabs, Zionists, French and Syrians. He had not had to change any viewpoint; he was listening sympathetically to all sides, expressing no agreement with any, trying to stay neutral and wishing for a peaceful solution which did not seem possible for Palestine. On the contrary, he predicted political intrigues, boycotts, and perhaps even pogroms as the anti-Jewish feeling would doubtless increase. His mother would be happy over how well he could keep still about things and be discreet, though she would doubtless get the full reaction when he returned home in the summer.

Constant rain made Albright and Worrell postpone their planned trip north into Galilee. On February 9 snow began to fall in late afternoon and continued through the next several days, rising to three feet on Wednesday the 11th. It was the coldest period in Jerusalem's modern history, where snow falls ordinarily once in five years. Ancient trees and roofs were broken down and the city was snowbound; there were many deaths from hunger and cold. The thaw that followed raised the Dead Sea level to an unusual height. There was still snow on the ground when Albright wrote his mother on the 22nd. People had floundered through waist-high

drifts, the natives crying in Arabic, "I die!" for they were not accustomed to such harsh weather.

In late February the School asked for permission to excavate at
Megiddo or Taanach when the mandate had been settled. Various
applications were being made—Dr. Reisner of Harvard for excavating Samaria, Dr. Fisher of Pennsylvania for Beth-shan, which
Albright had hoped the School would get, Dr. Bliss (whom Albright called the father of Palestinian archaeology) for Jericho,
and the British Palestine Exploration Fund for Ascalon, biblical
Ashkelon. Jerusalem was kept for British excavators.

By the time the heavy snow disappeared, William learned from
Ruth that Haupt was working on his behalf and he would not be
allowed to run out of money, though funds would come too late to
do much good; he did not dare spend any then on language lessons.
Ruth was gathering and sending him everything good she heard
about him, but he was glad she did not "press-agent" for him as
Sam Geiser used to do. Ruth's health was much better now, but
Sam was almost as blue as William had been in his first year at
Hopkins.

About the end of February William received his first letter
from home in nearly four months, and in reply said he wished his
family had written regularly as Ruth did, without waiting first to
hear from him after he reached Jerusalem. He reported that some
were trying to have him appointed Director of the School at a
$3000 salary. The committee had already offered him a lectureship
there, at only $1500, and he had turned it down. He was expecting
to reach home by July 15 and if he did, he could intensively tutor
Philip that summer, pushing him through a year of geometry and
a year of a modern language in six weeks. It would not matter if the
girls were older than usual at their graduations—Miss Stevens was
twenty-seven when she finished college (his first mention in many
years of his classmate Maude, the first girl to whom he was engaged, who evidently was six or seven years older than he). William
feared Ruth would be disappointed when Haupt failed to get him
the position in Jerusalem that he was trying to secure. He would
hate to bring a bride to a land under such a threat from either
Russian expansion or Islamic revolution. Also, remaining there
would make it harder for him to hide his real thoughts on the

political situation. While it was gratifying to hear, as he had recently heard from his old friend Bloomhardt, that Haupt considered Albright "the most brilliant man I have met in forty years," William said he thought Haupt's support and friendship would be more of a deterrent than a help in securing a good position. He was flattered that Haupt had given up some of his ideas to accept William's—a rare occurrence—and feared that Haupt's bragging would turn Ember and Blake into enemies from jealousy. He looked forward to summer on the farm after painful economy and constant suffering from his eyes during this time overseas. But he was learning much and in good health otherwise. His fluency in modern Hebrew and Arabic steadily increased.

On March 8, as Albright learned soon afterward, Faisal was crowned king of the Arabs in Syria. In 1916 Faisal had joined T. E. Lawrence ("Lawrence of Arabia") in the Arab revolt against Turkey. Faisal Ibn Husain would be King Faisal I of Iraq from 1921 to 1933, after the French expelled him from Syria in July, 1920 following a reign of only four months as king of the Arabs in Syria.

Albright prepared a paper for the first meeting of the newly formed Palestine Oriental Society on "Egyptian and Babylonian Elements in the Religion of Israel," but when the Society met on March 22 and nine scholars read papers at the afternoon session and four more in the evening, his paper was among four for which there was no time.

On Friday morning, March 26, Albright and Peters, who had returned from Mesopotamia two days before the POS meeting, left by first-class train for Haifa on Albright's first trip into Galilee. They arrived late that evening and stayed overnight in the Carmelite monastery on Mount Carmel. The next day they visited sites of interest there and on Sunday went to Afula, southeastward in the Esdraelon Plain, and spent the night at the Merhabiah colony of Jews. On Monday they rented horses for the day for 100 P.T. each and inspected the mounds of Megiddo and Taanach. That evening there was a *razzia*, or raid by Bedouin, against Afula, but no serious damage resulted. They returned on Tuesday to the Carmelite monastery and the next day by train to Jerusalem.

Albright watched the celebration of Nebi Musa (Moses the prophet) on April 2 with Omar Effendi El-Barghuti, a new Arab friend, and met an Arab poet from Baghdad. Two days later a pogrom or persecution began against Jews and lasted for three days. He told his mother on a postcard after it was over that scores had been killed plus hundreds wounded, but he and the other foreigners were safe. However, it might be necessary for him to come home earlier than expected.

The winter rains were almost over and it was possible to plan horseback trips. On Monday April 19 Albright and Peters started out in rain on horses and reached the Mar Saba monastery in the Wadi Qelt after four hours. Albright had purchased four tins of sardines as provisions the day before. On Tuesday they rode five hours down to the Dead Sea. After lunch and a swim in the heavy, oily waters they rode their horses two hours northward to Jericho and stayed in a hotel two nights. On the day between they took a rowboat ride on the Jordan River, then rode to Ain es-Sultan, Old Testament Jericho, and visited the prewar German excavations (1907-9 under Ernst Sellin and Carl Watzinger). Thursday they rose early and started riding north up the Ghor (Jordan Valley). With only a lunch break they stopped in the Wadi Farah about six o'clock after an exhausting all-day ride. On Friday they rode northwestward up the Wadi Farah and that night stayed in an Arab hotel in Nablus. After visiting the English church and hospital, in the afternoon they inspected Jacob's Well, Joseph's tomb, and the ruins of ancient Shechem. Albright had enough energy left to climb Mt. Gerizim, the Deuteronomic "Mount of Blessings." On Sunday they rode two and a half hours to Sebastiye (ancient Samaria) on its isolated small mountain and had lunch there. On Monday they rode their horses southward on the Nablus-Jerusalem road but turned aside to visit Shiloh and stayed overnight in the Greek monastery. On Tuesday they rode home, passing ancient Bethel, Muchmas, Anata, and other sites. Dr. Peters paid the main expenses; in exchange William acted as interpreter in Arabic for the trip. He felt rather weather-beaten after it was over, as he wrote his mother.

Wednesday Drs. Peters and Albright needed a good rest and allowed themselves to have it. The next day they did only local sightseeing in Jerusalem, visiting the Russian convent on the Mount of Olives and the Russian "Tombs of the Prophets" in two concentric circles of 36 underground grave niches on the upper slope toward the southern end of Olivet (Christian tombs of the 4th-5th centuries, though held by Jewish tradition to be the burial place of Haggai, Zechariah and Malachi). On Friday, April 30, they rode back out to Anata, Jeremiah's Anathoth.

Albright's next big trip with Dr. Peters began on May 3. On that day they started riding southward at eight in the morning, reaching Bethlehem in two hours and leaving their things in the Franciscan monastery where they would spend the night. The father who was their host had just spent eight years in Chile; William had a good visit with him in Spanish and learned that the political situation in Chile was then quite anticlerical. After a short ride southeast to Frank Mountain or the Herodium, one of Herod's fortress-palaces, they returned to Bethlehem and visited the Church of the Nativity, the oldest Christian church, its original having been built by Helena, the mother of Emperor Constantine.

The next day they left early, going south to visit Solomon's Pools (three reservoirs dating back at least to Herod the Great) and Hebron. They took off their shoes and entered the mosque, where they were treated courteously and shown the cenotaphs (memorials, not actual tombs) of the Hebrew patriarchs above the Cave of Machpelah where the patriarchs were buried. Christians could now visit the mosque by presenting a government pass; before the war, none but Moslems could enter.

Dr. Patterson, a physician from England who had been a missionary at Hebron for almost three decades, the next afternoon guided them to the ruins at nearby Mamre, or Haram Ramet el-Khalil. Albright copied a Greek inscription from fine Graeco-Roman ruins there.

For the three-day trip by horses westward to Gaza they were given a military escort, not only for their safety and favorable reception, but to avoid being taken for Jews. One soldier took them to Beit Jibrin, where the sheikh entertained them. Near the second-century B.C. Hellenistic town of Marisa they visited the painted tombs which Dr. Peters himself had discovered two decades earlier. Trudging through a veritable labyrinth, they saw the most important examples of Hellenistic mural painting to be found in the Near East. William's cave explorations on the eastern side of the mountains of Judea on the earlier trip had been somewhat more dangerous, he explained in a letter to his mother, but these caves at Marisa, which had belonged to a Sidonian colony, were larger and mostly artificial. He and Peters also spent several hours at the mounds of Marisa and Lachish.

With a different soldier next day they rode to Felluja, changed soldiers, and went to Tell el-Hesi, where Flinders Petrie had first excavated when he moved to Palestine from Egypt. After lunch there and examining the mound, they continued to Burer and spent the night at the military post. It took four hours to reach Gaza on Saturday morning, and for the first time Albright stayed in a Muslim house, the partly ruined house of one of Palestine's wealthiest men, Adil Effendi esh-Shawi. Major Mills, the governor of Gaza, an Oxford man, humanist and philosopher as well as efficient administrator, guided the party to the ruins, mound, and mosque and provided Albright with valuable folkloristic materials. William in his letter home described him as the finest kind of cultured Englishman, interested in archaeology and folklore as well as people and administration.

On Sunday he and Peters rode northward toward Ashkelon, a difficult two-day trip along the coast because the stubborn horses declined to get their feet wet by walking on the hard sand washed by the surf, preferring to stumble along in the nearby soft, dry sand. They stopped for examination of a mound, lunch, and a swim in the wonderful surf on that beach, then continued to Mejdel and spent the night in a flea-infested native khan (inn). Their muleteer Khalil was greatly worried by the unfriendly people of the Plain of Philistia through which they were now passing, for they took the scholars to be Jews and annoyed them, though without real harm. The usefulness of a military escort became apparent.

The next day they proceeded to Ashdod, the mound of which Albright considered most promising for excavation. After lunch at Tell es-Safi, which Albright thought was surely either Libnah or Gath, they reached Qazazeh and spent the night sleeping under a fig tree. The next day they continued inland into the Shephelah or foothills to Tell Gezer, which Albright especially enjoyed visiting. The Scottish archaeologist Macalister had secured important results in his years of excavation there. By way of Ramleh they arrived at Jaffa, to spend one day resting at the Cliff House. William closed his letter to his mother by repeating his plan to spend three weeks in France and arrive in New York in the last week of

July. He had now decided to give up visiting England and Germany, but he might stretch his time in Paris to four weeks. He also mailed a letter to Ruth, then did some shopping in Jaffa.

On Wednesday, May 12, Albright and Peters rode in the afternoon to Rishon Letzion. Meerensky, the director of that wine-grape-raising colony, was their kind host and showed them the wine factory, third largest in the world, which Rothschild had built. Instead of leaving next day they remained at Cliff House because Dr. Peters was feeling ill. William read Arabic newspapers and figured up his expenses—2.55 English pounds for three days at 85 P.T. per pound.

Friday they went up the coast to Tul Karim and found mosquitoes and fleas worse than ever before in the room they took. Saturday, May 15, William was conscious that it was the first anniversary of his engagement to Ruth. They rode on to Caesarea and had lunch in that ruined town. Hiring a guide so they would not again lose their way among the sand dunes, they rode to a Jewish colony, Zimmarin, and secured a room with two meals for 40 P.T. On Sunday morning they turned northeastward south of the Carmel range and headed for the pass near Megiddo, eating their lunch in a fig orchard. By evening they arrived at Taanach, and Albright found another ancient small jar when he examined the ruins. Their host was the sheikh, son of Sellin's Sheikh Said.

Monday they rode beyond Jenin and lunched at Silat ed-Dahr, then continued past the mountain of Samaria to Nablus and lodged in an Arab hotel. The next day they climbed Mt. Ebal (the Deuteronomic "Mount of Curses") in the morning and heard a lecture as they visited the Samaritans in the afternoon. To the Samaritan priest Albright gave 50 P.T. as *bakhsheesh*.

On Wednesday they rode southward on the Nablus-Jerusalem road, passing Bethel, and were found and taken in at Ramallah by Mrs. Kelsey of the Friends' Mission. In the wonderful evening they spent with the Kelseys at the mission, Dr. Peters related various experiences he had had in his many expeditions in the Near East.

Thursday May 20 they ended their eighteen-day trip, arriving in Jerusalem to find mail awaiting Albright, including a letter from Dr. Ember at Hopkins. He thought William's analysis of the Zionist situation was perfectly correct; he had always thought there would not be any marked improvement as long as there was military rule in Palestine. But he thought it only a matter of days before England would be given—or rather would take—a mandate for Palestine.

Albright's mail also included an April letter from Prof. Haupt, who had learned that Albright intended to return to the U.S. He advised him to remain in Jerusalem, because he believed he would be appointed Acting Director of the School, and in a year or two the "Acting" would be dropped. Even if Albright decided to get married, Haupt thought his bride-elect had better "make a pilgrimage to the Holy City" and be married there. Haupt was glad that Albright was studying Arabic so diligently, as he could live more cheaply and accomplish more with a good command of it. Dr. Nies shared Haupt's view that Albright would be the best man for the place and said Albright needed more money. Haupt was urging the Committee to give Albright at least $3000 a year plus $500 for entertaining, and he thought they would do this. The position would be as permanent as that of an associate professor at Johns Hopkins. Haupt mentioned further that he might retire in five years and there would then be an opening for Albright at Hopkins. He could naturally not give any definite promise, but thought Albright's chances were quite good if he proved successful, and Haupt was confident that Albright would not disappoint the expectations of his friends. He closed by suggesting certain archaeological explorations and advising Albright to keep on good terms with Clay. If he wanted to defend Worrell, he might write confidentially about him to Dr. Nies or tell Torrey and Bacon if he saw them in Jerusalem. Haupt had the impression for some time that Clay was not quite normal and thought he could do Albright a great deal of harm on returning to the U.S. He wished Albright every possible success and hoped he would take good care of himself—especially of his eyes, recommending Dr. Ticho as a good oculist in Jerusalem.

On May 26, two days after his twenty-ninth birthday, William wrote his mother about this new possibility. He was sorry he would not be able to reach home as soon as he had planned. The Committee expected him to stay longer because he had arrived so late. In view of the balance of $700 they had paid him in the previous six weeks he felt he must follow their guidance, above all because an offer would soon come from them for the next year. He would remain if they paid $2500, which was minimum in view of living costs. He needed to buy at least two or three hundred dollars' worth of clothing as well as books. He asked his mother to guess how much he had spent on clothes in the last five years, and answered the question— $150 including everything! Hence he was at the end of all and must buy new no matter where he was.

Ruth, he said, had announced their engagement a few weeks previously. Her parents made no objection, only fearing that if she became an invalid she might have to rely upon them again as had her sister Dorothy when she lost her health in missionary work in Japan. Because of this they probably would not want her to come to the Middle East, though actually the Jerusalem climate was much healthier than moist Japan's. William had suggested she stress that there was always the Virginia farm upon which to fall back, if necessary. He felt they would be adequately situated if her parents would pay for her outfitting and traveling expense to Palestine.

He said he would indeed regret giving up plans for going home, tutoring Philip and Shirley, and spending a year at Johns Hopkins, if it were not for this new opportunity to get a good start on a scholarly career. He seemed to be entering a new kind of life in which worry would replace tranquility and anxiety would substitute for obscurity. With a fellowship worth $400 one was already at the bottom! Now, however, he would have a reputation to sustain as biblical scholar, archaeologist, Arabist, Egyptologist, and Assyriologist as well as administrator. He might assist in excavations as well as write and lecture and serve as guide and translator. He had planned to continue doing research on fellowships as long as possible rather than doing all these other things, but felt fortunate in having two such influential friends as Drs. Nies and Haupt, both of whom were trying in every way to help him. He closed with a promise to cable his mother his answer when the offer reached him, if it was favorable enough to consider.

William attended a farewell tea for Worrell at Hotel Allenby, at which there were addresses in four languages. Before that, on May 25, the second meeting of the Palestine Oriental Society was held in which fifteen papers in French and English and one in Hebrew were read by Frenchmen, Americans and Jews—it was a broadly international group of scholars in Jerusalem. Clay gave the first paper, an absurd one on "The Amorite Name of Jerusalem," mispronouncing both German and English, showing how little Arabic

and Hebrew he knew, and making American scholarship a laugh-
ing-stock. Albright was embarrassed, but Clay had recently acted
friendly toward him, and he tried to do nothing to antagonize Clay.
Albright himself presented a paper on "Mesopotamian Influences
in the Temple of Solomon." It was well received—he had been careful to point out beforehand that his results agreed with the biblical
record.

When Albright wrote his father early in June, after a second
dental appointment on June 1—Ruth's twenty-eighth birthday—he
had not yet received the Committee's official offer; all he knew was
that they were offering him enough for "a young unmarried man
of economical habits." They could hardly expect him to travel, take
photographs for promoting the work of the School, etc., if they did
not pay enough. But the coming offer seemed better than the lec-
tureship he had declined. He would be Acting Director, solely in
charge, with a permanent appointment in view. He considered his
eyesight a great hindrance for administrative work, but with Ruth's
talents added to his own he might overcome that obstacle. He could
hardly bear the thought of being separated from her another year.
His five months in Palestine had given him a mere beginning of
what he wanted to do; a year and a half would see him master of the
spoken languages Arabic and Hebrew, and a real specialist in
geography and archaeology of Palestine as well as in modern Islam.

On Friday, June 11, Albright sent a cable to Prof. Montgomery
as well as writing a letter; the expected letter had finally arrived,
but the meager offer was not acceptable for a married man. A week
later came the great day of decision, as another offer had arrived.
William sent Ruth a cablegram to her sister's home saying he would
remain in Jerusalem; the salary was small ($2500.00).

The Chicago Expedition party of Prof. Breasted had been in
town for some days, and Albright went on local trips with them and
entertained them, as well as continuing to work with Haddad on
folklore. After hearing a lecture on demonology in Palestine by
Dr. Tewfik Canaan, who would become a family friend, Albright
spent three hours with this Christian Arab physician, trained in
Germany, and acquired wonderful folkloristic material from him.

Haupt's May 22 letter arrived the next day; he referred to Montgomery's last annual report which recommended that the Director
remain for a long term of years, if not permanently, and that there

should be a suitably paid librarian, and all staff salaries should be raised. He intended to suggest that if the Director was married his wife, if properly qualified, might be appointed librarian. Haupt reported news of his department: Snyder had failed his Assyrian exam and departed—Haupt thought it was hopeless. Dougherty had tried to prepare clay tablets following the directions in the notes on Ezekiel in the Polychrome Bible (Haupt's product, of which he was very proud, the text printed in different colors to show the original "sources"), and had very good success. Haupt hoped Albright was too pessimistic in his fear that Americans would soon be ordered to leave Palestine. While he would be delighted to have Albright in Baltimore the next winter, if he left Jerusalem there was danger that the Directorship would be offered to someone else when Clay returned. He admonished Albright to remember Ecclesiastes 10:4. (That verse reads: "If the anger of the ruler rises against you, do not leave your place, for deference will make amends for great offenses.")

On June 23, the day after William received this letter from Haupt, Prof. Haupt wrote to Ruth Norton that he was glad to learn Dr. Albright had accepted the position in Jerusalem. Perhaps the Committee would have granted the amount he had suggested if they could have done so, but their funds were inadequate. Dr. Nies might be willing to help, however, and the income could be increased by wise selection of a librarian. He agreed with her that she should take her Ph.D. the next year. (She had been thinking of giving up her doctoral work and spending some time at home for a change, to learn something about housekeeping and cooking, since she had been at home very little since the age of seventeen.) Haupt said he was sure the appointment would be of great help to Dr. Albright in his future career, and it would not have been easy to find a position anywhere else that would pay even that well and give him so much opportunity to carry on research. He had nearly finished preparing Albright's manuscript of his dissertation for publishing among the Contributions to Assyriology, but the Leipsic (as the name was spelled then) publishers had let him know of greatly increased prices.

Because of rising costs, the dissertation was never published—to Albright's satisfaction, because it contained "more Haupt than

Albright." Ruth later gave Haupt's letter to William to keep with other treasured early correspondence.

On June 26 another letter came from Montgomery, and Albright cabled his reply accepting the offer. He continued his studies with Haddad, his visits to sites of interest escorting visitors, and his exchanges of visits, having tea at the American Colony and attending a reception in honor of a general at Consul Glazebrooke's.

On July 2 his friend Dr. Georges Kukhi arrived to spend the summer with him in studies and visits to officials, colleagues, and important nearby sites. They were now the only ones at the School, with two elderly women (Frau Stahel and the Armenian Melisse, also called Meliki, meaning "Sweet") to look after them—one being a fine cook and the other a tireless scrubber, as Albright described them. Thus William and Georges were very comfortable and enjoyed the Jerusalem summer, with hot dry days and always cool nights. William had plenty to occupy his time, for now he could afford language tutoring lessons in addition to working on papers and cataloguing museums.

On September 6 William and Georges began a trip to Galilee, leaving for Haifa by second-class train. In a two-hour stop at Ludd (ancient Lydda) they saw many Polish immigrants. William's acquaintances in Haifa were all away from home, but he visited the elderly head of the Bahai sect and others on Mount Carmel, and on Wednesday morning he and Kukhi hired an auto to go to Nazareth, William being somewhat disgusted that at four pounds they were paying 100 P.T. too much. Passing Jewish boys and girls from Poland and Russia who were doing back-breaking work of crushing rock for road-building, they arrived in Nazareth, left luggage in a German hotel, and went on to Mount Tabor and climbed it. The next day they took the stage to Tiberias by way of Kefr Kenna (traditional but mistaken site for biblical Cana). They visited the tombs of Rambam (Maimonides) and Rabbis Ceni and Meir in Tiberias, and early Friday morning took a boat up along the shore to Mejdel (Magdala), visited the Wadi Hamam, tried to find Irbid, and returned to their German hotel in Tiberias. After lunch they took a steam launch to Samah at the southern end of Lake Galilee and the first-class train to Haifa. Early Saturday morning they caught the train back to Jerusalem. Both of them had mild colds after the Galilee trip, in which they had visited places prominent in the New Testament, taking snapshots and gathering material for the monograph Albright planned to write on Israel's early history. As he wrote about the trip to his mother, William thought she was even then getting acquainted with Ruth, and said he did not fear the result. If anything, Ruth would like them better than they would like her—but he was sure his mother would like her also.

Ruth was indeed visiting the farm in Virginia that September of 1920. A snapshot showed her looking shyly up with her head lowered, standing close beside Mrs. Albright, who was smiling with her eyes closed against the sunshine. In her thank-you letter Ruth expressed how much she had enjoyed the visit and how she had hated to leave. She hoped their reports to William would be as favorable as hers. Mails were becoming regular—her letters now reached William in about three weeks. She felt greatly relieved to see that he was more settled and happy, and thought he would not be again as distressed as he had been at the end of July, for now the Committee was friendly to him. (Then William had written home bitterly of problems being caused for him by a very high-churchman chairman [Clay] who was telling the Committee that William lacked "practicality" and he would not have appointed him if there had been anyone else available. William felt quite lucky to have his position as Acting Director, in view of such "friends.")

7

Acting Director of ASOR

At the beginning of October 1920 Dr. Charles C. McCown, Professor of New Testament Literature at the Pacific School of Religion and, like Albright, a Methodist, arrived to spend his sabbatical year as Fellow in the School. Dr. Albright learned that McCown had been a math professor at UIU in 1899-1900; he had been trained in Germany and was an excellent Greek scholar. While he was older than Albright, he did not resent being merely a Fellow, but William soon realized McCown should have been appointed Annual Professor.

At the end of September the truck he hired from Mr. Esch of the Syrian Orphanage came, and in eight trips they moved the cooperative library from its small room in the School to the Way House, now leased by the British School, where it expanded into two rooms. Then an extra room became available at the American School, for which William purchased at reasonable prices good pieces of furniture that had belonged to a former German official.

The full staff was now present, and there was much theological argument, though they were all liberals. McCown and Albright were liberal Methodists, Georges Kukhi was a fiery Unitarian, and Dr. Amos I. Dushaw, who with his wife and two small daughters had earlier arrived to stay at the School for some months, was a converted Jew, a graduate of Union Theological Seminary. Frau Stahel's late husband's niece, who was also her foster-daughter, Marie Meyer, arrived after being released from wartime internship in Egypt as a German. She became part of the School household and later was housekeeper in charge for a number of years. Both

83

women were Seventh-day Adventists, adding to the interdenomina-
tional character of the School.

William and Georges soon left for Egypt; William intended to
spend two weeks there studying and buying equipment. When they
arrived at Qantarah at eight in the evening, the Cairo train had already left, so they slept that night at the Marina Palace Hotel in
Port Said. Georges' cousin, Dr. Michel Kukhi, met them the next
noon in Cairo and saved them time by checking them off the list,
as he was chief inspector of public health. After a day at a hotel they
moved to a less expensive *pension*, and Albright began purchasing
clothing, compass, watch, pocket lens, a suitcase, paper and other
supplies, also a cane, flashlight batteries, and film rolls for Dr.
McCown. The shopping was done in between dental appointments.

William's plans for doing much study at the great Egyptian
museum and library and the French Institute of Oriental Archaeology were curtailed by a sore throat and influenza. But the weather
was marvelous, no warmer than a few weeks earlier in Virginia, and
the cool or cold nights were a pleasant surprise. He had found on
his Galilee trip in September how correct he was in not traveling
in summer. It was more comfortable to remain quietly in Jerusalem
or Cairo than to be on a farm in Minnesota or Virginia, or especially
in any large American city in the summer.

In Egypt the cost of living was continually rising. William tried
always to travel second-class, but even so he could expect to save
nothing from the $2000 stipend of this year, he wrote his father; the
added $500 for traveling would disappear rapidly in the trips he
planned to make in Syria during winter and spring. He had to give
up the Nile trip he had long hoped for, and even his next summer's
trip to America, unless he was fired from his post and found a job
in the U.S. He begged his mother not to mention anything of this
to Ruth, however, for she had her heart set on his returning. They
would by then have endured nearly two years of separation and it
was difficult to face another year, but he would not have any money
left on which to get married.

Some days after Albright returned from Egypt, on November 4
the third meeting of the Palestine Oriental Society convened, Prof.
Garstang being president and Albright one of the three directors.
The membership now exceeded two hundred. Albright presented
his paper on "A Revision of Early Hebrew Chronology," one of a

series in which he was confident, as he wrote his mother, that he was putting ancient chronology on a firm basis that would endure, lowering the dates of the Exodus and the Conquest by about two hundred years compared with the dates in her Bible margins. The paper appeared in the first volume of the society's journal, dated October 1920, and published soon after this meeting. Albright was elected vice-president, which meant that he would act as president during the winter when Garstang was away.

A day or two later Albright left for Ascalon at 6:15 A.M. with Phythian-Adams, Assistant Director of the British School. They arrived about noon and looked over the British excavations, and next morning went on up the coast to Mejdel, from where they caught the late afternoon train back to Jerusalem. Albright completed his article on the excavation results at Ascalon within the next ten days; it appeared in the 1922 volume of the *Bulletin of the American Schools of Oriental Research* (BASOR) edited by Prof. James Montgomery, President of the Schools.

The first rains (the biblical "early rains") began falling on November 10, aside from a most unusual shower in August. Albright settled down for a second winter in Jerusalem, for he knew that without strong military escort, trips to Petra and all of Transjordan were not feasible. However, there were many interesting sites to excavate in Palestine, with Mesopotamia uncertain and Egypt disappointing in what an explorer could glean any more. A reputable archaeologist with the backing of a responsible institution could now easily secure permission to excavate in Palestine. Albright wrote Dr. Nies these thoughts, hoping the School could soon find money for excavations, perhaps directed by Bliss; if they did not use him soon, his age being already nearly 62 and his health delicate, they would lose his experience. They should make the most of it by training younger men to carry on his work. Albright said he was much impressed with the site of Taanach; its remains led at once into the Canaanite period, and there probably were more cuneiform tablets hidden in its acropolis.

As for his own work, he told Dr. Nies it was proceeding well, with many articles in process and a monograph for which he wished to find a publisher, "Beginnings of Hebrew History." In it he thought he had solved finally the main questions, especially those concerning early chronology; he had recanted the novel ideas of his

"Historical and Mythological Elements in the Story of Joseph," which were due to Haupt. But, his freeing himself from Haupt's theories did not mean he thought less of him; he recognized that the training Haupt had given him was essential for his work. He was now bringing Genesis 14, Abram, the Exodus and the Song of Deborah into historical focus, owing to the results he had finally reached in Babylonian chronology, agreeing in the second millennium B.C. fully with Breasted's chronology of Egypt for that period.

The archaeological schools had arranged cooperatively a series of public lectures for the winter season. Albright attended Garstang's lectures at the British School and the next week at the French School; another on the modern Hebrew language by his neighbor, Prof. Eliezer Ben Yehudah, and one by McCown in the American School at the end of November. Albright's own series began after Thanksgiving Day. His first lecture was on the Old Testament, "The Religion of the Canaanites," at the British School; for his second and third, given at the American School on "Moses and the Prophets" and "Hebrew Poetry," he borrowed benches and chairs and had a full house. After his fourth lecture on December 16, Albright attended a debate between Omar Effendi and Sheikh Nassam. He and McCown also went on a two-day walking trip before Thanksgiving, north to Ramallah collecting folkloristic material, and he and Haddad, McCown and the Dushaws went on a Saturday in early December west to Ain Karim and collected good material of this type.

Life at the School was confined almost entirely to study and lectures in the next three rainy months. Eight inches of snow fell on February 24, and on March 4 three inches of hail pelted down. But, in late February and early March the School group was able to make short trips within ten miles of Jerusalem, especially visiting welis, shrines and holy sites. On March 10 Albright paid Khalil 20 shillings apiece for two horses and 12 for a donkey, and he and Dr. McCown rode all day to a village west of Jerusalem and back, not needing the donkey after all.

Dr. McCown was especially studying welis and other sacred places, preparing to publish the "first elaborate and systematic treatment of the subject," as Albright said in a report to the Chairman of the Committee, which was published in the September issue of

BASOR 1921, No. 4.[1] Albright explained how important it was to study the folklore of Palestine immediately, before the rapid social and economic changes taking place let significant and interesting details of it pass into oblivion. As they visited a village they were told, "The old men think so and so, but we boys don't think so." Yet the old ideas shed light on the mind of the Palestinian peasant, which was in many ways doubtless like that of the much earlier Canaanite and Israelite inhabitants of the land. Albright mentioned that he was cooperating in such studies with Syrian folklorists, especially Dr. Tewfik Canaan, Elias N. Haddad, Hanna Stephan, and Omar Effendi Barghuti, and was planning to collaborate with Mr. Haddad on a Palestinian Arabic grammar and conversation book set in the international phonetic alphabet.

On March 14 a walking party of eight set out for a trip to the Dead Sea. Besides Albright it included Drs. McCown and Dushaw, three other men and the wives of two of them. They walked the first day to the convent in the Wadi Qelt (Mar Saba Monastery) and paid 100 P.T. for lodging. They arranged for donkeys for the second night, visiting Tell es-Sultan (Old Testament Jericho) and Ain Duz on the way. Early on Wednesday morning they reached the Dead Sea, with two Christian Arabs carrying luggage. There they met the rest of the party—Dr. and Mrs. Canaan, Haddad, Linder and two Swedish ladies from the Swedish Mission, the Kelseys from Ramallah, Esch and several more, and also the hired motorboat. They went in the boat down to Engedi and visited that oasis site, then on southward and spent the night camping on the shore below Jebel Usdum (Mount Sodom, an almost pure rock-salt cliff), taking turns by twos to stand guard over the sleeping party. They found, contrary to what the manuals said, that the Dead Sea driftwood made a fine bonfire all night.

On Thursday they went in the motorboat across to the Mojib or Arnon Valley in a strong wind that caused a choppy sea which made several of them sick, especially Dr. Canaan. They had a fine lunch at the mouth of the Arnon on the eastern shore and returned on a calm sea, enjoying a delightful trip north to Judeideh, the port of Jericho. At ten P.M. the Jerusalem party began their walk back to Jerusalem! It took them eleven hours to walk the thirty miles, practically all of it uphill, for they climbed from the level of the

Dead Sea, nearly 1300 feet below sea level, up to Jerusalem, about 2500 feet above sea level. It is not surprising that they were nearly dead on arriving at nine the next morning.

In the September 1921 issue of BASOR, Albright reported on this trip on the Dead Sea: "Aside from Masada the archaeological interest of such a trip is not great, and the shores are too desolate to give an opportunity for folkloristic research. On the other hand, the natural beauty of the scenery is great, especially along the Moabite coast, where the cliffs strive to emulate the handiwork of man in their hues and odd configurations. Not a few archaeologists have been led by natives to supposed sculptures and inscriptions in this region, only to find on examination that Nature had played some of her strange pranks."[2]

On Saturday the 19th, in spite of the fact that he was still feeling in bad shape, Albright started out for Hebron in a hard rain with members of the School family for another horseback tour of Central Judaea and the Maritime Plain. They arrived at a hotel in Hebron late in the evening, having spent the morning at Mar Jirius on account of the rainstorm. On Sunday they visited Haram Ramet el-Khalil or Mamre in the rain and went down to Beit Jibrin for two nights. The weather turned beautiful in the Shephelah or foothills; the top of the Judaean ridge receives more rain than the Shephelah and the coastal plains. The *mukhtar* who entertained them refused any payment, so they gave 100 P.T. plus tips to his poor servant. The next three days they circled back to Jerusalem by way of Araq el Menshayeh, Esdud (Ashdod), Jebus, Aqir, Mughar, Qatra, Tell es-Safi, Deir ed-Dibban and Tell Zakariyeh.

In his report on the trip in the September BASOR, Albright said the purpose of the trip was "archaeological, topographical, and folkloristic"; "the six days we devoted to it were well rewarded in each of these directions." They found the famous painted tombs at Marisa, which the Department of Antiquities now kept locked, "in good condition, except that the colors have faded" in the year since Albright had visited them with Dr. Peters. "To our surprise and pleasure we found that the inscriptions are all in good condition, but we took the opportunity to collate them again. Even the curious exchange of notes between two lovers, hastily scrawled on the soft limestone walls of the most important tomb more than two thousand years ago, is still legible throughout, except in one place. We further measured and made drawings and a photograph of the pillar-altars, which have been hitherto neglected, despite their great interest to comparative religion. . . . The publication of the Gerza Papyri by Mr. Edgar has thrown interesting light on the origin of this Sidonian colony in the heart of the Shephelah, established in the third century B.C. as a station on the caravan route from the land of the Nabataeans to the port of Joppa. . . . it is in just such a place that we may expect to find inscriptions illustrating apostolic Christianity." In the next two days they visited nineteen villages in the Philistine plain, combing them for evidence of antiquity. "The results of this short trip show what is still to be done in Palestine in the way of archaeological and topographical research alone."[3]

Ten days later, as Albright reported in the same issue, "On the fourth of April, Professor McCown, Dr. Dushaw, and the Acting Director set out from Jerusalem on foot, with two mukaris and two donkeys to carry the equipment. Our intention was to traverse central and northern Palestine on foot, a very interesting experiment if it succeeded without sacrifice of health. The whole trip lasted twenty-three days, twenty of which were devoted to walking, leaving three days for rest"—at Nazareth and Tyre on the way north, and at Safed in Upper Galilee on the return. "Except at first, and on the rare occasions when we were able to find a European hotel or hospice, we subsisted on native fare, unleavened bread, cheese, eggs, and *leben,* with few variations. Oranges, obtainable in all the larger towns, proved a most welcome change in the monotony of peasant diet." They averaged twenty-five miles in nine hours of walking each day. "Our mode of travel gave us the advantage of being able to stop anywhere, and climb over precipitous tells, or through labyrinthine caves without worrying over the fate of our horses. . . . we gathered valuable material for the topography of the Plain of Esdraelon, the Plains of Accho, Asochis, and the western shore of the Sea of Galilee. We each secured important matter for publication; . . . the director specialized in topography. . . ."[4]

It was very rough country, mostly uphill or down, through weeds and stones, in a narrow winding path if there was any path— seldom on a good road. They did not sleep in the open because of robbers in those regions; instead they slept in villages or towns, among men, camels, goats, fleas, etc. They climbed every available mound or ruin-pile, measured it by pacing it off, and tried to date it approximately by looking at potsherds they could pick up. They had to gather quite an arsenal of visas and permits in Jerusalem in order to cross into French-mandated territory to reach Tyre. By the time they arrived there and had a second rest-day, William knew he did not want to make such a walking tour every spring. By then he had more respect than before for the horses that saved fatigue and enabled them to cover more territory.

His whole report of this walking tour makes fascinating reading. It was very rough country through the mountains of Upper Galilee down to Safed, which they reached on April 19, and rough again down to the Sea of Galilee, 700 feet below sea level, where they inspected the sites of ancient Chorazin and Capernaum, and continued down along the western shore of the lake. During the last part of the trip they "devoted less time to archaeological reconnaissance, and more to covering ground," as they were anxious to return to Jerusalem, since they were nearly exhausted.[5] From their hotel in Nablus, which they reached late on the 26th, they allowed their mukaris to take the two donkeys home alone while they made the trip by car in a little more than two hours.

The next day Albright called on the German scholar, Professor Gustav Dalman, who had returned to Jerusalem as head of the German Archaeological Institute. Though he was a quiet Christian gentleman who could be taken for a Swedish farmer, as Albright described him, he was one of the greatest orientalists in the world, but the British and French scholars ignored him except for trying to have his passport revoked. William intended to treat him with respect and esteem, although unable to bring him into the British School to see their cooperative library and museum. As he wrote his mother, William was still pro-German and not anti-anybody else. Prof. M. G. Kyle of Xenia Theological Seminary, St. Louis, had also come to Jerusalem to lecture at the School for some weeks. William was charmed with this leading conservative theologian and did not find him a fanatical or intolerant biblical scholar but a real Christian gentleman who never argued.

William told his mother near the end of his letter that on his return he received the astonishing news that Ruth and her mother were going to come to Palestine in August and they would get married about the first of September! He, at least, had expected their engagement to last five years, but it would be only a little over two.

He wished he could come home that summer to see all of the family; perhaps within six years, or sooner—if he was asked to make a lecture tour—he might return for a visit.

Saturday, April 30, the day before Easter, Albright went with Dr. McCown, Mr. Gelat, the School's legal advisor, and Consul and Mrs. Southard to the tiny Chapel of the Angel and edicule of the tomb of Jesus below the large dome of the Church of the Holy Sepulchre, to see the ceremony of the Holy Fire. Candles are lighted by the congregation from lighted tapers passed at noon by Greek Orthodox priests through tiny windows at each side, to commemorate the resurrection of Jesus. But, just before time for the "sacred" fire to appear, William felt ill and had to sit down. Although the symptoms were like those of malaria, it turned out to be what he called spring fever, not severe—probably what he would later call sand-fly fever. Toward evening he went to bed and remained there most of May Day. When he arose and ate breakfast on Monday, still shaky from the fever attack, the first news began coming in of the Passover pogrom against Jews in Jaffa. A peasant milk-woman brought in a wild report that forty thousand had been murdered; it later turned out to be about forty, but that was bad enough.

In mid-May Dr. McCown left for America by way of a visit to the excavations at Ascalon; Albright intended to accompany him that far on his way, but illness prevented him from doing so. Prof. Johannes Pedersen, a Danish scholar who had just arrived, visited him at the School instead. By the next day Albright was well enough to go to Ascalon and spend three days with the excavators, who were then working in the Philistine strata.

May 24, 1921, a Tuesday, was William's thirtieth birthday; it passed quietly. He was busy laying in supplies of wood for fuel for the next winter and preparing various papers to send off. On Ruth's twenty-ninth birthday, June 1, he rented a horse and rode to Wadi Farah and other sites and back with Professors Dalman and Pedersen and Pastor Linder.

Either that day or the next, a cable arrived from Ruth signed "Dr. Norton." She had just passed her doctoral examination the day before her birthday. After a pleasant session of answering questions on her dissertation topic and related matters, she was suddenly asked by one member of her committee a question about archaeology, to which she firmly replied that she knew absolutely *nothing* about archaeology. When Prof. Bloomfield came out to find her in the hall after her short wait and to report the committee's unanimously favorable verdict, he asked if she had heard the roar of laughter in the closed room a few minutes earlier. He explained that it occurred when he announced to the committee that Miss Norton, who claimed to know nothing of archaeology, was planning to go in July to Jerusalem and marry Dr. William Albright, the archaeologist! Her dissertation was a Sanskrit study later published; she did not gain possession of her diploma until 1926, however, because she was graduated *in absentia*, unable to attend the graduation ceremonies in early June. Instead, she had to go to Edgefield, South Carolina, where her sister Dorothy Peatross was making her trousseau. They were pressed for time, as she and her mother were to sail for Palestine on July 26.

William wrote his mother of the cablegram from "Dr. Norton"; he was delighted that her ordeal was over—she had been very nervous and frightened beforehand. He hoped her mother would not be so frightened as to give up the trip, by news of the bloody riots that had occurred in Alexandria, Egypt and in Jaffa, Palestine. They were to be expected every Easter for many years because of the historic festivals that converged on that season. William mentioned also the pogroms against the Jewish colonies in the Sharon and Philistine plains, with many casualties. The British cavalry and planes had arrived just in time to help the colonists repel the Arab raiders. The Egyptian riots had been anti-foreign, not merely anti-British, and the police and soldiers had been on the side of the mob in Alexandria, where it was a "holy war" against all Christians.

William wrote that on the previous day the body of Miss Lomax had been found in a cistern in the enclosure of the Garden Tomb and "Chinese" Gordon's Calvary. It was near her house where she lived as keeper, since the war, of the places considered by many Protestants the site of Jesus' crucifixion and burial. It was a restful garden setting contrasted with the dirty buildings shared turbulently by rival monks where the tomb of Christ was usually claimed to be (and where it more likely was located). Miss Lomax was about sixty and had been a missionary in South Africa and India—a dear old English lady who nevertheless savagely hated Germans, could smoke and drink whiskey like a man, and was not afraid of anything. Robbers were looting her house when, apparently, she surprised them. The body was not found for several days. William feared the atrocious crime would blight interest in that beautiful spot.

Albright worked hard on his papers alone for several weeks. Dr. Kukhi was to join him about the first of July for the summer. In the meantime Albright put Frau Stahel and Marie to work to improve the appearance of the School house and its furnishings before Ruth and her mother arrived. William admitted to his mother that he dreaded the wedding and all its complexities, feeling ignorant of how to do everything properly; he hoped such difficulties would take care of themselves when the time came.

He had some help by way of a rehearsal, however. Brown, on the staff of the British School, married a YMCA secretary; since both were English, the ceremony was in St. George's Cathedral, with Herbert Danby officiating. William was alarmed at the hour-long service and its high-church character; the mitre of the Bishop of Jerusalem was the last straw! Fortunately the Bishop would be away at the time of William's wedding, when Danby would again officiate. William asked his mother to send the best of his old clothing with Ruth when she came; his brothers were welcome to the rest if they could use anything, and Philip could have his dumb-bells. He gave his gas-iron to his sisters or Philip, whoever needed it. He asked his mother to pack carefully and send to him eleven large, heavy reference works in Greek, Latin, Hebrew and German that he had left at home.

As Haupt expected, the "Acting" was dropped and beginning July 1 Albright was Director of the ASOR.

After attending the bachelor dinner given for Brown at the Bristol Hotel, and next morning the wedding at the Cathedral and the wedding breakfast at Garstangs', in the afternoon of June 30 William checked into the English hospital and read in his room all afternoon. The next morning, Saturday, an operation was performed on him by Dr. Orr-Ewing and he remained in bed most of the following week. He received visits from Prof. Pedersen, who had returned from Syria, and Kukhi, who had come for the summer, as well as from Danby. On Sunday Albright left the hospital by coach, and found everything fine at the School. A few days later he wrote his mother, asking pardon for not writing more often

and explaining that from July 1 to 10 he had been in the hospital
for the circumcision operation, which he assured her was not as
simple at thirty as it was for an eight-day-old baby boy. He had
postponed it for years but now wanted to care for it well before his
coming marriage. (It is characteristic of the scientific detachment
of his scholarly genius that during all the months in Palestine he
turned his trained scientific observation upon himself and made a
careful study of his own nature. He recorded his objective observations in an Assyrian cuneiform code of his own devising, which he
later simplified by transliteration. Doubtless he never dreamed
that a half-century later a devoted disciple of his would innocently
and unintentionally crack his intimate code!)

He asked his mother about Mary's plans for the next year. How
he wished he could visit them all at home! But traveling was too
expensive and would become doubly so after he married—at least
$1500 for the fares. He would wait until they had to come; prob-
ably he would be asked to lecture in America in a few years. He
now wanted more than ever to remain in Jerusalem—the first
place, he said, where he felt that way. No other place in the world
suited him like Jerusalem; he loved not only its associations, but
the wonderful research opportunities there and its cultured cosmopolitan air. Not that he minded provincialism, but he heartily
hated narrowness. He was delighted to meet interesting persons of
every type and race. The variety and opportunity in Jerusalem
were unsurpassed. A monotonous life was not possible there. A
further advantage was to be able to get well acquainted with European scholars without the cost of travel. Scholars from many countries were able to meet there and exchange methods and findings,
rapidly increasing knowledge of the lands which were the cradle of
spiritual and material civilization.

In the preceding month the American School in Jerusalem,
which had been without a charter since its founding in 1900, and
was sometimes called the American School of Archaeological Research, was incorporated under the laws of the District of Columbia under the name of "American Schools of Oriental Research,"
the name already used on its *Bulletin* (BASOR). Now they could
hold title to property; the plural form of the name included the
projected School in Baghdad and others they might later undertake
to establish.

On the 13th of August Albright left by the 6:00 A.M. train for Egypt. Arriving at Alexandria twenty-four hours later he went to the Windsor Hotel to secure a room and reserve another for the women. Ruth and her mother had taken a ship of the French Faber Line from New York to Naples, traveled by train to Brindisi, and boarded a small Italian ship for Alexandria. Because William remained in Jerusalem, Ruth's family had never met him. Her father paid their fares over and his wife's return fare, and paid for his wife's trips through Palestine and Egypt—on which Ruth and William went as their honeymoon, with William as guide for the two women.

Tuesday afternoon, August 16, the *Dalmatia* docked and William met Ruth and her mother. Ruth's and William's happiness in being together can only be imagined. Her mother expressed herself as very much relieved when she finally could meet William and see them together.

On Wednesday, after reserving tickets to Jerusalem, he took the women riding in a carriage. Mrs. Norton paid the balance due on the Pullman tickets plus the charge for shipping Ruth's trunks to Jerusalem. Because of the annoyance caused by porters, William tipped them recklessly, for him, as they departed from Alexandria at 3:30 Thursday afternoon. When they arrived at Qantarah and had passed through the quarantine section, they found that the Alexandria ticket collector had removed the Palestine slips from their tickets, and they had to buy three new ones, this time getting a receipt from the stationmaster. They saw the palms of El-Arish and the desert baking in the August morning sunshine. On Friday, the 19th, they arrived in Jerusalem at noon, and it took two carriages to bring them and the luggage to the School. There were no customs to go through because the entire journey took place in British-controlled territory.

After visits to Consul Southard, the Cook's tour agency, and stores in the American Colony, William arranged for Ruth and her mother to be brought by carriage from the hospice to the School for tea in the afternoon. Sunday morning the three of them went to St. George's Cathedral to hear a sermon by Canon Waddy, who with his wife invited them in for morning tea afterward. They visited Canon Danby, went through the Jewish museum, then had afternoon tea at the American Colony and dinner at the School.

On Monday Georges Kukhi accompanied Mrs. Norton on a visit to the Church of the Holy Sepulchre while William and Ruth had a chance to talk in private at last.

William bought a ring from the goldsmith Cartine, made arrangements for their trip to Jericho, and took the two women to visit the Tombs of the Kings and the cooperative library and museum in the British School. Tuesday morning the three of them made a trip to Jericho, the Dead Sea, and the Jordan River. The next day they visited sites in Jerusalem—the Mosques of Omar and El-Aqsa, St. Anne's Church, beside which the Pool of Bethesda had been excavated, and the Praetorium, or paved courtyard of the Roman garrison building—the Tower of Antonia of Jesus' time— now below the convent of the Sisters of Zion. Thursday they made a longer excursion—to Hebron and Bethlehem, where they enjoyed visiting the mosque over the Cave of Machpelah and the Church of the Nativity. William and Georges took the women on Friday to visit Notre Dame de France, the Citadel, and other places in the city. Saturday they went riding to the Mount of Olives, visited the German and Russian buildings, the Garden of Gethsemane, and the Church of St. Mary at its foot.

On his last Sunday as a bachelor William took the women to Christ Church. In the afternoon, after making some last-minute purchases, he countermanded an order that had been given for champagne for the wedding reception; he was determined to have no liquor at their reception. Then he arranged for an auto to take the three of them on Friday to Galilee. They had moved their wedding date up from September 7, the anniversary of Ruth's parents' wedding, to August 31, William's mother's birthday, realizing that they all wanted to make a trip in Palestine and Egypt and that it would be easier to do so if they were married first.

August 31, a Wednesday, was therefore the great day. The wedding took place at 10:00 A.M. in St. George's Anglican Cathedral with Canon Herbert Danby officiating, followed by the reception. Four carriages were needed for the wedding party. Ruth wore a white dress, the type then considered a short dress, and a hat rather than a veil. The scholars of Jerusalem were almost all present—Pères Lagrange, Dhorme and Vincent, founder, director, and professor of archaeology of the Dominican École Biblique; the Garstangs and others of the British School; various Jewish scholars,

William's Arabic and Hebrew tutors and folkloristic colleagues, the diplomatic community and other friends.

A snapshot taken later that day shows a shy bridal pair sitting on the stone front steps of the School. Ruth, still in her longsleeved white wedding dress with square neckline, is knitting and looking coyly up at the photographer through round eyeglasses. William at her left in a light-colored suit, is sitting stiffly with hands on his knees, his lips pressed tightly together, and leaving a visible space between the two of them as he leans a little away from her. Small potted palms frame them in front of the double doors with shuttered, barred windows on each side.

Later that day Ruth and her mother moved their things from the hospice into the School house, into rooms vacated by School summer residents who had moved elsewhere. The next day William secured a new version of his passport, including his wife on it, and they completed preparations for the trip to Galilee.

Early on Friday morning in the hired car they went straight north into Galilee, over the road that the British army had built, through Nablus and past Sebastiye to the Esdraelon Plain and Nazareth. No road had yet been built up Mount Tabor; they drove through Kfar Kana to Tiberias and up along the west side of the Lake of Galilee to Capernaum, not yet as well excavated as it would be in following years by the German Franciscan fathers. They returned through the Jezreel or Esdraelon Valley to Mt. Carmel and Haifa, seeing all along the way young Jewish men and women, the halutzim or pioneers, immigrants mostly from Eastern Europe. These had come after the war to build the road, expecting that Britain would keep its word to provide a homeland in Palestine for the Jews. They were doing cheerfully the backbreaking work of crushing stones with hammers for the building of the new road. William's bride remembered learning much about "perfidious Albion" in those early years—things it was not easy to forget when one had seen them with one's own eyes.

Then the three of them took the train from Haifa down the Mediterranean Coast to Cairo by way of Qantarah East. Ruth was as unhappy and sleepless as always on that night train ride, for she could not get used to a train berth.

In Egypt they did not go south to Luxor—the weather was too hot and in those days that trip was too dangerous. They visited the museum in Cairo, and crossed the Nile to see the Pyramids, having a photo taken of them on camels. Another photo shows the two women with sun helmets, sitting in a carriage drawn by a horse with the Egyptian driver standing by its head. The Pyramids are on the distant horizon, and William, in white suit and white pith helmet, is mounted on a camel beside which its owner stands. A donkey waits at the right.

With not much time for sightseeing in Cairo, the three of them went up to Alexandria, where there was not much sightseeing to do. Mrs. Norton said goodby to her daughter and her son-in-law and embarked for Italy, where she visited Rome, Florence and Pisa before sailing home from Naples. Ruth and William caught their train and reached the Suez Canal just as the pontoon bridge was starting to draw aside. Ruth asked the man in charge if he could not allow them to cross on it before the ship came through. He replied, "No, ma'am; we couldn't get it out of the way soon enough." Ships went through at a certain slow speed. The two of them had to sit on their suitcases more than an hour and a half in the middle of the night while *five* ships went through! The Jerusalem train was being held for them in Qantarah East, however, and again they saw the palms of El-Arish and the desert, now in September heat.

At the School in Jerusalem Ruth and William set up house-keeping. In the following weeks telegrams and letters of congratulations flowed in from their friends. Doubtless the first to arrive and to await their return was a short handwritten note dated their wedding day, from Prof. Gustav Dalman: "Dear Doctor! I am so sorry that I got the kind invitation of Mr. and Mrs. Thornley Norton only now and could not arrange for being present at the ceremony of your marriage. But I hope you will believe that my most earnest wishes of blessing and happiness accompany you and Mrs. Albright to-day and in future. It was a nice time when your Institute and ours were living like two kindred families. I trust it will come again to the benefit of Palestinian Science, which, as I know from experience, grows best on the ground of happy family-life." The gentle scholar knew very well that he would not be welcomed by the British in their Cathedral on this or any other occasion.

A telegram from Johannes Pedersen in Copenhagen contained only three Latin words: *Vivas ver aeternum* ("May you live an eternal springtime!"). Dr. William Rosenau wrote from Baltimore;

Dr. Paul F. Bloomhardt typed a letter to his old friend from Buffalo, New York, referring to the time when, as they talked on the *George Washington,* William had shared with him the news of his great happiness in winning Ruth. He was greatly pleased at news of the wedding, and thought her trip halfway around the world in order to marry William outclassed for romance his own wartime marriage on notice of a day and a half.

Dr. E. Smeta of the University of California sent a note of congratulations "from the shores of the Pacific—gray and powerful as an American dreadnought— . . .to that biblical land of the Jordan River." The sentence could almost be a summary of William Albright's life progress thus far.

The September issue of BASOR announced: "Miss Ruth Norton was married in Jerusalem to Dr. W. F. Albright, Director of our School, on August 31. Miss Norton took her degree in Philosophy at Johns Hopkins in June. It is a pleasure to know that the School has now become also a home."[6]

8

Director of ASOR

Ruth and William Albright lived in the School house with two servants. Frau Stahel, originally from Ulm in Württemberg, could speak a little English, but when she learned that the new bride could speak German, she preferred to talk with her in her own language. This made Ruth feel that her German language studies had not been in vain. Marie, called Sitt Marie (Lady Marie), was able to direct part-time and occasional household helpers in many languages, having lived also in Greece and Turkey.

To reach the house behind its front courtyard one went through a long entrance path between high walls. A Jewish doctor and his wife lived in a house on the other side of the walled pathway. The doctor as well as other people thought Ruth a Jewess. William told her it was because of her dark curly hair, her very fresh complexion and her lively expression, with snapping dark eyes; also she was short and plump. When the doctor expressed much surprise on learning that she was not Jewish, she told him he need not be embarrassed. At the University of Wisconsin a fellow student had asked her if she wished to join the Menorah Society. When Ruth said, "The *what* society?" the girl answered, "Well, then, I don't suppose you do!"

Ruth began trying to raise some flowers in pots and tubs during the winter. She also ambitiously began studying Arabic. And, of course, there were many social obligations to fulfill. The Albrights had Thanksgiving dinner at the American Colony, and the next day entertained the American Consul and his wife; they also had dinner with the Governor of Jerusalem and his sister. By a tea they cared for their social obligation toward the High Commissioner, and William hoped that the bulk of such matters was out of the way for a while. He was glad to write to his family that Ruth was becoming impartial, more friendly with both Germans and Jews, especially the former, though at the beginning threatening to take sides against these groups. She had joined the Ladies' Club of St. George's and read a paper at a meeting. William wrote to Sam Geiser that Ruth was finding the city both interesting and instructive, and told of their wedding and brief honeymoon trip.

In his annual report Dr. Albright had expressed interest in a nearby mound, saying: "The excavation of the shallow mound at Tell el-Ful, less than an hour north of Jerusalem, would at least settle the question of the identity of the site, probably that of Gibeah of Benjamin."[1] The Trustees of the ASOR authorized him to excavate there, and provided $1000 as a special appropriation for this purpose. Before he could begin work, however, investigation had to be made of the property comprising about two and a quarter acres to the north of the Damascus and Herod's Gates, that was now owned in the name of the incorporated Schools, on which a new building was to be built with the $50,000 bequest from Dr. Nies's deceased wife, Jane Dows Nies. A Roman gateway had been found on the property, and before starting to build they wished to dig further and see whether they might find remains of a villa and perhaps even a mosaic floor. Prof. Clay authorized this project and suggested it be done on non-rainy days during the winter so that if Dr. Nies went to Palestine in the spring, the building construction might begin. From January 2 to 17 they dug on the lot, but found no further Roman remains, only distinctively Arabic walls, pavements, potsherds, and a lamp. Albright concluded that an Arab khan (inn) had been on the hill before the period of the Crusaders.

That first year only one student came, the Thayer Fellow, Mr. W. E. Staples from Toronto. Hence no formal classwork was carried on, but the work was done by conferences, lectures, walks, tours, and excavations. Albright and Annual Professor William J. Hinke of Auburn Theological Seminary gave a series of eight lectures at the School during November, Albright's on the post-exilic history of Palestine and Hinke's on the religion and cult of Israel. In December Albright gave five public lectures, and in January Hinke gave his five, the public series concerning the history and civilization of Palestine and the Near East. Prof. Hinke also gave some illustrated lectures in the YMCA series; Albright lectured for the English College on "The Rediscovery of the Ancient Orient" and to the Jewish Archaeological Society on Canaanites and Amorites. The lectures were well attended, contributing to the lively intellectual climate of the city.

Prof. Dalman had returned to Germany early in November, and soon afterward Prof. Albrecht Alt, his successor, arrived—a charming man as well as a good scholar, possessed of much-desired tact, which Dalman had lacked in spite of his gentleness. Albright considered Alt now the best scholar in Jerusalem, with the possible exception of Père Vincent.

ASOR President Montgomery stated in BASOR for January, 1922, that "affairs in the School at Jerusalem have moved prosperously. . . . We would speak in high praise of Dr. Albright's energy and faithfulness, along with his approved scholarship which enables him to be one of the leaders in the stirring intellectual life of modern Jerusalem. He has made good contacts for the School in all directions, and has known how to steer the bark of the School among the perplexing currents of the life in Jerusalem, where many forces, ancient and modern, are in competition and often collision."[2]

Late in January William wrote his mother that all was fine; life was going along just then without excitement. He had returned from walking with Ruth and the housekeepers through the market or *suq* inside the Old City. Ruth on her arrival had been unable to tolerate the odors and dirt that were always to be found in a native market, but now she was accustomed to the East and even considered the market an interesting place. The Annual Professor had injured his feet on a difficult walk northward to Anathoth and Michmash, and they had not been able to take any long walks for some weeks, but William hoped they could soon resume them. He enclosed some snapshots and said if he and Ruth looked as though they were quarreling, they were merely trying to be dignified.

At Easter time Mrs. Albright and Mrs. Hinke attended the Good Friday night service in the Church of the Holy Sepulchre, standing for hours before Calvary where the Franciscan service was held, with sermons in French and in English, and removal of a half-life-size figure from the cross. When the procession began to take the figure from Calvary to lay the body on the Stone of Unction near the exit doorway, the two women decided to try to leave. The officer in charge attempted to help them but could only manage to place them near the door. When it was finally unlocked, all the Greeks who had been shut out during the Latin service tried to enter, and all the people on the inside tried to leave. Ruth held onto the jacket of a soldier and followed him through the mob until safely outside, rejoined by Mrs. Hinke, both almost overwhelmed and exhausted.

The new School building was the subject of a prize competition at the Yale School of Architecture, with prizes set by Dr. Nies. The first prize was won by Mr. P. E. Isbell and his plans were unanimously adopted on February 18 by the Trustees of the Schools. Dr. Nies carried out his plan to go to Jerusalem that spring of 1922 to oversee the beginning of the building. He sailed with the plans on March 15 on the *City of Lahore* for Port Said, and arrived by train in Jerusalem on April 6.

When he showed the plans to Mrs. Albright, she could see at once that the American student's plan was not suitable for Jerusalem. He had made eleven entrances to the large building. The security problem would have been enormous. Buildings in that part of the world were surrounded by walls, with one or two well-guarded entrances. Ruth agreed with Dr. Nies that it was a truly beautiful plan, and tactfully suggested how it might be adapted for the actual conditions there, including the very essential water cisterns in the basement.

Another problem was the cost of this elaborate building as planned. Ruth said, "Dr. Nies, supposing there isn't enough money to pay for this?"

"That will be all right, because I myself will pay for what you need."

"But, Dr. Nies, you have told me that the doctor told you not to come to Jerusalem, because it is too high for your heart condition. What will happen if you let the contract, and then you die?"

"But I'm not going to die," was the Episcopal clergyman's reply. "The Lord has laid the burden on me to build this School, and He will keep me alive." He added, "Of course if I die, you would not get anything"—his will left what he had, beyond the $50,000 bequest for the School and a $10,000 bequest for a Jane Dows Nies

Publication Fund for the Jerusalem School, to his brothers, to go eventually to the School in Baghdad after the death of the last surviving brother.

During the winter when Prof. and Mrs. W. J. Hinke were there and also Mr. Staples, the Thayer Fellow, plus the two Albrights and Frau Stahel and Marie Meyer, Ruth as a new bride had decided to let the house run itself a while and observe, rather than try to take control in an unfamiliar situation. Frau Stahel did fairly well with the marketing and cooking. When the Hinkes left in mid-May, Ruth decided to have a try at managing things herself, and just then Frau Stahel took to her bed with a light attack of malaria. Ruth, with no experience of marketing or cooking, suddenly was faced with feeding a group of hungry people each day, including Dr. Nies, who suffered from arthritis and gout in addition to his angina attacks, and thus could eat no meat, nothing fried, not many eggs—and he also kept the fasts of the Episcopal Church. A friend came to her rescue and offered to do her shopping for meat, vegetables and fruit on alternate days for a small payment.

They were thus getting along passably well with no refrigerator and no ice, by purchasing two days' supplies of these items every other day. But Ruth still had to make her way into the Jewish bazaar for dry groceries, and the smells of the Oriental bazaars still bothered her more than William had let on to his mother, or perhaps more than he even realized. She was intrigued, however, by the clergy of the Greek and Latin Churches in their colorful regalia—an Australian monsignor in a cassock with cerise buttons; the Latin Patriarch in purple gloves with a large ring on the outside, blessing people as he progressed through the city; the Dominicans and the White Fathers all in white even in winter; the Franciscans in brown serge with, it was rumored, flannel undergarments even in ninety-degree temperatures, and no sun-hats, just the small round caps covering the tonsure; the Jesuits, Benedictines and others in heat-absorbing black; the Orthodox Jews from Eastern Europe in their fur hats and fur-lined coats with their ear-locks or long curls in front of the ears; dark-skinned Yemeni Jews with no hats, but the same kind of curls; and the peasant Arab women veiled and shrouded, in dark blue clothing brightened by cross-stitch embroidery.

The architect chosen for their new building was Mr. Ehmann,

trained in Europe and experienced in Palestine. He had erected the Augusta Victoria Hospital on Mount Scopus, which had become Government House and the official seat of the Palestine mandate administration; the Friends' Mission Orphanage at Ramallah; the German gymnasium in Jerusalem, and many other public and private structures. When he was Director before the war, Prof. George L. Robinson had already selected Ehmann as the best architect. However, illness now interrupted his work. Albright hoped to send the revised plans to America and have them back by the end of the summer so they could complete the cisterns and put in foundations before the next rainy season; it did not happen so rapidly, however.

Because Dr. Nies was there and could not travel, Albright held himself back from trips he very much wanted to make to see Dr. Fisher's excavation at Beisan, in order to keep temptation away from Dr. Nies. But Dr. Nies planned a trip to Ashkelon alone, any-way, which was prevented when a violent attack of angina pectoris struck him on the night of June 12. There was no telephone and no time to send for help. Sitt Marie ran next door to get the Jewish doctor. In spite of his physician's warnings, Dr. Nies had insisted in climbing all the way up the Augusta Victoria tower two days before he had the heart attack. His health had been deteriorating ever since he arrived in Jerusalem; it was too high for his heart condi-tion, yet the heat anywhere else in Palestine was too severe. This became a fatal dilemma in which he was caught.

As soon as they could secure more medical help, they called Dr. Canaan, whom Albright considered the best physician in Jerusalem, Dr. Neumann, and Dr. Orr-Ewing. They hired a night nurse; the Albrights cared for him themselves in the daytime. Dr. Nies seemed to be improving until the 17th; then at 6:00 on Sunday evening the 18th he died in William's arms.

As Albright wrote to Fisher, Dr. Nies was a remarkable man, uniting his own scholarship with generous support of that of others; a loyal, kind, and altogether delightful person whose death they keenly felt. They had his body embalmed and sent by special car to Port Said for shipment to America as soon as the official permission was cabled from Washington. Albright wrote a letter of condolence to Frederich Nies, Dr. Nies's brother in Brooklyn.

Thanks to a $1000 gift from Miss Juliana Wood, of Philadelphia, which was turned over to the School by the Trustees for this purpose, Director Albright was able to begin excavations at Gibeah —Tell el-Ful ("the hill or mound of the bean")—in the spring of 1922, in mid-March after the rains had ceased, and resume them in the summer after Dr. Nies's death. Albright employed forty peasants who lived near the site. The October 1922 issue of BASOR carried a photograph of the excavations at Tell el-Ful on the front page (and Prof. Clay's obituary for Dr. Nies; the December issue contained a photo of Dr. Nies in his ecclesiastical robes). Tell el-Ful was the first early Hebrew site of Palestine to be dug; before that, work was carried on almost entirely in large Canaanite mounds at the edge of the plains. Some ancient towns were buried under modern ones and thus could not be dug; others were unwalled, and their remains were washed away by the hard winter rains, or removed as building stone for nearby later villages. Peasants had opened some of the tombs on the eastern slopes of Tell el-Ful and the western slope of the adjoining hill, and had peddled to museums the bowls and jugs they found, dating from the period of the biblical city, 1200 to 900 B.C., which King Saul made his capital. There were at present no buildings on the mound, and it was shallow. In his preliminary report Albright was already able to say that in the top part of the mound there were "remains of at least three superimposed fortresses, all from Biblical times. Since the fortress is surrounded by a glacis [sloping wall] in an excellent state of preservation, it will be seen that we have here an Israelite migdol [fortress], the only one of the kind yet found in Palestine."[3]

In June of 1922, Upper Iowa University granted their alumnus in Jerusalem his first honorary degree, the Litt.D. In the last week of that month Dr. Albright interrupted his dig to go to Beirut and represent the American School at the inauguration of the new President, Bayard Dodge, of American University. The trip gave him an opportunity to study the collections at the local museums and to visit Byblus, where Pierre Montet had been excavating. He returned to Jerusalem by way of Damascus, with a side trip to the great Hellenistic ruins at Baalbek, and through the Hauran in northern Transjordania, a trip similar to the one he wished he could have made the year before with Prof. Johannes Pedersen.

Albright's Tell el-Ful excavation continued until the beginning of September. He made the daily trip back and forth—too exhausting an arrangement along with the work of sorting and labeling all the potsherds and other finds. Since he had no trained foreman there seemed no other way, but Ruth had already discovered, and had also been told by her doctor, that she must sleep in a separate room if she was to get any rest. When William arrived back from the dig late at night, he had to open his mail and study various things in their room, regardless of her—and his own—need of sleep. Ruth had known that she was marrying a genius and that geniuses are not easy to live with, and she simply adjusted herself to their life the best she could, in a way to protect his genius and productivity in scholarly work.

Albright reported later that "the only serious interruption occurred toward the end of August, when some of the owners of the property became unpleasant, refusing to abide by the agreement we had offered to make." His wife's memory a half-century later was that, with his terrible temper and intolerance of poor workmanship, he had insulted a native digger. Albright wrote: "They went so far as to demand up to four hundred pounds for the privilege of excavating the site! Having retained a well-known shyster lawyer of Jerusalem, they had a warrant issued for my arrest, and so several days were wasted in court proceedings." (At this time, Mrs. Albright was in the Bethlehem hospital run by the Sisters of Charity, with her first miscarriage. She had one of the several private rooms kept for French officials, and remained there two weeks, being treated like a princess.) "Needless to say," Albright continued, "I was released, and the Government proceeded to take steps for compulsory lease of the property. Meanwhile I proceeded with the excavations, until the imminent exhaustion of the funds forced me to suspend work September 2." After a small group of experts had assessed the rental value as *seven* pounds a year instead of four hundred, he "returned to the site November 7, working four days, with several members of the School present for part or whole of the time."[4] The full report would appear in an *Annual* of the Schools.

With the beginning of the 1922-23 academic year three Fellows arrived and regular classwork was organized in addition to excursions and lectures. The new Annual Professor was Dr. W. H. P. Hatch of the Episcopal Theological School in Cambridge, Mass. Dr. James A. Kelso, President of the Western Theological Seminary in Pittsburgh, also lectured. The Thayer Fellow was Mr. Voigt of

Yale, and Mr. Cooke of Yale and Dean Edwards of Missouri Bible College were the other students. Albright lectured in the first term on the topography of Jerusalem, the archaeology of Palestine, and the geography and topography of Palestine, giving also a course in North Semitic Epigraphy (inscriptions). Prof. Hatch taught Greek Epigraphy, and native speakers taught Modern Hebrew and Modern Arabic. Albright began lecturing, as well, in Egyptology at the new Hebrew University founded by Dr. Judah Leon Magnes.

The Albrights gave an "at home" tea on November 15 in order to have the new faculty members meet the School's friends in Jerusalem. They found themselves associating with the elite, for it was a small community in a foreign land, and because of Dr. Albright's official position and the contacts he had cultivated from the time of his arrival, they were included in all social affairs of the foreign scholarly community.

A month before that at-home tea Ruth took a serious step which for a while threatened their marriage. She, an Episcopalian, on October 15, 1922 entered the Roman Catholic Church and became a Tertiary of the Dominicans—that is, joined their Third Order, a lay group of men and women living in the secular world but actively supporting the Church in many ways and committed to the daily reading of the Divine Office in the Breviary, as well as to systematic studies in theology. She had been studying many months privately with the Dominican fathers of the École Biblique.

William's reaction at first was great regret that he had been so busy with his excavation at Tell el-Ful, visiting Beisan, and doing many other things, that he had not been aware of her studies and where they were leading. He felt sure that if he had realized, and had had time to talk with her and explain theology to her, he could have headed off this result, which at first to his strong Methodist-leaning background seemed a catastrophe. In view of his childhood in Chile and his terror of the black-robed religious of that area, who had much less knowledge, wisdom and tolerance than those in the same area exhibit at the present time, one can understand that he would feel an emotional reaction in spite of the fact that the priests and monks whom he knew in Jerusalem were of an entirely different type and that he greatly admired their scholarship and was on close personal friendship terms with them himself.

But, as so often in his life, William began to view the development philosophically and discovered that he could find good even in it. Many years later he looked back on this period and this event, recalling how interested he had become in comparative mythology and history of religions in the years following receiving his doctoral degree, and how this direction in his studies could have taken him into increasing subjectivity. The Thayer Fellowship which enabled him to go to Palestine after the war had changed the direction to studying modern Hebrew and Arabic, then explorations of topography and archaeology leading into excavation work of his own. He remembered how "liberal" he had become during his university studies, then marrying a very intelligent Ph.D. in a similar field, and thought he might have continued as a liberal, except for the fact that his topographical and archaeological work was continually confirming biblical tradition and undermining the extreme liberal views about the history of Israel then current; and the fact that his wife made the relative easy change from her Anglo-Catholic background to Catholicism, with a solid training in theology as a Dominican tertiary. He long had resisted her influence, he thought later, because of his hostility due to the kind of backward Catholicism which had conditioned his attitude since childhood, but he read for years the fine Catholic literature she provided in the household, and also read Neo-orthodox Protestant literature. Between these opposing pulls he had become quite stable in the middle position, adopting the ideas of either side as they coincided with his own convictions as a scholar.

Ruth's spiritual advisor was Père Vincent, whom her husband considered the greatest Palestinian archaeologist. One time about the end of her first year of marriage she remarked to Père Vincent that she was only William's second wife. He looked questioningly at her, and she explained, "Years before he met me he was already married to Pallas Athena"—his scholarly work. Père Vincent threw back his head and laughed heartily, agreeing with her.

In the previous summer Prof. Ember, then in Germany, wrote to his former Egyptian student and colleague asking him to write a scientific article for the Haupt *Festschrift* for which he was one of the editors, and also to write an appreciation of Prof. Haupt and his scholarship and works, including biographical material. Albright in reply expressed great unwillingness to write the appreciation, suggesting that there were other Assyriologists in a better position than he to write it. But Prof. Ember did not give up easily. In October he wrote again, saying that it need not be long nor "a panegyric like Montgomery's eulogy of Jastrow," a scholar and Trustee who had died. "A sober, truthful, and restrained statement could be preferable. The least that I could expect of you would be that you send me some reminiscences of your connection with the Oriental Seminary. How about a congratulatory message in Assyrian? I know that Prof. Haupt would be greatly delighted if you would prepare such a message." Dr. Albright reconsidered his objections; he would not consent if there were an older student of Haupt's still in touch with his contributions to Assyriology, but he would do his best, and send something for criticism. He added that he would be happy for a chance to show how he appreciated Haupt's scholarship and his remarkable contributions, especially in view of the fact that he was now opposing almost all Haupt's critical views in Old Testament studies of his more recent years.

A few days later Albright wrote Haupt a letter, thanking him for the "Biblical Studies" which had just arrived. Tactfully he said he wished that he could agree with him more nearly on many items, but—for better or worse—he had in general gone back to views that were already full-blown in his mind before he entered Johns Hopkins. He gratefully gave Haupt credit for teaching him to be a philologist and to rate accuracy and soundness in this area very highly, but he feared that his historical viewpoints had remained the same as they had been previously. He might be able to follow Haupt more closely later, but not at present, at least in biblical questions. Yet he could never forget the unequaled training he had received there at Hopkins; he appreciated it deeply and owed it much, and therefore hoped for Haupt's pardon that he was going astray in his application of methods he had learned from him.

After this diplomatic effort to cushion Haupt's reactions to his papers now about to be published, Albright told of resuming and amplifying regular classwork in the School, and of his successful excavation work at Tell el-Ful, where they had found the burned fortress dating to the period of the Judges of Israel, also Saul's fortress of the royal period and a much later Maccabaean fortress. They had found seven separate building periods dating from about 1200 B.C. to about A.D. 70.

Albright sent off his appreciation of the career of Prof. Haupt to Prof. Ember, saying he hoped it would be satisfactory, for he had taken great pains with it. The editing of the volume took several years; Ember unwisely showed Albright's article to Haupt, who wanted a number of items inserted about his activities in learned societies, without Albright knowing he had suggested it. Albright refused to add anything, for then Haupt would know he knew of the suggestions, and in any case he had not intended to be exhaustive. It would finally be presented just in time, before Haupt's death, a few years later.

During the fall of 1922 Albright was also working every spare moment at the museum on deciphering the inscription on a weathered stele of Sethos I that Alan Rowe had found as he excavated at Beisan. At the December 7 meeting of the Palestine Oriental Society Albright read a paper on "The Beth-shan Stele of Sethos I." His term as president expired, and Père Dhorme, Director of the French School, was elected president, while Albright was made assistant editor (with Danby) of the society's Journal.

At the end of December Albright and most of the School group went to Egypt for two weeks. He was in Cairo from December 30 to January 8, but missed seeing Alan Rowe there because he thought he was still with Dr. Fisher excavating in Luxor. When Albright reached Luxor, Fisher told him that Rowe was in Cairo, but on returning there Albright became ill and left early for Jerusalem, thus missing a number of scholars he had planned to visit, among them Prof. Breasted. In Cairo before going to Luxor, Albright spent most of his time in the library studying. He was with a party of six in the four days he spent at Luxor and hence did not try to see the inside of the newly discovered tomb of Tutankhamen (which Howard Carter and the Earl of Caernarvon had opened only a few weeks earlier after Carter's discovering it on November 4). Fisher and Winlock showed the party around their excavations. Albright recognized that a great impetus had been given to archaeology and its popularization with the sensational finds in the Theban tomb of Tutankhamen.

On March 9 the entire School group made a trip down to the Dead Sea. Twelve joined in hiring a motorboat and trailer, and this time they allowed three days instead of two—and they did not walk. They reached Judeideh, the port of Jericho, soon after seven in the morning and took their boat southward, spending several hours at the mouth of the Arnon and then going to Mezraah, the port of Kerak. They spent the night there, then made the boat trip southward around the Lisan or "tongue" the next day with a choppy sea which Albright in his report said "made progress difficult and introduced an exhilarating atmosphere of danger into the situation. After some minor accidents, we passed Cape Costigan safely, and at once the sea became calmer. In the afternoon we made a brief run down to Jebel Usdum and the Salt Grotto, and returned to spend the night at the southwestern end of the Lisan. The third day we spent in visiting Masada and Engedi, returning late that evening to Judeideh. The trip proved very interesting to most of the party, though some of the more timid ones were rather badly frightened at times. The morning of the fourth day was given to a tour by way of the Jordan and Jericho."[5]

Albright's reports of tours and archaeological digs in his years in Palestine were written for the general reader in not too technical a style, in order to appeal to many people and increase the influence and support of the American Schools of Oriental Research.

Instead of being able to make the usual spring trip south and west into the Shephelah, Dr. Albright was busy with a small excavation of two of the four mounds or tumuli at Malhah several miles southwest of Jerusalem, for which Mrs. William M. McKelvy had provided the funds, seventy pounds ($340), on her visit to Jerusalem in mid-winter. He began excavation of the tumuli on March 26 with about thirty workmen and worked until rains and an Arab feast put a stop to it on the first of April. He intended to resume after the spring trip northward, but had to nurse a severe attack of sand-fly fever for three weeks in May and June. He still had two-thirds of the funds and hoped to continue later, but difficulties over use of the land developed with the owners, which with other obstacles prevented his ever coming back to complete the investigations. He had found potsherds which were characteristically eleventh-century in date, and Philistine pottery. "I am able also to show," he wrote to Montgomery on April 7, in a letter that Montgomery quoted in the April BASOR, "that the tumuli were not erected by natives, but by an invading army, so the probability that they were raised by the Philistines during the age of Samuel, Saul and David is very great. . . . The significance of these provisional finds at Malhah is of much importance. For the Bible student they illustrate the operations of the Philistines as recorded in the Books of Samuel, especially the campaigns of David so briefly summarized in 2 Samuel 5. And for the archaeologist in the Mediterranean civilization they give an added link connecting the Philistines with the far-off shores of the Aegean civilization."[6]

Early in April, after the end of the biblical "latter rain," the members of the School left on their annual spring trip northward, returning on April 26. Albright reported it in the same issue of BASOR: "The entire trip lasted eighteen days, and proved very successful, all members of the party expressing their enthusiastic approval of the trip and the way it had been conducted. . . . The journey, which we made with horses and tents, carried us from Jerusalem to Timnath-serah, Aphek, Caesarea, Dor, the Wadi Arah, Megiddo, the Plain of Acre, the Plain of Asochis, Nazareth, Tabor, Beisan, the Sea of Tiberias [or Galilee], Gadara, Jerash, Araq el-Emir, Madeba [the latter four in Transjordan], Jericho. We avoided the automobile routes and 'tourist' points as much as possible, in accordance with the system of trips which I have outlined before. I succeeded in keeping all costs, including fees, tips, hotel bills, where incurred, etc., down to a pound a day.

"The scientific results of the trip were not inconsiderable, especially for the historical geography of the country, on which I have gathered much new material. At many tells and sites hitherto little or not at all investigated we made large collections of potsherds, and I examined many thousands of sherds in the course of the journey. . . . All the members of the party were profoundly impressed with the great significance of potsherds for dating of sites; several members of the School have acquired a considerable knowledge of the intricate but exact science of historical ceramics. I may add that this is the first long trip made by any archaeological school in Jerusalem in which potsherds have been properly studied and utilized."[7]

Several tragic losses took place that year, two of them while they were away on this trip: one the death on April 17 of Mrs. Anna Spafford, head of the American Colony. After family tragedies—death by drowning of four daughters and by scarlet fever of their only son—the Spaffords had left Chicago in 1881 with their remaining two daughters to spend the rest of their lives in service to the needy in Jerusalem. They did what later was called settlement work— teaching and nursing. During the war they nursed wounded soldiers of both sides and ran soup kitchens; they managed a hotel, stores, and other means of raising money for welfare projects, and later established a baby hospital. The older daughter Bertha helped her widowed mother and continued her work, aided by her husband Frederick Vester and their six children. Bertha Vester became a well-known painter of wildflowers of Palestine and a friend of Lowell Thomas, among many famous people. The Albrights knew her and her mother and others of the Colony. It was Bertha who had provided the white surrender flag—half of a hospital sheet fastened to a stick—when Turkish Jerusalem surrendered to the British in 1917.

On April 23, just before the group returned from Transjordan, their legal advisor, Antoine Gelat, first dragoman or interpreter of the American Consulate, died. Earlier in the winter Ezekiel Ben Yehudah their neighbor, the leader in restoration of Hebrew as a modern living language, died; Dr. Albright's tribute to him was published in the JPOS for 1923. And in the group's absence Prof. Alt had left Jerusalem for the University of Leipzig.

At the April 3 meeting of the Trustees held in Princeton in connection with the AOS meeting, an additional $100 was appropriated to Dr. Albright for his dig at Tell el-Ful. Also, "It was voted, with warm terms of appreciation of his work, that Director Albright be given a sabbatical year upon completion of his six years of residence in Jerusalem."[8] Mr. Samuel Feigin, who was about to receive his doctorate in Assyriology at Yale, was granted the Thayer Fellowship for 1923-24, and Dr. Clay was appointed Annual Professor for that year in place of Prof. Haupt, who earlier had resigned for health reasons. The Albrights could now look forward to a trip to America in several years, while still living in the dream-come-true world of the lad in Chile so many years before.

After the other lecturers of the School and the students had mostly departed by the end of May, and Albright recovered from his sand-fly fever attack of May and early June, he spent a week at Beisan working on the decipherment of two additional steles that had been found, and a week in Beirut and Byblus studying

the finds from the Egyptian temple excavated there. He became a
more confirmed Egyptologist than ever, as he wrote to Prof. Alt—
recognizing that knowledge of Egyptian was necessary even for
archaeological work in Palestine.

In late August he spent eight more days, with the extra $100
given him, in excavating Tell el-Ful, bringing the work to a close
so that in the fall he could prepare the results for publication in an
Annual.

By mid-September Prof. Clay had returned to Jerusalem and he
and the Albrights were working hard revising the plans for the
new School building. Clay left for Baghdad with his party on the
4th of October, Albright going with them part-way and returning
alone from Syria. On learning that Clay had visited Carchemish
with Woolley, Thureau-Dangin and Dhorme, the three groups
having apparently met accidentally at Aleppo, Albright regretted
very much that he had turned back to Jerusalem at Beirut instead
of going farther into Syria with Clay's party.

As the Clay group was returning from Mesopotamia a few weeks
later, two cars carrying them became lost in the desert between Hit
and Palmyra and plunged over a precipice more than three yards
high into the wadi. The Arab driver was killed, but the rest were
not injured seriously; Clay himself had some broken ribs. Dr.
Judah L. Magnes, Chancellor of the new Hebrew University, was
with the party and told Albright of the accident on his return early
in December. When the telegram arrived, Albright thought the
party was delayed by quarantine or by research in that neighbor-
hood; when he heard the full story, he considered their deliverance
from death nearly miraculous. Dr. and Mrs. Hewett were more
seriously injured (he was Honorary Lecturer, coming from the
School of American Research at Santa Fe), but by the time they
came through Jerusalem on their way home they had nearly recovered. Prof. Clay was able to give two lectures before leaving
with the Hewetts the day after Christmas.

On the last day of 1923, Albright wrote to Prof. Max L. Margolis of the University of Pennsylvania, who was to be Annual
Professor the next year, '24-'25, giving information on schools for
their daughter and places to live. He suggested that if they did
not need a separate kitchen and would not mind having a child

about a year old in the same house, they were welcome to live in the School house with the Albrights, in the room reserved for either the Annual Professor and his wife or for the Fellow.

The child Albright referred to as being about a year old in the following academic year was Paul Norton Albright, born on December 12 in the Hospital of the Sisters of St. Joseph in Jerusalem. His father came to the Hospital about 4:30 to see Ruth, but she was so worn out and suffering so much just then that she sent him away, not wanting him to see her in pain. She did not have time to tell him it would not last much longer, so he went home and went to bed. He was greatly surprised on coming the next morning to learn that only a couple of hours after he left, at 6:20 P.M. his fine son weighing 8¾ pounds was born. The nuns thought it terrible that he was not named Marie-Joseph, as he was born on the feast-day of Joseph and thus should be named for him and Our Lady. He was named Paul Norton, for Ruth's father, also for William's next-younger brother and Ruth's older brother.

By late January Ruth wrote a long letter to Mother Albright telling the happy grandmother about her grandchild. He had gained a pound and a half and was the image of his father except that he had her eyes, and was bald except for a fringe of hair at his neck. She described the amused smile on his lips, his energetic demonstration of his lungs, and how completely he occupied her time, including a long walk each day in his carriage at his father's insistence (on non-rainy days). Sometimes she pushed the carriage to the garden of the nearby convent, where he could lie in the sun under the hood while she visited with the Sisters or walked about in the only real garden available. She wondered how Mother Albright had ever managed with *six* children. She wished her mother-in-law could see William as he bent over his little son's bed—it was a sight to cure sore eyes, and although William was not vocal in his admiration as were the others, she could tell his admiration in his eyes. She and the baby slept in a separate room so that the baby would not disturb William's rest, but he came first thing every morning to see how they were.

Dr. Melvin Grove Kyle, president of Xenia Theological Seminary in St. Louis, had offered $2000 to finance an expedition to study the southern Dead Sea region and search for Zoar, the location of Sodom and Gomorrah, and Paran. Albright replied, extremely pleased over the cable making the offer. Further word had arrived and been forwarded by Ruth to William while he was with Clay's party in Beirut, so that William was able to invite Prof. Alfred Ely Day, dean of the American University, a geologist who well knew the geology of that region, to join them.

While the academic year had opened late with three students on December 17, after Clay's group returned from Mesopotamia, the usual lectures were compressed into two months and ended in mid-February when Kyle and his party and Prof. Day arrived to begin the Dead Sea expedition. On the morning of February 15 the party left Jerusalem in four Ford cars packed with equipment, including several hundred pounds of canned food. In Amman that evening they set up tents in the open square before the Emir's palace and spent part of the next day in negotiations with the Government. Within an hour everything was worked out with the Director of Antiquities, Dr. Riza Tewfik Bey, formerly professor of Philosophy in the University of Constantinople, and they received the necessary letter for the Governor of Kerak. They had intended to rest there that Sunday, but late on Saturday a strong west wind brought rain and promised snow. Outdoor camping in February on the highlands of Transjordan is anything but desirable, and they quickly struck their tents, loaded their cars, and rushed south by a desert trail over dangerous, half-built roads. After delays because of car troubles they reached Kerak late in the evening of the 17th, very happy to see the lights of that Moabite city on its height. The missionary who was to have arranged for their entertainment was ill, but Père Mallon, a member of the party, was able to find them a place to stay at the Latin parish house, where they had use of a kitchen and dining room and soon were eating a hot dinner.

They spent two days at Kerak preparing for their trip down into the Ghor, hiring "nine horses and a dozen pack animals, mainly mules, to carry our equipment and barley for the horses and mules," as Albright explained in his report in the April 1924 BASOR. They had an escort of two soldiers assigned by the Governor of Kerak, Reshid Pasha, "since the district into which we were going has a long-standing evil reputation." They went down "the precipitous slopes of the Wadi Qneiheh to the Dead Sea, but it required a day and a half to make this short distance, owing to the difficulty of the path. Hardly had we started downward when one mule fell over the precipice and was dashed to pieces several hundred feet below; this accident taught the muleteers caution, but two other mules stumbled over the edge and rolled down hill until further progress was fortunately interrupted by boulders. Much to our surprise the equipment escaped serious damage, and the surveying instruments were quite uninjured."[9]

Dr. Kyle's account in his fascinating little book *Explorations at Sodom* reveals that it was *his* bed that went down in the load on that unfortunate mule and was recovered, "but the mule himself did not recover!"[10]

They reached the very bottom at Ghor es-Safi early on Friday afternoon February 22, and began their archaeological investigation of that interesting district, spending a week there. They also covered the adjoining district to the south thoroughly as well as exploring several valleys and foothills. The weather was delightful; later it would have been so terribly hot that the exploration would have been completely impossible.

"Our principal objective here," Albright wrote, "was the identification of the site of Zoar, placed by the unanimous testimony of biblical and post-biblical, as well as Arabic sources at the southeastern end of the Dead Sea." He concluded, since only Byzantine and Early Arabic sherds were found at the traditional site, that biblical Zoar was now under the slowly rising waters of the southern end of the Dead Sea.

"From February 29 to March 4 we devoted ourselves to the exploration of the Ghor el-Mezraah and the adjoining districts, including the famous Lisan. . . . The day before Dr. Kyle's departure from Mezraah, March 2, was utilized in a voyage by motor launch from Mezraah to Jebel Usdum (Mt. Sodom) and back."

Dr. Kyle reported Arab hospitality at Mezraah: "At the port Mezra'ah, the port of Kerak, the harbor-master—if he can be dignified with so high-sounding a name—was a young Arab of high rank, a sort of nobleman. He received us with ceremonies becoming his rank. After many salaams and much hand-shaking, a servant appeared with a bowl of warm milk, 'a lordly dish' it was; whether the milk was cow's milk, or goat's milk or sheep's milk or was from the donkeys or the camels or the horses, they did not say—and I do not say. Probably my quizzical expression betrayed my thoughts, for

Dr. Albright passed close by me, and said in English *sotto voce,*
'Drink it; it is a ceremony.' I drank, and we cemented our friendship in _____'s milk."[11]

On March 3 Dr. Kyle returned to Judeideh on the motorboat
they had hired. For Albright and the rest of the party, "as so often
in archaeological research, the real find came at the end, just as
we were about to return to Kerak. . . . we found first a large open-air
settlement of the same period [the Early Bronze Age], secondly a
strong fortified acropolis, more than a thousand feet long, and
finally a group of fallen limestone monoliths, six in number, with
fragments of a seventh. Strewn over the plain to the south of the
acropolis [about five hundred feet above the Dead Sea near Bab
ed-Dra] were thousands of hearths and enclosures, both rectangular
and circular, to judge from the foundations, which are alone preserved. Everywhere were potsherds and flint artifacts." Père Vincent and Phythian-Adams agreed with Albright's date of around
2000 B.C., down to about 1800 B.C., "characteristically Early Bronze"
with "indications of early Middle Bronze techniques"; later terminology for those centuries would be Middle Bronze I and II A.
There was no deposit of debris, so Bab ed-Dra was not a town.
"The presence of the group of *massebot,* which must have been
dragged for miles to be placed where they are now, furnishes the
solution of the puzzle: Bab ed-Dra must have been a holy place,
like the later Israelite Gilgal near Jericho (*pace* Sellin), to which
people came on annual pilgrimages. The numerous hearths and
foundations of enclosures are then the remains of the festival
booths, called *sukkot* (succoth) in Hebrew, where the pilgrims lived
during the days of the feast. The fortress was presumably erected in
order to protect the latter from sudden razzias."

After discussing where these worshippers might have come
from, hardly the nomadic population of the Plain of Moab, Albright concluded: "It therefore seems highly probable that Bab
ed-Dra is a link with the biblical Sodom and Gomorrah, and that
an exhaustive excavation of the acropolis would furnish us with
much data of value for the reconstruction of their culture, and
doubtless for the clearer understanding of the depravity which
tradition ascribed to them." This identification was "supported by
the fact that it was once for all abandoned at about the time when
biblical tradition places the destruction of these towns, early in

the second millennium B.C. . . . ." The steady rising of the waters
of the Dead Sea, and the fact that the floor of the sea south of the
Lisan jutting out from the eastern shore is on the average less than
four meters deep, together with the constant depositing of silt and
mineral salts on the bottom, raising the floor as the surface level
rose, led Albright to conclude that any ancient mounds underneath
were now deeply buried. With the leveling action of currents and
storms their inequalities had doubtless been eliminated, so that
there was little possibility of ever recovering the exact locations
of Sodom, Gomorrah, or Zoar.[12]

After their return to Kerak on March 5 they made a short trip
to Jebel Shihan. "The most interesting point visited on the return
journey was Ader, about an hour and a half northeast of Kerak. . . .
At Ader we discovered the first Moabite temple known thus far,
though only the foundations are preserved. . . ."[13]

They left Kerak on the 13th and arrived in Jerusalem the following morning. The expedition had cost only about $1400 but
produced gratifying results. Dr. Albright concluded his report with
the suggestion that other institutions might cooperate in similar
expeditions with the American School and publish their results
jointly, dividing any finds between the museum of the Palestine
Government and that of the institution cooperating with the School.
He emphasized the scientific, nondenominational nature of the
School, giving the same "friendly reciprocity" to scholars of
every kind, "Protestant or Catholic, Jew or Gentile, liberal or
conservative."[14]

On the page opposite the close of Albright's report appeared
the newly adopted seal of the ASOR—a circle with the name lettered around the edge, and inside it the Egyptian *ankh*-sign for
"life" which enclosed the Babylonian cuneiform "star" representing deity. This remains the ASOR siglum, adopted by the Trustees on December 27, 1923.

The School group left on April 2, 1924, for a ten-day trip
through the western and southern areas of Judaea. On the third
morning they visited the very large site of Tell Beit Mirsim, which
was especially interesting to Albright. He thought it was Debir or
Kiriath-sepher, a Canaanite royal city, captured by Caleb's son-in-
law Othniel. He found no indication of any post-exilic settlement
there—one would dig immediately into Israelite levels, and some

walls were showing above ground. "What an opportunity for the excavator, . . .!" he exclaimed; *he* would later be the excavator, together with Dr. Kyle. He closed his report in the October BASOR, "If we could always find as many new things as we did on this trip, we should be kept busy registering our discoveries."[15]

In April and May the School members made various trips in northern and central Palestine, part of the time in Galilee going on foot. From April 28 to May 5 several members of the School accepted Prof. Garstang's invitation to attend his five informal lectures on the "Methods and Practice of Archaeology." Albright lectured in May at the École Biblique on "Archaeological Researches in Moab and the Problem of the Cities of the Plain." Then the school year ended and people left on their way home to America.

In May Albright thought he had a hidden fever; his health seemed a bit shaky and he was more reconciled than earlier to their plan to spend the summer in Europe. Their building construction had again been postponed until at least the end of the summer. They had suggested to Prof. Clay that only two of the three wings be built first, so that there would be funds with which to equip and operate the larger plant while waiting for more funds to be raised for the third wing. Clay approved and let them know he would try to secure the Delco Electric System for the new building.

In June Mrs. Albright and baby Paul had quite an adventure that changed their plans for spending the summer in Europe. The Papal Legate was in town to open a new wing in the Italian Hospital, and that Saturday afternoon the Orthodox Jews, restricted by their Sabbath regulations from traveling more than a certain distance, stood on the hill in their quarter, Mea Shearim, and watched the colorful procession including the Latin Patriarch go with the Papal Legate into the nearby hospital. The crowd remained there waiting for the exit of the procession. Ruth was wheeling little Paul in his pram across and along the street at the edge of this crowd, when a Moslem taxi driver came past. He probably was thinking contemptuously about these Orthodox Jews, "Well, if you can't walk, I'll see if I can make you run!"—he had utter scorn for them—but he made a serious miscalculation in attempting to brush close to the crowd and scare them. He did not see until rounding the corner, too late, that Ruth was just lifting the baby carriage up the tiered sidewalk. His fender or bumper caught

Ruth behind the left knee as both were moving in the same direction. She went down with her head in the dry gutter. Her first thought was of her baby, and as she pulled herself up and saw her toes, they disappeared. The driver, in panic, had backed up to take his victim to the hospital, and had run over both her shins.

The jolt had bounced the baby up out of the carriage into the arms of a sailor from the *Iron Duke*, which was in the roadstead off Jaffa. Though forbidden to go ashore as far away as Jerusalem, a number of sailors who were Catholic did go, as it might be their only opportunity to visit the holy shrines and, as it happened, to see the Papal Legate. One of them was walking around the watching crowd and happened to be at the right spot to catch baby Paul. He handed him to a Jewish woman in the crowd.

Ruth sat where she had been thrown and demanded, "Where is my baby?" People clucked, "Don't worry—everything is all right —the woman there has it." Ruth said firmly, "I will do nothing until I have my baby!" The crowd expected her to become hysterical, as any Arab or Jewish woman of the Near East would have; when they saw how calm and determined she was, they gave the baby back into her arms. Instead of taking her to the government hospital, however, which served the Arab population, they took her in the taxi to the police station in Mea Shearim, doubtless thinking she was a Jewess. Since Ruth and her accident were more exciting at the moment than the Papal Legate, the space in front of the police station was soon filled with people from the crowd, discussing, giving advice, wanting to help, but unable to communicate with her or she with them. Time went on and on, while the driver was inside the police station. Finally a man in black, with hat and side curls of an Orthodox Jew, emerged from the station and authoritatively strode to the taxi where Ruth was sitting. He said, "Lady, you give your baby to my wife; she got good milk." Ruth refused, though the baby was crying for food and she wanted desperately to nurse him herself.

Finally the taxi driver also came out. He then took her to the government hospital, where she was examined, but nothing was done except make an official notification. At last she and Paul were taken home—at least three hours overdue from their walk. William and the two housekeepers were by then in quite a stir of worry. Frau Stahel and Marie put Ruth into bed and the baby was fed at last.

Dr. Canaan came; he found a bruise on the back of her head that had bled, so she had to have painful antitetanus shots the next morning, a prospect not exactly conducive to a peaceful night's sleep after such an exciting, upsetting afternoon and evening.

The next day the police came to see her at home and in William's presence were shown the bruises on her head and legs and given a full account. In court she appeared only as a witness in the criminal case of the state, her own civil case being in abeyance until the criminal case was decided. Her claim for damages could be presented later. But she never made any claim, though she followed her lawyer friend's advice not to let it be known that she would not press it. It would do the careless driver good to stew in jail over how much money might be claimed from him while he was earning nothing.

After the chauffeur was released from his several weeks in jail (a heavy enough sentence because of the lack of earning), he came to the house and made a polite apology to Dr. Albright. Being Moslem, he would not have expected to speak to her personally. She was still in bed, recovering. The effects of the accident lasted for years, and the immediate effect was to cancel their plans to spend the summer in Europe. Ruth with baby Paul spent some time recuperating at the Franciscan convent at Qubeibeh, the Arabic name for ancient Emmaus, seven miles northwest of Jerusalem on the Roman road. William joined them there after two weeks in which he studied and worked alone at home, and all three returned to Jerusalem about the last of July.

On September 15 construction finally began on the new School building. When finished it would consist of three buildings around the sides of a rectangle, the largest, main building facing southwest on the street along the long side of the rectangle, and the two wings running back along the shorter ends, with an inner court at the rear. A loggia around the court connected the buildings. The south wing was to be built only as far as the basement at that time. The main building contained a large library and assembly room on the first floor, and a hostel of nine bedrooms with lavatories and a salon on the second floor. The north wing would serve as the Director's house until the south wing was built some years later, and would have the refectory on the first floor, with the Annual Professor's apartment upstairs, used temporarily by the Director. All the buildings had basements, so there was room for two large cisterns and storage space as well as a photographic room and an apartment for the housekeepers.

Before the fall term began, Albright wrote a very special letter on September 20, 1924, to Prof. Robert W. Rogers, suggesting how desirable it would be for a closer relation to exist between the American School and Drew Theological Seminary. He outlined the way the School was cooperating with about fifty other seminaries and universities, among whom only two were Methodist, yet all the Fellows from 1919 to 1923 had been Methodists. He outlined their program of lectures, trips, and excavations and their cooperation with French, British, Jewish and German institutions, and explained the advantages of membership.

In closing he took advantage, as he said, of writing this letter, to express his great debt to Prof. Rogers. He explained how at the age of ten, as a Methodist missionary's son in Chile, he had run errands to earn enough money to buy his *History of Babylonia and Assyria,* which was for many years his favorite book and which he had practically memorized. Then, when he was seventeen, he had written to him for information about Hebrew Bibles, and he had never forgotten Prof. Rogers' kind, courteous and helpful answer. As a result of the inspiration he had received from him and his writings, he had learned by himself several Semitic languages and had been accepted in Johns Hopkins as a Fellow in 1913 because of a paper about to be published in a scholarly German publication. He had come to Jerusalem in 1920 and was now Director of the School and hoped to remain there many years longer, and gave credit for any scholarly success he had won largely to Prof. Rogers, to whom he was glad at last to be able to express his gratitude.

The fall trip by horseback after two weeks of lectures, made by a party of ten and lasting from October 21 to 28, was reported by Albright in the February 1925 BASOR under the title "From Jerusalem to Gaza and Back." To close his interesting report Albright wrote, "While less new material was secured on this trip than usual, we collected a good deal of topographical data, and brought home a large quantity of pottery and flints. Incidentally, the members of the party enjoyed themselves thoroughly, and became enthusiastic supporters of our horseback trip programme."[16]

No excavations were conducted under School auspices in the

1924-5 academic year, and in fact very little was done in Palestine by any organization. Projects were suspended, awaiting the raising of more funds and the return of personnel. Albright was unable to resume digging of the tumuli at Malhah because of the attention needed by the new building construction. On November 6 he gave a paper in the POS meeting on "The Fiscal Organization of Israel and Judah." Prof. Max L. Margolis, the Annual Professor, from Dropsie College, was elected president. On December 22 the Institute of Jewish Studies was opened and Albright gave a speech following the German address (for probably the first time after the war) given by Dr. Hertzberg of the German School to the assembled notables. In Albright's speech he said, "This unity of Jewish scholarship in diversity can hardly help but prove an example and an encouragement to us all. . . . May we join earnestly in our common studies, free from prejudice, and working only for the attainment of our scholarly ideals! We look forward with pleasure to a healthy and active rivalry in the search for ultimate Truth that is our common goal. We hope that our new colleagues will advance with giant steps, exciting us to friendly competition, and thus creating a stimulating atmosphere of scholarly productivity."

Before Prof. Margolis gave his presidential address on "The Name 'Nazareth' " in the January 8 meeting of the POS, at which Albright for once did not present any paper, a tragedy had occurred in the Margolis family. Just before Christmas one of his young twin boys suddenly died. The mother and the other two children returned to the U.S. in January and Prof. Margolis moved into the School. He departed as early in the spring as possible, in late March. All of them at the School were upset by the tragedy. Ruth with Paul and her maid went to spend a week beside the Sea of Galilee at Tabghah.

Early on February 7, 1925, Dr. Albright and the School members left on horses on the way south to Hebron, Engedi and Masada. They made an exhausting day's climb down beside the waterfalls at Engedi carrying only what they absolutely had to have with them, and next day tried to climb Masada. By the time they succeeded in finding a cleft in the southwestern side and scrambled up to the top, it was so late that they had little time to study the remains. (In March of the previous year Albright and a party had been there, but only Dean Edwards and one of the Fellows, Mr. Cooke, had succeeded in reaching the almost inaccessible top from the eastern face. Albright, who tried from the great stepped northern face, did not succeed.) The party did not return to their base camp on the top of the cliff at Engedi, where their horses and mukaris waited, until nearly midnight, after climbing and walking almost sixteen hours with nothing to eat or drink from noon onward.

Albright was a pioneer explorer in his day. Now the Israelis take their youth on annual spring pilgrimages to this historic mountain-top and bring tourists over good roads. There is even a chair-lift up the eastern side where Josephus's serpent-path is again usable, and on the Albrights' last visit to the land they would be taken to the top of Masada in a helicopter, with its famous excavator himself as their guide!

The party returned to Hebron and then to Jerusalem by way of Mamre and Beit Sur, ancient Beth-zur, a large site that Albright found attractive; he would later excavate it. On March 12 the group again visited the Shephelah, this time by the early and late trains, walking from site to site in the middle of the day.

The group of nine left on March 25 on horseback for their spring trip. It took them into northern Palestine and across into the Hauran of Transjordania. In his report in the October 1925 BASOR, entertainingly written like his earlier ones, Albright said that "all worked to make the trip as instructive and successful as possible. If one were to be singled out for special praise, it would be, without doubt, Mr. McFadden, whose zeal in collecting pot-sherds and flint artifacts was only equaled by his skill in frying bacon." Albright had to leave the party in Nazareth in order to be present, with Mrs. Albright, at the formal opening of the Hebrew University in Jerusalem, for which he was the representative of the American School, Johns Hopkins, and the Smithsonian Institution. He took the train from Nazareth to Jerusalem and returned by train on the second of April, the day after the ceremonies—first having a tetanus shot because at one point he unfortunately found himself between an Arab stallion and a mare, and got an ugly bleeding wound on his upper left arm near the shoulder.

He caught up with his touring party at Tiberias and in a few days they entered French-controlled Syrian territory and visited sites in what is now called the Golan Heights, working their way southward from the sources of the Jordan River on Mount Hermon and returning to the west bank by way of the Beisan excavations. "Wednesday morning we sent our pack-train directly to Jericho," he wrote, "while we crossed the Jordan at ed-Damieh by the primitive cable-ferry, in order to visit Tell ed-Damieh. Despite an interruption by some truculent Bedouin of the Sunur tribe, who suggested that they would like to kill us and throw us into the Jordan, but finished up by smoking a friendly cigarette with us (in Ramadan! [the month when Arabs do not eat, drink, or smoke before sunset]), we examined the mound thoroughly. . . . Of late years the Damieh ford (no longer, however, fordable) has become much more interesting to biblical scholars, thanks to Professor Sellin's demonstration that it, and not the Jericho ford, was the original place of the Israelite crossing. . . ."[17]

On March 7 Albright had given a paper in a meeting of the Jewish Archaeological Society on Egyptian officials in the land of Israel before the days of the Judges. On May 7 he presented "The Jordan Valley in the Bronze Age" at the meeting of the POS. Lectures had closed in mid-March; the students departed at various times following their return from the Spring Tour, and during May and June Albright had more time to devote to preparation of articles for publication, as well as to the rapidly progressing construction of the new building. A photo in the April BASOR showed the foundation and basement walls; the October issue carried a photo of walls up nearly to the top of the second story of the front of the main building, and the fully roofed left wing.

The first of a series of annual Summer Schools was held at the American School, combined with a pilgrimage—studies and tour through Palestine and Syria—in the Papal Jubilee year of 1925, with arrangements for an extra stay in Rome. Director Albright lectured during this summer school twenty-seven hours and took the party to many places of interest in and around Jerusalem as well as accompanying them on their trip in Syria. Six days after the summer school began, on July 22, the Albrights left the house on Abyssinian Street, which the School had rented for more than fifteen years. The furniture was stored in the basement of the unfinished Nies building until after the summer school; Ruth and Paul and the housekeepers went out into the country to stay for a few weeks' rest while William was busy with the lectures and trips of the summer school. Then they settled into the north wing, the main building not being ready for use until November. City water was connected in early August; they secured electricity temporarily by a line from the French School on the other side of the road.

Mrs. Albright retained vivid memories of the move into the new building on what was the birthday of one of her great-grandmothers. The third house, built only up to the first floor, contained in the basement an apartment for Sitt Marie and her elderly aunt, Frau Stahel, and extra storage space. The cisterns, of course, were empty and there would be no water for months. The water for the city system was at that time brought up from the Auja River in tank cars, dumped into the Pools of Solomon, and piped north into Jerusalem. In the upstairs of the main building there were two toilets, two showers, and one bath in the hostel, all in separate small rooms rather than together, so that the bath and showers could be closed off when water was scarce; people would have to use pitchers and basins. Before guests arrived that fall they secured water that could be used for flushing toilets, but with empty cisterns there was no water for showers or baths. The resulting misunderstandings in the dry seasons on the part of Americans not used to such inconveniences, and unable to realize the scarcity and undependability of the water supply, were probably the worst public-relations part of their lives in Jerusalem. When the guests found their showers and bath locked, they asked Mrs. Albright whether *her* bathroom was also locked. She said no, for the basin was in the same room with the tub in their apartment (the toilet was separate, European-style). "Well, then, why should ours be locked?" they demanded.

"If you had ever been through one of these droughts we have, you would not worry whether the director's family, with that kind of experience, will use the tub," was her reply.

Rain was late in starting that winter. The first rain did not come until January 17, 1926, and it started at tea-time while they were entertaining several guests. Marie, who had been promoted to housekeeper when they moved into the new building and her aunt was pensioned, told Mrs. Albright it looked like rain (which it already had a number of times, in vain). "Shall I open the pipes?" she asked—to let the first water run out, carrying away the dust of the roofs. Mrs. Albright replied, "No, there won't be that much rain in proportion to what we need, and it will settle." Then the rain did begin, and soon Mrs. Albright could not endure any longer to sit at tea with the others who were chatting about this and that, not realizing that a *miracle* was happening! She said, "Excuse me," and slipped out. In a few minutes Dr. Albright also excused himself and slipped out after her—and then the guests came out, to find them (they must have thought them crazy!) with Marie in the main front hall, bending over the iron plate that covered the entrance to the cisterns, smiling as they listened to the beautiful sound of rain-water gurgling down the pipes into their empty cisterns for the very first time!

Americans who came had problems not only with the scarcity of water in the fall, but with the Eastern-type food. When they became hungry enough, they let themselves be persuaded to taste the Turkish and Greek dishes that William and Ruth were enjoying, and eventually they too liked rice instead of potatoes, the *kusa makhshi,* the bitter-cured olives, pressed cheese, and the *lebban* (similar to yoghurt). No alcoholic drinks were served in the American School, because it was an American institution and Prohibition was in force. The Albrights always "ran a dry house," for they did not intend to give anyone an opportunity to charge that their reason for being in Jerusalem was to escape the restriction of Prohibition. Mrs. Albright considered it one of the greatest benefits an American could have, to go to such a place and find out how 95 percent of the world really lived. But it was especially hard on the type of guests they often had for short periods, who were "big frogs in little puddles" at home, but here were merely transients and had no influence with the permanent British, French and other foreign residents with whom the Albrights, as permanent residents with a responsible position, were social equals.

Word of the death of Prof. Clay was cabled to Jerusalem in mid-September, 1925. Albright mentioned it in letters, saying that for Americans his death meant a heavy personal loss, not without scientific relief; it was to be hoped that now the rifts in American Assyriology would be mended. Clay's student, Prof. Raymond P. Dougherty, the new Annual Professor, had arrived from Goucher College, Baltimore, and in October he and Albright left on a lengthy trip to Iraq, studying the tells of the Middle Euphrates region so they could establish the old topography of the area.

No students came to live in Jerusalem at the School that fall, leaving Albright free to carry out this planned trip to Mesopotamia.

Dougherty, who was soon appointed Clay's successor at Yale, was Annual Professor in both the Jerusalem and the Baghdad Schools and remained in Baghdad, continuing to survey southwestern Babylonia after Albright returned in mid-December.

They had left for Haifa on October 15 and gone by train to Beisan, then back to Megiddo, visiting the digs at both sites. There was a misunderstanding at Megiddo and Albright was forbidden access to the mound, so they drove in a Buick up along the Mediterranean to Beirut and stayed a week at the American University there, making side trips to Jebeil (Byblus) and other sites. From Tripoli they went eastward by train and used another car for day trips out from Hums, continuing by train to Aleppo. They had originally intended to go by horseback down the Euphrates Valley, but changed to a Ford which they used for sixteen days for about $165 with an Armenian chauffeur who, Albright reported, "never complained once during the entire journey!"[18] They started down the valley on November 1. A main purpose was to try to find the site of Mari. Albright thought their attempt entirely unsuccessful, yet described Tell el-Hariri as a large mound covered with Early Bronze Age sherds, and thought it surprising that such a site was not mentioned in the ancient sources. He considered it too far downstream to be Mari, but kept the possibility in mind, and it later proved to be indeed Mari—an ancient scribe had mixed the order of several sites as he mentioned them, thus confusing Albright at first. Monsieur André Parrot would prove it to be the ancient Amorite Mari when he began excavations there in 1933.

The "ban" on Albright's presence on the mound of Megiddo still puzzled and bothered him after his return in mid-December. Dr. Fisher, who now was connected with Megiddo as archaeologist, wrote to Prof. Montgomery about it and told Albright that he, Fisher, would always be proud to show Albright his excavations; he was ready to resign his position and work only at the School, if that became necessary. Albright himself wrote to Prof. Luckenbill of the University of Chicago, the institution sponsoring the Megiddo excavations. Luckenbill, expecting Albright to remain longer in Mesopotamia, let his letter wait and get buried on his desk; he did not reply for many months, even as he had done previously with a letter from Albright. Finally a letter of April 19, 1926, arrived, apologizing for his long delay. Luckenbill still could not figure out what he had said that could have been interpreted by someone at Megiddo to mean he should exclude Albright from the site, but he did remember that they at Chicago had been quite put out by a circular letter sent from the ASOR headquarters. It concerned publications, the list headed by Yale's volumes, and down in about tenth place a mention of the University of Chicago's publication of their Megiddo dig. Not a word had been said to them before their sudden inclusion in such a list. Otherwise they felt ignored except when "the hat was passed around for contributions." Luckenbill agreed with Albright that "the death of our old friend Clay has removed one of the main obstacles to peace in the field of American Oriental studies, it's a hard thing to say, but true." He closed by assuring Dr. Albright that he had "the highest regard for you and your work. We may not always come out at the same place, but anyone who works as you do, has my best wishes."

This tardy reply must have brought great relief to Dr. Albright, who made every effort to keep peaceful relationships on all sides. He replied on June 15, over a week after seeing his wife and son off for the homeland on their furlough, that the Megiddo affair had turned out as he surmised. He himself had had nothing to do with the offensive list of publications. He had long ago concluded that the attempt to exclude him from the Megiddo tell did not originate with either Prof. Luckenbill or Prof. Breasted, but was the result of some misunderstanding. He was only sorry that, as he had learned later, it nearly shattered the expedition there!

Little Paul was two years old when Albright returned from Mesopotamia. The Hazard Fellow, Samuel Rosenblatt, came that winter, later joined by Dr. Sheldon Blank of Hebrew Union College, and Albright started several courses for them on his return; one or two others listened in to the lectures that winter during the rainy season. Rabbi Rosenblatt later, as a colleague of Albright's, recalled hearing Paul speak a mixture of German, English, and Arabic, and remembered tall, already bald, thirty-four-year-old Dr. Albright as a little absent-minded, but always kind and affable, though he had no use for phonies.

Paul and his mother left for America and her family in Columbus, Ohio, on June 6; before Albright departed on September 6 he taught in the Summer School. Early in June there came the horrifying news that Professor Ember's wife and youngest son had died in a fire at their home the night of May 31. He died also, in the hospital, during the funeral of his wife and son. His library was destroyed. At first it was thought that his great work of twenty years on Semito-Egyptian affinities was lost as well, but it was saved from the fire, though badly burned, and could be partly published a few years later.

Prof. Romain Butin of Catholic University arrived in August to be Acting Director during Albright's sabbatical leave. Albright left as scheduled from Port Said on the *Kaisar-i-Hind* for Marseilles. As he started his journey after nearly seven eventful and important years in that place where he had thought to stay six months or so, and then return home to his *real* work, his thoughts must have been interesting. Life had opened up unexpectedly rich and satisfying during those years. Some thoughts about it and the contrast between his status on arriving and that which he now held must have been in his mind as he boarded his ship, though his mind was undoubtedly also busy working on innumerable archaeological and philological problems.

9

Furlough

After landing in Marseilles, Dr. Albright proceeded by train to Paris, where he enjoyed talking with French scholars and editors, with whom he had been in correspondence for years, and studying the Oriental collections in the great Louvre. He traveled up into Germany, visiting the university and museums and meeting scholars in Berlin, and attending the European orientalists' meeting in Hamburg. There he met Prof. T. H. Robinson, of Cardiff, Wales, President of the Society for Old Testament Study. He invited Albright to their international meeting at Oxford at the end of the following September on his way back to Palestine, expressing great pleasure in meeting him at last. Albright replied to the letter of invitation which was forwarded to him from Jerusalem (Prof. Robinson had forgotten to ask for his address in America) that he would have to be back in Palestine earlier, but suggested that the next Annual Professor, J. M. P. Smith, of Chicago, might attend on his journey. Robinson was sorry Albright could not come: "You are not the only desirable visitor we shall miss through having our meeting so late." He said he was "afraid we are not all absolutely at one in wishing for agreement between the late enemy countries, but the feeling is so strong amongst us that we can afford to disregard the minority. Gressmann's visits to England this year have been a tremendous help."

Dr. Albright arrived in the U.S. in time to rejoin his wife and go to Baltimore for the fiftieth anniversary celebration of the beginning of Johns Hopkins in downtown Baltimore in October 1876. However, Albright was ill and unable to attend the banquet, and Mrs. Albright could not attend either because little Paul was also sick. She heard afterward from friends what had happened. The master of ceremonies during the toasts called out, "Is Mrs. Albright in the hall?" And again, "If Mrs. Albright is in the hall, will she please stand up!" When there was no response, the toastmaster said, "I'm very sorry she isn't here, because I wanted you all to see the only person who has ever gotten *two Hopkins Ph.D's in the same summer!"*—hers at the end of May, 1921, and Dr. Albright at the end of August by marriage!

Albright's fine plan of first spending a couple of months with his parents at the Virginia farm vanished into thin air when he returned on October 20 and found that a series of lecture trips across the nation, which he was to carry out on behalf of the American Schools of Oriental Research, would begin on the 29th in Philadelphia, where he made his headquarters for the furlough year. On that same Friday he lectured to the University of Pennsylvania and the Phi Beta Kappa Society of Philadelphia. After lectures at Crozer Theological Seminary in Chester, Pennsylvania and Catholic University in Washington, from November 8 to 18 Albright made a swing through the Midwest, lecturing at McCormick Theological Seminary, Garrett Biblical Institute, the University of Chicago, and the University of Michigan. Then he returned east for a brief rest and the Thanksgiving holiday.

Albright attended the celebration of Prof. Paul Haupt's 68th birthday on November 25. On that occasion the *Festschrift* that had been in process several years, edited in his honor by Cyrus Adler, president of Dropsie College, and the late Aaron Ember, was presented to Haupt. He had taught forty-three years at Johns Hopkins. Three weeks later, on December 15, 1926, Paul Haupt suddenly died. Albright's "In Memoriam Paul Haupt" appeared early in 1928 in the German series Haupt had edited, *Beiträge zur Assyriologie und vergleichende semitische Sprachwissenschaft* 10, No. 2. Born in Görlitz, Silesia, November 25, 1858, he had earned his Ph.D. at the University of Leipzig in 1878 and began teaching in 1880, from 1883 on at Hopkins and, for half the year during many years, also at Göttingen. The *Festschrift*, luckily not delayed too long, contained a copy of his portrait, painted by one of his sons and presented at the celebration of his fortieth year; it now hangs on a wall in Gilman Hall. Dr. Cyrus Adler, who was Haupt's first Ph.D. graduate, was "the first person to have received the degree of Doctor of Philosophy in Semitics from an American University," as he said in his Commemoration Day address on February 22, 1923, when the portrait was presented to Johns Hopkins. Perhaps Haupt was best known as the editor of the "Polychrome Bible," the text of which was printed in different colors of ink to show the different "sources."

Albright resumed his lecture trips November 29 at Wellesley College in Massachusetts and lectured at Yale on the 9th of December, with several other stops in between at Haverford College in Pennsylvania, and again in Massachusetts at Mt. Holyoke College and Smith College, and the Oriental Club in New Haven, Connecticut. On the 10th he spoke at Vassar College in New York, on the 14th at Jewish Institute of Religion and Columbia University, and on the 15th lectured at both Boston University and Brown University, Providence, returning to Harvard the 16th and speaking in nearby seminaries on the 17th.

After the Christmas holidays with his family, Albright spoke on December 28 at the meeting of the Society of Biblical Literature in New York. He had been invited to sit with the ASOR Board of Trustees that day, and "a hearty vote of thanks was extended to Dr. Albright for his assistance to the Trustees in sharing with them the proceeds of his present lecturing tour." "On motion of Dr. Albright," as BASOR reported in the February 1927 issue, "the Executive Committee was asked to request and receive from the Union Theological Seminary the archives and materials deposited in its custody by the American Palestine Exploration Society, an organization which operated in Palestine in the 'seventies."[1]

At the Corporation meeting later that same day President Montgomery "noted that the occasion marked the twenty-fifth anniversary of the School in Jerusalem. The year had been signalized by entrance into the new Nies Building in Jerusalem; and the current volume of the *Annual* had celebrated the anniversary with historical sketches. He referred to Dr. Albright's valuable work in Palestine, ..."[2]

In the evening the ASOR group met with the Society of Biblical Literature. A good audience attended at General Theological Seminary in spite of stormy weather. Albright and others spoke on various excavations that had been carried on that year in Palestine, and Professor Dougherty on his explorations in Mesopotamia, the lectures being beautifully illustrated.

In Prof. George A. Barton's report on "Dr. Albright's Lectures in America," he stated that "great interest has been manifested wherever Dr. Albright has lectured. His vivid presentation of the facts illustrated by his new and excellent photographs have given many a new realization of the possibilities of Palestinian archaeology as a source of information of Biblical life and history. Doubtless many who have seen his face and heard his voice will take, in the future, a much greater interest than hitherto in the work of the School at Jerusalem and in the whole field of Biblical archaeology."[3]

Tall and not quite so thin as formerly, almost bald and now thirty-five years old, Dr. Albright was an effective lecturer. He once explained that because he could not see well enough to read a lecture or paper acceptably in public, he simply talked to his audiences. If he wore his reading glasses to see the manuscript, he could not see the people, and if he wore his distance glasses to see the people, he couldn't see the manuscript to read it.

On December 29 Albright lectured at the Archaeological Institute of America in Cambridge. There was a respite until January 11, when he spoke at Cornell, the next day at Auburn Theological Seminary, and on Thursday the 13th at the Archaeological Society in Syracuse, New York, where he had been in the "limited service" just over eight years earlier. After further lectures in Rochester and Pittsburgh, he took the night train to Illinois for lectures in Naperville and at the Archaeological Society of Chicago. By the 28th he was in Salt Lake City, lecturing to the Archaeological Society and the University of Utah on the same day.

On Saturday January 29 he wrote to Dr. Weidner in Germany that during his time in America he would give more than a hundred lectures. In this large country, days of travel were needed to go from one lecture to another in some cases, and he lacked any time for research, study or writing. Thus he had to decline the request to write several book reviews; he was eagerly anticipating returning to Palestine.

At the beginning of February Albright's lectures were in the States of Washington and Oregon. He spent the 7th to 9th at Pacific School of Religion in Berkeley, California, McCown's institution, and the following days at other schools in the Bay area, Fresno, Los Angeles, and San Diego. On the 26th he spoke to the Archaeological Society in Santa Fe, New Mexico.

In Santa Fe a letter from Prof. C. W. E. Miller, of the Classical Seminary of Hopkins, caught up with him. President Goodnow had appointed a committee of three to consider the needs of the Semitics department since Paul Haupt's death. Albright's name had been mentioned as a desirable candidate for a position on the department's staff; he requested a list of Albright's publications at his earliest convenience.

Albright replied that he had given about seventy lectures so far in the four months since he had returned from Palestine. He had not intended to become a candidate, as he was happy in the research opportunities available to him as Director of the School in Jerusalem—he had been able to work in Mesopotamia and Egypt as well as in Syria and Palestine. But as the Schools' financial outlook was not too good then, the temptation was strong to take an American university position, with more security possible. He could not, however, give a complete list of his publications until he returned to Philadelphia at the close of April. From memory he mentioned that he had published more than fifty articles, aside from reviews, in American journals; reports of expeditions and excavations in BASOR; some twenty papers in JPOS, and about thirty articles in scholarly journals in Europe.

Suddenly a new development was possible in his career, and it must have given both the Albrights some restless nights.

In early March he lectured in Colorado and Missouri, and on Thursday afternoon, March 10, he arrived at the home of his old friend, Dr. Sam Geiser, in Dallas. He spent four days with Sam and Bess, their son David and baby Phyllis, and on Friday Albright lectured at Southern Methodist University, where Sam then headed the Biology Department.

Sam claimed in a letter reporting those wonderful days to their old friend "Dr. Danny" Parker that they had a whale of a time and nearly ran "Bill's" legs off. He took him to meet people at the Dallas University Club, the Athletic Club, the Scottish Rite group in Texas, and to a luncheon in his honor at Southern Methodist University. His old friend made a grand impression, and Sam could hardly stop marveling at how he had developed in the years he had been overseas. Drs. McIntosh and Scheussler, who had taught William at UIU, were telling everyone including the janitors how he had been their student, and Prof. Heuse, who had not happened to teach Albright anything, felt rather left out. On Sunday morning Geiser took Albright to breakfast with the dean of their School of Comerce and Finance, and that noon all those formerly of UIU had a banquet, at which "Bill" spoke again. Finally on Sunday night he left for his next lecture at St. Louis on Tuesday March 15 (with a day between for a much-needed rest).

In mid-April Dr. Albright lectured at Hebrew Union College in Cincinnati and remained to attend the meetings of the American Oriental Society the 19th to 21st. "Tribute was paid to the late Prof. Haupt by Dr. Albright" at the first meeting, as the JAOS recorded in the Proceedings.[4] At this meeting Albright presented a paper on "Canaanites and Amorites," defining the terms historically, geographically and linguistically.

On Friday April 22 Albright lectured at Lake Erie College, Painesville, Ohio, Ruth's *alma mater*. With further lectures in Washington, D.C. and at Bethlehem, Philadelphia and Gettysburg, his tours drew to a close. There were other lectures besides those that had been published in a list in BASOR for that February; he gave informal talks to groups of students at the educational institutions he visited, and a woman in Buffalo, New York, a city which was not on the list, sent a clipping from the *Courier-Express* stating that "Buffalo has recently had the honor of a visit from Dr. W. F. Albright of the American Institute of Archaeology and Director of the ASOR in Jerusalem. At a dinner Dr. Albright deeply interested those present in his account of the excavations being made in Palestine and the wonderful increase in archaeological work in Biblical lands, now that they are no longer under Turkish control."

His lectures were completed in the first week of May. The news note in the April BASOR said, "On this tour he gave over a hundred lectures and addresses, and we are deeply indebted to him for making this valuable presentation of the cause of the schools. His audiences recognized that he spoke with authority, and he held their attention by his clear and straight-forward discussion of his subjects, which were admirably illustrated by his pictures. He will now take a well-earned vacation, and expects to return with his family to Jerusalem in August."[5] Actually he gave 125 lectures.

The Albrights had not informed either his family or hers of her conversion to Catholicism in late 1922, but waited until they could all be together. The news of this development caused the beginning of a rift that widened as time went on, not only between her and his family, but also between her and her own parents, two brothers, and sister. The family members of both sides, however, greatly enjoyed having their rather famous relatives home for a visit, and were delighted with little Paul.

During the year in America, Paul turned three. One time he and his mother were visiting the home of her sister Dorothy, whose husband was then the rector of the Episcopal church in Wellsville, New York. His cousin Patricia, about a year older than Paul, was a very knowing little lady who had been to New York and other places. She somewhat looked down on her little cousin from Jerusalem, though Paul did not realize this. She asked him, "Have you been to New York?"

Paul asked, "What's New York?"

"You don't know what's New York? New York's a place where you can see lots of things, and you can go to the *thoo*."

"What's the *thoo*?"

Patricia said, "Don't you know what's the *thoo*? It's where you have to go to see lions, and tigers, and elephants, and camels, . . ."

Paul stopped her right there. "No, you don't go to the *thoo* to see camels! You just look out the window!"

Doesn't *everybody* have camels passing outside the window?

Prof. William Rosenau sent Albright his hearty congratulations, having heard that he had been offered the professorship in Semitic languages, to be Haupt's successor. He was delighted at the honor being given Albright, well-deserved, he thought, and looked forward to being associated with him. Also Prof. Frank R. Blake wrote expressing how happy all of them were in the department, and sending congratulations.

These congratulations, however, gratifying though they may have been to Dr. Albright, were premature. Sam W. Geiser wrote early in May. Could it be that the "poor kid" who, fourteen years before, in the spring of 1913, lamented to him the supposed fact that he would need shortly to leave forever his chosen profession, teaching, and go into consular service for the Government, had actually had the opportunity of declining the offer of the chairmanship Haupt had held at Hopkins? He had been right in his estimate and encouragement, though of course he had nothing to do with the success his old friend had achieved. But if there were the slightest reason to fear that Bill would become like his predecessor, Sam would not hesitate to call down the wrath of the gods to destroy him first! He thought Bill was doing absolutely the right thing in choosing to return to Jerusalem.

Paul Bloomhardt wrote on May 16 (William had seen him at the AOS meeting in Cincinnati). He was delighted that their *alma mater* was recognizing Albright with the offer of the chair, and congratulated him. He was sure that he would perform a far greater service to Oriental studies than his predecessor, and thought there would be pressure brought upon him by other orientalists in America to accept the chair, in the view that his presence would do more to stimulate such studies than another seven years away in Palestine. However, Albright could best judge between those alternatives, and he wished only to say that he hoped Albright's decision would not be influenced by the hostility from some quarters at Hopkins.

Sam wrote again, hoping Ruth was enjoying her stay with her own family. He had appreciated so much their visit that spring and predicted that he would visit Albright in Palestine before his next return. He was most delighted at the certainty of Albright's going back to Palestine and said he had made the best possible choice. It was much better to starve as a scholar (an echo of William's youthful ambition).

Albright replied to his enthusiastic old pal's latest letter from Beach, Virginia, on May 31, a week after his thirty-sixth birthday. He and Ruth and Paul had been at the family farm for several days, all feeling better in the cooler weather, and he himself was, he claimed, eating like a horse. Probably they would stay there through July. He had remained in Philadelphia until the 23rd to finish writing some papers. Part of that time Ruth had been in Baltimore, and they met in Washington to stay with a friend a couple of days. He said his father, who was sixty-eight, was in good health; they were as close as the antipodes, but he knew his father meant well. His mother was in fine health now, also. He gave Ruth much credit for tact in handling the situation with his parents, and said she seemed healthier than he had ever known her to be.

Albright told Geiser that the chair in Semitics had not after all been offered to him. He had been made aware of this by an odd letter from Dean Joseph Sweetman Ames, who apologized that Albright's name had been printed prematurely in the circular of the University. The Trustees had approved the appointment all right, but only if the president found the necessary support financially— which was only an excuse to eliminate the chair entirely. Thus several chairs were now dropped; there would be no more depart- ments of Indo-European, Sanskrit, or Semitic philology, and why? Because President Goodnow and another man in the administra- tion were intent on the establishment at Johns Hopkins of a School of Law, and were turning finances in that direction. Thus he had been spared having to choose between that chair and his post in Jerusalem; but actually, as Sam knew, his mind had already been settled. It was a hard period for humanistic studies; a utilitarian wave was sweeping through and would affect other than philolog- ical departments. Those interested in the humanities and scientific research would have a difficult time stemming the tide, but it could and would be accomplished if they worked hard and intelligently enough.

The background of all that confusion was that after Haupt's death a small part of the next catalog edition had been printed, carrying the name of William Foxwell Albright as chairman of the Oriental Seminary. Then the presses were stopped and the name was removed for the remainder of the edition, and Dean Ames sent a letter intimating it had been a mistake. Albright kept his letter and a copy of the catalog listing his name, for he intended to take the matter up with the American Association of University Profes- sors if anyone else was elected for the position after his name had appeared. Mrs. Albright never at any other time in his long career saw him more disappointed and more active in protecting himself. It had come like a bolt out of the blue—a copy of the catalog was sent to him as usual, and there was his name, and then came the retraction. He felt that news concerning it would hurt his profes- sional career, and therefore reacted defensively. But outwardly he was philosophical, preferring to continue his work in Palestine— which he really did wish to continue.

In mid-June Albright wrote to a friend at Harvard that he had not exactly had an easy time making his decision between accepting the chair at Hopkins and keeping on with his work in Palestine, but both he and Mrs. Albright were too involved in the latter place and work to give it up. They were going to go back for at least another year or two, and he hoped permanently—although the unendowed condition of the School, and its status, being at the mercy of scholarly and institutional jealousy and intrigues, made his situation anything but secure.

On July 11 in mid-afternoon a severe earthquake shook Palestine. The Albrights were alarmed over the newspaper reports and greatly concerned about their staff and the School building in Jerusalem. No cable came with bad news, however, and they felt somewhat relieved. The center of the quake had been to the north around Nablus. Those killed in Palestine numbered 200, with 356 injured seriously and 375 slightly; in Transjordan 68 were killed and 102 injured, according to reports a week later. Government House and the Allenby Bridge had been somewhat damaged; at the School some plaster ceilings were cracked, but the walls and the cisterns remained intact, and everyone connected with the ASOR was happy for the sturdy construction.

During the earthquake of July 11 a cliff slid into the Jordan River at ed-Damieh, blocking the flow of water, so that people south of there crossed on dry land—just like the Israelites in Joshua's time —for 21½ hours before the water broke through and flowed down the riverbed again.

Ruth and Paul left the Virginia farm on the 18th of July to spend a little more time with her parents and her sister's family. They and William met in New York before their sailing date, August 5, on the *De Graesse*.

As William mentioned to Paul Bloomhardt in a letter from Paris, they had a fine voyage, though Ruth was *hors de combat* much of the time (she was always a bad sailor for the open ocean). He reported that Prof. Daniel D. Luckenbill had died from typhoid on June 5 in London, and Prof. Chiera was to replace him at Chicago; he urged his old friend Paul to continue his interest in biblical and orientalistic studies, hoping to see him return to them as a career, though he expected him to do good work in any field he was in.

After shopping some days in Paris, buying furniture and equipment for the School in Jerusalem, the Albright family sailed for Palestine and "home."

10

Tell Beit Mirsim

Before leaving on his furlough, Dr. Albright had collaborated with Dr. Kyle, President of Xenia, on the first season's dig at Tell Beit Mirsim in the spring of 1926. On October 31, 1924, Kyle had written of his interest in what both of them tentatively identified as biblical Kirjath-sepher or Debir, and said that nothing would please him more than to cooperate with the American School in excavating it. He probably could come in the summer of 1926. There was about $600 left from the $2000 he had raised by lectures for their expedition to the southern end of the Dead Sea, and he thought he could raise more. Albright replied that nothing would please *him* more than for them to work together on an excavation at that site. However, the summer of 1925 was already planned and the summer of 1926 fell in the beginning of the Albrights' sabbatical leave. Fall of 1927 or spring or summer of 1928 would be the earliest possibility. As an afterthought, Albright suggested that Kyle might be able to come in the *spring* of 1926; if so, they could have their first campaign of six weeks, costing about $2000, before the Albrights' departure.

That is the way it worked out. Albright found he could schedule his trip to Mesopotamia with Prof. Dougherty in the fall of 1925, since no students appeared except belatedly the Hazard Fellow, Samuel Rosenblatt. Kyle let Albright know he had raised $3000 for the excavation, and Albright replied on September 19, 1925, expressing his pleasure at learning that Kyle was actively planning for their dig and already had the money in *site* (the spelling mistake betrayed his mind as rushing ahead of his typing fingers). They would be able to pay fifty laborers for about ten weeks. If it had to be a shorter period because of bad weather in mid-March, they could employ more men and speed up the work. Tell Beit Mirsim was fifteen road miles southwest of Hebron and five northwest of ed-Dhahariyeh on the main road and had an orchard beside it in which they might be able to pitch their tents. They might even find a route for a Ford to come south from Beit Jibrin, which lay on a main road.

In February Prof. W. F. Badè, Dean of the Pacific School of Religion, where McCown taught, arrived in Palestine ready to begin excavating at Tell en-Nasbeh, just to the north of Jerusalem, which he and many others thought was biblical Mizpah. Albright followed Robinson in locating Mizpah at Nebi-Samwil rather than Tell en-Nasbeh, and had other possible identifications in mind for the latter site; but after encouraging Badè to come and letting him know some scholars thought it was Mizpah, he decided to keep quiet about his own opinions on the subject. As events unfolded it seemed that Albright was probably wrong this time.

Albright applied to Prof. Garstang for a permit to excavate at Tell Beit Mirsim, following Dr. Fisher's plan of operation. The permit was promptly granted, and also exemption from Import Duty on articles they brought in for use at the excavation. President Kyle arrived at the end of the first week in March ready to finalize preparations. The rainy season was not yet ready to relinquish its hold on the area, however.

As the negotiations which began on March 15 came to a successful conclusion for leasing the site of Tell Beit Mirsim, and the staff was ready to begin work, they assembled at Hebron for the signing of the lease. They had to wait over Tuesday, eating unleavened Passover bread at their Jewish hotel, in order to see the governor and also to get the promised camels, both available only the next day. Dr. Albright hired a horse which they named Bucephalus (after the steed of Alexander the Great) and the rest of the staff with the *mukhtar* (head man of the village) were to go by automobile, but then the auto was delayed until after they ate one more lunch in civilization.

For their first night they were invited to be the *mukhtar's* guests at his village near Tell Beit Mirsim. "It was an evening of true patriarchal hospitality," Dr. Kyle wrote in his fascinating book published in 1934 on the four seasons at Tell Beit Mirsim, *Excavating*

Kirjath-Sepher's Ten Cities.[1] (The contents were his James Sprunt
Lectures of 1932 at Union Theological Seminary, Richmond, Virginia.) Their camp was pitched high and dry, with a view over
meadows filled with spring flowers toward the "nether springs"
mentioned along with the "upper springs" in verse 15 of Judges
1:11-15. It is the story of Caleb's promise to give his daughter
Achsah in marriage to the man who would capture this Canaanite
city, called "Debir, formerly Kiriath-sepher." Othniel captured it
and won Achsah as his wife. She asked her father for springs of
water as well as the city, and he gave her both "the upper springs
and the lower springs." The presence of these, along with other
features, helped Albright and Kyle identify Tell Beit Mirsim with
Kirjath-sepher or Debir.

As Albright reported in the October BASOR in 1926, they
"pushed work vigorously, with a maximum force of seventy laborers. . . . Nowhere in Palestine has the writer seen such ideal conditions for precise stratigraphical results. The site is free from en-
cumbrance, and exhibits three very strongly marked burned levels,
belonging to three complete destructions of the city by fire."[2]

After they had worked from April 1 to 18, they were interrupted
for a week by the Archaeological Congress that had been organized
for that spring in Syria and Palestine. Albright was general secretary
as well as a delegate for American institutions, and had organized
the Palestine section besides presenting a paper. It was the first time
since the war that German scholars took part in an international
gathering of archaeologists and orientalists. Albright attended the
sessions held in Jerusalem, but when the delegates were touring
elsewhere he was busy at Tell Beit Mirsim.

He reported: "Our work was only once seriously interfered
with, when a terrific wind and dust storm forced us to suspend
work for a day and employ our entire force in saving the tents,
which were badly damaged, but could be taken down in time to
escape destruction.

"Relations with the natives were excellent; two strikes were
attempted, but proved quite abortive. We were constantly receiving invitations to dine out, many of which we accepted. These occasions were welcomed by the writer as providing an opportunity to
record the local traditions about the origin and history of modern
Dura, which was occupied by the ancestors of the present inhab-

itants about 1600 A.D. The saga of Dura offers extraordinarily interesting parallels to the traditions of the Old Testament, but has not hitherto been known to Western scholars.

"After it was found possible to reach our site by car from the Beersheba road, we had numerous visitors, including most of the scholars then in Palestine. . . ."[3]

When the excavation closed down in early June, Albright was quite exhausted. He wrote to Prof. Alt that the whole expenses had been no more than 800 English pounds, and they expected to continue later. No inscriptions had turned up yet, but they had worked out the whole history of the site, and he was practically certain it was the site of Kirjath-sepher.

Albright's report in BASOR was written in a non-technical way, and it is helpful, for an understanding of his work, to see his outline of the history of the site as clarified in the first season. Subsequent seasons refined and deepened this knowledge but did not seriously change the picture he had already acquired. He wrote:

". . . Thanks to the careful study of the pottery from the successive strata and sub-strata, it is possible to describe the history of the town already, though names and personalities naturally elude us as yet, owing to the fact that no inscriptions have been found. Since, however, there are at least a hundred thousand cubic metres of debris on the site, we need not be discouraged by the meagerness of our epigraphic finds during three weeks of work [preceding the Archaeological Congress].

"Our site seems to have been organized as a town toward the end of the third millennium, perhaps not until about 2000 B.C. After a comparatively brief occupation, as indicated by the average depth of about half a metre in this stratum, the town was destroyed by fire at some time in the latter part of the Middle Bronze Age. The site was soon reoccupied by a population accustomed to building strong fortifications. The revetment of the Canaanite wall of the second period was probably about seven metres high, and its polygonal construction is strikingly reminiscent of the glacis [slope] of the Middle Bronze wall of the fourth city at Jericho. The east gate was then situated in a great tower surrounded on the outside by a massive sloping revetment. We may date this construction about the seventeenth century B.C., as at Jericho, while the previous destruction took place at the same time, in all probability, as that of the third city of Jericho, about the eighteenth century B.C.

"The Late Bronze stratum on our site averages about two metres thick, and at the east gate exhibits two successive building phases, apparently separated by an incomplete destruction of the gate. Until the work is further advanced we cannot even suggest a date for this event. The Late Bronze pottery on our site is characteristic, with intrusive Cypro-Phoenician ware (wishbone-handled bowls, base-ring ware, etc.). The masonry of this period seems markedly superior to that of the following one—quite natural when one remembers the difference between a Canaanite 'royal' city and a provincial Jewish town.

"The second catastrophe which overwhelmed the city came during the transition from Late Bronze to Early Iron, i.e., in the thirteenth or twelfth centuries B.C. Since this is precisely the age of the Israelite irruption (cir. 1225 B.C.), we need have no hesitation in combining the two events. The town which arose from the ruins was approximately the same in extent as the preceding Canaanite city, but was not so well built. The Israelite wall was only about two metres wide, on the average, while the glacis was formed by a series of rounded bastions built of much smaller stones than were used by the Canaanites. The masonry of the gate, though using some of the large blocks—one over two metres long—of the older fortress, is relatively inferior in every respect. The gateway itself is, however, very interesting, and exhibits the same indirect ingress as that still familiar to tourists who pass through the Turkish gates of Jerusalem.

"After a period of peace, Tell Beit Mirsim was attacked by some enemy, who partly destroyed the gate, and broke down the wall just north of it. The breach was never repaired, and we do not yet know where the new wall was built. The approximate date of this occurrence is fixed by the fact that the new constructions at the gate are built with their foundations a metre higher than the old ones of the Iron Age, and that this metre of debris contains little, if any, pottery from the second phase of the Early Iron, while the pottery above this stratum is almost exclusively from the latter phase. We must, therefore, date the partial destruction in the Early Iron between the early tenth and early ninth century B.C. There is no trace of fire, so the conqueror was possibly satisfied with the capture of the place. We are reminded of the fact that Shishak, king of Egypt, 'took the fortified towns of Judah' (II Chr. 12:4), as confirmed by the famous Shishak list at Karnak, in the fifth year of Rehoboam, that is, about 923 B.C. The discovery at Megiddo of a fragment of a stela of Shishak, recently announced by Professor Breasted [Albright was careful to state that this item concerning Megiddo had been officially announced by an authorized person from Chicago University, and not get himself into a misunderstanding again], shows that some of us have been too sceptical with respect to the Shishak list, and that the towns mentioned in it were really captured by this Pharaoh.

"In the second phase of the Early Iron there was a partial restoration or rather reconstruction of the gate, and a reservoir was installed just to the north of the main entrance. The reservoir was fed by an aqueduct formed by large stones hollowed out in the middle and laid side by side so as to form a continuous channel or water pipe. The stones are shapeless, in contrast to the perfectly hewn blocks of similar installations in the Roman Age.

"The 'high-place' just now being examined can hardly be described until it has been studied in more detail. It is already possible to state that it was in use down to the final destruction of the city by the Chaldaeans, and also that it had been destroyed and set up again at least once. Highly interesting finds may be expected from the continuance of our excavations at this point.

"The final destruction by fire in the latter part of the second phase of the Early Iron may confidently be connected with the Chaldaean conquest of Judah in 588-7 B.C. There was no occupation thereafter, aside from a few unimportant installations, which may safely be postulated from the Byzantine sherds scattered sparsely over the surface, but never found below ground. As will be seen, we have an extraordinary opportunity here for highly interesting discoveries, and best of all to the archaeologist, excellent conditions for the study of pottery, since the strata are horizontal and exceptionally well defined.

"The identification with Debir or Kirjath-sepher now seems to the writer practically certain, since the archaeological evidence is just as favorable as the literary and topographical material. . . .

"With the excavations now in progress at Megiddo, Beth-shan,

Shechem, Shiloh, Tell en-Nasbeh and Tell Beit Mirsim, we may confidently expect fresh light on biblical Palestine. Palestinian archaeology is only in its infancy, and the outlook has never been so attractive as today. Students of the Bible and of oriental archaeology can do no better than follow its development with the closest attention, for it holds the secret of the correct understanding of both."[4]

After their furlough the Albright family returned to Jerusalem on September 8, 1927. He had been away exactly a year and had remarked in letters months earlier that he felt out of touch with what was going on and feared it would take him a while to catch up. He found the School in good condition after Prof. Butin's Acting Directorship and the month's leadership by Dr. E. A. Speiser while enjoying a vacation from his exhausting work in Mesopotamia. A large group of fourteen students came that fall. It included a future Director of the School, Rabbi Nelson Glueck, Ph.D. of the University of Jena, who was on the staff of Hebrew Union College Cincinnati (of which he would later be president). Some local students joined the group for lectures and tours. The Annual Professor was Prof. J. M. P. Smith of Chicago.

Albright took the School group "to Eastern Galilee, where a beautiful week in December was devoted mainly to a study of the ancient sites. We made the German hospice at Tabghah our base, and for nearly a week we enjoyed the charm of one of the most delightful spots in Palestine, where nature and man vie with one another to make the stay agreeable. . . . From this base we made trips on foot, by car, or by boat to nearly all the most interesting points on the Sea of Galilee as well as from Beth-shan in the south to Hazor in the north. While the weather was too dry for the suffering ground, it was ideal for our purposes, and the wind subsided for a whole day in order to make our trip on the lake feasible."[5]

Albright had searched for the site of Hazor in vain for some years, "though able to disprove the identifications previously suggested by others . . . It was reserved for Professor Garstang to discover the correct site in the fall of 1926, just after the writer's return to America. Garstang and Vincent then studied the site carefully, and produced the conclusive archaeological proof, fully supported by the literary evidence, that Hazor is to be identified with Tell el-Qedah and the great enclosed terrace to the north of it. This is in our opinion the most important topographic discovery which has been made for many years. . . . Hazor was a very large city in the Late Canaanite period, a city some eight times as large as Megiddo. The statements of Joshua [chapter 11] are thus more than confirmed."[6]

They studied other Bronze Age mounds, such as a newly discovered one north of the Sea of Galilee, and el-Kerak, ancient Bethyerah, the "City of the Moon," at the southwestern edge of the Lake.

During the winter rains, the program went on at the School with lectures and, when possible, short tours. Mrs. Albright continued managing the School with a larger staff of efficient helpers than in the former rented building. There was not yet a municipal supply of electricity; the School still obtained theirs by a line to the French School. No taxis were available; the native people went to bed at sunset and rose at dawn.

Mrs. Albright therefore had to make careful plans. Having calculated when her second child was due (after three miscarriages since Paul was born), she moved into the mission hospital in Jerusalem about four days ahead of that date and spent each night there, not risking a night emergency with no means of transportation. Daytimes she was free to do anything she wished. During her stay there was an earthquake lasting a few seconds and shaking the buildings laterally. The nuns of the hospital came rushing into her room—the maternity room used only for European and American women—to calm her down, but found her entranced by the interesting happening.

On February 27, 1928, the Albrights' second son was born and named Hugh Norton. Then, the only time while Ruth lived in Jerusalem, it snowed. And she was not allowed to get out of bed! But she did get up when the nuns were elsewhere, and she did see the snow on the windowsill and on roofs and streets!

Albright and Kyle resumed their excavation at Tell Beit Mirsim on April 2, 1928. The October BASOR which contained Albright's report of their second season showed their tent camp in a photo on the first page, and five other photos—Arab neighbors including the *mukhtar*; the tremendous discovery of the first Canaanite serpent-goddess stele, found in stratum D; a number of scarab seals; dye-plants discovered in stratum A; and the impression of the Eliakim seal found in stratum A which identified the ancient owner as "servant of Jehoiachin," last king of Judah in 597 B.C. when Nebu-chadnezzar captured Jerusalem and deported captives. Their campaign continued to the first of June; Albright's report outlined the further knowledge gained from each stratum as compared to the first campaign.

With the help of Dr. Fisher, now Professor of Archaeology in the School, Albright and Kyle secured a well-trained Egyptian surveyor and two foremen to supervise the laborers—an improvement over the first campaign when the two scholars had done these things as well as everything else. "During the second campaign," Albright reported, "we devoted almost all our efforts to the clearance of an extensive area south of the East Gate, which we excavated, stratum after stratum, until we had reached the bottom of the fourth level from the top. We also continued the clearance of the top stratum in two other areas, where, however, we were very careful not to dig below floor or foundation level. In order to avoid possible error in numbering the lower levels, we have lettered them A, B, C, D, etc., from the top stratum downward. The stratification is exceedingly clear, since the strata are almost invariably separated by burned levels. Strata A and D are remarkably well preserved, practically complete plans of the excavated areas being available; while B and C are poorly preserved and only partial plans could be drawn. The reason lies unquestionably in the almost immediate reoccupation of B and C after the destruction of the preceding towns. Consequently there was no chance for the surface of the ruined site to become level through the action of the wind and rain, which produced an evenness of terrain which subsequent builders had no object in disturbing. City D must have lain in ruins for a considerable time before a new town was built on the site, while A, of course, was never disturbed, since the site has been absolutely abandoned for more than twenty-five hundred years.

"Little was added to our knowledge of the first stratum, which we now call F. . . .

"The period which we previously called the second, and which we divided into two phases, now proves to have had three phases, one antedating the construction of the great Canaanite wall, and the two later ones following it. Since E has not yet been excavated to any extent, we can only say that the pottery belongs without question to the second half of the Middle Bronze Age, but that its affinities are rather with the first half of this age than with the early Late Bronze, so that it cannot be placed too late. . . .

"Our most interesting discoveries were made in the following D stratum, the best preserved layer in the mound, next to the top one. Owing to the abundant pottery finds, supplemented by a collection of seven scarabs, all found in this level, there can be no doubt that this city was built sometime in the seventeenth century, and was destroyed sometime in the sixteenth, probably toward its close. We find the black pear-shaped juglets still in use, but more sparingly than during period E. Cypro-Phoenician ware has also come into use. . . . There is practically no native painted ware, and no Mycenaean imported ware has been found in this stratum. The scarabs all belong to the Hyksos period, or to the very beginning of the Eighteenth Dynasty. Both scarabs and pottery prove conclusively that stratum D was destroyed before the reign of Tuthmosis III (1501-1447 B.C.). It may be added that Rowe's recent discovery at Beth-shan of two temples from the time of Tuthmosis III establishes the ceramic chronology of northern Palestine, from which that of the south differs very little, back to the first half of the fifteenth century, in strict accord with the general conclusions of previous students of Palestinian pottery."[7]

In the palace they uncovered in stratum D, only part of which they were able to excavate in the second season, their most important find in the debris which fell from the upper story when it was destroyed by fire was "the lower part of a limestone stele, about 30 cm. wide, and at least twice as high, representing the serpent-goddess of the ancient Canaanites. The figure of the goddess, barefoot, and clad in a long dress, reaching to the ankles, is preserved as far as the waist, below which one elbow projects. A large, well-modeled serpent is coiled around the legs of the goddess. . . . This is the first object of the kind found in Palestine, and is, in fact, the first native Canaanite representation of a deity yet discovered, aside from the Astarte figurines and similar small objects. . . .

"Numerous smaller objects of interest were discovered in stratum D, but none of them approach the value of the serpent stele. A quantity of ivory inlay, some of which was itself inlaid with ebony, or some other dark wood, was found in the courtyard of the palace, suggesting the richness of the furniture with which the upper story was once equipped. Bronze weapons, jewelry, vessels of alabaster and faience, etc., were also found. . . ."[8]

They found not only Cypro-Phoenician pottery in stratum C, but also many sherds of Mycenaean pottery dating to 1400-1200 B.C. In the B stratum they found typical Late Bronze Age styles ending before Philistine ware began to appear, indicating an interval of time. The Philistine pottery "probably began to be imported into the Shephelah of Judah shortly before 1150 B.C.," Albright wrote. "We can, therefore, date the fall of city C about the same time as the latest possible date for the invasion of Canaan by the Israelites, and, in view of the total change in the character of the fortifications, as well as in the culture of the following period, we may confidently ascribe the burning of city C to the incoming men of Judah. . . .

"City B was built in the ashes of C, many of whose walls were built on the old foundations, while the new fortifications, built almost immediately, as we can now show, were very hastily and badly constructed. . . . We may safely ascribe the building of both town and fortifications to Othniel, the conqueror of Kiriath-sepher, and the first recognized 'judge' of Israel.

"In view of the insecurity of life in southern Judah in the period of the Judges, it is not surprising that we find a rather low level of prosperity in B," the town which the invading Israelites rebuilt. "The most striking characteristic of the culture of B is the appearance of iron sickles and plough-shares, none of which occur in the previous strata. At the same time the use of flints, common even in C, dies out entirely, just as everywhere else in Palestine during the twelfth century. . . .

"All through the middle of this period, from about 1150 to the early tenth century, Philistine pottery was imported in quantities. Since we know that Judah was tributary to the Philistines in the eleventh century B.C., in the time of Samson and Samuel, this is not at all surprising. There can be little doubt that the culture of the Philistines influenced Israel to a much greater extent than is commonly realized."[9]

The burned level of B's destruction they now definitely ascribed to Shishak's invasion in 924-3 B.C., forming the transition between Early Iron I and II. City A, the last city on the site of Tell

Beit Mirsim, lasted from about 900 B.C. for a long time. Albright thought that the seal of Eliakim, which they found in that top level, "proves that it was standing in 597 B.C., so that it must have been destroyed either in the Chaldaean invasion of that year, or in the final catastrophe of the years 588-6. It therefore was occupied for not less than three centuries," with very well built houses—"better than either ordinary Canaanite or Arabic houses," Albright said.

"The principal industry of the town was weaving and dyeing woolen garments. Three new dye-plants were found in the second campaign, all exactly like the first one discovered. In each there was a pair of massive round stones, hollowed out to make dye-vats." They found much pottery "from the seventh and early sixth centuries B.C. Articles of domestic use appeared in abundance. Several baskets-full of iron tools and implements were found. Toys were numerous, including clay figurines, rattles, and whistles, which make just as shrill a noise today as they did twenty-five hundred years ago. Five carved stone cosmetic palettes illustrate the wiles of the women of the day; in one of them powdered malachite was found, employed to color the lower eyelid green, while powdered antimony (kohl) was used to darken the rest of the eye. . . .

"Several short inscriptions were discovered in this stratum. Two stamped jar handles, bearing the well-known inscription 'Belonging to the King, Hebron,' both exhibit the 'flying roll' design of the later seventh century royal stamps. They belong to the fiscal administration of Judah, and illustrate the use of standard measures of oil and wine as a kind of currency. . . . Another sherd contained the first letters of the name 'Uzziah,' in a very large clear script, cut into the clay.

"The most important single discovery made this spring, after the serpent stele, was a jar-handle containing the impression of the seal of Eliakim, servant of Joiachin. The impression is perfectly clear; the letters of the original seal were beautifully cut, and not one is in doubt. . . . We may . . . date it to the year 597 B.C. with entire confidence. No other early Hebrew inscription yet found can be dated so exactly as our seal impression."[10]

(However, decades, later, after Albright's death, one of his outstanding students, Dr. Frank Cross, Jr., challenged both the date and the identification of this seal, dating it to about 700 B.C. with no connection with the last king of Judah. Also Prof. Yigael Yadin, an outstanding Israeli archaeologist who was a great friend and admirer of Albright, came to the conclusion that Albright had made mistakes in dating the various strata and the famous solid wall; that it was actually later than his strata G and F because it cut through the buildings of those levels, which Albright would have seen if he had done more study of sections against walls. Yadin said, "It is tragic for me that my article on this subject appears rather after his death, because, knowing Albright, I would have enjoyed his reaction to my article even if he would have cut me to pieces afterward. It would have been for me the most important thing to see his reaction. If he accepted it, obviously that would have been a great satisfaction, but even if he were against it, knowing Albright and his scientific integrity, I would have liked very much to see on what grounds he based his refusal to accept it. My article does not even a little bit diminish what I think he did—I compare him to the other two greats, Petrie and Vincent. Albright was far superior to both of these other two great giants in vast knowledge of the whole Near Eastern comparative material. I think he may be considered to be the true developer of what we call, whether one agrees to this definition or not, biblical archaeology.")

Dr. Albright wrote his BASOR report for non-specialist readers. In closing he mentioned that "the publication of the results of the first two campaigns is in an advanced state of preparation. The importance of the results already attained will there appear even more clearly. Palestinian archaeology owes President Kyle a profound debt of gratitude for making these two campaigns possible. No biblical students of the future will be able to overlook their results. Let us hope that nothing may happen to prevent the continuation of this important work."[11] The publication of these campaigns would still be used decades later by Albright's students to teach their students pottery chronology, for Albright in these excavations at Tell Beit Mirsim firmly established the relative chronology of Palestine by the potsherds found in clearly marked layers or strata in this ideal site.

President Kyle in his own fascinating book on the excavations told a story on Director Albright: "Matching pottery, putting together the broken fragments found in the ruins and making complete vessels, beats crossword puzzles and, among archaeologists, has more fans, and more sorely obsessed also. The Field Director of our staff, Dr. Albright, is an expert, and matching pottery has so bewitched him that he was caught at the lunch table a day or two ago unconsciously trying to match fragments of orange rind!"[12]

The third campaign at Tell Beit Mirsim took place in the summer of 1930, after the Albrights lived in Baltimore. Running from June 16 to August 16, as Dr. Albright reported in the October 1930 BASOR, "the excavation was continued for forty-eight working days, with a maximum force of 120 locals, and an average of about 90, who received from twenty to forty-five cents a day. The ordinary able-bodied laborer received forty cents a day, besides occasional backshish for finding objects. We moved about twice as much earth as we had during our second campaign.

"We found that the summer is well adapted to excavation in so favorably situated a point as our mound, some 1600 feet above sea-level. In the afternoon there is almost always a cool west wind, and we seldom found it necessary to discard our blankets at night. Life under canvas proved much more agreeable in summer than we had expected. We were also most fortunate in working after a rainy winter, since the well in the valley south of us lasted two months longer than it had during our first two campaigns. Such excellent water is not often found in Palestine; it was not even considered advisable to boil it until the last fortnight of our campaign."[13]

Albright related the additional finds and knowledge gained from the strata in sequence in this campaign, comparing them to those from the earlier spring-time campaigns. The outstanding finds of the third campaign were "the stone lion and the table of offerings . . . found thrown down on end in an open space filled with debris of C. The lion is of limestone, and measures about 60 cm. in length; it was presumably one of a pair of lions which once flanked the entrance to a shrine, or the throne of a divinity. Artistically, the execution is obviously inferior and provincial; archaeologically it represents one of the most important objects of genuinely Canaanite workmanship yet discovered. As the first stone lion of pre-Roman date to be found in Palestine proper it is extremely interesting; it was found on the last day of excavation! Not half a metre away we had previously discovered a stone table of offerings, with three lions carved in relief stretched out around the rim. There can, of course, be no question that this object also comes from a sanctuary, probably not far away. The conditions of discovery show that they must have been thrown out at the destruction of the Late Canaanite city, perhaps by the Israelites. The table of offerings is also unique as an example of genuine Canaanite art, though it also betrays ultimate Egyptian influence. We may safely date them to the early part of the C period, roughly about 1400 B.C."[14]

In concluding his report Albright stressed "the importance of the American School in Jerusalem as a base for archaeological work. Without its facilities we should have been put to considerably more expense and loss of time than we were. . . ."[15] The report was illustrated with a front-page photo of their camp and photos of a stratum-C house courtyard of about 1800 B.C., the Canaanite lion from stratum C, about 1400 B.C., the Canaanite offering table with lion's head from the same date, Mycenaean pottery pieces from C dating about 1400 to 1200, and the set of game pieces they found in stratum D, dating from approximately 1600 B.C. The New York *Times* of August 27, 1930, under headlines "Amazing Art Work Dug Up In Palestine" and "Scientists Are Jubilant," carried a Jerusalem dateline August 26 story about the stone lion. An editorial on the 21st commented that this "little land has become the cynosure of all eyes both historical and archaeological. . . . It is chiefly because no other ancient land, not even Greece, has so dear a place in the geography of the people of Christendom—Jew and Gentile.... So does history repeat itself as news, with the archaeologist as the reporter. What happened 3,000 years ago is the freshest of news this morning."

For the fourth season of excavation at Tell Beit Mirsim, Albright sailed early in May of 1932 on the *General von Steuben*, a steamship of the Norddeutsches Lloyd Bremen line. Near the end of the voyage, on May 10, he wrote a letter on ship stationery to his parents, saying it was his twenty-fourth long sea voyage, disregarding short ones he had made. The weather was rough, making the ship roll and pitch. He had not sailed on a German ship since the *Herodot*, of which he said his parents would have vivid memories (that may have been the one on which they returned from Chile, which had to be fumigated at sea because of stopping at a port where bubonic plague had broken out). Early in the Depression as it was, he said his round-trip cost was almost $60 less than the preceding year for second-class passage; he hoped prices in the Near

East had likewise fallen. Only for the 1930 season had he paid his own way; his present trip would probably cost the Schools less than $400.

He wrote his parents that he had been very tired as he departed, having just finished his volume on the pottery of Tell Beit Mirsim and sent it to the printer on the last day he was in Baltimore. He gave it to the printer at 3:00 P.M., packed his books to make his office at Johns Hopkins available for someone else during the summer, wrote some letters, and after supper at home, packed for the trip and left the house (in northwest Baltimore) by taxi at 9:30 P.M. to go to the train station. It was a relief to find the ship quiet, not having tourists on board but business people or those going to visit relatives, and hence not the rowdy types. He promised to try to be a better correspondent than he had been lately, but in any case his parents would get news through William Franklin.

William's sister Mary had married William Franklin Stinespring on April 4, 1928. The first of their two sons was born March 16, 1929, and was three years old by the time his father went to Palestine to join Albright's fourth season of excavation at Tell Beit Mirsim. Dr. Stinespring had earned his Ph.D. under Prof. Charles C. Torrey at Yale that spring and was interested in Near Eastern languages, especially Arabic.

Long afterward Dr. Stinespring vividly remembered being a tenderfoot on an archaeological dig with his already famous brother-in-law, whom he hardly knew. After a week in Jerusalem, becoming accustomed to the country, he was taken to Tell Beit Mirsim. "The first impression that I had of him was his breadth of knowledge. I knew he was a good linguist and a good book-scholar, but I didn't know that he had so much practical knowledge, such as surveying, architecture, drawing—draftsmanship necessary for drawing potsherds, all this kind of thing. Everybody consulted Albright about everything, except that the cook did not consult him on how to cook the food! (Sometimes they did discuss menus, although there wasn't much choice—the only meat available was goat, which was bought on the hoof. Sometimes we'd go out in the morning and look at the live goats, one of which we were going to eat for lunch! Both goatmeat and the method of preparing it were new to me.)

"The other impression that I got at first," Albright's brother-in-law continued, "was the enormous amount of dust. But we got used to that. I soon acquired the job of photographer; Albright inquired very closely of me, as he did of every new recruit, about the various things which I had done. When he found out that I was a photographer of sorts, he put me in charge of photography, and I was able to escape the heat and some of the dust because the darkroom which had been set up was partly underground and therefore cooler—the most comfortable place in camp. I was afraid that some may have thought Albright was showing favoritism to me because I was his brother-in-law; those who really knew him knew that he never showed favoritism to anybody. He had an uncanny way of finding out everyone's talents and putting them to maximum use. It was one of his many secrets for carrying on an excavation at a very low cost. I am sure that Albright set an all-time world's record for amount of archaeological knowledge gained from a given amount of money."

When William Stinespring married Mary Albright he "was only vaguely aware that she had a brother who had some connection with Johns Hopkins University." He confessed that he "was never able to get interested in potsherds as Albright was. He could pick up two or three and then knew just about when the particular layer in which they were found could be dated. He communicated his enthusiasm for this aspect of archaeology (begun by Sir Flinders Petrie but carried to perfection by Albright) to many of his students and followers, most notably Dr. Nelson Glueck, whom in many ways Albright considered his best pupil.

"When the campaign that summer came to a close, we went back to Jerusalem and photographed many of the potsherds. Also we went through the photographs and negatives which we had taken on the tell, to get ready for the publication. It was at that time that I became much better acquainted with Prof. Albright. We worked very carefully on the photographing, because he was trying by these displays of different types of pottery to show his ideas on the chronology of the site."

Albright's report on "The Fourth Joint Campaign of Excavation at Tell Beit Mirsim" appeared in the October 1932 BASOR. It was similar to his previous reports, adding the new information gained level by level on the history of the site. "It must be confessed," he said, "that the writer began the fourth campaign with some trepidation, since he had already read the proofs of the pottery volume before the opening of this year's excavation. Though a great mass of new pottery and scarab material was discovered, illuminating several hitherto obscure periods, few changes in the dating of ceramic types are required. It goes without saying that a large number of new types were recovered this summer, and that previously known types are illustrated by a much larger number of examples."

Before beginning work he had made a trip with Père Vincent to Megiddo and Samaria and found at Megiddo that their "pottery chronology agreed throughout with that of Mr. Guy. At Samaria we found the same to be true, on comparing our views with those of Mr. and Mrs. Crowfoot and of Dr. Sukenik. . . . During the course of this campaign both Professor Fisher and Père Vincent visited our camp and examined the pottery in detail; agreement was complete throughout. . . . The just published volume on the pottery of the first three campaigns furnishes detailed comparative evidence for the correctness of our chronology, and shows at the same time how homogeneous the pottery of Palestine was in most periods."

After reporting on the new information from the various levels, Albright wrote, "It will be recalled that the excavation of Tell Beit Mirsim was originally undertaken because of the writer's identification of the site with biblical Debir or Kiriath-sepher. This identification has not yet been conclusively demonstrated; . . . This summer we obtained permission from the Department of Antiquities to make soundings at Zaheriyeh ('Dahariya'), a large village on the main road from Hebron to Beersheba. . . . The soundings . . . prove conclusively that Zaheriyeh is not the site of a Late Canaanite fortified town, though there was a small settlement there in the period of the Jewish monarchy."

Albright concluded his report on Tell Beit Mirsim by saying, "We hope, *Deo volente*, to continue our work at this important archaeological site with a fifth campaign, in which we shall devote special attention to the problem of the fortifications, which prove to have had a much more complex history than we had supposed hitherto."[16] This was never to take place, however. His collaborator, President Melvin Grove Kyle, who raised the money to support the excavations and presided over the staff at the tell, died in May of 1933. Albright said of him in his obituary in the October 1933 BASOR: "To few men is it given to combine such ecclesiastical and scholarly distinction as Dr. Kyle attained with such simplicity and purity of character. . . . Dr. Kyle was one of the very few really tolerant men whom the writer has known. He possessed that rarest of all qualities, the instinct and art of befriending those whose religious and scholarly views diverged sharply from his. Often he converted enemies and ill-wishers to warm friends and admirers, solely through the cumulative force of personal contact. The writer used to meet Dr. Kyle occasionally, before coming to Palestine in 1919, at learned society meetings. In those days, the fact that we were apparently at antipodes with regard to most crucial biblical and oriental problems seemed to preclude all real friendship. In the spring of 1921 Dr. Kyle came to Jerusalem with his family for a stay of several weeks as lecturer in the School, during the writer's year as acting director. The acquaintance then developed soon ripened into friendship.

"In 1924 Dr. Kyle provided the money for our first joint expedition, devoted to the exploration of the Dead Sea Valley. This was followed, in 1926, by the first joint campaign of excavation at Tell Beit Mirsim, an undertaking in alternate years thereafter (1928-32). . . . Never did cooperation continue more harmoniously over so long a period. Though we were together in the field during almost the whole duration of each campaign, and were in constant correspondence between expeditions, there was never a breath of ill-feeling and never the slightest friction between us. We seldom or never debated biblical questions, but there can be no doubt that our constant association with the ever-recurring opportunity for comparing biblical and archaeological data has led to increasing convergence between our views, once so far apart. To the last, however, Dr. Kyle remained staunchly conservative on most of his basic positions, while the writer has gradually changed from the extreme radicalism of 1919 to a standpoint which can neither be called conservative nor radical, in the usual sense of the terms."

Albright closed with a poignant farewell to his faithful collaborator, "Ave, anima candida!"[17]

At the excavations, there were occasional interruptions in the steady diet of hard work, however. John Bright was a member of the last season's dig at Tell Beit Mirsim and recalled decades later that his "first impression of Prof. Albright was one of complete awe. Frankly, though I needn't have been, I was scared of the man. The range and depth of his scholarship and interests, which he exhibited in table conversations over the evening meal in the main tent— which conversations often went on until bedtime—left me speechless. Much of it was over my head, and I dared not open my mouth. But I soon learned that questions—even dumb questions—always received courteous and patient answers. Albright never 'put down' a student if that student was honestly trying to learn. I have never been sure just how many languages he could speak, but I remember well one day at the dig, when visitors of various national backgrounds were present, that the conversation leaped from English to French to German to Hebrew to Arabic and back again, with Albright the only one present in command of all."

Bright remembered that Albright, though he never participated in sports, "had a physique that would do credit to a professional athlete. He could, and on occasions did, walk any of us into the ground. I remember once when we were on a field trip in the School station wagon and had stopped to examine a mound— I think it was Tell el-Ful, where he had dug some years previously. We parked the car and walked to the top of the tell, a distance of several hundred yards. When he finished showing us what there was to see, he declared confidently that he could beat any of us back to the car, whereupon he took off running. I was aghast, for, knowing he was half blind, I feared he would stumble and fall. But there was nothing to do but take off after him. I was put to it even to keep up with him (though I was still in my early twenties and had been on the track team in college), and he wasn't even winded!"

Bright recalled Albright as "essentially a serious-minded man, not given to wisecracks and banter. But he had quite a fund of supposedly true anecdotes, mostly having to do with colleagues or others whom he had known, and mostly humorous, which he loved to recount. And he was on occasion not above indulging in the broadest of practical jokes. The classic among these is surely the incident of the lizard soup, which took place at Tell Beit Mirsim in 1932. News had been received that important visitors, including the American Vice-Consul, and others, were coming to view the dig and would remain for dinner. This seemed to Albright the ideal time to have some fun. Plans were laid. Albright paid some of the Arab potsherd boys to catch a couple of the lizards that swarmed all over the place. Nelson Glueck was to conceal one of the (now deceased) lizards on his person, and during the soup course surreptitiously slip it into his soup, and then with the next spoonful fish it out for all to see, crying, 'How did this lizard get into my soup?' Others of us were coached to feign illness, while still others—while exhibiting disgust—were to pretend to carry on with a stiff upper lip and eat their soup as if nothing had happened.

"All went as planned. Glueck played his part masterfully, pulling out the lizard with a roar of shocked surprise and looking as if he were going to be ill. Albright shouted with well simulated anger, 'I told that cook never to make that lizard soup again!' He then called for the cook and spoke to him sternly in Arabic. Actually, he made casual conversation about the meal, but since none of the visitors understood Arabic the effect was the same—and as might be predicted. Pale faces were everywhere, some looked ill (and it was not feigned), and one may even have stepped outside. Albright, then seeing that matters had gone far enough, explained that it was all a joke, and everybody laughed.

"Everybody, that is, except Aage Schmidt. Dr. Schmidt, who had not been present when the prank was planned, was an eccentric Dane, well trained in archaeology but somewhat odd. He was also a man of devout Christian principles who opposed killing and violence of whatever sort. He turned to Albright and addressed him long and solemnly in German. My German was rudimentary at the time, but I caught the drift of what he said, and afterward others filled me in: it was a stern rebuke to Albright for taking the life of one of God's innocent creatures needlessly. Albright blushed to the top of his bald head and kept stammering as Schmidt went on: 'You are quite right, Herr Doktor! You are quite right, Herr Doktor!' When Schmidt had finished, Albright apologized. But I don't think he was really sorry, for I have since heard him relate the incident with apparent glee!"

11

The Commuter,
Baltimore-Jerusalem

President Frank Johnson Goodnow, who had been in office at Johns Hopkins since October 1, 1914, having been inaugurated on May 20, 1915, announced his retirement effective at the end of June 1929. As his successor, Dean Joseph Sweetman Ames was chosen. Since the spring of 1927 when Dean Ames had been one of those carrying on the difficult negotiations with Dr. Albright concerning the position left vacant by the death of Paul Haupt, further negotiations had taken place.

The Trustees of the American Schools of Oriental Research announced in BASOR for April, 1928, that "Dr. Albright has presented his resignation of the Directorship of the School in Jerusalem, the resignation to take effect next year, in July, 1929. He has accepted the call of Johns Hopkins University to the chair of Semitic Languages, lately occupied by the distinguished Professor Haupt. The Trustees must accept the inevitable, recognizing the honor paid to Dr. Albright and appreciating the full measure of invaluable services he has given to the School since his connection with it, which began in 1919. . . ."[1] The successor chosen was Dr. Chester Carlton McCown, by then Dean of Pacific School of Religion, who accepted for two years and who, Albright said, was the one he himself would choose.

A second decision had reversed the first one made by the Albrights in the spring of 1927 while they were in the U.S. on furlough. The steps leading up to the new decision began with a cable on January 19 following their return to Jerusalem. There were exchanges of cables and letters, after his acceptance and their agreement to postpone the effective date to July, 1929. Misunderstandings had to be clarified concerning the salary and the possibilities for him to carry on archaeological work in Palestine part of each year. Albright wrote to Prof. Miller of the Classical Seminary, chairman of the faculty committee concerned with filling the vacancy, saying that the resignation of President Goodnow would mean a real loss to the institution. He hoped that the succeeding president would be as sympathetic as Goodnow had been toward the humanities. For himself, it was a relief that they had accepted his deferred date—he would hate to return leaving unfinished business of all kinds behind. He said he would loyally do his best to cooperate in the university and to keep its well-known atmosphere of harmony and productivity. He would attempt to make friends for the Oriental Seminary and archaeological sections, as these were rather exposed outposts of scholarship among the humanities, and he would continue to support and cultivate sound methods in philology.

When Albright wrote on June 24, 1928, thanking Prof. Miller for his letter that had set his mind at ease that the salary was really to be $6000 and not $4500 (too little to live on in America where they would no longer have the use of a furnished apartment, with board, maid and laundry service included), Albright reported that earlier in the month he had concluded his second season of excavation at Tell Beit Mirsim. Now he was anticipating spending less strenuous years of study, teaching, and scholarly production at Johns Hopkins. He remarked that his duties in Jerusalem had increased from year to year, encroaching more and more on his research and writing.

After the close of Summer School, Albright, in poor health, left with Professors Chiera and Speiser for a month in Europe. He attended the Orientalistic Conference at Bonn and the Oriental Congress at Oxford, giving a paper at each. Chiera and Speiser returned to America before the end of September. By that time Albright had returned to Jerusalem, having traveled with his wife from Beirut where she met him, through the Lebanon mountains to Baalbek and Damascus on the way to Jerusalem.

President Montgomery wrote in the December 1928 BASOR

that "in the School in Jerusalem we face the crisis of losing our Director, who has served us there single-heartedly since 1919. . . . For his ten years of service it can simply be said that, while others have come and gone, Dr. Albright has been the School in Jerusalem." At the December 27 meeting of the Trustees they adopted a resolution of appreciation for his services, and the same resolution was adopted later that day at the meeting of the ASOR Corporation and also reported in the December issue. In part it said: "Taking charge at a time when stability in the management of its affairs was greatly needed, he instituted and maintained a policy of which the wisdom has been abundantly shown. By his energy and prudence in directing the routine work of the students, arranging and conducting expeditions, exploring and excavating ancient sites, and publishing the results of the School's scientific work, the good name of our institution has been preserved and its prestige steadily increased. . . ."[2]

For a few weeks during the last academic year that the Albrights were in Jerusalem, his old Hopkins classmate and student, Rev. J. Edward Snyder, was there, along with other short-term students. Director Albright took the School members on a trip through Galilee from November 19 to 24. His spring horseback trip, however, was almost washed out by intrigue. One of the staff members was of an envious and spiteful nature and persuaded most of the School members not to go, but not to let Albright know this until the last moment. The few who went, left with Albright on April 10 and returned on May 2, "in better health than when we left," Albright wrote, "and all the more convinced than ever that horses and tents are still indispensable to successful exploration in Palestine."[3]

In the small, closed foreign society there, consisting of only about a thousand residents, everyone knew everyone else and small things became blown up out of proportion. For a long time there was a well-known running "feud" between Mrs. Albright and Mrs. Danby, the wife of Canon Danby who had performed the Albrights' wedding ceremony. At tea parties and other gatherings the other ladies eagerly inquired of each other the latest news on this score. William Albright came to the conclusion early in his married life that he simply would never understand women, and that the best thing to do was to keep himself strictly out of their affairs and controversies; let them battle things out among themselves, while he tended to his scholarly matters. He had enough problems at times in those affairs in which he was directly involved.

Mrs. Albright often shielded her husband from unpleasant-nesses that occurred in the course of the work, however. One of his lifelong problems was that he could not see the expression on the faces of people to whom he was speaking, in order to judge the effect he was producing in time to change or modify it. This was at the root of the problem that resulted in only a small group going on his last spring horseback tour. Without having consulted the staff, he announced that several wealthy Jewish families from America who were coming to Jerusalem for a two-week visit would be housed at the School while they were away on the horseback trip. The jealous staff member, who had already moved himself and his family to another residence in order to embarrass the School financially, had no great love for Jews, and succeeded in persuading most of the members not to join Albright's tour. Mrs. Albright managed very well, however—she sent her German nanny with their two boys out into the country to stay the two weeks, and let the one large family have the Albright apartment while she moved into two rooms. The visitors hired a kosher cook in the city, giving the School cook a vacation, and brought Mrs. Albright's meals to her. They enjoyed the use of the whole building for their group except her rooms. She was treated like one of the family and taken to concerts given in honor of the visitors. They made a handsome gift to the School before they left.

The threatened letter of complaint reached Philadelphia in due time from the angry professor, and the letter from the ASOR of-ficial who knew only one side of the story arrived in Jerusalem, quoting the angry professor, as Mrs. Albright knew it would, while Dr. Albright was off on the horseback tour. She had no inten-tion of ever letting him see the letter, for the ASOR official who sent it, basically a very fine person, would never have written it if he had understood the whole situation. She pondered overnight what to do, and early in the morning wrote him a short note send-ing back his letter with it, since she could not destroy it. When she returned from mailing it at the nearby post office, one of the dis-tinguished visitors was in the front garden sunning himself. Learn-ing of the reason for her early errand, he offered to care for the matter himself, as he was a Trustee, and was perplexed when she said she could not turn the letter over to him. On hearing what she had done, he threw back his head and roared with laughter, complimenting her on knowing how to clear up difficult situations.

Before leaving Palestine in mid-1929, Mrs. Albright took Paul, then five and a half years old, and drove in a small party with Father Jaussen north on a farewell trip to the Christian shrines in Galilee, where churches are built on so many sites of events in the Gospel stories. As they were riding up through the country Mrs. Albright was deep in conversation with Père Jaussen, when Paul suddenly said, and repeated it to get her attention, "Mummy, I know the difference now!" Finally she answered him, "Yes, Paul, what difference?"

"I know the difference between the sheepses and the goatses!"

"Well, what is the difference?"

"The sheepses are the white goatses, and the goatses are the black sheepses!"

The two are customarily seen together in flocks on almost any hillside—in chapter 25 of Matthew, the parable of the last judgment is based on this fact—and the observant child had figured it out. His proud father enjoyed telling this story still many decades later, highly amused over it each time.

The April 1929 BASOR reported that "Director Albright expects to leave Jerusalem on July 12, and will assume his new duties at Johns Hopkins University with the fall term. He will be greatly missed in the Holy City, where with his long stay of full ten years he has proved himself one of its most eminent scholars. Dr. Albright has been elected a member of the American Philosophical Society, an honor accorded annually to only sixteen American scholars and scientists. . . ."[4]

The new Director, McCown, reported in the October issue of BASOR, "You will be interested, I think, in some of the events which marked Dr. Albright's departure. It was the signal for numerous expressions of good will for him and the School which he has served so long. In addition to various private affairs, the Hebrew University at a public meeting presented him with a parchment engrossed in Hebrew and certifying his election as a life member of its Institute of Oriental Studies. Addresses were made by the Chancellor of the University, Dr. J. L. Magnes, and by Dr. Joseph

Klausner stressing Dr. Albright's neutrality in the vexing racial and religious problems of Palestine and his services to Oriental studies. His ability to use Modern Hebrew and his not infrequent addresses to Jewish audiences have given him a unique position among non-Jewish scholars in Jerusalem. Just before their sailing the Palestine Oriental Society gave a reception for Dr. and Mrs. Albright which was held, by invitation of Bishop and Mrs. MacInnes, in the gardens of the Cathedral of St. George. Dr. Herbert Danby, who since the founding of the Society has been its secretary, and Bishop MacInnes spoke, the latter presenting to Dr. Albright in the name of the Society a beautiful silver casket, the work of the Bezalel School of Art. [Mrs. Albright, with son Paul and his wife, spent two weeks at the School, living in their old apartment, a little over a year after Albright's death, and Mrs. Albright gave this silver casket to the School to keep in her husband's memory. The School was renamed over a year before his death the "William F. Albright Institute of Archaeological Research." She also made a generous gift for renovation of the library, in particular to provide better lighting and more private study carrels.] Both speakers referred to Dr. Albright's services to the Society, which for some years has met regularly at the School, living in their old apartment, a little over a year after second president, as vice president, as treasurer, and throughout its entire existence as a member of its editorial advisory board. He has given a large amount of time to assisting various Arab and Syrian scholars in Jerusalem, so that their unique knowledge of the country and its folklore might be made available to Western scholarship. The representative gathering of men of all religions, races, and languages at the reception testified to the very high esteem in which the retiring director of the American School was held."[5]

The son of the self-supporting Methodist missionaries in Chile had early received the training that enabled him to foster the remarkable growth of the School under the precarious financial conditions during his decade of service there. All the tributes were due and fitting. Before leaving Jerusalem Albright was able to settle a long-standing boundary dispute with a neighbor and win by June 15 the main battle for tax-exempt status for the School.

As Pres. Montgomery gave the twenty-eighth annual presidential address, printed in the December BASOR in 1929, he not only mentioned the keen appreciation of Albright shown by the community in Jerusalem, regretting that the ASOR had not been able to support him with more means, but also expressed their "deep obligations to Mrs. Albright for her part as mistress of the School and for her bravery and ability in meeting the cares of the day of small things; our small appropriations were cheerfully received and most carefully expended. For them we desire all happiness in their new home in this country. We feel a compensation of pride that in losing our Director we contribute a successor to the eminent scholar, the late Professor Paul Haupt."[6]

In closing his annual report Dr. Albright mentioned improvements they had made and the arrival of Dean McCown, the new Director. "But we cannot emphasize too strongly that he must be properly supported in America, and not hampered at every step through lack of money. It is no easy task for the Director of the School to teach, guide parties, excavate, investigate, receive an endless stream of visitors, carry on an extensive correspondence without a secretary, act as sole librarian, accountant, etc., if he must even then provide the miracle each year by which the School may escape a serious deficit."[7] Albright was speaking out of his own life and experience. He closed with many expressions of appreciation to friends, officials in Jerusalem, and President Montgomery.

Thus with an appreciative and triumphant send-off the family, now numbering four, nearly two months after Albright's thirty-eighth birthday, on July 15 embarked for America and a new kind of life.

At first they leased the house at 3302 North Calvert Street. It was a reddish-brown brick, three-story, narrow row house facing east, only several blocks east of the Homewood Campus of Johns Hopkins University, and it was on and near main streetcar lines (now buslines). Since they had no car—because of his poor eyesight Dr. Albright never possessed a driver's license, and Mrs. Albright did not yet at this time—it was very important for him to be able to walk daily to the university and to reach other places by streetcar, transferring several times if necessary. They moved in early in August.

At that same time troubles broke out in Palestine. On the 16th and the 23rd of August, following the Ninth of Ab fast that commemorates the destruction of Jerusalem and the Temple by the Roman general Titus in A.D. 70, and also the day when the army of Nebuchadnezzar broke through the walls of Jerusalem and began destroying the city and Temple in 586 B.C., there were local riots in Jerusalem and throughout the land. In Hebron and Safed nearly the whole Jewish population was massacred, for there was no Haganah—Jewish self-defense force—in those towns. Mr. Harold M. Wiener, a good friend of the School, was killed in his car near Herod's Gate trying to rescue two Jewish friends. The School and its members were safe, being in an "Arab" quarter; they took custody of a valuable manuscript to protect it during this period. The disturbances had been triggered this time by disputes between Jews and Moslems over rights at the Wailing Wall, the western wall of the ancient Temple area.

A story in the Baltimore *Sun* quoted Dr. Albright as saying that "despite the antagonism between the two races, the Arabs have profited more from Zionism than have the Jews in Palestine," and "The relative importance of the recent troubles in Palestine is frequently lost sight of by those who entertain violent antagonism toward one side or the other. . . . We should realize that Palestine is a typical Near East country, where religious differences stir passions that are equally excited by other causes elsewhere. When I left the United States the last time race riots were in progress in East St. Louis and, as I recall, they were rather more serious than the recent outbreak in Palestine." "Zionism has unquestionably aided the Jews culturally and spiritually throughout the world," he said, "but the Arabs have been the material gainers from the influx of Jews into Palestine. They sell their products at heretofore unheard-of prices. The Jews have brought money and modern methods of agriculture and industry to the country and the Arab peasants are the most prosperous in the Near East. But it is never pleasant to be jolted out of a happy rut and the Moslems realize that they are no longer in the saddle. This seems to me to be at the root of the trouble."

At the time Albright left, no one expected such outbreaks within a month, "except those in the councils of some Arab leaders," the paper quoted him as saying. "I speak the tongues of both races and because I have kept out of politics have been able to keep warm friends among both Arabs and Jews. The propaganda of both sides embroiders the truth to suit its own case, but the Arabs have suffered at the hands of too ardent friends who have frequently exaggerated to such an extent that they have caused outsiders to lose faith in the cause they would help."

The article closed with Albright's plans for his department at Johns Hopkins: "Dr. Albright plans to link the seminary closely with the work of the research school. He plans to go to Palestine in May and return in September and expects to make annual visits to the Near East. As newly organized, the seminary will devote much time to positive research into Bible history and literature instead of to higher criticism. It will go after new information in historical episodes as described in the Bible, helping to carry on researches begun ten years ago."

At this time and for many years, the Oriental Seminary under Prof. Albright's chairmanship was practically a one-man department. Dr. Frank R. Blake, Rabbi Rosenau, and Rabbi Samuel Rosenblatt taught part-time. There were not many students in those Depression years; the stock market crash occurred at the end of October the year the family returned to the U.S. Albright continued some of the courses he had long been teaching in Jerusalem, including Archaeology and Ancient History, and added others more directly concerned with Old Testament studies, though different from those of Prof. Haupt, his predecessor in the William Wallace Spence Chair of Semitic Languages. His archaeological investigations had brought him a long way back from the extreme higher criticism of Haupt, following Graf-Wellhausen views, and he was now fully persuaded of the essential historicity and factual reliability of the Old Testament records and references to events and places. He was a considerate and inspiring teacher, though his students were often terrified by his immense erudition. He demanded their best, but was always more than willing to help them individually as long as they were willing to work seriously.

On December 6, 1929, the Albrights' third son, Stephen Foxwell, was born. Mrs. Albright came home with the new baby by the 20th, in time for Christmas with the older boys. The first months in America had not been easy, filled with family illnesses and the problem of finding reliable household help. When Stephen was a few weeks old, Mrs. Albright's business sense told her that it was not good policy to continue paying rent for their leased house on North Calvert Street. She began to look around for a house to buy, and on March 3, 1930, the family moved to northwest Baltimore, to a high, two-story, squarish, cream-colored stucco house with screened porch at the right side, set in a shady yard, No. 5703 Cross Country Boulevard. They rented their row house on Calvert until their lease expired, and Dr. Albright was still on a main transportation line for the six or seven months per year that he was in the city.

Prof. Albright sailed at the beginning of May for his third campaign at Tell Beit Mirsim. Before leaving he presented a paper at the meeting of the American Philosophical Society in Philadelphia on "A Millennium of Biblical History in Light of Recent Excavations." Together with Prof. Speiser's paper on "The Earliest Civilizations of the Near East" it shared the rating of "two of the most notable papers delivered. . . ."[8]

It must have seemed like "returning home" for Prof. Albright to live again in the Jerusalem School before and after camping at the mound for his third season at Tell Beit Mirsim.

At the end of 1930 Prof. Albright, as planned, took over editorship of the *Bulletin of the American Schools of Oriental Research* from Prof. Montgomery, who had edited it since its beginning in December, 1919, just as Albright was arriving in Egypt and Palestine. He continued as editor of BASOR for almost forty years; it became and remained the chief outlet for his ideas and work in progress. Gradually it became more technical. Beginning with his first issue, that of February 1931, a Table of Contents appeared on the front page or on the second page each time.

At the Executive Committee meeting of the ASOR, at which Albright was present, on December 31, 1930, Dr. Fisher was reappointed Professor of Archaeology at the Jerusalem School, with an increase in salary; it was voted to find a housekeeper for the School and free the Director's wife from this demanding and amorphous work. As McCown's two years were soon to end, Prof. Millar Burrows of Brown University (later of Yale) was appointed Director. "The President then expressed his desire that Professor Albright be given some appointment that would connect him permanently with the School in Jerusalem, in recognition of his long and devoted service there. It was voted to elect him adjunct professor at the School in Jerusalem, without stipend."[9] This would involve his giving some lectures when he was there half-years.

The excavation project for 1931 was the first campaign at Beth-

zur, north of Hebron. Albright had asked Prof. Ovid R. Sellers
to be director, in order to relieve him of many duties so that he
could concentrate on the archaeological work. Dr. Nelson Glueck,
Dr. A. Saarisalo, and a number of students formed the staff, and all
sailed at the beginning of May, arriving in Palestine before that
month ended.

The October 1931 BASOR, which contained the report of the
campaign, carried on its front page a lovely photo of the School
taken from the south showing the completed south wing, the new
Director's House. A photo on page 3 showed the Beth-zur mound
from the southeast, with the tent camp of the expedition on the
slope in the foreground. Other photos illustrated the report, showing "stamped jar-handles with Hyksos scarab impressions," "A
cosmetic spoon illustrating egyptianizing Canaanite art of the second millennium B.C.," "Stamped jar-handles of the Jewish monarchy (800-600 B.C.)," "Ancient wax impression of the seal of
Gealyahu, son of the king," "Ruined foundations of the Maccabaean citadel of Beth-zur," and "A dye-plant of the Maccabaean
age." The campaign ran from June 1 to July 29, with digging for
nearly fifty working days, the average force being over one hundred
laborers from the local Halhul clan. They "cleared nearly 8000
square meters of the summit to bed-rock, and filled almost the entire area again before the end of the campaign. . . . The denudation
of the ruins is partly due to the fact that the town was repeatedly
abandoned after being destroyed, and partly to the fact that the
builders of the Byzantine and Arabic Beth-zur employed the more
ancient site as a convenient quarry. . . . As a result of these circumstances we have no continuous stratification on our site. . . . The hill
rises in rock-terraces, one above the other, so that the town was
built like a gigantic *ziqqurat*, or temple-tower, and the debris from
one terrace fell down into the next. We therefore find an almost
incredible mixture of sherds of all ages, except where house walls
and floor-levels are well preserved. More than half the baskets of
sherds exhibited this mixture; the sherds had actually been shuffled,
so that sherds of *all* occupation-periods were found in each of these
baskets. Happily we found respectable areas of well-preserved stratification belonging to every single age, and in occasional better
preserved Hellenistic houses, as well as in all late cisterns, we found
large quantities of absolutely homogeneous pottery—seldom, how-

ever, complete. Since the pottery of Beth-zur is identical in type with that of Tell Beit Mirsim, where conditions of stratification are ideal, we were seldom in any doubt as to our dating, even when we found a mass of mixed debris containing MB [Middle Bronze] lying over a perfectly clear and distinct Hellenistic deposit . . . our ceramic chronology was confirmed and made more precise by the aid of nearly seventy stamped jar-handles of all periods, and 279 coins."[10]

Albright and Sellers in their joint report sketched the reconstructed history of the site. "No definite proof of a general destruction at the time of the Exile, or of a following period of abandonment, has yet been obtained," they stated, "but the indications pointing that way are numerous. . . .

"The occupation of the town in the Persian period seems to have been rather sparse. As will be recalled, it was a district capital in the time of Nehemiah (Neh. 3:16), B.C. 444. . . .

"The great importance of Beth-zur was not in the biblical period proper, but in the Hellenistic age, and especially in the time of the Maccabees. . . . For towns like Beth-zur and Gezer the removal of the garrison meant extinction, since the local population had already been forced out by the repeated vicissitudes to which military occupation had subjected it."[11] The excavators concluded that the garrisons had been removed after John Hyrcanus reconquered the coastal plain.

Articles on the Beth-zur excavations appeared in the New York *Times* on July 3 and 10, speaking of Maccabean relics from a "Fortified Town Which Was Alternately Greek and Jewish" and "was abandoned before the time of Christ," and the fact that "the site is 3,300 feet above the sea level and the highest excavation site in Palestine."

On his way back to America from the Beth-zur dig, Prof. Albright attended the Eighteenth International Congress of Orientalists at Leiden, Holland, from September 7 to 12, along with a few other American scholars. To Albright's regret, only a small group of German scholars were present, among the total of seven hundred. Prof. Albright gave a paper on "Exilic and Post-exilic Judah in the Light of Palestinian Archaeology."

In reporting on his summer's work in the October 1931 BASOR, Editor Albright said he had arrived on May 21 and departed on

August 30. "June and July he spent with the Beth-zur expedition, after the close of which he continued the archaeological explorations begun in 1930, on a grant from the American Council of Learned Societies. In pursuance of this work he made successful soundings at Deir Ghassaneh in central Palestine (the probable site of Zeredah [birthplace of Jeroboam, I Kings 11:26]), and visited numerous points in Western Palestine, Transjordan, and Syria, with many interesting discoveries and observations. It was an unusual pleasure to follow the steady development of Palestinian archaeology. . . ."[12]

At Hopkins Prof. Albright began his classes, then went away for some days in October, giving the Carew Lecture series at Hartford Seminary Foundation in Connecticut. His subject was "The Bearing of Archaeological Discoveries in Palestine on the Bible."

Editor Albright featured a fine illustrated article on the 1931 work at Jerash by Dr. Fisher in the February 1932 BASOR. He also reported that "Professor Nelson Glueck of Hebrew Union College had been nominated as Director of the School in Jerusalem for the year 1932-3, for which time he would be able to secure leave of absence." Albright was present in the Executive Committee meeting on December 29 when "President Morgenstern, as Chairman of the Committee on Personnel, stated the Johns Hopkins University had consented to an arrangement by which it would permit Professor Albright to devote one-half of each year to the service of the School in Jerusalem. The Committee nominated him as Director of the School for an indefinite term beginning July 1, 1933, with the understanding that each academic year should be divided between the School and Johns Hopkins University . . . the Annual Professor each year should be a person who could take charge of the work during the time of Professor Albright's absence."[13]

Before leaving in late spring of 1932 for his fourth and final season at Tell Beit Mirsim, Albright published in the April BASOR his article on "New Light on Early Canaanite Language and Literature." It told succinctly the story of the discovery of Ugaritic and its decipherment, work having begun at Ras esh-Shamrah (ancient Ugarit) on the coast of northern Syria only three years earlier. His account is fascinating to read, concluding with his evaluation: "The new material will, of course, revolutionize our knowledge of Hebrew lexicography and poetic usage; no future Hebrew dictionary which does not include the rapidly increasing mass of material from Ugarit will be of value to the serious student of the Hebrew Bible."[14] For the rest of his life Albright emphasized the discovery of Ugaritic as one of the most influential and important for biblical studies. He called the language deciphered on the tablets found there Ugaritic, and classed it under Canaanite, to which Biblical Hebrew also belongs; some others would consider it a third dialect in Northwest Semitic along with Canaanite and Aramaic.

Between duties of teaching and heading the Oriental Seminary, Albright in the preceding year had spent some days in February 1931 in Richmond, Virginia, not far from his parents' home, giving the Richards Lectures in the University of Virginia. His family came to hear one of them, proud of him though not fully understanding all he said. He immediately afterward prepared the lectures as a book manuscript which Revell published early in 1932—*The Archaeology of Palestine and the Bible,* a small book of 233 pages. Dedicated "To my Wife, who has borne the burden and the heat of the day," it was revised in 1933 and 1935. In the preface to the third edition Albright said that "the rapidity with which the first two editions have been exhausted is very gratifying, especially in view of the lack of illustrations and the modest scope of the book. Thus our efforts to be succinct and clear, as well as to provide full documentation for every statement, have evidently filled a real need among students of biblical and related subjects.

"Owing to the limitations of space, we do not attempt to discuss any phase of our subject exhaustively. In the first chapter we have stressed the methods of archaeological research in Palestine rather than the results. In the second chapter we have illustrated the first by describing the first three campaigns of excavation at Tell Beit Mirsim. The work of the fourth campaign in 1932 is briefly described in the Supplementary Notes.

"In the third chapter we enter a bitterly disputed field, the bearing of archaeology on the Bible, selecting the three most difficult and controversial phases of this question, precisely because of their obscurity and the need for archaeological illumination. In the four years since these pages were written, much new material has accumulated, some of which is referred to briefly in the Supplementary Notes. Our standpoint, though independent, is so closely related in part to that of the school of Alt and in part to the views of Böhl and Jirku, among continental scholars, that sharp criticism from more orthodox critical scholars in America was inevitable. The parallel trend of biblical scholarship in Germany has since become so evident that our views no longer seem strange to most of our colleagues in America. Eppur si muove!"[15] (Albright occasionally used this Italian quotation from Galileo in letters, also, to indicate that in spite of opposition, things nevertheless do move!)

The official publication of the Tell Beit Mirsim excavations appeared in the *Annuals* of the ASOR, Nos. 12, 13, 17, 21-22, in the years 1932, 1933, 1938 and 1943. It was a landmark publication, a standard work that has been in constant use by Palestinian archaeologists ever since. By great good luck or incredible intuition, Albright had chosen to do his major series of excavations at a site whose history coincided with the entire history of settlement in that land down to the Babylonian Captivity in 586 B.C., and whose strata were so clearly separated by the repeated destructions that their pottery could serve as the definitive chronological time-clock, supported in every segment by comparative material from other sites.

After his fourth season was over, on August 20, 1932, Albright wrote by hand a letter to his mother, sending affectionate regards and his best wishes for her seventy-first birthday. He said it was very hard to write while an excavation was going on, and she had probably heard news from letters William S. had written to Mary. His health was better than it had been in summer for years and so he could hope to be better than usual in the fall—which would be fine, since, as his mother knew, Ruth would be *hors de combat*.

Dr. Albright's younger sister Shirley lived with the family in Baltimore that winter and took graduate work in the English Department at Johns Hopkins, having earned her B.A. earlier from Lincoln Memorial University at Harrogate, Tennessee. Interested first in library science, she shifted to study of English and returned to teaching in schools near the farm in Virginia. But she was present to help Ruth that fall after William returned from what turned out to be his last campaign at Tell Beit Mirsim and plunged into a new term of teaching at Hopkins.

On November 2, 1932, Dr. Albright wrote his parents a letter to report what he called real news—their fourth son, David Foxwell, had been born the evening before at about 10:30 at Mercy Hospital, weighing 10½ pounds. Ruth and the baby were doing well and would remain three weeks, to avoid the leg-vein trouble she had suffered after the birth of Stephen. As for himself, Albright said his health was better and he had accomplished more that fall than for several years; the year before, he had not recovered from the Beth-zur dig until in November. The two little boys were fine—he had just spanked them for making great noise after being put to bed—and Paul was improving in behavior and learning rapidly. Shirley was studying eight or ten hours a day but keeping well.

During 1932 in JBL a scholarly debate developed between Prof. Albright and Prof. Torrey of Yale. Albright argued that the pre-exilic Jewish towns and villages of Palestine were destroyed in about the early sixth century and most of them were never reoccupied; it was not merely a temporary destruction but a permanent one. In concluding the exchanges Albright expressed the highest respect for Prof. Torrey's work, "not because his views are always correct, but because of the breadth of his knowledge, the originality of his views, the soundness of his philological method, and the unequalled brilliance of his exposition. The combination of such qualities would make any biblical research important, even if erroneous historical premises were to invalidate part of the results."[16] Exactly the same sentences might have been written by one of his scholarly opponents concerning Professor Albright and his work!

Beginning in January 1933, Paul, who was then nine and attending school in Baltimore, brought home the four minor communicable diseases and generously shared them with his younger brothers and even his mother. She, with what help Shirley had time to give, before the end of May had to cope with four cases of chickenpox, four cases of whooping cough, one case of measles, and five attacks of mumps—Ruth herself having the fifth. William wrote his old friend Sam Geiser in April that his wife had been for more than a week the most swollen sight he had ever seen. William had arrived home from Palestine about five weeks before David's birth and left again before mid-June of 1933 to return to Palestine. Ruth did all the night-service for the children in order to let her husband have his necessary rest. It often seemed to her that his scholarly obsession was a tyrant. He could spend nearly half a year in Palestine, return home, and then think he should and could wield a heavy hand, be the master of the household, and punish the boys for things that she allowed them to do. His hair-trigger temper was well known. Standing between him and the boys, as she needed to do in order to spare him for his work, she inevitably brought up the children to be more hers than his, though he would always be proud of them, especially after they were grown men. In spite of sometimes feeling tyrannized by his work, Ruth felt that William was a gift from God to turn Bible study back toward truth, and that she was on earth in order, as much as possible, to make him a human being!

In the February 1933 BASOR, Editor Albright reported on his surface explorations in Palestine since 1930 and stated, "This topographical research has now attracted untrained men into the field, some of whom have unhappily published their results, none of which are of the slightest value. We must regretfully mention the work of A. Jirku, who has made several journeys in Palestine and Syria, and has published the observations made in the first ones. He began by accompanying Alt and later the writer on their annual horseback trips through the country. Immediately after the close of his trip with the writer, in which he had not taken the slightest interest in the pottery, except to note down the results of the writer's examination of the sherds collected by the latter and the other members of the party, Jirku undertook independent trips in northern Palestine and Syria, where he fixed the dates of the sherds examined himself. Needless to say nearly all Jirku's conclusions are absolutely wrong, as the writer can assert with confidence, since he had previously visited a number of these sites himself, and has since had an opportunity to see some of the pottery which Jirku imprudently identified—invariably without success." Albright could be very plain-spoken when it was a matter of protecting the work of serious scholars. "The value of this research for the history of occupation, as well as for the identification of ancient lands, is obvious," he continued. "In the hands of Alt, it has already been made to play a very important part in the reconstruction of territorial history. It is also about to prove decisive in many problems of the date of documents and institutions. . . . These and other parallel studies will so advance our knowledge of the development of political, social, and religious institutions in Israel that no biblical scholar can afford to disregard the progress of research in Palestinian archaeological topography."[17]

On June 7 Albright sailed from Baltimore to spend the last six months of 1933 in Jerusalem as Director again. Dr. George Ricker Berry of Colgate-Rochester Theological School had been appointed Annual Professor; Dr. Fisher was on the staff as Archaeologist, and Dr. Stinespring was there as Thayer Fellow after having been Two Brothers Fellow. Albright also lectured in the Summer Institute from mid-July into August. Mary had joined her husband and was to "keep the record book" at the Jerash excavations directed by Nelson Glueck. As Albright had written his old friend Sam Geiser in April, he had suffered from his eyes much of the time that year, worse lately because of an occulist's honest error followed by inexcusable carelessness on the part of the best optician in the city. But now the situation was corrected and he hoped not to lose much more time because of his eyes—a rare mention of his poor eyesight in contrast to constant complaints in earlier years.

Mary was hostess of the School during the time she was there with her husband as he alternated with her brother in the directorship from 1933-1935. Dr. Glueck during his year as Director had asked Dr. Stinespring to have his wife and son come over, as Mrs. Glueck was then finishing her medical course in Cincinnati. Mary and Forrest came on an Easter cruise ship and immediately organized a clean-up of the School as well as changing the menus to more American-type foods, a change appreciated by the residents.

As Dr. Albright left home in early June, necessarily taking with him for the trip what money was available, the only thing Ruth could see to do in the immediate future was what he had suggested: to go with her three boys and baby David to the Virginia farm along with Shirley after the close of her classes, and spend the summer at the farm. The "bank holiday" had been declared in March as Franklin D. Roosevelt became President; many banks had closed permanently. People who had money in a bank could not draw it out. The situation for millions was desperate. Ruth asked William's parents and his brother Finley if she and the boys could stay at the farm that summer, as she simply had no money. She said that when William's salary finally could reach her she would give half the amount to them. They accepted the arrangement, but she felt that they did not really believe her statement that she was without money, and this was confirmed a half-century later. Ruth was deeply hurt both times. A further strain was thus placed on the in-law relationship. Living on a farm, with food always available, they simply could not understand that city people with good positions could actually be penniless during that time of financial panic. Later she and William were able occasionally to add a permanent improvement to the farm home. For her it was not the most happy time. For the boys, however, it was a wonderful summer, the first of many that the older boys would spend with Uncle Finley and Aunt Shirley, the younger ones being included also as they became old enough to profit from the farm life away from home for a couple of months and to be of a little help with the work, not merely an extra burden.

In one of her visits during the last years before the death of William's mother in 1936, Ruth persuaded his parents to deed the farm to Finley and Shirley, the unmarried children who had remained to make the farm productive and to provide a home for their aging parents. Her tactic was psychological: she said that they surely would not want their farm, after their death, to be divided up among all their children and in-laws (knowing that the rather rigid-minded parents did not care for the wives of Paul and Philip or the husband of Mary any more than they did for her). The tactic worked; the farm deed was put in the names of Finley and Shirley. On returning from France after World War I, Finley had made it his ambition to restore the worn-out tobacco farm, reforest part of it and make it produce good crops. He learned about farming from Government bulletins of which he collected many stacks, and from a kind old Negro neighbor who gave timely advice, for example telling Finley when the corn was ready for harvesting. In the year of William's death, Finley and Shirley would deed the whole farm over to the local Council of Boy Scouts with life rights to approximately half of it. Finley passed away January 21, 1974, 28 months after his illustrious oldest brother.

Once again as Director, Prof. Albright left Baltimore on June 7, 1933, and reached Jerusalem on the 29th after having interviews in Paris with French scholars. The Henry J. Cadbury family of Haverford College was at the School from mid-May to mid-July. After Albright's arrival he often talked with his sister, Mary, who with her family lived in the Director's wing. She helped him on various phases of his work as well as being hostess, and the whole group of residents ate meals together. Mrs. Cadbury became suspicious that something was going on—the Director, who was there without his wife, was spending a lot of time alone in his study with Dr. Stinespring's wife! Finally at the dinner table she demanded once again of Mary, "Are you *really* Dr. Albright's sister?" Dr. Albright burst out laughing and asked Mary to hold her table napkin over the upper part of her face, covering it down to the end of her nose, and he did the same, covering his upper face. Both were laughing as they did so, and the obvious truth became perfectly clear even to Mrs. Cadbury. Their smiles were carbon copies.

The Baltimore *Evening Sun* of January 9, 1934, carried a story under the heading "Stammerer's Prayer Unearthed, Haverford Expedition Scientist Baffled by Inscription Till He Uses Mirror." It said: "Members of the excavating expedition of Haverford College knew all about ancient writings, but the characters on a small clay tablet from the ruins of the Biblical town, Beth Shemesh, stumped them. Dr. W. F. Albright sat up nights working on the inscription— then he got a hunch. He held a [the] tablet before a mirror. The characters formed the words of a prayer. The doctor read: 'Oh, El, cut through the backbone of my stammering. I desire that thou shalt remove the spring of the impediment."

Mary, on returning from the Jerash excavation, was still recuperating from sand-fly fever (papateche fever). Dr. Judah Magnes of Hebrew University offered the Stinesprings his cottage at Netanya on the Mediterranean coast in hopes it would hasten her slow convalescence, since most of her life had been spent at much lower altitudes than that of Jerusalem. After a week there she returned a new person, and her brother looked at her in amazement. He decided he had better accept the invitation of the Mohls, who owned the cottage next-door to that of Dr. Magnes. (Mrs. Mohl before her marriage was Sophia Berger, who worked with Henrietta Szold, American founder of the Hadassah Medical Organization in 1912, to save German-Jewish children from Hitler's grasp by bringing them to Palestine and caring for them.)

Therefore, early in August Dr. Albright went down to the coast to be a guest of the Mohls. On his first dip in the Mediterranean, a large wave knocked him down, injuring his back. The Stinesprings received a telephone call asking for William S. to come in the sta-

tion wagon with a mattress on the floor to take Dr. Albright back to
Jerusalem. "It was some time before he could force himself to get
up and lead a fairly active life," Mary recalled later. "He seemed to
be in constant pain until after the operation on his back." The
needed operation for his ruptured disk did not take place until
twelve years later, after the problem was repeatedly misdiagnosed.
Late in 1945 he finally had the vertebrae fused.

That summer of 1933 he returned to work at the site of his first
dig, Gibeah of Saul, Tell el-Ful. Previously he had left walls standing and masonry quite intact, but the 1927 earthquake had caused
much to collapse. While this fact was to be regretted, it made possible further investigation of the fortress interior. Work began during the first week of September and continued almost a month. This
time there was no legal problem over leasing the site from the many
joint owners. With his much greater knowledge of pottery chronology Albright could make some refinements and corrections now,
yet there was much corroboration and very little need for change,
which must have been satisfying to him. He was always, however,
willing to make changes whenever the discovery of more evidence,
by himself or anyone else, necessitated it.

There were ten students in the academic session; Albright lectured twice a week until he left on January 3 to return to Johns
Hopkins for the spring semester. Dr. Stinespring was Acting Director in his absence, and as he later recalled, "I was not too fond of
administrative work; it was always a great relief to me when he got
back to Jerusalem from Baltimore. I was always grateful to him
that if I had made a decision, he stood by me completely, but I only
made decisions on things that I absolutely had to decide on." He
never became fascinated by potsherds, and "was happy just to photograph the pots and let him worry about what their date was."

Before leaving Palestine Albright and his party joined Mr.
George Horsfield, of the Transjordanian Antiquities Department,
and his staff in making soundings at Ader in Moab during a two-
week campaign in mid-November. They explored the Bronze Age
city which, since he and Kyle had first visited it nearly ten years before, had been partly occupied by Bedouin who almost completely
destroyed the ancient temple for building material—a matter of
heartbreak, Albright called it, to an archaeologist.

During the early spring of 1934 Dr. Albright had one of his not infrequent slumps or periods of depression, though he was able to carry on his work and keep planning for the future; perhaps his frequent back pain was a cause. Mrs. Albright felt that something had to be done. She "connived" with her old Pennsylvania teacher, Prof. Franklin Edgerton, by then long at Yale, to secure for her husband the offer of the Chair in Assyriology which had become vacant by the death of Prof. Raymond P. Dougherty in the previous July. Not that she meant for him to accept it, by any means! It was a ploy to accomplish two purposes: to lift him out of his depression, and to secure from Johns Hopkins a much-needed raise in salary. The strategy worked fine—in fact, too well. Albright was elected Laffan Professor of Assyriology and Babylonian Literature and head of the Semitic Department at Yale, the same chair Prof. Albert T. Clay had held. He was on the point of accepting, even though it would mean a narrowing of his fields of activity to a specialty almost confined to Assyriology—and he knew that his eyes could not take constant work over cuneiform texts. Yet he was so close to saying yes that Ruth had to take drastic steps. She confronted him directly and pronounced her ultimatum: She was not going to leave Baltimore, and he was not either! Another version is that if he accepted the offer he could go to Yale, but she and the boys were absolutely not going anywhere; they were staying in Baltimore! That secured the desired result on Albright's part, who knew nothing of her hand in the matter; and Johns Hopkins, alarmed over the prospect of losing a professor who was bringing fame to one of its smallest departments, came through with a sizable raise (from $6000 to $7000) before he actually declined the offer. At news of the raise Ruth lifted her youngest in her arms and exclaimed, "David, you have a famous father!"

Albright did decline the offer, but to have received it buoyed up his spirits tremendously. He suggested in place of himself a Gentile German scholar, Albrecht Goetze, who had in the preceding year been dismissed by the Hitler government from his professorship at Marburg University because of his refusal to cooperate with Nazism. Prof. Goetze in his long and distinguished career at Yale never knew, while he and Albright had polite scholarly "feuds" over chronology and other points, that his very position in

America (where he became a naturalized citizen in 1940) was due to his erudite antagonist! Both would die in the same year, a month apart.

Prof. Goetze was not to be the only scholar whom Prof. Albright would help to a position in an American university after he had fled from Nazi terror. Rabbi Rosenblatt, Albright's colleague in the department, would say much later, "I know that when Hitler came to power, Professor Albright, because of the discrimination that was practiced, left the Deutsche Morgenländische Gesellschaft, where he was an honored member (that was the most prestigious orientalist society in the world at that time), and I know personally that he must have helped at least five hundred scholars that came to this country—provided them with positions or recommended them very highly, so that they were able to continue their work in this country, thanks to his deep interest."

Prof. Albright sailed from New York on June 12, 1934, on the American Export Line S.S. *Excalibur* for Jaffa, arriving on July 1, ready to undertake the Kyle Memorial Excavation at Bethel. In November of 1927, immediately after the Albrights returned from furlough, he had conducted preliminary soundings at Beitin, north of Jerusalem, to see whether the tradition was correct that it was biblical Bethel. He and his staff found many iron and bronze artifacts from the time of Israelite occupation and earlier, carrying on the work for two weeks with money given by Mr. Harold Wiener before his tragic death in the riot two years later. As Albright reported in the October 1934 BASOR, they "rented a fig orchard just north of the modern village, with its southwest corner within two metres of the shaft which we sunk in 1927."[18]

Young George Ernest Wright, just graduated as a student of Ovid R. Sellers from McCormick, the Presbyterian seminary in Chicago, and John Bright, Albright's student who was already teaching at Union Theological Seminary in Richmond, were on the Bethel staff. Dr. Stinespring remembered that around the camp and at the School they were called "Wright and Bright, the Gold-dust Twins"! James L. Kelso was codirector.

Wright, on his first dig that summer, was tremendously impressed with Albright and vividly recalled the dig decades later, after he himself was a famous archaeologist: "The incredible thing about Albright that summer was not only how he was completely native; nothing fazed him. He never got sick; he was as strong as an ox—could eat anything, drink anything, anywhere, just as Glueck learned to do. And this dig was completely a one-man show. He was at it day and night, overseeing every single thing, working hours upon hours by himself out there in the field after the dig was over, taking notes and working out every detail of the relationship of walls to walls, and so on, working this all out in his head, then doing pottery with everybody around, teaching everybody the rudiments of pottery chronology while he made notes on the pottery at the same time. It was an incredible performance, a one-man show."

Albright was, however, ill during that campaign and lost a couple of weeks because of a bad carbuncle on the back of his neck, which finally had to be operated on, and an attack of dysentery, which responded to immediate vigorous treatment, as well as a short lumbago attack, as he wrote his parents. He nevertheless managed not to lose weight as he usually did, and reported success in the campaign at Bethel. They found firm proof that the destruction by the Israelites, who immediately rebuilt the city, had occurred in the thirteenth century B.C. This, their greatest historical discovery, should end most of the controversy over the date of the Hebrew conquest. He told his parents of his new monograph which should—and did—appear that fall: *The Vocalization of the Egyptian Syllabic Orthography,* Vol. No. 5 in the new AOS series. (It was widely opposed for many years, but in the last decade of his life Albright had the satisfaction of seeing its increasingly general acceptance by scholars.)

In his report in the December 1934 BASOR on the Bethel excavation, which ran from July 9 to September 15 with from 20 to 75 laborers (Arab men, women, and boys), Albright wrote that "there were few unsolved problems of stratigraphy remaining when the campaign closed, ...

"We may also observe that the vicissitudes of Ai and Bethel cannot be separated; the two towns are so close together that only one could have any importance—or could in fact exist in more than ephemeral fashion—in a given period. The name *Ha-Ai* means simply 'the ruin' (*par excellence*) in Hebrew. Bethel fell into the hands of the Israelites, who burned it to the ground, somewhere in the thirteenth century. In the tradition, since Ai was the precursor of Bethel, and was also destroyed by a foe who burned it to the ground, some eight centuries before, the former replaced the latter. . . . Bethel and Ai are so inextricably combined in the stories of the Israelite Conquest in Joshua, that some explanation such as we have given, seems necessary."[19]

John Bright, who had also been with Albright at the last dig at Tell Beit Mirsim two years before, recalled that Prof. Albright chose to "conceal his linguistic ability in connection with the 1934 dig at Bethel. When it came time to negotiate with the village elders for the use of their land, Albright pretended to know no Arabic and commissioned one of the Arab foremen to conduct the negotiations on his behalf, hoping thereby to secure more reasonable terms. But then, the matter concluded, he was in a trap. He couldn't deny himself the use of Arabic in addressing the laborers through the entire campaign, but if he used it he would advertise himself as a liar. So he gave it out that he was studying Arabic diligently, sitting up late at night in his tent to do so. After a day or two he would attempt simple Arabic sentences, taking care to mispronounce words and commit grammatical errors as he did so. Each day he got better at it, till at the end of a week or ten days he spoke it as fluently as the Arabs did. They were amazed and thought him a genius—which of course he was, if not in the way they thought!"

The first meeting of the season of the Palestine Oriental Society was held at the School on October 25, 1934, and Albright was elected president for the second time. Between November 8 and 20 Albright, Stinespring, Carl Kraeling and A. M. Honeyman made a thirteen-day trip to the north and east which, as Albright reported in the BASOR for February 1935, "was most successful and there was not a hitch or a delay in the schedule, in spite of rainy weather on the North-Syrian coast. The itinerary carried the party to Balatah, Acre, Beirut, Tripoli, Jebleh, Lattakia, Antioch, Rihaniyeh, Aleppo, Dura Europus, Tell el-Hariri (Mari), Abu Kemal, the petroleum pipe-line to Palmyra, thence to Hums, Baalbek, Damascus, and home."[20]

After returning, Albright "gave the annual presidential address at the meeting of the Palestine Oriental Society. As his subject he chose the same topic which he had treated in a presidential address before the society in January, 1922: 'Palestine in the Earliest Historical Period.' Attention was called to the remarkable increase in our knowledge, especially during the past three years, so that it is now possible to fix the chronology of Palestinian culture in broad lines back to the late fourth millennium. On December 17th the writer gave an address on 'Recent Archaeological Work in Palestine,' before the University Women's Association, and on the 18th he gave an illustrated lecture on the 'Excavation of Bethel' at the Y.M.C.A."[21]

From December 1 to 13 Albright and his staff were on an expedition to Petra, south of the Dead Sea, with Mr. and Mrs. George Horsfield (Mrs. Horsfield, formerly Agnes Conway, had excavated what was named the Conway High Place at Petra). George Ernest Wright, a Fellow at the School, vividly remembered some facets of the Petra trip that Albright did not include in his report in the February 1935 BASOR. "That was a transition period in Albright's life; I was coming into his period of 'civilization'—he was still making mistakes once in a while on *either* and *neither* [pronouncing the first syllable as *eye*], but he was purposely teaching himself, since going to Hopkins in '29, to be a civilized Easterner. He started to curb his temper—he was noted for having a horrible temper, which I'd seen him lose twice in '34 when I was there. Once it was against a cleaning lady; it went on in Arabic and I could only recognize the word 'Shut up! Shut up! Shut up!' The other time was in early December when he was taking the whole large group at the School to Petra. After staying overnight in the Palestine Hotel in Amman, we had a convoy that left at six A.M. and went down the desert road. The instruction was for each to follow the car ahead, the taxi driver leading the way. I was the driver of the Model-A Ford right behind the taxi driver, and Albright was in the Model-A station wagon right behind me with a kind of cautious fellow driving it. There were two or three other cars behind him. It was just beginning to get light when we started, and this taxi driver shot off through those empty streets of Amman just about as fast as he could go. I didn't know where I was going; I was just determined I wasn't going to get lost! We wondered where the others went, and waited half an hour for them to catch up. Finally the taxi driver said, 'Well, I bet I know which way they went. You stay here and I'll go find them.'

"So half an hour later they all came, and I got it from Albright!

I've had no one blow like that since my father, who had the same kind of temper. There was no rationalism to it, he just blew! Then we spent the day riding alongside the railroad—there wasn't any regular road. We stayed overnight in a cave in Petra, and the next day Albright started to give everybody the tour, having become his jolly self again as soon as we had arrived in Petra. When we left to go home, only those remaining who were to dig with him, Albright shook hands all around. The way he shook hands with me was such as to let me know, 'Well, let bygones be bygones!' He never said a word of apology, but I recognized his intention."

The spring semester was filled not only with teaching and preparations for returning to Palestine, but with lecturing to various groups and meetings, on recent excavations in the Near East. When Prof. Albright sailed on June 11 on the *Excambion,* Mrs. Albright and their four boys went with him to spend six months in Jerusalem, this time living in the Director's House. No major excavation was planned; Albright worked mostly on preparation of the Bethel material, and other things, for publication. Sir Flinders and Lady Petrie moved into the School as permanent residents during that June, remaining until his death in July, 1942.

Paul was eleven and a half years old. He had been used to seeing his father only five months or so at a time in Baltimore. When Prof. Albright was at home and needed to give a lecture or go on an errand, he had to ask his wife each time what streetcar lines to take, and she would give him full details. Paul drew his own conclusions. But in Palestine that half-year, in meetings of the Palestine Oriental Society and other groups there was a great deal of discussion, as usual, about archaeological and linguistic details. Often the Jewish scholars would come, two or three at a time, to have Prof. Albright adjudicate their problems or controversies. Paul did not realize what a well-known scholar his father was, but he was learning by experience that a large number of people consulted him as an authority, and he was duly impressed. One day at lunch time Prof. Albright was called away from the dining table to settle one of these questions. When he came back he was laughing and said something off-hand as he sat down to finish his meal. Paul looked at him and said, "Dad, you ought to live in Jerusalem all the time. Here you know everything, and at home you're just plain dumb!" To which his father replied with a roar of laughter.

While the Albrights were there, at the end of August the probability that Dr. Judah Leon Magnes would resign as Chancellor of the Hebrew University he had worked so hard to found and foster caused great consternation among Gentile as well as Jewish friends of the institution. Prof. Albright gave an eloquent speech on the 29th, reported the next day in the New York *Times,* saying: "In my opinion it will be a catastrophe for the Hebrew University and a disgrace to world Jewry if Dr. Magnes is forced to resign his post as chancellor because of lack of funds. . . .

"When I arrived in Jerusalem sixteen years ago there was no Jewish science or scholarship here worthy of the name. In the ten years since the founding of the university the situation has changed with the most startling rapidity and Jerusalem has become the foremost centre of Jewish research and learning in the world.

"What the university means to the Jewish people is now clear to all far-sighted people. What it means to Palestine is becoming evident even to the man in the street. . . . I know of no man possessing these two qualities [prophetic vision and international-mindedness] in such measure and in such a happy combination as Dr. Magnes. His idealism never yet has faltered and his breadth of interest and sympathy never has narrowed. . . . The university and the Near East need Dr. Magnes." It was Dr. Albright at his fiery best, defending a valued friend and institution with all the eloquence at his command. Dr. Magnes remained with the Hebrew University as its president until his death on October 27, 1948, in New York at the age of 71.

Prof. Albright left his family in Jerusalem and went to Rome from September 18 to October 3 to attend the Congress of Orientalists. He had been appointed chairman of the U.S. delegation by the State Department; he was also the American member of the Consultative Committee of the congress. As Albright reported in the December 1935 BASOR, "Assyriology was extremely well represented, but most of the papers of value were rather too technical to be described here. The Old Testament was very badly represented, and most of the papers in this field were of little significance."[22]

President Millar Burrows (succeeding Prof. James Montgomery, after his long tenure, as ASOR president) in his annual report in BASOR for December expressed regret for the Stinesprings' departure from the School to take up teaching at Smith College. He mentioned the welcome increase of books with Sir Flinders' library stored in the School and the Petries as welcome residents, and then said: "One note of deep regret sounds through what otherwise might be a paean of almost unqualified rejoicing. Prof. Albright's resignation as Director of the School in Jerusalem is as unwelcome as his return to that position in 1933 was welcome. All we can say about it is that we realize how hard for him and his family the arrangement of the past few years has been and how fortunate we have been to have his services so long. Knowing that his devotion to the School will be undiminished, and assured that his help in excavation and publication as well as his counsel in administration will still be ours, we are the better able to be reconciled to what we cannot help."[23]

Dr. Nelson Glueck was appointed Director for a term of three years. Editor Albright in making the announcement of this appointment in the February 1936 BASOR called it "a most fortunate event in the history of the School. . . . Professor Glueck is the first young Palestinian archaeologist to receive all his training in connection with the Schools,"[24] and praised his personal qualities and characteristics which assured the School of excellent management. In closing his last annual report Albright said, "In many ways the writer must count the past year as the most successful of the ten years during which he has directed the School. But its success is mainly due to the efficient and loyal collaboration of officers, members of the staff, and students of the School. To them we again extend our hearty thanks."[25]

The Albright family left Jerusalem on December 29 and sailed on the S.S. *Exochorda*, arriving in New York on January 23, 1936. Dean McCown had been appointed Acting Director until Dr. Glueck would take over on July 1. When Prof. and Mrs. Albright, Paul, Hugh, Stephen and three-year-old David boarded their ship it was the close of a period in their lives.

Later Albright looked back on his years in Palestine and his shift in 1926 from surface explorations to archaeological excavations. His earlier skeptical view of the historical tradition of Israel had repeatedly been jolted by the discoveries he made which confirmed biblical details as being historical rather than legendary. He found himself closer to Hugo Winckler's Pan-Babylonian viewpoint and strongly opposed to Julius Wellhausen's ideas that Israel developed in isolation from the ancient Near Eastern civilizations, and that its development had been a unilinear evolutionary one. He more and more insisted that the tradition of Moses and mono- theism already in the time of Moses were substantially historical, and he continued building on these basic principles throughout his life. He had not lost his interest in Assyriology and Egyptian, however, and resumed such studies on returning to Johns Hopkins in 1929. When the Arab rebellions and the Second World War, from 1936 on, made it impossible to carry on excavations in Pales- tine, he had turned his researches more intensively in the direction of the philosophy of history.

12

The Professor

A rather different kind of life began for the Albright family in 1936. Instead of the constant direct connection with the School in Jerusalem, they now followed its progress and life from the distance of correspondence and reporting through BASOR. That journal became even more of an outlet for the comprehensive studies that Prof. Albright carried on, replacing the popular-type preliminary reporting of explorations and excavations he had published in it during past years. All the boys except David were then in school, attending one or two of the fine Catholic schools in Baltimore. Dad was now going to be at home year-round, except for frequent trips to learned society and committee meetings, and lectures at various schools, clubs and other organizations.

The Baltimore *Sun* of January 22, 1936, carried an AP story from Boston dated the 21st, saying that "the fall of Lacish [Lachish], ancient city in Southwestern Judah, has been established as occurring in the year 589 B.C., Prof. William Albright, of Johns Hopkins University, Baltimore, announced today. Professor Albright, returning aboard the liner Exochorda, from his sixteenth year of research work in the Holy Land, said establishment of the date was important, and that the city was the last to fall to the Babylonians before they reached Jerusalem." The ordinary newspaper reader might have wondered why it was important—what it had to do with his life in America in 1936—but the learned professor was going to have an opportunity through voluminous reporting in the next decades to educate him as to the importance of such events—how such knowledge illuminated ancient history and confirmed the historicity of biblical narratives.

194

William's mother died on March 16 and was buried in the little cemetery behind Wood's United Methodist Church on Hickory Road not far from the Virginia farm. On her tombstone her last name is spelled "Allbright"—a few years earlier her husband had returned to the former spelling of the name. He would outlive her, but not happily, by just over eight years, recovering from a broken back in the autumn of 1938, and dying on April 24, 1944. If Zephine had lived another year and a half, she and Wilbur would have reached their fiftieth wedding anniversary.

A month later, on April 15, Prof. Albright as President of the American Oriental Society delivered an address in New Haven at the annual spring meeting, titled "How Well Can We Know the Ancient Near East?" His address was published in JAOS the following year in volume 56. He referred to the late James Henry Breasted's brilliant career, which he said had caused America to be in the forefront in the efforts to recover the Ancient East. Since such studies had quickly declined in German universities following Hitler's rise to power in 1933, America was becoming the center of academic research in this area and many universities had established departments to foster it. He cautioned concerning the artificial nature of this interest, however, saying that it rested too heavily on a few scholars' ability to organize and promote its study rather than on a spontaneous demand. He warned that his fellow scholars needed to be aware of the danger of an unexpected onslaught from some direction, such as one of the actual or potential enemies who surrounded them and who thought that by doing away with their department they could increase their own budget and overcome some small deficit.

The Dansville, N.Y., *Breeze* of April 18, 1936, announced, "Woman Lecturer Coming Monday." ". . . Dr. Ruth Albright, . . . will give an illustrated lecture in St. Peter's Parish at 7:45 o'clock . . . Dr. Ruth Albright has been associated with her husband, Dr. William F. Albright, . . . and with him has spent much of the larger part of the past sixteen years in that land. . . ." There were *two* Drs. Albright lecturing in America on Palestine.

One of the first students to earn a Ph.D. under Prof. Albright's chairmanship of the Oriental Seminary was Abraham Bergman (later Avraham Biran), in 1935, a native-born Israeli (a "sabra") whose great-grandfather had emigrated to Palestine in the 1880's and whose family had helped found early settlements of Jews in the land, such as Rosh Pinnah, Petah Tikvah, Rishon Letsion, Zichron Yaakov, and Binyaminah. He recalled that "with the rise of Hitler, long before Hitler began his outright anti-Semitic activities, Albright sensed that something was wrong, and as a sort of private battle he declared a boycott of German books. He told us once in a seminar that 'from now on I am not buying any German books.' It was very difficult for a man like Albright—he needed the tools, and the most important things in his field were published in German."

Bergman had met Albright in Jerusalem in the late '20's. In his young days he had walked through the whole country of Palestine from Dan to Beersheba, visiting all the biblical sites. With his ability in Hebrew as well as that background, when he transferred from the University of Pennsylvania to Hopkins, really at Albright's urging, he had advantages over the few other students there. "Albright used the same method that he continued for years afterward," he recalled. "He had seminars, he gave lectures, he taught us everything. We studied cuneiform, hieroglyphics, history, and Bible with him. Those were pre-Ugaritic days—it was just beginning, the first tablets having been found in 1929; word was leaking out, and in fact Albright used to bring to us some of the newest information. He didn't teach us Hittite. That was during the rise of Hitler, and Albright invited Emil Forrer (a refugee professor) to come for a term. Forrer taught us Hittite, including hieroglyphics and history of the period, and Frank Blake taught us Hebrew grammar, syntax and phonology. He was very famous for his grammar of Tagalog. Blake suggested that he and I sit down together and write a Hebrew-English dictionary, not the usual kind, but a dictionary of idioms. We worked on it for several years, but I don't think Blake ever published it. Albright then was spending part of each year in Palestine." Biran would later be Director Biran of the Department of Antiquities in Israel and head of the Rockefeller Museum (then only recently built and opened) north of the Old City of Jerusalem, not far from the School property.

In May of 1936, as Ernest Wright much later recalled, "Abe Sachs and I were both taking exams, I taking my Master's exams, he taking his written exams for the Ph.D. My Master's thesis was finished; Sachs had not yet started on his Ph.D. thesis. And Albright gave us the exams—with an unholy glee! He would come every half hour to see how we were doing, and would pat us on the back, both of us at the same time, and say, 'Don't worry, boys! I'm going to pass you anyway!' "

John Bright was another of the few students at that time. "All of Albright's students," he recalled much later, "can testify to his extreme thoughtfulness of them and personal concern for them. I had to leave the Tell Beit Mirsim dig in 1932 a few days before it ended in order to get back to Richmond for the opening of school. As I was putting my things into the station wagon which would take me to Jerusalem, Albright called me aside out of earshot of the rest and said, 'I say, Bright, have you enough money?' Fortunately, I had; but I was touched that this great scholar should make such an offer to a young fellow whom he had known for scarcely two months and whom, for all he could know at the time, he might never see again.

"I had this personal concern of Albright's for his students illustrated to me again in the spring of 1936. I had entered Hopkins in the fall of 1935, but by the following spring I had run out of money, and, it being the depths of the Depression, saw little chance of finding any more. Besides, I was discouraged." (As Wright said, Bright was most distracted over the language learning, which he called "that crazy business—this stupid bit of put-on. I'm supposed to become a scholar under this guy? And put up with Julius Lewy too?"—Prof. Julius Lewy, a distinguished German orientalist, a professor driven out of Europe by the Nazis, who became Professor of Assyriology at Hebrew Union College in Cincinnati, was substituting for Albright in the fall semester of 1935, while the Albrights were in Jerusalem for their last stay.) Bright continued, "I saw no course but to withdraw. When I went to his office to inform him of my decision, Prof. Albright immediately offered me a loan. I could not accept it, both because I saw no prospect of ever being able to repay it, and because I shrewdly suspected that he could himself ill afford it. But that was the sort of man he was. It could not be put down to some special fondness on his part for me, for others of his students have told me of similar experiences."

Wright explained about Professor Lewy: "Bright and I put on a vendetta against Julius Lewy. We considered him a Jew who was just like a Nazi, a Prussian. He was unmerciful in his criticism of us, and when Albright was away, Bright and I just boycotted him.

We would never speak to him, we would never go near him; we would go to class and do what we could, and if he criticized us, O.K. We just walked out. Lewy had the German manner of lecturing. When the hour came, he waited one minute, then he'd march out of his office into the podium and start lecturing. When the time came to stop, he marched right back into his office, and we never went near him. Never, until Sachs let the cat out of the bag. Lewy asked Abe Sachs what Bright and I had against him. Then Lewy invited us to a *Christmas* party, and broke down and became a human being! We were friends from that time on!"

About Prof. Lewy, Albright in later years loved to tell the "yeenius" story. It was relayed by his students, to whom the formidable European scholar substituting for Albright had given an outrageously difficult assignment. When they protested, he replied that *he* could easily do it, and they answered, "But you are a genius, Professor!" He did not deny it; he raised his hand and solemnly said, "Ah, but I vass not *born* a yeenius! I *became* a yeenius by hard vork"—meaning, "Go, and do thou likewise!"

Bright said, "Prof. Albright was in a real sense a father to his students. He could be cutting in his evaluation of colleagues in the field (once when the name of a well-known biblical professor in a well-known university was mentioned in his presence, he snorted, 'The man's illiterate!'). He did not suffer fools gladly (once a part-time student kept interrupting in a seminar with comments aimed at impressing Albright with his cleverness. Albright finally turned toward him and loudly said, 'Shhh!'). But if you had the honor to be one of his 'boys' he was with you all the way. He never called bad work good, but he could be amazingly tolerant of a student's limitations, as I, perhaps as much as anyone, have occasion to know. Nor did his interest in his 'boys' cease with their graduation, but rather followed them throughout life; encouraging, taking time to read their work and offer constructive criticism, praising them in some cases, at least, far more highly than they deserved—as I, again, have occasion to know. I think he invented the term 'the Baltimore school' (which he was about the only one to use) partly for modesty's sake, so that he would not have to refer to himself so often, but also to identify with those of his students who carried on in his tradition."

Of the students in the thirties, Wright would become a great archaeologist and professor at Harvard, Sachs would be a well-known professor many years at Brown, and Bright, at Union Theological Seminary in Richmond, after conquering the languages, would become one of Albright's best historians, publishing in his *History of Israel* (1959) the basic views of the "Baltimore school," i.e., the "Albright school."

"Recollections of Albright as a teacher are general impressions rather than tangible incidents," Bright said, and voiced the opinions of many students as he continued, "It must be said that as a pedagogue he was not at his best. Of educational method he knew nothing and, I suspect, cared less. His lectures were a catena of brilliant divagations upon which it was impossible to take coherent notes. (When he gave the Sprunt Lectures in Richmond, he spoke from copious notes—on the back of an envelope. And I'm willing to bet he didn't adhere even to those.) In seminars his mind would range over the frontiers of scholarship, driving the student (at least, this student) both faster and farther than he was able to go. It is small wonder that many first-year students became deeply discouraged and were tempted to quit. Yet, from another point of view, Albright was the greatest teacher I ever had. The student who stuck it out knew that he had served his apprenticeship under a master craftsman. He had had the opportunity to observe great scholarship at first hand and he learned more than he realized by osmosis, as it were. If he was made keenly aware of his limitations, he also learned to stay within those limitations and not pontificate upon subjects over which he did not have first-hand control. And he learned how to learn for himself, and thus perhaps how to remove at least some of the limitations. Above all, he learned scholarly integrity: that shoddy work simply will not do. To say that Albright taught me much would be the understatement of a lifetime. I owe him a debt that I can never repay."

George Ernest Wright published an article on "The Chronology of Palestine in the Early Bronze Age" in the October 1936 BASOR, No. 63. He expressed in a footnote his "gratitude to his teacher, Prof. W. F. Albright, for constant advice and for putting at his disposal unpublished materials."[1] Albright continually stimulated and encouraged his more advanced students to begin publishing on their own.

One of Albright's first doctoral graduates, Bergman/Biran, also commented on Albright's encouragement of his students, "but it was more of the old type, the Hebrew method—you 'sit at the feet of a master.' If you can grasp anything, it is your good luck; if you don't, it is your bad luck." After his graduation Dr. Bergman went to Jerusalem as Thayer Fellow during Albright's last term there. "There wasn't any money then, so they gave me the title of Thayer Fellow without any stipend. When I was still at Hopkins and we were talking to Albright once, we said, 'Professor, look, everybody has done so much about the history and the identification of sites; what's the use? We are going to start now; there is nothing to discover any more!' He gave us one of those looks of amazement as though to say—but he wouldn't say it because he was a polite gentleman—'You idiot!' 'Now look at me,' he said. 'I was there in 1920 and '21 and was also thinking that everybody had already discovered everything [just as he had feared as a boy of ten in Chile], and merely around Jerusalem I went out to Me Niphtoah, and Gibeah and Gibeon, and I wrote an article, publishing new identifications. The field hasn't been touched!' "

Bergman/Biran continued, "When I was Thayer Fellow, Albright suggested that I go and do a dig at Anathoth, the hometown of the prophet Jeremiah. There was another Fellow there, a Methodist minister named Edward P. Blair. Albright said to Blair and me, 'Why don't you go to Anathoth?' There is a village called Anata about five miles northeast of Jerusalem, and the identification of Anata with Anathoth was usually accepted, but nobody had really checked it archaeologically. So we went down and began excavations, but found only Roman-Byzantine pottery. It was not a very large excavation; in fact, I said to Albright before going, 'Now, Professor, you know we don't have much experience.' Albright said, 'Look, don't you worry; I'm going to give you this Arab foreman; *he* knows—you just don't interfere with him!' Which is again typical of Albright—sink or swim, that was his method."

Bergman published an article on his dig in the April 1936 BASOR, with their negative findings concerning Anata and their investigation of the idea that perhaps an opposite hill, called Ras el-Kharrubeh, which means "the top of the carob tree," which did have some Iron-Age pottery, might have been biblical Anathoth instead of the hill of Anata. His article expressed doubt that Ras el-Kharrubeh could, after all, have been Anathoth, as it had no sign of burning or general destruction and never had a large occupation at the top of the hill where an Israelite settlement would be expected. "Albright in his inimitable way added a footnote," Bergman/Biran recalled much later, "in which he implied very politely that I was talking nonsense! He knew so much, but he gave one a chance—that was typical of Albright."

Editor Albright was famous for his "Additional Notes" and upheld the view that the site of Ras el-Kharrubeh was indeed Anathoth, following Alt's view confirmed by his own examinations in later years. He had found just as much denudation of the hilltop at Tell el-Ful, and said it was "hard to overestimate the effect of more than two thousand years of denudation on such exposed summits, bearing the ruins of unwalled villages, at the top of the watershed ridge in central Palestine. Further excavations at Ras el-Kharrubeh would certainly reveal numerous grain-pits and caves, cisterns, cavities in the rock, etc., with Iron I and II pottery. There is no reason to suppose that Anathoth was occupied before the age of Saul. . . ."[2] Albright signed his name to his note, not merely his initials, but when Bergman came back with a rejoinder, Albright published it in the October issue—but could still have the last word with another Additional Note!

Wright recalled life in the department at Hopkins in those days. "Cyrus Gordon, Sachs and I (and Bright for one year) had this great thing: on special occasions, especially at birthdays, it was to invite Albright over to the newly-built Levering Hall [the YMCA building on campus]—once or twice we even hired a room upstairs—and we would have lunch there and would get Albright to tell stories. That was a marvelous time! We heard those stories three times over, but it was always enjoyable, and every so often Albright would throw in a new one. The one about Koldewey and the knotty-tailed cats [inbred in Babylonia] should be put in writing by somebody who has a good memory! One of the things about Albright as a teacher was that while he was incredibly bad from any official standards of pedagogy, he had a way of loving gossip. So when he'd start on somebody ('who shall remain nameless'), he'd tell you the whole story of this scholar or archaeologist—all his strengths, all his weaknesses, Koldewey and his knotty-tailed cats and all, and that's what you learned about Warka! Now if you want to know what the *dig* at Warka is all about, you go on into the library and hunt that up for yourself. What was important at Warka? I only learned that on my own. But when you came out of his courses you *knew* all the great scholars; you were in the family. You knew the gossip about them, their greatness, their weakness, and so on."

Wright recalled that what "got him" about Albright "was his tremendous, simply fascinating lectures" when he was in his first months of study with him in '34 in Jerusalem. "Albright's incredible mastery of material was something I found I could absorb—his way of putting together topographical history and archaeological history. He taught me pottery so that I suddenly had a fascination for pottery. That fall I did the first really original first-rate job I had ever done on ceramic chronology, so I had it made with Albright. He had this way of looking way down on you, but if you got a good idea then he threw you clear out of focus the other way. He thought I might be good at archaeology, but that I was no good at languages or anything else. So I entered Hopkins in February of 1935, having the Nettie F. McCormick fellowship. About the 21st Albright wrote my former teacher, Ovid Sellers, and at the end said, 'Congratulations on your student Wright; he just caught me in a Hebrew mistake the other day!' This happened in a case where I knew my paradigms off by heart, and Albright rattled off some of them, and got one wrong, and I caught him—I was kind of ambitious! From that time on I was 'a great linguist too,' which of course I wasn't."

With such enthusiastic reactions from his few students in the middle thirties, there began to grow the "Baltimore school," as Albright modestly called it, of young scholars who found that he opened exciting new worlds of scholarship to them, and who considered his ideas and methods tremendously persuasive and, as Wright said, "incredibly fascinating."

Wright recalled that Abe Sachs "had been there a year before me; he had gone through the new Hopkins program, which was to go straight through from high school to the Ph.D., with no stop for a B.A. Sachs and I were the first pair that really ran Albright [like the Cross and Freedman pair a decade later]. Those were the most wonderful years of my life, those two and a half years and two summers at Hopkins, where Albright was always the genial companion. He never was a severe critic of either Sachs or me. He never corrected me on anything in my dissertation. I was no good at anything else; the manner in which I got through my German examination was typical of the way Sachs and I operated.

"Sachs was one of these walking encyclopedias of everything. In April or May of 1935 Albright said to me, right out of the blue, 'Look, I'm going to be gone next fall; I guess you'd better take your German exam.' I had never had any German; I picked it up more or less on my own, and read nothing but German archaeological works in the American School all fall every morning. I kept reading as much as I could in the spring semester at Hopkins. So Albright pulled down off the shelf a book belonging to Abe Sachs—we had access to Albright's office, walked in and out whenever we pleased, and sat there and used his library; privileged students could do that. He opened the book and I looked over his shoulder and stumbled along, reading this German. Albright said, 'Well, I guess it wouldn't hurt you to study, read some more German over the summer,' which was certainly the understatement of the year. But Sachs, who was sitting there [Albright would give these impromptu reading exams in front of anyone who happened to be in his office] said, 'But Julius Lewy is going to be here in the fall in your place! He'll *never* pass a German exam under Lewy!' Albright said, 'Well, that's right. I've passed worse!' That's how I got through German!"

During the years of the second World War there were a few students in Albright's department who became well-known—Jacob M. Myers, Roger T. O'Callaghan, Dr. Harry M. Orlinsky as a post-doctoral student, Cullen I. K. Story, and a few others. The post-war period brought students in great numbers as GI students began flooding into American colleges and universities.

David Noel Freedman, who would later collaborate with Prof. Albright on numerous publication projects, including the great *Anchor Bible*, vividly recalled his first meeting with the Albrights. It created a trauma in him. He had had rather rigid religious training at Princeton Theological Seminary, quite incompatible with his earlier training, which had been a scientific intellectual inquiry. He thought he had to choose between the two, but found that Albright and his type of studies offered a synthesis; it seemed like the kind of answer that makes sense in our day. He had been graduated from Princeton in 1944 and then had gone out to Washington State with his young wife to pastor a pair of small churches as a national missionary. On recommendation from his teacher, Prof. Gehman (Old Testament professor at Princeton Seminary, who had been a student of Prof. Montgomery at the University of Pennsylvania), Freedman wrote to Albright asking about the possibilities for qualifying as a beginning student at Johns Hopkins. He told what he had studied and the languages he could read (Latin, Greek, Hebrew, Syriac, and French). Albright responded saying it was hard to say who qualified for the Oriental Seminary; he would define the main qualification as willingness to work hard. He cited a brilliant student, a Jesuit (Roger T. O'Callaghan) who had come in three years earlier without knowing anything of Hebrew or any other Near Eastern language, and he was ready to complete his work in that autumn of 1945 knowing in a superior way both Hebrew and Arabic, as well as having made a fine start in Egyptian, Sumerian, Assyrian, Ugaritic, Aramaic, and so forth; and his dissertation was a great contribution to a field of history. (Titled *Aram Naharaim*, it was later published in Rome in the *Supplement* to *Orientalia* in 1948; Albright had contributed massively to its content and development.) Albright further cited another man (Cullen I. K. Story) who, without a college degree but with four years at Dallas Seminary, had hitch-hiked from Des Moines to Baltimore and within four years had earned his M.A. degree with a very good thesis. He warned Freedman that he would have to study German, but he could do so by himself with aid from Albright—half his students had to work at it intensively for a couple of years in their course. Since Freedman already had a reading knowledge of a number of languages, he could well begin, but whether he would want to continue, Albright could not predict, adding that most of the students who possessed any determination and ability did so.

Thus Mr. and Mrs. Freedman at the end of the summer drove across the country just as wartime gas rationing ended. Leaving Neil and their baby girl with her family in Princeton, Noel drove to Baltimore, where it was very difficult to find any place to stay. He reached Hopkins in late afternoon and came into Gilman Hall by the south side entrance, going down half a flight and walking into Albright's dingy old office at the far end of the hall. He had never seen Albright before, and Albright immediately shattered his image of him as a solid, stocky person with a red face, a fighter (Albright was only the latter). Noel walked in and met a tall, ascetic type of man who by that time had achieved a considerable reserve, if it was not his natural shyness.

The first thing Freedman noticed in the office was a tremendous collection of old wrapping paper, boxes, large envelopes and string, way up on the top shelves above the books lining the walls. He would never forget it (and years later after Albright's funeral, when finding the same kind of collection stored in Albright's study and bedroom, would almost swear that it contained the very same items). (Ernest Wright of a decade earlier remembered that in his time the upper shelves in the office were given to packets of reprints of articles, and in the closet was all the string and paper; you opened the door and . . .!)

Albright and Freedman began talking about four o'clock. It was a very cordial, friendly conversation about what courses he would take—and he learned for the first time that there were no choices. Students took eleven courses, twelve hours, per year (the seminar was two hours), all on Tuesdays and Wednesdays. Everything was fine, and Freedman was going to get up and leave, but Dr. Albright said, "Let's read some Hebrew." Freedman hadn't looked at a Hebrew Bible in over a year, so tried to decline with thanks, but Albright took the Bible off a nearby shelf, and Noel received his entrance exam. Albright opened the Hebrew Bible to Genesis 17 and handed it to Freedman, saying "Read." Noel saw at once that it said something about "Avram," that he was so many years old. Freedman tried to think, not what the Hebrew meant (99 years) but what the English said. Finally he ventured, "A hundred." Albright looked at him and said, "You're close!"

By then it was growing dark and Albright had learned that Noel had no place to stay, so he said he should come home and stay overnight at their house (they had moved in 1937 around the corner onto Sulgrave Avenue in Mount Washington). Noel drove the two of them there. The Albrights had a garage but at that time no car. Noel drove his car into the driveway, and Ruth came out of the house to meet them. William introduced Noel to Ruth and then said, "Put the car in the garage." Noel got back in and started to drive into the garage, and Ruth said, "Don't you want to back it in?" Noel thought that might not be a bad idea and started to back out and turn around, but William said, "Don't be silly; he doesn't know the garage, so he should drive in forward!" By this time Noel, as he later told the story, was thinking, "What have I got myself into with this pair? Maybe I'd better leave the car in the driveway! Or put it in sideways!" That was his introduction to the Albright ménage.

Noel and his family settled in Baltimore; he was the only new full-time Ph.D. student in the department in 1945-46, and there had been none in 1944. That made him eligible for the Rayner Fellowship in 1946-47. Bob Hansen, a classmate of Noel at Princeton, had come in 1943 and though a bright student, was, as he claimed, totally paralyzed by Albright. Frederick L. Moriarty also came in 1945 but was there for only one or two years and took an M.A., while Jacob M. Myers was then almost at the end of his course, working on his dissertation.

That fall Albright had his long-delayed back surgery, and Prof. A. L. Oppenheim substituted for him in the Oriental Seminary. In exchange Albright taught the winter quarter in the Oriental Institute at Chicago University. Finally a woman physician who did not meet Albright gave the correct diagnosis from a description of his trouble and referred him to the right surgeon. Dr. Otenasek fused the vertebrae together, and for once, Albright obeyed as to post-operative procedures and made a good recovery. During the weeks of bedridden convalescence, when he was naturally depressed and nervous, Ruth spent hours—up to eight or more a day—reading to him, not technical material in his field to keep him up to date, however, but detective stories, something with the thread of a plot, to hold his attention and interest and yet not tax his mind but rather keep it from strenuous scholarly thinking. He was ever afterward grateful to her for her devoted care and companionship during this long, trying period. As the result of the operation he was stiff and straight for the rest of his life; his erect way of walking and sitting was well remembered. Noel visited him and read Hebrew with him during his convalescence—after the disastrous reading exam Albright had decided that Noel should work with him on Hebrew. They read Samuel together, and Noel was always impressed that this great man would take time every week to read Hebrew with an entering graduate student in a personal tutorial.

There are tales about Albright's months in Chicago. As Dr. G. Ernest Wright, who was then teaching at his *alma mater*, McCormick Seminary, recalled, Albright always thought that was a very rich period, because he got to know all the people in the Oriental Institute—Thorkild Jacobsen and others. (As Freedman said, "*We* got to know Oppenheim.") Jacobsen afterward told marvelous stories of Albright as a student of Sumerian in his class. He had never before had such a student. When Albright asked a question, it was something that Jacobsen normally could not answer—it was much too good a question. So Prof. Jacobsen would say with a straight face, "I'll speak about that at the next hour." And then, as he told it, he would go home and work steadily until the next class hour, a day or two later, and have some answer ready to give Albright! In any case, both men came out of the experience with simply incredible admiration for each other. Jacobsen always claimed afterward that he had never in his life had any such threat as when Albright would very courteously ask a question. When he did Thorkild Jacobsen would fairly blanch!

With the beginning of the new academic year in '46, as Freedman expressed it, "a whole flood of new people" came to the Oriental Seminary. In his second year Noel had to teach (for his fellowship) this "whole flood of new people" Hebrew Rapid Reading. It was in this year that he gained a close friend and got onto the right track in Albright's department. Frank M. Cross, Jr., who had been a student of G. Ernest Wright at McCormick, enrolled. It was soon apparent to Noel that Frank was somehow on Albright's wavelength, and that he had better get acquainted with Frank. Noel's reaction to his first year was that it had been a complete disaster (like Albright's own less valid reaction to his first year with Haupt, and like John Bright's estimate of his experience). "I had to give two seminar papers that year," Noel later related, "and I'll never forget the look on Albright's face after each one of them; I'd totally missed his point, simply because he'd never told me what he wanted. One was on musical instruments; Albright wasn't interested in musical instruments—he was interested in words, etymologies. Well, that was one total disaster, for I had got hold of a book by someone who was trying to interpret Israelite music in the light of mediaeval Jewish music, and I had never heard of Albright's dictum on that, that there was a complete break. *I* didn't know that Albright was interested in all this Phoenician and Canaanite stuff! The other seminar paper was on Iron Age houses, and to show where *I* was, I did *not* even refer to Tell Beit Mirsim!"

Frank Cross had met Albright for the first time during his quarter of teaching at Chicago University. Wright had taken Frank to the Oriental Institute to introduce him to Albright, who said something Cross never forgot: "I have read every word of your thesis." Cross said, "It struck me, 'Why on earth wouldn't he read it? He was the judge of the thesis"—one of two submitted for the Nettie F. McCormick Fellowship. Only when Ernest later explained it to him did he understand that if Albright had read every word, this was something very unusual.

As Freedman said, "Generally he could tell by the third page that it was not worth reading!" Freedman described how Albright would often read a book that came to him in the mail, at the time when Freedman was acting as Albright's amanuensis or secretary, as students did who were on the Rayner Fellowship, and helped him open his mail. "He immediately started at the back end, with the Index, looking up the entries under *A*, checked the references, and put the book down!" (He also had a self-taught ability to read a page at a glance, long before the development of dynamic-reading methods and courses.)

Cross countered on Albright's way with a new book: "No, he read the footnotes to books first, normally; if the footnotes were all right, then he would read the book." Continuing about his thesis, he said (in the conversation among Albright students of three decades, after Albright's death): "At all events, Albright apparently thought there was something new in the thesis, and I wanted to know what it was, and I didn't know how to ask him, because to give away the fact that I didn't know what I had that was new . . ."

Freedman chimed in: "It suited Albright's whole approach to scholarship perfectly, because it had a thesis, just like the classic German monographs."

Wright explained: "It started in with an analysis of the background, a Wellhausenist analysis of the Tabernacle tradition; it then demolished that analysis and put up an entirely new thesis—a historical reconstruction with new ideas on terminology . . . Albright told me that Cross's paper was infinitely superior to that of the man he was competing against, who had only written about a hundred pages. He said very carefully, 'This thesis is better than the average doctoral thesis in any given year produced in this country or abroad.' "

Cross continued his tale: "Well, at any rate, when Albright began to discuss the thesis with me, I was immediately lost. He began to remark on Ugaritic parallels."

Wright said amid the laughter, "That was the latest stage of Albright's life at that point, you know. In my time, '35 to '37, he was reading the stuff and keeping up, but he hadn't started teaching it yet."

CROSS: "He would carefully vocalize the Ugaritic for me, and of course with my ear I got nothing, just absolutely nothing, and I didn't know *what* to do. I was terribly embarrassed."

FREEDMAN: "And knowing Albright, he probably gave you three pronunciations of each word!"

CROSS: "At all events, that was my first meeting with Albright. Ernest prepared me well enough when I went to Hopkins to know that I would be completely despairing of any point in my going on to get a degree, before the first year was over. So I survived because of the warning; I'd say, I *knew* I was going to feel this way; I *knew* this guy would overwhelm me."

FREEDMAN: "You will never convince me you were nearly as frightened as the rest of us!"

WRIGHT: "He was! It was also the way he started at Harvard" (where he, along with Wright, has been a professor for a number of years).

FREEDMAN: "The only time I sensed that Frank was in the same boat I was in, was in that famous or infamous Accadian class. There were three of us in it, about two o'clock in the afternoon. We used to work and work and work, and it was always devastating. We were reading Sennacherib's prism, and we'd prepare faithfully and do it all, and then the Old Man would start, call on one—and as long as there were three of us it was more or less tolerable. One read and the second worked feverishly on the next section, so the guy who had just read could relax for a minute. But the third kept threatening to drop out. We begged him and we bribed him, and told him we'd do all his work and give him the papers and everything, but he finally did drop out!"

CROSS: "His hand shook so much with the text that he could not see the signs!" (He did earn his Ph.D. in due time, however.)

FREEDMAN: "With that, of course, you're right under the gun, because while one guy is reading the other is looking ahead, but the Old Man might interrupt at any moment. And no matter how well you prepared and how much you looked up, it was like a different world. He'd start rereading the text, retranslating, everything new, and you'd ask, 'Where did this come from?'—'Haven't you heard?—Landsberger; I have a private communication . . .' and all that!"

WRIGHT: "That was the trouble with you fellows. You were trying to be linguists, where his great love was! I wasn't going to be a linguist . . ."

CROSS: "You were just lucky! We had to go on the philology thing. I had no trouble in Hebrew at all, but the Accadian was devastating."

FREEDMAN: "Neither of us ever became specialists in Accadian, because the worst of all was that finally the Old Man started falling asleep, right in the middle of class. It was always right after lunch, and whoever was reciting would just drone on. Finally the Old Man would wake up. He wouldn't admit he had been asleep, so he didn't know where the place was; and that must have killed half the hours. We never really learned much Accadian, but it was a devastating experience!"

WRIGHT: "I had this syndrome in me: 'I can't become Albright; I'll just wait around and do what he tells me, and maybe I can get something through, just pass.' But I found this crazy thing of Albright's, where he overvaluates someone."

FREEDMAN: "I can confirm that, because he told me that the only real disappointments he had had in life were his students! That came largely, I think, from this over-estimation."

Cross spoke of Albright's work in topography. "One time Noel and I were in his office and Albright was reminiscing, and finally said, 'You know, isn't it interesting? The greatest topographers in the whole of Palestinian geography, all their names begin with A.' He said, 'There's Alt, and there's Abel,' and then he started turning red!"

Cross also remarked about Albright's pedagogy. "You remember his teaching of Ugaritic, Noel? He began the first class by putting up on the board *malku, malka, malki, malkuma, malkima,* and he said, 'All right, you know the noun! Then he put up *yaqtulu,* etc. . . .'"

FREEDMAN: "He couldn't stay on it!"

CROSS: "This was his analysis of Ugaritic grammar; it lasted one period and a half, at which point he said, 'This is boring! Let's read text!' With that, we suddenly plunged into text; we knew no grammar—"

FREEDMAN: "We knew nothing!"

A student from the '50's, who was a member of this group telling Albright yarns, Ted Campbell, chimed in: "Well, the only difference, I think, between my experience and yours is that we didn't have the hour and a half of grammar at the beginning!"

CROSS: "Well, Noel and I collected all the lexicons; we got all of them we could find for all the languages, and sat down together and worked at this. That is when we learned Comparative Semitic philology—this is when *Early Hebrew Orthography* was actually born [one of the two eventual joint dissertations by the Cross-Freedman pair]. We were trying to stay ahead of Albright, who required us to vocalize this stuff. And no matter how we vocalized it, of course he corrected it, and we never knew why. We would ask why, and we never got an answer which really explained."

FREEDMAN: "Or tied to anything. That is so true. I remember sitting in Blake's classes, and I got there late. I didn't get there late that year—I got there a *year* late! Because he had already started his [three-year grammatical lecture] cycles the previous year."

CROSS: "They *all* did this! You got on the merry-go-round when you got on."

WRIGHT: "I got on at the right time!"

FREEDMAN: "I didn't understand this *qatala* and *qatl-qitl-qutl* business; I didn't know where it came from. Because he always said, "Now, this word (we would have some Hebrew word), well, the *o* represents an older long *a,* and the long *a* represents a short *a,*' and I wanted to know how *he* knew! He never explained this. And I discovered later with my own students it was the same thing—this great mystery, where the grid came from, where the forms originated—and finally you had to tell them, 'It came from the mind of some German who figured that's the way it ought to have been!'"

While the group roared with empathetic laughter, Cross exclaimed, "Not to mention Blake's Tagalog illustrations!"

FREEDMAN: "Oh, my! But Albright was even worse! Because he had this historical sense, so he had some obscure inscription somewhere..."

WRIGHT: "And Amarna..."

FREEDMAN: "You know, all these things which you're supposed to *know*. But I was very deeply influenced by Blake. I am convinced that without Blake I could never have understood anything Albright did. The big turn-around for me—because there was a time when I thought Blake was really better than the Old Man—came when I discovered that Albright knew everything Blake knew, just as well or better than Blake knew it—and that *he* only *started* from there! I was deeply impressed by that. Albright had studied, as Blake had, with Haupt, who was terrific on structure."

CROSS: "Albright knew Brockelmann by paragraph, which always astonished me."

FREEDMAN: "But Albright knew, too, that it was from the inscriptions and the strata and all the rest of it that you were going to reconstruct the languages of these people, and that you could never do it from the Blake approach."

CROSS: "In our day you got a key to Albright's office at a certain moment. In the case of Noel and me, Albright always did nothing but what he did it for both of us together. My favorite story in this regard is when Noel finally passed his examinations, defended his dissertation, and at this point Albright shifted from one's last name, and he addressed Noel as Noel. And I happened, of course, to be there, right out in the hall waiting for Noel to come out, so Albright looked around at me, and you could see gears grinding. So he called me Frank, and till the end of the term he called me Frank. The next fall when I arrived, and Noel was gone, I was Mr. Cross, until *my* exams, at which point I became Frank again!"

Prof. Albright was the kind of teacher about whom legends soon began to grow. His students in various decades remembered his faith in old-fashioned mustard plasters. John Bright recalled, "Prof. Albright, although a man of rigid scientific method, had some eccentricities that certainly did not derive from the world of science. I became aware of what was probably the most far-famed of these only a few weeks after the Tell Beit Mirsim dig began in 1932. Coming to the main tent for breakfast one morning a few minutes early, I found Albright sitting there applying a mustard plaster to his shin. I asked him what was wrong with his leg. He replied that nothing was wrong with his leg but that he felt a cold coming on. I was afraid to let my reaction show. Albright continued to put faith in this remedy all his life. Years later he visited Richmond to give lectures and stayed in our home. One morning he asked my wife if she would get him a mustard plaster at the drug store—he felt a cold coming on. He was serious in his conviction that it was the only efficacious remedy."

Later students also remembered about the mustard plasters. Several of them in their conversation about him mentioned them, and Frank Cross said, "It's a perfect example of what should be suppressed!"

Ted Campbell, from Albright's last years of teaching at Hopkins, replied, "But it's the most perfect example of empirico-logical thinking I know of!"

FREEDMAN: "Oh, absolutely! It's fantastic!"

WRIGHT: "It's like me and chewing gum; if it works, it works."

CROSS: "He said that to put the mustard plaster on the chest was purely psychological."

WRIGHT: "No, it actually happened. He had a terrible cold one winter, and he put it on his chest so many times—it worked, but his chest got so sore that he couldn't put it on there any more. There was no place left to put it on, so he put it on the calf of his leg, and it worked! So if it works, it works, and he doesn't care where he puts it. It sets up a tension in one's system . . ."

FREEDMAN: "Improves the circulation of the blood."

WRIGHT: "And that's what does the work!"

FREEDMAN: "What difference does it make where you put the plaster?"

CROSS: "Pure superstition; absolutely pure superstition! One time I knew he had one on his calf, and I don't know why, but this particularly horrified me. I had scientific training in my background, and the notion that the Old Man had a mustard plaster on his calf so horrified me, I didn't know what to do."

CAMPBELL: "Well, you see, by my time these things had become legendary. They contributed to the character of the awe that we all felt, because we also sensed that there was a kind of curious aspect about the Old Man, a centrality about him . . ." He continued, "There's another thing that indicates the character of this later period, and that is that he very carefully called everybody by their first names from the time we got there. Another story from that last year has to do with his parsimony. In addition to the small salaries in the department, the thing that bothered us the most and I think sort of got the reformer's zeal going in us, was this business about the library. You see, he had been accustomed to this kind of routine that you men have known, where everybody either had a key to the library or there was a good deal of passage in and out. But when you had thirty and forty students around, as in his last year, you couldn't do that. Albright would always answer you, if you couldn't find a book in the library, that it was in his office and all you needed to do was to find a time when Nancy [Renn-Lapp, his first woman student who worked also as his secretary for her part of the Rayner Fellowship, which was shared that year] was there and you could go in and get the book. 'Red' Sinclair finally became greatly disturbed by this, because none of the excavation reports were available, and he wanted to continue the work he had been doing on Megiddo; it turned out that it wasn't checked out to anybody —the library had never gotten it. He went up to see the librarian, and the librarian said, 'Well, Mr. Sinclair, I'll be glad to cooperate with you all I can, but we have received back from Dr. Albright the request sheet for books that he would like us to buy, blank. He said on it, "We don't need to buy any of these because I own them myself." ' Red said, 'Well, don't you think it's kind of curious to just take that from a professor? You can't afford to let your library be dictated to by considerations like that.' The librarian said, 'You give us the list of things we need, and we'll buy them.' So Red Sinclair became the buying agent for the library at that point, for *reams* of stuff! He would come around on a day when we were all in seminar, and during the break would collect suggestions from people about things that ought to be bought for the collection. That intense feeling about money that the Old Man always had—"

CROSS: "But Albright always assumed that the end of the department would come when he retired, and he always assumed that the library did not have enough money to buy these expensive books."

FREEDMAN: "And there was a certain egotism in this. He never expected them to retire him. He expected to be asked to continue indefinitely. It was a great shock to him that they let him retire at the stipulated age, two years beyond 65. The fact is that Albright had a kind of reverse theology about chastisement, that anything that went wrong he rationalized as providential; it was meant to be that way in order to humble him. But it never worked that way, because he really brooded and was rather bitter about disappointments, but he created an elaborate façade; everything fitted into this all-purpose theology of his. And other people could suffer for it severely."

WRIGHT: "I have always thought that the greatest non-academic thing I got from Albright—and I've said this repeatedly to students —is his continual teaching that you fight, you struggle over an issue or with a cause, with whatever it is. But when you come to the point that you can't do anything about it, you just *accept* it as the providential work of God—you just accept it! And it all becomes so easy then, instead of fighting the impossible. I don't know, that kind of thing was built into me under Albright, and it so fitted my Calvinistic conception of Providence that I have always found that strengthening, that example of Albright—it *was* an all-purpose theology. I can see now what I didn't know then, how it worked to the detriment of the department, in the low salaries of his staff, in not building up the library with adequate books and not having adequate staff in the department when the great numbers of students came—it all worked backwards in the last years."

FREEDMAN: "It was a kind of inverted pride in adversity, most of which was self-imposed."

The group returned to talking about their terrifying language exams with Albright. Cross said: "When Albright gave me my French exam, I began to read, and he said, 'Mr. Cross, I can't stand it! Can you translate?' And I translated; as it happened there was not a single word on this particular page that I couldn't translate; I translated it right off. And he looked at me and said, 'All right, you're passed.' But he added, 'Don't ever attempt to speak French to anyone!'" Cross continued, "For my German examination he gave me Brockelmann's *Syrische Grammatik*."

WRIGHT: "I had that in the seminary with Sandy Sellers, learning Syriac! Look up the Syriac, then look up the German!"

CROSS: "Albright said, 'Will you translate the title?' And I said, 'Yes, this is 'Syrian Grammar.'' And he said, 'Syrian?' And I said, '*Syrische*—Syrian!' And he said, 'Can you think of an alternate possibility?' And I said, 'Assyrian Grammar!' Albright said nothing, and he paged over into the Introduction. 'Would you read the introduction?' "

There were sighs from the group, who had just been howling with laughter. Cross concluded, "Well, those were dreadful times, the tests of language!"

Noel referred to his disastrous first year, saying, "If I'd had any gumption I'd have left! I just didn't have even *that* much energy."

CROSS: "I can see, Noel, that it was important that I came that next year!"

FREEDMAN: "When all these new people came, can you imagine me conducting Hebrew Rapid Reading with this crowd? But then I discovered to my amazement that Cross, though he was new, yet knew more about Albright and about what was going on than *I* did after I had been there a year!"

CROSS: "Ernest really got me ready."

FREEDMAN: "Victor Gold was there that year too, but the other guys were mostly strangers. I decided I'd better talk to this Cross fellow and find out how to get through to Albright, how to get connected. Somehow we found we could work together. That was a very big thing for me, because from then on my seminar papers were on the track. At least there was something that we could talk to Albright about."

CROSS: "I think probably Noel and I are unique. I am sure there has never been a joint thesis, and then a *second* joint thesis, in the history of American education. And the astonishing thing is that Albright didn't blink. It was perfectly all right." (Freedman later thought that Albright saw they complemented each other and that the total was greater than the sum of the parts.)

FREEDMAN: "He picked the subject, and it all came about on that one seminar paper on Deuteronomy 33. When we hit verse 26, the Old Man couldn't contain himself. Here were students who had discovered the secret of that tenth-century orthography which nobody else in the world, apparently, could figure out! And we had figured it out in the most simplistic way, like, look at the end of the word! Or, '*this* means *that*'! He got up, I remember, and went to the board, and went over it two or three times. I *know* he was trying to figure out to himself how *he* could have missed it! He told us, 'You've got to publish that!' That was our first joint publication, and it was in No. 108 [December 1947] of BASOR, which is the thinnest *Bulletin* ever published, because Albright went on some expedition and left us to publish that issue, with our article in it."

WRIGHT: "Oh, I remember that!"

FREEDMAN: "We were both shaking in our boots. Cross was already published—he had been in the *Biblical Archaeologist* [edited by Wright] in '47, but BASOR—this was the ultimate; nobody gets into BASOR because in those years Albright was publishing only Albright! [Not quite true!] And that was our start. After that the Old Man treated us both with extraordinary deference!"

Another student from those years, Frederick L. Moriarty, S.J., wrote much later to Freedman: "More important to me than any letters from Albright is the grateful memory, after exactly 25 years, of the debt I owe the old Master for his contribution to my formation. I guess you could sum it up in one word—inspiration. He gave us momentum, drive, a basic interest in the field, and this has sustained me over the many years since those days at Hopkins which I always recall as among the most precious of my academic life. As for general memories the most vivid I have are of his excitement, enthusiasm for any new data or discovery or plausible hypothesis which might advance the frontiers of learning in our area. Do you remember the day that you and Frank Cross made your 'rider of the clouds' proposal in Deuteronomy 33:26? The Old Boy practically jumped out of his chair. I never forgot that."

Freedman said of Albright's expedition (to Egypt and Sinai) at that time, "This trip undoubtedly saved our dissertations on Hebrew orthography and biblical poetry. With Albright out of the way, we were able to complete the manuscripts before he returned. Then instead of chewing them up piecemeal, as he would have had he been around, he gracefully accepted the whole thing with only a few corrections and suggestions."

CROSS: "One of the things that I was surprised to find out was the way in which Albright developed his articles. I had always thought of him as writing his articles first-draft and sending them off, and that was the impression you had, is that not right, Noel?"

FREEDMAN: "Yes, he always typed them out, . . ."

CROSS: "We always saw him typing them, between classes and

what-not, and we got the notion that there were no drafts, there were no revisions, nothing of the sort."

WRIGHT: "Well, that's the way it was when *I* was there; he gave us to understand that you save a lot of time by working very carefully on that first draft, and type it out (with carbon copy) and it was the *last* draft."

CROSS: "Ernest, that just isn't so!" (The fact is, Albright used both methods. On some things the first draft was the final; on others he wrote and rewrote and gathered notes for years before publishing.)

CROSS: "We have now seen Albright's last articles"—after his death.

FREEDMAN: "I found, for example, this one on 'The Greek Intellectual Revolution,' which revolutionized *me*—it took us three months to fill in those footnotes, and Cross solved the final problem with the last six footnotes, for which nobody could dream up any kind of data—cross them out! That's all! Which I hadn't been able to bring myself to do. On the final draft there were all these numbers for footnotes, but no footnotes. But on certain issues, like the date of Sanchuniathon, he had lengthy notes, three separate ones giving three totally different dates, all worked up, all ready to go! And finally he had decided which way to go!"

WRIGHT: "The interesting thing about my relationship with Albright was that I suppose it was ten, twelve years before I was weaned. I remained a student of Albright's—submitted everything I wrote to him before I printed it, that is, every serious thing, for about ten years or more. The only things I didn't submit to him were when I got to the point of *The Old Testament Against Its Environment,* where I was trying to correct his theory of monotheism in the first chapter, and *God Who Acts,* and things like this; I was on my own in those things and didn't go to him."

FREEDMAN: "Well, we were all very much that way for a number of years. Everything we wrote we first sent to the Old Man, and he offered his criticisms."

Many of the yarns about Albright could be repeated from different students in other decades, for the events happened more than once. For example, Dewey M. Beegle in the early '50's remembered Albright's sleeping in *his* Accadian class while he sweated and struggled to translate Sennacherib. When the twitching of Albright's little finger signaled that he had wakened, he asked Beegle a few questions on grammar in the early lines he had translated, and then proceeded around the long table having the students, who had been highly amused at Dewey's struggles, recite in turn. Albright was totally unaware that Sennacherib was retracing his steps!

Dr. Robert F. Ogden, who was a student at one of Albright's summer seminars at the School in Jerusalem while serving as a member of the Syria Mission of the Presbyterian Church (USA), recalled that at that time Albright, after questioning him on his previous studies, remarked, "What we need now is a popularization of archaeology." "I believe it was his way of urging me to keep my feet on the ground, and to eschew any 'ivory-tower' attitude to future study. Since this interview occurred at a time in my life when direction had become a sort of major question, 'What should I go in for, as a field of study?' this contact with such a dynamic personality left a great impression on me. The course of lectures which followed deepened that impression that here was a field and a method to which a life study could well be dedicated." Later Ogden became a graduate student of Albright at Hopkins. "I have often wondered if every candidate had such a grilling. For the next hour at least, he tested me in the biblical languages and in the ancient and modern languages used in research about which I had some knowledge. In some cases as Accadian and Ethiopic, he only asked what I had done or not done. One thing he did say, 'I shall not presume to examine you in Arabic.' Of course he had heard me speak it in Jerusalem. His conclusion took me completely by surprise: 'I think you could do it.' This I believe was a reference to the amount of residence time that would be necessary. I have always thought that along with the sly twinkle in his eye was the unspoken 'if'—I applied myself! What a challenge! In one brief hour he had not only found out what had been done but staked out the course for the year ahead, not only in scope but in a coupling of the objective in material to be covered with the spirit in which the work was to be approached. In a very real sense life began with that year at Hopkins. I was thankful to be able to work under the inspiration of such a personality."

Another who had the typical Albrightian interview and grilling on languages was Carey Moore, who entered Hopkins in Albright's department in 1956, having been a student of Albright's former student Dr. Jacob M. Myers at Gettysburg. When Albright pulled a Hebrew Bible out of his revolving bookcase saying, "Let's see how much you remember," Carey realized "that he was not interested in grades which may or may not accurately reflect past knowledge and performance, but in what I really knew, what I had actually retained." After translating from Samuel and reading also from a Greek New Testament and a Latin Vulgate, "Dr. Albright pulled out what was for me at the time not the most engrossing book, a Hebrew Grammar in German. With his help I 'translated' a passage on segholate nouns. We rounded out the oral exam by my reading and translating from the French edition of *From the Stone Age to Christianity*.

"Throughout my 'ordeal' Dr. Albright was very friendly and supportive towards me, but at the same time quite insistent on accuracy and precision as I translated the various passages. When we had finished, he said, 'Well, it looks like you remembered something from your courses. We'll start classes here around the end of September.' Looking back, I realize now that that one hour interview indelibly impressed upon my mind the crucial fact that a biblical scholar must have a genuine command of a number of languages, ancient and modern, and that ultimately it is what a student really knows that counts and not just the courses he has 'taken' or the grades received. Albright's de-emphasis on grades and courses taken (one automatically got a 'P' for 'passed' for any course one enrolled in), together with his high expectations in the grueling prelims and dissertation, made it easy for all but the most self-disciplined and inwardly motivated students to 'goof off,' with the end result that the weak student never had the requisite knowledge to pass the prelims, let alone attempt a dissertation. Only the self-disciplined and inwardly motivated would survive, and such qualities are a prerequisite for continuing research and writing long after the degree has been conferred."

While Albright's students relished their experiences with their fabled professor and loved to tell both hair-raising and amusing tales on him, they had learned methodology and caught inspiration from him that would control their careers during the rest of their lives.

13

A Wider Audience

On May 31, 1936, Dr. Albright received his second honorary doctorate, the Doctor of Hebrew Literature, at the eleventh commencement program of the Jewish Institute of Religion in New York. (His first, a Litt.D., had been conferred by Upper Iowa University in 1922.) In his address, as reported in the New York *Times* of June 1, "Dr. Albright warned against the misuse of knowledge, asserting that some of the doctrines of national socialism in Germany had their roots in the misapplication of ethnology and other sciences. 'I believe we stand on the threshold of a renaissance of the historical studies, comparable in some ways to that of the Middle Ages, which opened the way ultimately to the age of invention and industrial development,' Dr. Albright said. Turning to conditions in Palestine, he expressed hope that the joint efforts of scholars of all races—especially Jews and Arabs—would bring light to the leaders 'from whom go out the impulses which ultimately percolate down into the masses.' "

A few days later at Jewish Theological Seminary of America, of which Dr. Cyrus Adler was president, another D.H.L. was conferred on Albright as well as two other Semitic scholars. The award to Albright was "in recognition of his work in the field of Semitic scholarship, and of his distinguished services as Director of the American School of Oriental Research in Jerusalem," as reported in the New York *Times* of June 8.

In mid-June Dr. Albright sailed for Europe. The *Times* of the 25th carried a small wireless dispatch with dateline Amsterdam, June 24, stating that "among the scholars receiving honorary degrees today in connection with Utrecht University's tercentenary were Dr. W. F. Albright, Orientalist of the Johns Hopkins University, Baltimore, and Dr. W. B. Castle of Boston." The Th.D. degree Albright received there was his first doctorate of theology. Such honors would be sprinkled through the decades from then until he had received nearly thirty in his lifetime.

That year beginning at Easter-Passover season in mid-April there were again Arab uprisings against Jews in Palestine, continuing until mid-October after Yom Kippur, the Jewish New Year season. The troubles kept simmering, only cooled by the outbreak of World War II and the involvement of the Near East in the conflict. For this and other reasons Albright found it impossible to return to Palestine for almost eighteen years. His activities turned in other directions, to more intensive lecturing and writing. In February of 1937 Prof. Albright gave the Lyman Coleman Foundation lectures at Lafayette College, Easton, Pennsylvania.

Albright, attending the Easter, 1937, meeting of the American Oriental Society in Cleveland, found it "interesting to note that nearly half of the papers presented in the Near-Eastern section came from former members of the Schools in Jerusalem and Baghdad. At such meetings the influence exerted by the Schools cn the development of Oriental and Biblical studies in North America can be easily estimated, and proves to be very great indeed."[1]

Prof. Albright opened an institute on biblical and post-biblical literature at Jewish Theological Seminary on his forty-sixth birthday, May 24, 1937, with a paper on 'The Bible and Archaeological Discoveries." Several newspapers the next day quoted him as saying that archaeological discoveries made at Nuzi, Northern Mesopotamia, and at Ugarit, Syria, "prove that the patriarchal stories of Genesis do not reflect the culture of Israel in the period of the divided monarchy (about 700 years after Moses), but were handed on in substantially their present form from a much more remote age."

In mid-1937 the Albright family sold their home and bought a somewhat larger house at 2305 Sulgrave Avenue, just around the corner across the wide, curving Cross Country Boulevard on which they had lived seven years. G. Ernest Wright and Emily DeNyse spent their honeymoon in that house. They were married on July 31 after he had received his Ph.D. in June. "The Albrights had just bought the house, and that was the only time they ever went down to Virginia to spend a month with his father," he recalled much later. While they were in Virginia they let the newlyweds have the use of their new house. The three Albright boys, out of school for the summer, plus younger David, reveled in the country freedom. In following summers for many years at least two or three of the boys would go back to spend a few weeks at the farm.

After the family returned from the month in Virginia, in the late summer of 1937, Prof. Albright had an operation on his crippled left hand. Specialists thought they could straighten it and make it more useful. An outstanding specialist at the University of Maryland Hospital performed the operation, but unfortunately the hand was worse after the surgery than before, though the surgeon had done many mending operations successfully. The one good feature was that, no longer being so tightly curled, the hand was less likely to catch on something and involve Albright in an accident. His students well remember his characteristic pose at the blackboard with the hand tucked behind his back, or seated at the end of the long table in his seminar room with the hand slipped under his right elbow as he lectured, arms folded, gesturing only with the right hand.

Editor Albright announced in the February, 1938, BASOR a new journal, *The Biblical Archaeologist,* edited by Dr. G. Ernest Wright to fill the need of "a non-technical, yet thoroughly reliable account of archaeological discoveries related to the Bible"[2]—a need filled at first by BASOR, which had been growing steadily more technical. In the first issue of *The Biblical Archaeologist* Albright's contribution was a short article, "What Were the Cherubim?" By this time his lifetime bibliography contained about 360 items, ranging from short notes, encyclopedia articles, book reviews, and obituaries of scholarly colleagues, to longer articles in many scholarly journals, *Annuals* of the ASOR, monographs and books. His *Archaeology of Palestine and the Bible* had appeared in its third edition in 1935. His second volume on Tell Beit Mirsim, *Annual* volume 17, on the Bronze Age, came out in 1938.

However, the work that enabled Prof. Albright to reach out to a surprisingly wide audience of readers was his 1940 book. He modestly mentioned in the October 1940 BASOR that "since there have been numerous requests for information about my forth-

coming book, *From the Stone Age to Christianity*, I take this opportunity to announce that the book is now in press and will
probably appear in early November...."[3]

This contained a grand synthesis of all the archaeological, historical, geographical, topographical and other information which
William Albright had been gathering through two decades. He
wrote the book to enter in competition for the $30,000 Bross prize
at its fiftieth anniversary, but won only third prize. "It was entirely too new as an aspect of biblical study for it to receive first
prize," Mrs. Albright commented long afterward, "but it received
the second honorable mention, and William received a letter from
Scribner's asking to see the manuscript, because they had a contract
with the people who gave the Bross prize that they always printed
the winner and also had first chance at the next two. In correspondence concerning the book, William wrote that he had spoken in
various places, his lectures had been well received, and so on; but
the manuscript was returned with regrets. The head of their religious book department, on consultation with readers, had decided
that it would perhaps sell 450 copies at best!

"He was so upset—really angry—at this stupid attitude that he
asked me whether I could help him out, because I had not long
before received my inheritance from my mother. [Ruth's widowed
mother had died in the spring of 1937 of a stroke, only a year after
the death of William's mother.] I said certainly, I would pay for
the printing, binding and publication of the book, and we would
see what would happen. The Johns Hopkins Press was then run
that way.

"One of the first reviews was from overseas, from a German
Catholic missionary priest in southern Brazil who wrote and told
him how magnificent he found the thing. Some of the reviews were
absolutely absurd; but the book caught on with his students, and
we soon had to reprint. Far from having a sale of only at most 450
copies, it went into thousands, and later Noel Freedman took it
to Doubleday Anchor Books and it was accepted in that paperback
series. Then it began selling by the tens of thousands and is still
going [over 80,000 by the time of his death]. It is now translated
into many languages—German, French, Italian, Spanish, Portuguese for Brazil, Polish, Hebrew, and others. It was taken by the
Catholics, by conservatives. Scribner was no longer conservative in

its religious section as it had originally been, and they and their modernistic readers couldn't believe their eyes when they saw this 'return to the Dark Ages,' 'unscientific' work succeeding. Some of the reviews were horrendous."

"I think it was this book," Mrs. Albright commented, "that for the most part attracted the Catholic students who came to his department in Hopkins. They came at first because they were desperate. These men wanted their degrees and were studying in Rome, but had to come home because of the war. That started the first two or three who came, and then the success of these fathers was so great that at one time five of William's Jesuit students were in Rome at the Istituto Biblico, and at the same time the heads of the departments of Bible in all of the five or six provinces of the Jesuits were either William's own students or *their* students. The whole record starts from this one book, because it actually turned the line of march, one might say, of biblical studies right around."

Mrs. Albright gave a reason for William's success in his career: "It was largely due to the fact that, like so many people who are physically handicapped, some other faculty is strengthened. William was able to cultivate a magnificent memory so that he had an almost instant recall of where to look for some scholar's paper on a certain subject. His work depended a great deal on his own knowledge of the field and his knowledge and estimate of other scholars in that field. His correspondence was enormous and it included a large number—in the tens of thousands eventually—of the offprints of articles of other scholars, and exchange of scholarly writings. These he was able to read rapidly—he had taught himself how to read rapidly since he had difficulty in reading for prolonged lengths of time. But he had the memory and knew where to find something and what each man actually stood for. He was one of the few people who was not afraid or ashamed to change his mind, for he was only after truth."

The Baltimore *Sun* in its December 22 announcement of the book said that "in the 300-odd pages of this work, Dr. Albright traces the growth of man's belief in God from prehistoric days to the time of Christ, analyzing the progress made against the historic backgrounds and changing philosophies of the periods covered...." He dedicated it to Dr. Samuel Wood Geiser.

From the Stone Age to Christianity was favorably reviewed in

JBL in the latter half of 1941 by Fleming James. After outlining the contents, he said: "To deal in detail with this comprehensive and amazingly erudite book, or to do justice to its brilliance, is not possible here." He pointed out "three features which seem to the present reviewer of chief significance": "The first is the author's philosophy of history, as set forth in Chapter II. . . . The second feature is the author's high estimate of the biblical tradition. . . . The third feature is the place the author ascribes in history to Moses and Jesus. . . . The author holds that Moses was a monotheist, . . . Jesus likewise represented an abrupt break. . . . Jesus actually was what Christians from the first believed him to be. . . . The book bristles with challenges which will undoubtedly be taken up. Perhaps the author goes in places too far. But his main contentions rest on solid foundations which will not easily be overthrown."[4]

In his review of the later paperback edition, the British scholar Prof. H. H. Rowley said, "The vast learning of Professor Albright is apparent throughout the work, in which the development of man's idea of God from prehistoric times to the time of Christ is traced. Notable is the author's recognition of serious historical value in the patriarchal narratives and his treatment of Moses as a real figure of history. . . ."[5]

Albright's new book was selected by the ASOR for the free book to be sent to their Associate Members, with Glueck's *The Other Side of the Jordan* as alternate. A favorable review by Albright's old friend Dr. Paul Bloomhardt in the January, 1941, Alumni Magazine mentioned that *From the Stone Age to Christianity* might well have its subtitle, *Monotheism and the Historical Process,* as chief title. "The book will be read with a keen human interest by all who are personally acquainted with Dr. Albright since to them it will appear, whether so intended or not, to be a kind of *apologia pro vita sua.*" A shorter review in the Baltimore *Sun* of March 23 stated, "The Bible was responsible for Dr. Albright's interest in archaeology; . . . And archaeology in turn has stimulated his interest in the Bible, for the foundation of his latest book rests upon archaeological research. . . ."

For Prof. Albright's fiftieth birthday, May 24, 1941, a committee of his former students in America and Palestine prepared a surprise. Dr. Harry M. Orlinsky as chairman arranged, and later published at New Haven, an "Indexed Bibliography of the Writings of W. F. Albright." It contained about 90 pages with two columns per page and was priced at a dollar. When it appeared in mid-September many copies were sold immediately. His bibliography contained about 500 items up to that birthday. It was "dedicated to Professor Albright as a great scholar, inspiring teacher, and loyal friend with the hope that a long and fruitful career remains ahead of him."

A Foxwell Reunion was planned for July 4-6 in Wisconsin that summer. Aunt Ella wrote to William inviting him and his family to attend. On June 2 he replied with a long newsy letter, saying he regretted their not being able to do so. It would have been pleasant for him to meet the cousins he had not seen for years and all the second cousins he had never met. He hoped there would be another reunion when they could attend, and that Aunt Ella would still be there for it. (She was—in 1963—when he, Ruth and Hugh did attend.) He referred to his fiftieth birthday a week previous, which he called the dividing line between early and late middle age, and expressed relief that now he could act as an elderly man without pangs of conscience. As for his sons, they were all flourishing. He said he was sending Aunt Ella a copy of *From the Stone Age to Christianity;* it was about ready for second printing, selling much better than he had expected, though it was difficult reading for most people. Most of the reviews had been flattering. He noted that he and his wife felt the same as Aunt Ella did about the war in Europe; this time he was violently anti-German.

For his carbon copy of the letter to Aunt Ella, Albright frugally used the back of a spoiled sheet headed "The Role of the Canaanites in the History of Civilization," the title of his article contributed to the Waldo H. Leland Volume, *Studies in the History of Culture,* which was published in 1942. He closed that lengthy chapter by saying: "There can no longer be any doubt that the Bible has preserved much of the best in Phoenician literature, especially lyric and gnomic. Without the powerful influence of Canaanite literary tradition, we should lack much of the perennial appeal exerted by Hebrew poetic style and prosody, poetic imagery and vivid description of natural phenomena. Through the Bible the entire civilized world has fallen heir to Phoenician literary art."[6]

In 1942 Albright's next book, *Archaeology and the Religion of*

Israel, was published by the Johns Hopkins Press. It consisted of the Ayer Foundation Lectures he had given beginning in mid-April the previous year at Colgate-Rochester Divinity School in Rochester, New York. The school celebrated its hundredth year with the annual spring alumni convocation at which Prof. Albright gave four lectures on "Archaeology and the Ancient Near-Eastern Mind," "The Archaeological Background of Old Testament Religion," "Archaeology and the Religion of Early Israel," and "Archaeology and the Religion of Later Israel." In preparing the lectures for publication he added another chapter, making it the third of the five, "Archaeology and the Religion of the Canaanites."

In his Postscript to the fifth edition years later, Albright explained that complete recognition of the historical character of Israel's religion must underlie any serious investigation of it, and that in this respect the Judaeo-Christian tradition is unique. No other great world religion is thus historically based. He said monotheism was an essential element in the religion of Moses from the start, and was empirico-logical (implicit and practical, not explicit and intellectual). It could not become explicit until Greek logical thought developed in the sixth century B.C.

Albright referred to the Israelite prophetic movement as another element that could now be much better appreciated because of archaeology—it was easier to recognize Israel's prophets as being neither religious innovators nor pagan ecstatics, but rather leaders in teaching repentance, conversion, and communion directly with God in a constant personal relationship.

Albright dedicated this book to "James Alan Montgomery, . . . Gentleman, Scholar, Friend," who was still alive (he died early in 1949). The book went into a number of editions. Translations appeared in German and in other languages later. The Anchor Books paperback edition in English, the fifth edition, was published in 1968.

The next major publication of Dr. Albright was *The Archaeology of Palestine,* published in England as a Penguin Book, and in the U.S. as a Pelican paperback, in 1949. He began with a chapter on "The Art of Excavating a Palestinian Mound," and one on "The Discovery of Ancient Palestine," then followed with historical periods in sequence as evidenced by their archaeological remains. He had written it in the autumn of 1947 and revised it in the following year. The publisher's description in other Pelican books states that "this book is written for the reader who wants an up-to-date, authoritative, and clearly written account of the subject. The author has been engaged in active excavation and research in this field since 1920, and he has utilized his command of it to write a survey which emphasizes the most important and most interesting phases of Palestinian archaeology. Besides summarizing the results of the archaeological work of the past twenty years, during which the subject has been revolutionized, he brings the reader up to date with references to the very latest finds. . . . A final chapter on 'Ancient Palestine in World History' places the book in the full current of the philosophy of history, showing how profoundly archaeological research is influencing historical and religious thought."

Prof. Albright sometimes paid students for helping with proofreading on his publications and for making the necessary indexes, as well as for helping with his letter-writing and other office duties. The university never provided him with secretarial help and only sparsely with supplies. Even in a later decade an urgent letter could not go out when it needed to be sent because his student assistant was waiting for the janitor to bring around the allotted two sheets of carbon paper for that day!

For his friend, Chancellor Louis Finkelstein of the Jewish Theological Seminary of America in New York, Albright contributed a lengthy chapter, "The Biblical Period," to *The Jews: Their History, Culture, and Religion,* edited by Dr. Finkelstein and published by Harper & Brothers in 1949. Dr. David Noel Freedman made arrangements in 1950 for it to be published by the Biblical Colloquium, mainly composed of Albright's former students, and in 1962 for it to be reprinted, in revised and expanded form, as *The Biblical Period from Abraham to Ezra, an Historical Survey,* in the Harper Torchbooks paperback series. Albright explained in the foreword to the latter that "the text was originally written in the summer of 1947, just fifteen years before the date of the present revision. In order to include some treatment of new finds and their significance, as well as a brief account of my own recent work on such figures as Abraham and Samuel, the book is nearly half again as long as the chapter on 'The Biblical Period.' . . ."[7] It filled such a need that it quickly sold among Albright's students and former students and their classes in various schools. It also has been translated into many languages, including Japanese.

In the preceding year, 1948, Chancellor Finkelstein had included Albright in his *American Spiritual Autobiographies,* with a photo accompanying Albright's own view of his early life, education, and development of career and philosophy. (This autobiographical sketch was reprinted, along with papers and studies on a number of topics, in Albright's 1964 book *History, Archaeology and Christian Humanism,* published by McGraw-Hill.)

Through the years of World War II Albright was an active participant in conferences on such subjects as "The Near East and the Jews" or "The Role of Palestine in the Rehabilitation of the Near East." He gave the latter address in Cleveland on January 18, 1942, and was quoted in an interview with the Cleveland *News* as saying that "settlement in Palestine is the only solution for the Jews of Europe." Beginning in 1939, at the end of every summer for a number of years Prof. Albright was co-chairman, gave papers, and otherwise participated in the annual "Conference on Science, Philosophy and Religion" sponsored by Chancellor Finkelstein and others and held at Columbia University. He took part in the oral discussions that followed the papers and added his signature to occasional statements that were drawn up to be presented to the State Department.

Toward the end of 1942 Prof. Albright spoke at a United Palestine Appeal Conference held in October at the Hotel Statler in Boston. He cautioned the New England delegates "against regarding the problem of a Jewish floating population as a purely Jewish problem. Instead, it must be regarded as 'an integral part of the reconstruction problem of Europe and of the whole world,'" as the Boston *Herald* reported on October 12. On November 1 Albright was among the speakers over WGN, Chicago, on the "Northwestern Reviewing Stand" discussion on "America and the Near East." In mid-December he was one of the principal speakers at "an all-day conference of Christian clergymen and laymen of all denominations to consider various phases of the problem of Jewish immigration into Palestine and the re-establishment of a Jewish National Home in the Holy Land."

Through 1943 and early 1944 the issue of Palestine as the main

hope of Jews for a homeland was especially agitated because a
deadline was drawing near. Neville Chamberlain's White Paper in
1939 had limited immigration to Palestine to only 75,000 for five
years from May 1939, and after March 31, 1944 no further immigration would be allowed except for those that might be left over
of the 75,000. Now that the full impact of the Holocaust under
Hitler was widely known, all humanitarians, not only Jews, were
much concerned to save all Jews who could yet be rescued. Many
conferences were held, papers written, and statements presented
to Congress and to President Roosevelt—and Albright was active
in most of these. In early March of 1944 he told a group gathered
at a Washington hotel for the purpose of "mobilizing American
Christian sentiment in favor of the free entry of Jews into Palestine
and the reconstruction of that country as a free and democratic
commonwealth," that "we are not going beyond our rights in
stating to our Government our conviction that the White Paper
conflicts with American sentiment and American interests."

During the war Albright taught classes in Arabic and geography
for soldiers training to be sent to the Near East, and did various
other work for governmental agencies concerned with that part
of the world. In the second World War the Government came asking for his expert help, in contrast to the first World War when he
was so unfortunately drafted into the "limited service."

The family contribution to the war effort besides Prof. Albright's was of several kinds. The oldest son Paul in the army was
transferred to an officer candidate detachment and eventually, after
being a paratrooper, saw service in Germany. At the family home
on Sulgrave Avenue the boys dug a larger garden area and planted
more vegetables than usual. Mrs. Albright participated in volun-
teer services as much as possible, besides doing her work at home
with less help. After the war ended many people were busy packing
boxes of food and clothing or sending CARE packages to destitute
people in Europe. The Albrights sent these to scholarly colleagues
without regard to the position they might have taken in Nazi
Germany before and during the war. In fact, Albright chose to send
packages especially to several who he knew had been sympathetic
to the Nazis, though he lost respect for them on that account, because he knew that other American scholars would refuse to send
them any such help.

Albright's own views on minorities were known from his many addresses and articles on the subject. In one paper, published as "Some Functions of Organized Minorities in Approaches to National Unity," in the 1945 publication of the papers of the Fifth Symposium of the Conference on Science, Philosophy, and Religion in Their Relation to the Democratic Way of Life, he gave five arguments for the encouragement of minorities. He said they tend to be more productive, proportionally, than majorities; they are a stimulus to the majority, which otherwise would settle into rather an inert mass; reform and progress characteristically proceed from individuals or small groups, and thus are more likely to come from within organized minorities; such minorities form in any developed society strong balance wheels, not only politically but also in religion and education; negatively they are valuable as touchstones for democracy: the success of Hitler's propaganda against minorities gave the first indication of fatal weakness in democracy in Germany. Albright drew the conclusion that the success of democracy in America depends on its continuing to foster its minorities.

Albright had always been sensitive in the matter of minorities because of his boyhood as a Protestant missionary's child in Catholic Latin America, then as a Christian in Moslem Palestine with close friendships in the Jewish group, and finally back in the U.S. with a wife and family who were Catholics in a predominantly Protestant land. And from 1933 on he was actively interested in and engaged in helping Jewish victims who were a minority in the lands under Hitler's domination. The Albrights began then also to interest themselves in the problems of Negroes (as they were then called) and other ethnic minorities in the U.S. He considered it difficult to find solutions for problems of minorities, and better to emphasize their positive values, which are usually overlooked. They are actually, he felt, assets to any nation possessing organized religious or national minorities.

During some of the years under President Isaiah Bowman (1935-1949), Johns Hopkins adopted a sort of quota system on admission of Jewish students, against which Prof. Albright fought continuously until it was abolished. Nahum Sarna, of Brandeis University, recalled that when Albright was in a reminiscing mood he told Sarna that "in the 1940's the Trustees or the administration of Johns Hopkins made a decision to limit the number of Jews to be allowed into the University, and Albright led the opposition to this practically single-handed. He went to the President and to the members of the Board of Trustees, and without help from the rest of the faculty, including Jews on the faculty, he got them to rescind this decree, as he called it. And he was extremely proud of that." Although the number of Jewish students in Albright's own department was small—usually only one or two at a time—it was a matter of principle with him.

Albright had hoped to dig again at Bethel in the summer of 1938, but the periodic riots and outbreaks of actual warfare continued, making such work much too dangerous. Instead he went to Brussels as a delegate from America to the Nineteenth International Congress of Orientalists which met there in September, 1938, and read a paper on "The Northwest-Semitic Tongues before 1000 B.C." In 1947 he planned to make a trip to Palestine and even had a British visa in hand, but it was canceled by the outbreak of war between Arabs and Jews over the UN decision to partition Palestine. The future held several trips to Palestine in store for him, however; but first there would be high adventure in some unexpected directions.

14

Adventures in Sinai and South Arabia

Under unusual circumstances during the war Prof. Albright had made the acquaintance of a temporarily halted but dynamic young fellow who would have a great influence on Albright's career. As Wendell Phillips himself told the story in the last *Festschrift* or volume in honor of Prof. Albright (1971), "It was early in the winter of 1943, while visiting two student friends at Princeton Theological Seminary, that I picked up the copy of Professor Albright's *From the Stone Age to Christianity*, which enticed me to visit the author. My unexpected visit to Professor Albright's office was met with warmth, kindness, and generosity. This first visit terminated with the Professor autographing a copy of the book which had first directed me to him. Several years later, after wartime invasions and battles, I ended up with polio in the Marine Hospital in Baltimore, where every afternoon, unrecognized by the staff, Professor Albright devoted one of his precious hours to keeping up the spirits of one very sick young man who might never walk again."[1]

Wendell had been in the merchant marine for five years, in every main theater of operations in the war, and contracted polio after the Okinawa invasion in the spring of 1945. He was flown to the appropriate hospital in Baltimore for treatment. That hospital happened to be the one just south of the Homewood campus; it is now a Public Health Hospital. During his time of service, Wendell had dreamed in lonely watches of someday going to Africa in search for fossil man and apes.

234

After arriving in the hospital, Wendell sent word to Prof. Albright, and the professor went over to visit Wendell. It immediately became a daily habit. Albright would spend an hour in the afternoon talking with the young fellow about field archaeology and other things, to help him pass the weary weeks and months of his stay in the hospital. This was only a few months before Albright's own back operation and similar experience of being bedfast.

Wendell, a slender, enthusiastic person, eagerly drank in everything he could learn from Albright. As soon as he was well, he returned to California and to school, graduating in paleontology at the University of California. A born promoter, he soon had rounded up support for and organized a South African Expedition of the University of California. What happened next was told by Albright in his fascinating report in the February 1948 BASOR:

"About the middle of August this past summer Mr. Wendell Phillips, leader of the African Expedition of the University of California, came to see us in Baltimore, as he had often in previous years. This time, however, he came to invite me to join his expedition as archaeological adviser to the newly established Egyptian phase. Having already made my plans for an exceedingly busy winter, I tried to turn my back on temptation, but Wendell was too persuasive, and shortly after midnight my last defenses collapsed. President Isaiah Bowman of the Johns Hopkins University gave me leave of absence during the middle of the academic session, and Professor Carl H. Kraeling of Yale University generously relieved me of the duties of acting president of the Schools during President Burrows' absence in Palestine. Of course, there were many difficulties to be surmounted, and many new ones arose as we approached the middle of December, when we hoped to begin our proposed visit to Sinai. The time for planning was far too short and it was impossible to get much of anything done either in America or in Egypt during the late summer; I was already so overwhelmed with previously accepted commitments that there were only a few free moments to review the literature and to make specific plans for work; soon afterwards the cholera epidemic swept northern Egypt and for a time threatened to make the work of the expedition impossible; in early December the Palestine crisis again threatened to spoil all our preparations. But these and many minor problems and obstacles merely stimulated Mr. Phillips to greater efforts; in retrospect one rubs one's eyes and wonders what *did* happen to brush the difficulties away. . . .

"I flew by Pan American World Airways from New York to Damascus, via Newfoundland, Ireland, London, Rome and Istanbul, leaving the morning of November 26th, 1947, and arriving in Damascus early on the morning of the 28th. From Damascus I flew directly to Cairo, arriving there on the 29th. . . .

"The first half of December I divided between Cairo and the Faiyum, where the headquarters of the African Expedition had been established in the commodious house built by the University of Michigan excavators at Kom Aushim (ancient Karanis). While in Cairo I devoted myself to the study of the advances made in the field of Egyptian archaeology since my last previous visit, more than twelve years before. . . . In fact the array of discoveries since then has almost dwarfed the finds of the preceding twenty years. . . .

"On December 15th we were finally able to get off to a good start on our Sinai expedition. . . . we continued working in Sinai until January 17th, when we returned to Cairo. During the last five days we enjoyed the companionship of Drs. John C. Trever, Willard A. Beling and William H. Brownlee, from the American School of Oriental Research in Jerusalem. . . . the party was able to move about freely (except, of course, along the Palestine border) and to carry on its work without interference during the five weeks of the reconnaissance. A young soldier was assigned to our party, and he proved to be both helpful and uncomplaining, in spite of occasionally trying conditions of temperature and food. . . ."[2]

They first explored the prehistoric and historic settlements in the north, using el-Arish as their base, though because of the warfare just to the northeast they had to cut that part of their work a little shorter than intended, allowing more time for the south. Albright mentioned the shifting sand-dunes of the area, broken by some eroded mountain ranges. "After the effective domestication of the camel in the late second millennium the population of this region increased rapidly, since Sinai is full of plants which provided food formerly for great herds of camels, and which still support smaller herds, decreasing in number as the development of motor transport makes the camel less and less useful as a beast of burden. . . .

"From Dec. 24th to January 17th we made our base at Abu

Zeneimeh (Zelimeh) on the western coast of Sinai, where the manganese mining headquarters are located. . . . From the beautifully situated rest-house at Abu Zeneimeh, we made numerous shorter and longer excursions in our trucks (one-and-a-half-ton and two-and-a-half-ton vehicles with six-wheel drives) to explore the *wadis* which promised most, . . . None of the members of the party had ever visited southern Sinai before, and all were greatly impressed with the extraordinary beauty of scenery and wealth of archaeological remains. Numerous color photographs illustrate the former, while Dr. Field and I devoted ourselves to archaeological and anthropological research. Dr. Field proved the most valuable member of the expedition, as he contributed tirelessly to every phase of the work: physical and cultural anthropology, prehistory and historic archaeology. . . ."[3]

Dr. Henry Field's equally fascinating account of the trip to Sinai appeared in the National Geographic Magazine in December 1948, titled "Sinai Sheds New Light on the Bible." It contained fine photographs by William B. and Gladys Terry, who were each a combination of Expedition photographer, camp manager, and truck driver.

Albright considered that "the most valuable new discoveries in southern Sinai were in the Merkhah district south of Abu Zeneimeh and at Serabit el-Khadem. . . .

"Near Merkhah, a little more than five miles south of Abu Zeneimeh along the coastal road, we found a small Egyptian settlement, about 100 by 50 metres in extent, which had served as an embarkation and debarkation point for Egyptian mining expeditions sent across the Red Sea to Serabit el-Khadem. Soundings proved that the site had been so badly denuded by wind erosion that remains are mostly on the surface. . . . they can be dated by contemporary Egyptian material from Harageh and other sites to the fifteenth century B.C. (or possibly a little earlier). . . . the real significance of the find lies in a different direction. The edge of the site toward the sea lies only a little over a hundred metres from the sea, and less than five metres above mean Red Sea level (the hillock on which the settlement stands is only two metres above high tide). This naturally means that the shore line has not risen more than a metre or two (if at all) during the past 3500 years, thus confirming for the northern part of the Gulf of Suez what Nelson

Glueck has found to be true of the northern part of the Gulf of Aqabah . . . neither the northern end of the Gulf of Suez nor that of Aqabah projected north of the present shore-line, though both may easily have been located a little south of it. . . . A flying visit to the vast site of Tell el-Maskhutah and the smaller (but still large) site of Tell Ertabeh convinced me that Gardiner's identification of them with the Succoth and Pithom of Exodus, respectively, is correct. The geography of the Egyptian phase of the Exodus thus approaches a definitive solution."[4]

Another discovery Albright made supported Aimé-Giron's identification of the Baal-zephon of Exodus 14:2, 9 as near Daphne or modern Tell Defneh, ancient Egyptian Tahpanhes, southeast of Tanis. "Biblical Pi-hahiroth, between Baal-zephon and Migdol (now Tell el-Heir) is thus to be located not far from modern Qantarah, on the shore of the Lake of Reeds (*Yam Suf*, also mentioned in thirteenth-century Egyptian sources as a body of water near Raamses) in the north. . . . In any case, the new discoveries prove conclusively that we must give up the now traditional southern crossing, and separate the Red Sea completely from the Sea of Reeds in Exodus. Incidentally, the topography of the Book of Exodus now becomes far more logical than it had been previously. In my opinion these discoveries do not affect the problem of the identification of Mount Sinai in any way.

"Our second unusual new discovery was in connection with our reconnaissance of Serabit-el-Khadem. Thanks to our reëxamination of the publications of Petrie and the three Harvard expeditions on the spot, as well as to the perspective given by our exploration of the region around, we were able to correct previous ideas about both date and function of the proto-Sinaitic inscriptions. Since these documents form by far the oldest body of documents in our own ancestral alphabet . . . , this correction is obviously significant. We are now able to fix the date of these inscriptions about the fifteenth century B.C. (cir. 1500 in round numbers), three centuries later than the standard date of Alan Gardiner, but in entire agreement with the original date given by Sir Flinders Petrie himself. Moreover, we have also been able to show that many of the inscriptions are of mortuary character, having to do with offerings for deceased persons; the 'incubation' theory of Petrie is just as impossible as the 'stone shelter' hypothesis of his successors. The group of mines and the neighboring burial cairns where nearly all the proto-Sinaitic inscriptions were found between 1905 and 1935 belong to about the fifteenth century B.C., and are thus contemporaneous with the Merkhah port described above. The miners who worked them cannot have been Bedu, as most of us have too easily assumed, since the local nomads have never been of any use for sustained operations of such difficulty and danger; the miners were captives or laborers levied from Canaan, and their language was thus one of the Canaanite dialects of the day, just as their script was the Canaanite linear alphabet, intermediate between the inscriptions of the 17th-16th and the 13th centuries B.C."

To Albright's immense satisfaction, "owing to these considerations it has been possible for me to work out a fresh decipherment of the proto-Sinaitic inscriptions, which appears to make excellent sense throughout and to yield a South-Canaanite grammar and vocabulary absolutely normal for the period in question. . . .

"...The trip to the traditional Mount Sinai occupied several days, but was extremely interesting from every point of view, in spite of the bitter cold. Father Nilus and his colleagues did everything possible to make us feel at home; we saw the manuscripts, climbed Djebel Musa (Mount of Moses), and some of our party attended services. . . . we did not reach the Monastery until the evening of the Greek Christmas instead of on Christmas Eve, as had been planned. Another rather exciting experience was the trip to Serabit, in which after winching our trucks through the last [stretch of] sand we finally found a good camping spot in the Wadi Serabit directly under the Egyptian temple. Our horizontal distance was insignificant, but the vertical distance was considerable and the journey took about an hour and a half each way, mainly along a gorge lined with a series of cliffs, each surmounted with a sloping talus of loose shale and boulders. Some of us had quite enough of this kind of mountaineering after two or three round trips. . . ."[5]

Albright in closing mentioned meeting many old and new friends in Egypt, and thanked Wendell and his colleagues of the staff "for one of the most delightful and rewarding experiences of my life. The Sinai Expedition has proved to be an unqualified success, in spite of the initial obstacles which threatened to make it impossible."[6] His article in the February 1948 BASOR was illustrated by seven photos.

Isaiah Bowman, a geographer by profession and near the end of his incumbency as President of Johns Hopkins, wrote to Dr. Albright on April 13, saying that he had read with great interest Albright's report on the Sinai expedition. He considered several of its points important and interesting for geology and geography —namely concerning the stability of that Gulf coast. Whenever President Bowman contacted Dr. Albright it seemed to be with reference to some scientific aspect of his work which he could appreciate. His interest in the humanities was less apparent.

Stories on the expedition appeared during January and February in various papers—the New York *Times* on January 6 and 22, the Providence *Journal* on the 22nd, the Dallas *Times Herald* and the Los Angeles *Times* of January 23, and the Baltimore *Sun* of February 8, among others. A mid-February story by Burke Davis in the *Sun* said, "Dr. William F. Albright, . . . was back in his classroom today with a fresh Egyptian suntan and news of one of the most important archaeological achievements in recent years. . . ."

In the April BASOR Albright published his article on "The Early Alphabetic Inscriptions from Sinai and Their Decipherment," a subject to which he returned about once in every ten years thereafter, updating the material with additional inscriptions found and additional letters deciphered.

He was appointed Annual Professor at the School in Jerusalem for 1948-49, subject to resignation in case it should become inadvisable for him to go to Palestine. The war over the establishment of the State of Israel indeed prevented his keeping this appointment. But opportunities to return still lay in his future.

A year later Wendell Phillips incorporated the American Foundation for the Study of Man, with Prof. Albright as First Vicepresident. Headquarters was established in Washington. The next adventure on which enthusiastic Wendell took non-reluctant Prof. Albright was the South Arabian Expedition sponsored by this foundation. The Baltimore *Evening Sun* of December 23, 1949, reported that "Prof. William F. Albright, of the Johns Hopkins University, will lead phases of field research for an archaeological expedition which sailed today from New York, bound for unexplored areas of southern Arabia. . . . Professor Albright said one object of the trip is to learn more about the mysterious civilization of southern Arabia in the age of the first spice trade with Mediterranean countries, about 3,000 years ago. 'The first object, however, must be to build up a succession of types of pottery characteristic of different periods, from the earliest times to the Middle Ages,' he said. . . ."

Frank Cross, in conversation with other Albright students, said, "I remember that the first time any of us knew that Albright was going to South Arabia was when he announced in class, 'It looks very much as though we will *not* be going to South Arabia!'—the most Albrightian remark conceivable!"

Noel Freedman responded, "There was an element, I'm convinced, of sympathetic magic, which goes right along with the famous mustard plasters, that this was the way you exorcised the evil spirits. This was the way he deflected them—the way you avert the evil eye in primitive cultures by saying, 'This child is ugly, this child is despicable. . . .' "

Ernest Wright parodied: " 'I don't think we're going to make it on January 14th'; but Wendell Phillips saw to it they *made* it on the 14th!"

CROSS: "On Albright's desk there was a big sign—'Leave for South Arabia,' with the date, and then in small letters below, 'Remember to take Ruth.' "

Amid the laughter, Ted Campbell exclaimed, "You're kidding!"

CROSS: "That was actually on his desk; we all saw it. Ruth was going to spend the time in England or somewhere."

When Albright wrote to Noel on January 3, 1950, he said he should be airborne for Arabia the next week. The New York *Herald Tribune* of January 14 headlined: "Dr. W. F. Albright Will Fly to Arabia; Is Leaving Today to Join Study of Man Expedition." The article mentioned that "Dr. Albright speaks at least twenty-five languages ["speaks" is not the right word, but people often misuse it in such a scholarly connection] and is the author of more than 600 books and scientific articles. . . ."

The expedition collected most of its supplies and personnel at Aden and boarded the S.S. *Velho* to steam for thirty-six hours along the southern coast of Arabia to Mukalla. Another staff member met them with a small canoe out in the harbor facing the "white city crowded onto a narrow shelf between the blue harbor and tall red-brown cliffs," as Wendell Phillips described it in his fascinating book *Qataban and Sheba,* with subtitle "Exploring the Ancient

Kingdoms on the Biblical Spice Routes of Arabia." Prof. Albright
with his "twenty-five languages" was aboard the *Velho*. Bill and
Gladys Terry were in charge again, and Gladys, who could drive
any truck and fly almost any plane, was convoy pace-setter after
they transferred into their "thirteen specially built Dodge Power
Wagons and started for the interior," leaving Mukalla at 2:00 P.M.
on Monday, February 20, 1950. "Professor Albright became ill,
but since we were only sixty miles from the sizable city of Seiyun,
where there would be good accommodations, we drove on."[7] At
"the beautiful city of Seiyun, capital of the Kathiri state . . . arrangements had been made for us to stay at the rather bizarre but
sumptuous palace of Saiyid Abu Bakr, . . ." Albright remained
there until he recovered, and caught up with the rest of the party
at Timna, "strong and healthy, so eager for immediate work that
he was somewhat disappointed to learn that we had not already
taken care of all diplomatic formalities." These included a banquet
by Sherif Hussein bin Ahmed, followed with entertainment in a
large courtyard by two Yemenite dancing girls. It reminded Wendell of the gypsies dancing at Abu Zeneima rest house two years
before on Sinai, when "as Professor Albright was obviously the
most elderly man present and the girls had been told by fun-loving
Henry Field that he was loaded with piasters, the dancers directed
most of their activities in his direction. It was quite a picture, with
our Professor sitting there, Gladys perched [rather for protection
of him] on the arm of his chair, and the gypsies dancing as close as
possible to him. The Professor's face became redder and redder,
and his one comment on the performance was, 'My, what marvelous control!' "[8]

Prof. Albright's purpose at Hajar bin Humeid was to find the
basis for the chronology of Qatabanian and other civilizations on
the Arabian peninsula. He and his crew made a cut 64 feet square
on top of the mound and cleared one level of occupation after another, taking any objects and potsherds found to their workroom.
After photography of a cleared level was completed, Wendell would
remove Prof. Albright with force, if necessary, for his own safety
and in order to get the rest he needed—and also in order to let the
demolition work proceed without his jumping in eagerly to see
what might be coming to light in the next level. It was no easy matter to keep up with the Professor, who at five in the morning was

already cheerfully stirring about assembling everything for the day's work and thereby waking all the less ambitious expedition members. In addition, his frugal philosophy considered all beyond absolute necessities to be frivolous concessions to weakness.

Some of the huge, fat, hairy spiders that invaded their camp in Beihan proved when measured to be more than seven and a half inches across. An Arab boy usually made "a running leap through the air, and with his bare left foot smashed the spider against the wall." When this happened one evening, with Albright working at a nearby desk, "the rest of us felt somewhat shattered by the experience," Wendell said, "but the professor was so absorbed in his work that he did not even look up." Especially if he did not have his glasses on, Prof. Albright could be "singularly unconcerned about the spiders, . . . At such a time, he is quite nearsighted and spiders disappear from view, which was perhaps the most effective way of handling the whole situation. But it was hard on the rest of us. One evening I passed the Professor's room as he was about to retire. He was sitting on the edge of his bunk, and his glasses had been laid aside. To my horror, I saw a huge Beihani spider leisurely walking across the Professor's pajama leg, unknown to him. . . . the spider continued on his way unhindered—probably to my room—and the Professor lay down and fell asleep to dream of inscribed potsherds."9

The unearthing of a green bronze lion with a fat cupid on its back, and an inscription in ancient Qatabanian characters on the base, caused great excitement. Prof. Albright, Prof. Honeyman and Dr. A. Jamme bent their heads over the inscription, muttering to each other, and a very excited Albright read it aloud slowly to the crowd gathered round. He explained the significance of the discovery to their chronology, settling the dates of Qatabanian kings and giving dates for the masonry they were finding. The lion was copied from a Hellenistic type that the Greeks made not much earlier than 150 B.C. The same King Shahr Yagil Yuhargib who had redecorated the House Yafash had placed this lion there (for the same pair of craftsmen was credited with both works) and thus the king's date was only a century or two B.C., rather than several centuries earlier than that. Within a half hour *another* lion and cupid came to light!

As they neared the end of their time Prof. Albright, whom

Phillips described as "a tireless dynamo of energy," would have worked double shifts, day and night, if it had been possible for him and the others. Wendell worried about Albright's health and felt a responsibility to keep him from working himself to death, for as he said, "expeditions come and expeditions go, potsherds are found or they remain in the ground, but there is only one Professor Albright and there will never be another."[10]

They had not found much pottery, and Albright had concluded that the ancient Qatabanians used far less than the ancient peoples of Palestine, Syria, Mesopotamia and Egypt. He found many more inscriptions, however, than he did in Palestine. Finally at the end of their expedition Albright found some pottery fragments on which he pounced with a happy cry. The many inscribed pieces showed a script he could accurately date in the third century B.C.— the same script as that found in earlier tombs they had dug. Now he was content to let that season come to an end in spite of the fact that the mound still rose 35 feet and contained probably seven levels that would go back another thousand years or more. By the end he had become so familiar with types of masonry and script that he could approximately date their finds as rapidly as they came to light.

Stories on the expedition appeared in newspapers in Toledo on March 2, in Norfolk, Virginia on March 19, in New York on April 2, in Montreal on April 4, and in many others.

After flying back to Baltimore on May 1, Prof. Albright wrote a postcard on the 15th to Noel Freedman, saying he was gradually recovering from the illness that had laid him low as soon as he returned. The Sinai and Arabian expeditions, which were both extremely successful, had surely been a little too strenuous for him; nevertheless he would not have missed the last four months in South Arabia for much, though he was now so pressed with work that he had to turn down some very enticing invitations coming from overseas.

Years later his student Bill Moran recalled when Albright left for and returned from the South Arabian expedition. "I'll never forget the scene in his office on the day before his departure to South Arabia. He was at his desk composing an article for the survey of Old Testament studies edited by Rowley, right off the top of his head, and a number of us were assembled for things like checking BASOR galleys. He was constantly interrupted but never lost patience, for the simple reason his patience wasn't being tested, since his concentration remained unbroken. It was a prodigious performance.

"I remember his returning from South Arabia and taking up his lectures on archaeology and history. The first day back he started off about archaeology, only to be informed by someone in the class that it was the day for history, the archaeology lecture being two days later. 'I apologize. Now just where were we in the history?' On being informed, he launched into a detailed lecture on Assyrian campaigns of the ninth century B.C.!"

In the October 1950 BASOR Editor Albright presented in ten pages his "Chronology of Ancient South Arabia in the Light of the First Campaign of Excavation in Qataban."

On the following January 22, 1951, Prof. Albright flew to Cairo to join Wendell Phillips' second Arabian expedition. At Timna while Wendell was away, Albright was working near House Hadath and was called to come up and look at an object the workmen had just found. It was lying face down on the lowest floor of that house, having evidently fallen from above when Timna was destroyed. The bronze statue sat on a stone seat; one missing arm was found nearby, the other fell off as they lifted it after spending over an hour clearing away around it with knives and finally soft brushes. About a meter high, the bronze figure showed an aristocratic lady, though not so beautiful as "Miriam," the name they had given to a beautiful translucent alabaster head from the first century found there in the first campaign. The pedestal inscription was more important to Albright than her appearance; it named the king of Timna, Warawil Ghaylan Yuhanim, son of Shahr Yagil Yuhargib, as well as the woman, Lady Bar'at, living at the time he reigned. Thus Albright was able to date the destruction of Timna down near the time of Christ, as well as the *terra sigillata* ("sealed earth") pottery found near Lady Bar'at—a Roman type coming into the eastern Mediterranean between 31 B.C. and A.D. 14, the period of Augustus' reign and of Herod, who reigned in Judea when Jesus was born. Potters' names were not stamped on their products after about A.D. 70.

Another great discovery was the proper order of the ancient South Semitic alphabet, inscribed in a central court at the temple site, on paving stones of the colonnade running around three sides. The order was much like that of the later Ethiopic alphabet.

They also worked again at Hajar bin Humeid, and Prof. Albright found the pottery sequence he had been hoping for which provided a framework of chronology for South Arabian archaeology as his finds at Tell Beit Mirsim had done for western Palestine. Hajar bin Humeid had apparently first been settled about 1000 B.C.

Wendell Phillips was invited to Yemen for an audience with the king in order to discuss going to Marib for excavations. He wished Prof. Albright to go with him and his party, and Albright was immensely tempted to do so. But the possibilities of delay in his scheduled return to the U.S. were too great, and reluctantly he parted from Wendell at Aden.

James L. Swauger of the Carnegie Museum in Pittsburgh recalled his first meeting with Prof. Albright at a Cairo hotel on February 4, 1951. While he was unpacking his bags there was a knock on the door. "I opened it to see a very tall, nearly bald, most pleasant man. He peered at us from behind very thick lenses. He was most flattering and gracious in announcing his pleasure at my presence. There is the measure of the man. In relation to archaeological work in the Near East, I had not attained even unto obscurity, and here was the foremost American authority on biblical archaeology, a world-renowned scholar whose name, as I learned later, was an 'Open Sesame' to any scientist or institution concerned with such matters, Chief Archaeologist of the Second Arabian Expedition, who had the extreme courtesy to come to greet *me*! I was his slave from that time forward. One felt he was in the presence of genius, of course, but also that he was in company of a man so instinctively sensitive, kind, and humble that the genius was exalted because of the man, and not the man because of the genius.

"He was delightful in the field," continued Swauger. "Quick to point out errors, abrupt in dismissing irrelevant arguments, swift to condemn mistaken procedures, his essential dedication to truth, to accuracy, to expanding knowledge always came through in a mantle of goodness so that one could not rise to anger with him. . . . There were, of course, many small quirks that one remembers. He was tall, and the doors of our mud castle in the Wadi Beihan were not. Often at meal times an idea would come to his mind and, as if hypnotized, he'd rise and start for the door with his rapid walk and his face drawn in thought, and from the rest of us there'd come a shouted chorus of concern, 'Professor, your hat,' and if we were lucky, he'd remember to put on his *topi* and duck before going through the door. If we were not, he'd crack the lintel with his head, rear back, look startled, clap his hand to his forehead, and duck through the opening intent on getting to his reference or the artifact whose significance he'd just realized, or to dash off a note to a colleague about some puzzle they'd been working with for thirty years. And he had, as I recall, a romance with sugar-coated cereals.

"His warm personality, his demonstrated command of several fields, and his thoughtfulness toward others were components of a unique individual who attained the leadership of his field without a trace of self glorification. We shall not see his like again," concluded James Swauger.

While Prof. Albright was overseas on the second Arabian expedition, the editorship of BASOR was entrusted to Prof. E. A. Speiser, as Guest Editor, who with perfect timing brought out the April 1951 issue No. 122 several weeks early "In Honor of WILLIAM FOXWELL ALBRIGHT On His Sixtieth Birthday, May 24, 1951," as stated on the front page. The contributors were an elite group who prepared scholarly articles in their specialties in his honor rather than merely encomia and eulogies. Albright thanked them in the October issue, No. 123, saying, "This was the best possible tribute, since the writer would have objected most strenuously to a heavy expenditure of time and money on the part of his friends, especially since he still has, *Deo volente*, years of active scholarly work ahead of him." (Yes, two decades; and several volumes of *Festschriften* would in those years be dedicated to him.) Since Speiser had brought the issue out early, Albright said he "was overwhelmed by congratulatory letters from friends all over the world, and has had many books and papers dedicated to him. Such tribute is far more heart-warming than a costly volume which would cause expense to many and hard work for others. He thanks these friends, one and all, for their kindness."[11]

Wendell Phillips published a fascinating article on the campaign in *Collier's* that spring with good color photos and an inset by Lowell Thomas saying that "Wendell Phillips is a brilliant heir to the great explorers of the past. To me it is thrilling to see a

young man [he was then 29] take his place in a field which has
provided the world with a large part of its vicarious adventure.
Wendell is a phenomenon—a rare combination of adventurer and
executive. He uses an incredible persuasiveness, gift of organization,
mass of scholarly information and leaping imagination to organize and run expeditions. . . ." Wendell's article spoke of Dr. Albright as "fearless to the point of carelessness."

The Dallas *Times Herald* of April 25 carried a story that Wendell Phillips had "obtained permission from the Imam of Yemen
to excavate the site of Marib, probably the capital of the Queen of
Sheba's legendary kingdom. . . ." But in that expedition, a year
later, Albright did not participate, and Wendell and his party had
to leave most of their equipment and supplies and flee for their
lives from hostile natives.

Dr. Sam Iwry, who had come as a refugee from Poland by way
of China in 1948 and graduated under Prof. Albright in 1951, then
becoming a lecturer in the department, vividly recalled Albright's
return from the second South Arabian Expedition. Iwry was conducting the departmental seminar in Albright's absence, after Albright had given "five or six tremendous lectures to prepare the
students for the theme of the seminar, early Hebrew poetry. Then
he assigned papers which were to be read in six or eight weeks in a
certain order. There were about fifteen to eighteen men attending.

"They read their papers and some of them were really marvelous. Everyone participated freely—more freely than when Albright
was present, because some of them felt a little constrained with him
but in my presence they could ask questions and discuss. Some of
the papers were so good I was sorry he wasn't there—he would have
been beaming. I wrote him one or two letters telling him everything was going all right, and he answered me.

"One day, a Wednesday, when he was about to return, the seminar was going on, and around 9:30 or 10:00 he came in with a
satchel and a coat. You could see that the man was just now off the
plane and had come by taxi, realizing that he could still attend
part of the seminar. The consternation it caused! The fellow who
was reading his paper fell completely flat on the floor and had to be
revived. Then I stepped out of my place to give Albright his right-
ful seat, but he said, 'No, no, no! You sit and conduct the seminar,'
and he sat on the side like a visitor. But I could not make this fellow

continue reading his paper! Finally after he gave a few more words I opened the topic for discussion—and nobody wanted to open his mouth and discuss! Some of them were new people who didn't know Albright very well, and they were afraid to speak.

"While I was struggling with this seminar, the door opened and Mrs. Albright stood there! In a very stern way she looked at me and then at her husband, and said, "Sam, come here! I want to talk to you.'

"I went out. She said to me, 'I thought you had more sense; don't you understand? A man of his years comes home from such a long journey, through so many countries, and was traveling all night on a plane. He has first to go home and rest before going to the office and classroom. Couldn't you send him home right away? Don't you know?—He may be a great intellectual, but he's not intelligent!'

"As if I could make him go home!" Iwry exclaimed. "According to her, when he opened the door and we all became speechless, including myself, seeing him come in all of a sudden, I should tell him, 'Dr. Albright, I am sorry, you have no right to enter this place; go home!' "

15

Mr. Dead Sea Scrolls

On October 21, 1936, the Baltimore *Sun* published an article stating: "The world for three decades has possessed, without knowing it, a fragment of the Old Testament in Hebrew which was written before Christ, it has been determined by Dr. William F. Albright, . . . This fragment, the Nash Papyrus, long has been recognized as the oldest Hebrew copy of the Aramaic script in which it is written; however, Dr. Albright has discovered it was from a much earlier period. It was written less than a century after the writing of the latest books of the Old Testament. . . ." Containing the Ten Commandments and the *Shema Israel*, used as a Jewish prayer, it had been bought early in the twentieth century by an Englishman, Walter L. Nash, from natives in Egypt and presented to the Cambridge Museum. In 1937 Albright published in JBL an article titled "A Biblical Fragment from the Maccabaean Age: the Nash Papyrus." Years later this study proved foundational.

The spring of 1948 at the Oriental Seminary was both interesting and suspenseful. Sam Iwry and Siegfried Horn (a German missionary in Java when the war broke out, who had been interned by the Dutch there and the British in India for seven years, and had rejoined his wife and come to America after the end of the war), along with Noel Freedman and Frank Cross, Mitchell Dahood (a Lebanese-American Jesuit), Bill Moran (another Jesuit), and several others, were all members of Prof. Albright's seminar. The topic every Wednesday morning that year was "The Apocrypha in the Mid-Twentieth Century." As Sam Iwry recalled, "Albright felt that in 1948 we should take a new, fresh look at the Apocrypha, their role in searching the Near Eastern mind, especially in the pre-Christian times, and see how we can now evaluate them. The seminar was quite promising, with fine students, and everybody got a piece, some book of the Apocrypha or the Pseudepigrapha. Albright looked at me—this was my third month of sitting in the seminar—and said, 'I have something just for you. You will take the Damascus Document, and you will examine it afresh. I know that one of your great teachers at the Warsaw Higher Institute for Judaic Studies dealt with this, and maybe you will be able to come up with something new.' The man was Poznanski—he had been a teacher of my teacher. I was very happy to reexamine this Hebrew document, which had been found in a Cairo synagogue *genizah* (storeroom for worn-out manuscripts) in 1897 and published in 1910. R. H. Charles had received a lot of scolding for including this book in the Apocrypha. I spent quite a bit of time on it, and when my turn came a paper was ready—in bad English, of course, but by then they were all used to me. I read the paper, concluding that this document is genuine, not a hoax as Solomon Zeitlin and others had said, and that it goes back to the Second Commonwealth. I enumerated about sixteen points showing why I thought the document is genuine. Albright was impressed and said the paper should be published, and even asked Cross and some of the other students to edit it for publication.

"A week or two later at the seminar the telephone rang in Albright's office. The call was from Jerusalem. Dr. John Trever told Albright about the scrolls that had been brought to the School for evaluation, and the little fragment of a scroll that he had chipped off and that it was already possible to read. There was no question about the identification of the Isaiah scroll, but what was this other? He mentioned the two lines; on the long-distance phone it wasn't too clear and the fellow who read the lines did not pronounce Hebrew well. Albright hurriedly called me from the seminar room into his office, took up the phone and said, 'Tell him to spell it!' So the man spelled it out to him and as Albright repeated the Hebrew letters I recorded them. And I immediately read the first five words and said, 'This is related to the Damascus Document!' Nobody except those thoroughly acquainted with the document—and I had just freshly been dealing with it—could get this connection.

"There was an immediate reaction," Iwry continued. "Albright believed at once that this was a very great find. The biblical books alone were not yet any indication that it was an *old* library that had been discovered, for they were not yet really examined and biblical books could always be everywhere."

Albright and Iwry returned to the seminar in progress, Albright bursting with his news. Siegfried Horn recalls that Albright came in and said he had some tremendous news but could not tell it. Bill Moran recalled later that "Albright walked back in and announced that he had just learned of the most sensational archaeological discovery of modern times, but unfortunately his lips were sealed. Later he interrupted the seminar to say that, despite the secrecy he must keep, he could tell us that it concerned Palestine. Such proclamations came at regular intervals throughout the morning and lunch, until I think we knew about 90% of that secret. He simply could not contain himself."

Dr. Trever airmailed to Prof. Albright two small Leica photographs of a column or two of the scrolls that had been brought to the School on February 18, 1948, by Metropolitan Athanasius Yeshue Samuel and Father Butros Sowmy of St. Mark's Monastery, for evaluation. As Dr. Albright used to tell the story, within an hour of first looking at them he knew it was a genuinely ancient discovery; these scrolls dated from the last two centuries B.C. and the first century A.D. Actually, as he confidentially told his editorial assistant a couple of decades later, he knew it in the first ten minutes! But he would not dare tell it that way, or people would think it was a superficial judgment! As Mrs. Albright related the story, it may have taken him twenty minutes to form a judgment, and nineteen of those minutes were spent trying to find his 1937 article on the Nash Papyrus, with photograph, somewhere on his loaded desk! It was an example of his memory for form and detail. He had recognized in these tiny Leica prints four letters with distinguishing characteristics that were older than those he had discussed and dated in the Nash Papyrus nearly a dozen years earlier.

Noel Freedman recalled, "After Albright received the pictures of the Isaiah A Scroll from Trever, he called Cross and me into his office—said we were the first to know—and showed us the pictures and said the manuscript dated from about 100 B.C., earlier than Nash. The date still stands. Cross and I were flabbergasted; I remember that we spent the whole evening transcribing the two or three columns so we would have the readings. The material was from the end of Isaiah, chapters 61-63. The thing that interested us most, of course, was the orthography, which was very full—vowel-letters all over the place, confirming a view of Wellhausen, also held by Albright, that the Maccabaean period saw the most extensive use of *matres lectionis* [certain consonants used to indicate vowel sounds]. We incorporated the information into our joint dissertation on Hebrew spelling—a very happy confirmation of our work just when the thesis was nearly finished."

In a conversation among some of Albright's students, after Ernest Wright had remarked that he always said, "Watch out for Albright's hunches," Noel responded, "Well, look at the Nash Papyrus—a really pivotal study at the right time, a decade before the discovery of the Dead Sea Scrolls"—it paved the way for his immediate recognition of their genuineness and real value.

Dr. Siegfried Horn, who with Albright's recommendation and blessing later transferred to Chicago to complete his doctoral work in the Oriental Institute, wrote in his diary at the time: "It was a great surprise when Dr. Albright told us that a few days ago some parchment scrolls had been discovered . . . [including] a complete manuscript of Isaiah copied near the beginning of the second century B.C. . . . We students saw photographs of these manuscripts and were greatly excited. The spelling differs from that found in the Masoretic Bible, but otherwise the text agrees remarkably well with the known Hebrew Bible text, although it seems occasionally to support readings found in the Septuagint. It will be interesting to see how far the results of the textual criticism of the past will be supported or revised by this new find. It is wonderful that finally, after a long period of waiting, Biblical scholars possess pre-Christian Hebrew Bible manuscripts for which they have longed more than for anything else. The age of great discoveries does not seem to have passed."

Rabbi Samuel Rosenblatt was there as a part-time teacher "when the Dead Sea Scrolls were discovered and Prof. Albright called us into his office to speak about 'the most momentous discovery in modern times pertaining to the Bible.' "

It was not long until the news began coming out in scholarly journals so that Albright's lips were unsealed (not that he had very successfully sealed them). In the April BASOR No. 110, published

late as was quite usual, Editor Albright signed his name as First
Vice-president and Acting President, with date May 19, 1948, to a
note on the discovery: "We had hoped to include in this number a
statement by President Burrows [who was Director of the ASOR
in Jerusalem that year but away from the city when the scrolls
were brought to the School in February] on the sensational discovery of Hebrew rolls. Readers of the *Bulletin* will surely have
noted brief news releases [in the public press] from Burrows and
Sukenik on this subject. . . . Since this is unquestionably the greatest manuscript find of modern times, we await further details with
the keenest interest, hoping devoutly that nothing happens to the
rolls which are now in the possession of the Hebrew University.

"According to the news from Sukenik the rolls were discovered
by Bedouin in a cave near the northern shore of the Dead Sea during the past winter. Apparently they had been concealed in pottery
jars, wrapped in linen and covered with pitch for protection against
the elements. Certainly some of the rolls are in a remarkable state
of preservation, though at least one is very much the worse for
wear. Four of the rolls, one of parchment and three of leather,
were purchased by the Metropolitan of the Syrian Orthodox Monastery of St. Mark in Jerusalem; they are said to be safely out of
the country, after three had been fully reproduced by Dr. John C.
Trever, who is an expert photographer. The Hebrew University
bought a number of other rolls; in all there would seem to be at
least eight and possibly more. The most important of the rolls
owned by the Syrian Monastery is a complete scroll of the Book of
Isaiah. Dr. Trever sent the editor two photographs to illustrate
the script of this parchment, which is easily a thousand years older
than that of the oldest Hebrew biblical roll hitherto known. The
script is materially older than that of the Nash Papyrus of the
Decalogue, which is itself earlier than the most archaic square
character of the Herodian Age yet known from contemporary
graffiti. With respect to the form of individual letters the script is
similar to that of the Edfu papyri and ostraca from the third century B.C. Sukenik is quoted as saying that some of the rolls are
over two thousand years old and that none is later than the fall of
Jerusalem in 70 A.D. The Isaiah scroll now in the Syrian collection
thus goes back to about the second century B.C.; in other words, it
may be early Maccabaean, while the Nash Papyrus is late Macca-

baean, from the first century B.C. (additional evidence for this date has accumulated since the editor's article of 1937).

"Among the rolls being studied by Burrows, Trever and Brownlee is part of a commentary on Habakkuk and a 'curious manual of ritual and discipline' from a still unidentified Jewish sect. The Sukenik material is reported to include another text of Isaiah, a book of hymns resembling the Psalter, a historical narrative of an unidentified war, and the original Hebrew of several apocryphal books hitherto known only from Greek translations. It is easy to surmise that the new discovery will revolutionize intertestamental studies, and that it will soon antiquate all present handbooks on the background of the New Testament and on the textual criticism and interpretation of the Old Testament. We congratulate the fortunate scholars who are preparing these rolls for publication, and hope that nothing will happen to prevent complete salvage of an almost incredible discovery!"[1]

Prof. Albright's annual seminars for the next years were focused on study of the Dead Sea Scrolls, as they were immediately called, and his public lectures turned largely to this subject. BASOR was full of articles studying the orthography, the paleography, the dating of the linen wrapping, the pottery, and other aspects of this "incredible discovery."

In a conversation of Albright students, Frank Cross, who later became a specialist on the paleography, or shapes and dating of letters, of the Scrolls, remarked, "Albright was in Arabia when I had my oral examination [1950], and it was a catastrophe" (though of course he passed). They started telling tales of their oral examinations under Prof. Albright. Noel Freedman said, "I turned in the dissertation April 1st [1948], had the writtens during April, and about May 1st the orals. And I'd never want to go through anything like *that* again as long as I live. But I'd survived the writtens, and then for the orals there was really nothing you could do."

CROSS: "There was certainly no way you could get ready."

FREEDMAN: "Well, *I* thought there *was*. I reread *From the Stone Age to Christianity* as light reading the night before the orals—like reading the telephone directory—and that nearly finished me. Next day I went staggering in there, and they had this murderous collection of people. If you were an Albright student you had two and a half strikes against you, for he used to go to these other departments' exams quite innocently and ask some questions that destroyed the candidates! It was usually pertinent, perfectly legitimate, and just destructive!"

CROSS: "And *never* innocent!"

FREEDMAN: "It was deeply resented by these professors, so naturally they sharpened their knives for *his* students. The rule was, there had to be a majority outside the department to pass the candidate. They could ask anything under the sun."

WRIGHT: "Ah, it was a very terrible ordeal!"

FREEDMAN: "Defense of the dissertation was a minimal feature. First you summarized the thesis, and that was the end of the subject as far as anybody else was concerned." Freedman had trouble because of Albright's helpfulness when he asked the principal sources for the Canaanite language in the second millennium B.C. "I *thought* he said or meant the *first half* of the second millennium; therefore I locked out Ugaritic and Amarna, which was obviously what he wanted to hear about, and tried to rack my brain for some source of Canaanite in the *first* half of the second millennium. I finally dredged up out of my foggy mind these references I had seen the night before to the *Aechtungs-texte* [Execration Texts], and mentioned them. In the 1940 edition of *Stone Age* he had mentioned only the first edition, and he asked me for the second set. I didn't want to tell him it wasn't in *Stone Age*! Then a different inspiration hit him. He asked, 'What are these texts about?' I didn't know what they were about! So then he said, 'What does it mean, *Aechtungs-texte*?' He should have realized when I used the German that I didn't know what the English was—he didn't translate the term in *The Stone Age*. But not Albright! You could see the consternation all over the room, and I was convinced I was a dead pigeon—and why? Because he was trying to help!

"Blake started asking questions," Noel continued, "and that saved my neck. He asked me a few grammatical questions, which I tossed off with ease, and I was beginning to feel a little better. Then he asked me about the pronunciation of the letter *tav* in Hebrew according to the Massoretes, the Sephardim, and the Ashkenazim—and disagreed with my correct answer, so that Rosenblatt came to my defense, and Blake grew purple! After it was over, and fortunately the members of the committee forgot about the first part, they said, as Albright later told me, 'What kind of a student is this?—he corrects his own professors!' So it came out as a happy ending to a dismal beginning."

Wright said, "I think in my time, in June of '37, the university wasn't as sensitive against Albright as you say they became because of his questioning of their candidates. I had just conquered the world with my dissertation! I supposed that my thesis should pass me; and lo and behold, Albright questioned me only ten minutes, Blake twenty! He would start off and ask a question and then start in on the answer, giving me the first half of the first sentence, and then I knew what he wanted—it opened up the whole thing! Abe Sachs went in right after the committee left the room and picked the ballots out of the wastebasket and pieced them all together, and he knew that I had passed unanimously!"

Sam Iwry at a different time mentioned what happened when a candidate failed the oral examination. Albright would ask Sam (after he was teaching part-time) to go with the unhappy young man to the train station—not to leave him alone, but stay with him, talk to him, and put him on his train. Then Albright would start to tell, by way of excusing the failure, how the young man's schools had not really taught him well. He was compassionate for the failures as well as enthusiastic about the successful ones—while at the same time impressing them with the fact that they did not yet know it all.

Mrs. Jean Tomko, librarian of the Classics and Semitic sectional library on the same floor in Gilman Hall with those departments, recalled how Albright once in great perplexity came in looking for a young man. On being excused from the room while the vote was taken on his oral examination, the young fellow had run on out of the building, convinced that he had failed. Albright was desperately trying to find him in order to congratulate him on passing!

Sam Iwry had his orals in the spring of 1951 after Albright had returned from the second South Arabian Expedition. "There came up with me Victor Gold and Mitchell Dahood and (a little bit before, but we took the written examination at the same time) Bill Moran. At that time came a letter from Frank Cross and other friends addressed alphabetically to these 'victims,' saying, 'Your Day of Judgment has arrived,' and telling us how to handle it. But Albright had seen that beautifully written letter! Because it was addressed to the department, with all the names in a long line, he thought it was for the Oriental Seminary and opened it, and then gave it to me!" Sam recalled that Albright decided to give him questions on a certain morning on history and archaeology. He typed them and Sam stood behind him looking on. He suggested that he answer orally and spare Albright (and himself) his bad English in laboriously written answers. Albright agreed, listened, and after seven or eight answers he removed the paper from the machine and said they were not the correct questions for Sam. He would have the list ready that afternoon.

"I came in the afternoon; there was an envelope addressed to me and I took it into the other room to write. These were completely different questions and I could have kicked myself for what I had done to myself. If I hadn't opened my mouth but had accepted the first set of questions, I would have answered easily and quickly. This was a horrendous set of questions! When I returned my paper to him, he looked at them and said, 'I knew that it was all right, but I wanted you to know, scholarship doesn't come so easily!' And he smiled. 'Of course you passed,' he said right away. I asked, 'In other words, did I pass on my first batch of questions, or on my second batch?' He said, 'It doesn't make any difference!' "

The Baltimore *Evening Sun* of May 29, 1948 carried a story from Cincinnati saying that "Dr. William Foxwell Albright, professor of Semitic languages at Johns Hopkins University, was awarded an honorary doctor of Hebrew laws degree here today at commencement exercises of Hebrew Union College. . . . Five honorary degrees, including Dr. Albright's, were conferred by Dr. Nelson Glueck, recently inaugurated as president of the college— oldest Jewish seminary in America." This was Albright's seventh honorary doctorate; other papers carried the story in following days. His fifth, after a ten-year gap from three bestowed in 1936, had been an honorary Th.D. in 1946 from the University of Oslo, for which he made a quick trip to Norway; his sixth had been an LL.D. from Boston College in 1947.

Two months following his seventh honorary degree at Cincinnati, the Albrights were on their way to Europe for the sixth International Congress of Orientalists in Paris. Ernest Wright and Roger O'Callaghan made the trip with them in 1948, "the first one held after the war," as Wright mentioned in a conversation of Albright students. "Here were all the big guns you've ever heard of. O'Callaghan could speak anything he could hear; he got us across Europe in the most entertaining manner. But the big thing about that Congress was, all the old boys were gone. Only Frankfort appeared too, but went home two days early because he couldn't stand it— for Albright was the center of everybody's attention! Albright was in everything—everybody was crowding around Albright—everyone wanted to know Albright. All the young scholars whom Albright had corresponded with and helped in all those years—now they were in positions of power, and the man they wanted to meet and know was Albright. He was in the center of his glory."

On returning from Europe on August 16 Albright wrote his former student, Jacob Myers, that he had caught a cold in his head and ear and was delayed a day or two before even going to the office in the university to get mail that had piled up. He and Ruth had had a very interesting four-week trip to Paris and Rome. The Orientalistic Congress in Paris had been greatly successful, with 900 people attending when about 300 had been expected. He was now trying to avoid everything that would take him away from Baltimore before the first of October, since he had been away so much during the past twelve months.

To Noel Freedman, who following his graduation was about to begin teaching in Western Seminary in Pittsburgh, Albright wrote that he and Ruth had had a great time in Europe. While he was in Paris fifteen days, she was there ten; he was in Rome twelve days, and she had preceded him, spending seventeen there. Though the attendance at the Congress was three times as large as anyone had expected, no one was present from Germany and hardly anyone from Eastern Europe—naturally none from Russia. Only a few Americans were there, and few biblical scholars, though almost a hundred Egyptologists and a somewhat lesser number of Assyriologists. Albright had met more than a hundred friends and recent acquaintances. Most of the time in Rome he spent reading the scholarly literature in German that had appeared since the start of the second World War. He commented that going by plane made the trip expensive, though living on the Continent was the opposite. Nevertheless they would not have missed this very worthwhile trip for anything.

The October, December, and February issues of BASOR at the

end of 1948 and beginning of 1949 were full of studies of the Dead
Sea Scrolls. In the year-end SBL meetings in New York, Prof. Solomon Zeitlin, of Dropsie College, led the opposition to Albright and
his group who recognized the authenticity of the Scrolls. Zeitlin
and a few others claimed they were medieval forgeries. On visiting
Prof. Albright not many months after the news first came out, Prof.
Zeitlin refused even to look at the Leica prints and see the ancient
letter forms; by some unknown means he knew they were hoaxes
without even seeing them! It was a stressful SBL meeting that year,
and Zeitlin continued his bitter opposition through the following
years. The excitement snapped Albright out of slow recovery from
a virus attack, as he wrote Noel in mid-January; he remarked that
the Scrolls were becoming ever more interesting but it was too
soon to try to refute Zeitlin; time would take care of him, with new
data flooding in.

In early March of 1949 a new method of dating ancient remains
was announced, discovered "when scientists found considerable
carbon-isotope 14 in Baltimore sewage," as an AP story reported.
"Dr. William Libby of the Institute of Nuclear Research, University of Chicago, is trying to determine just how far isotope 14
can be trusted as a time-clock. If his experiments are successful,
Prof. William F. Albright of Johns Hopkins University (Baltimore) hopes to try out the new technique in Egypt and the Bible
lands. The key to the theory is radioactivity. . . ." Prof. Albright
was always eager to utilize new discoveries and new methods.

The Albrights went abroad again that summer, for Dr. Al-
bright's first foreign lecture tour in England and Scotland. On
June 30 he received his eighth honorary doctorate, an LL.D. from
St. Andrews University in Scotland. Other honors had come that
spring, when he was "elected foreign member of the Royal Danish
Academy of Sciences, honorary member of the British Society for
Old Testament Study, and corresponding member of the Finnish
Oriental Society," according to a notation in his clipping files in
the Hopkins Alumni Records Office. He was already honorary
member of several foreign Oriental societies, and in the next few
years more were added to the list, as well as several national
Academies.

The Philadelphia *Inquirer* of August 14, soon after the Albrights' return from Britain, headlined, "Scholars Debate Ancient

Scrolls." The article stated, "A spirited academic debate over the authenticity of the Hebrew scrolls, found in a Palestine cave and purporting to be books of the Old Testament, is contained in the current issue of the Jewish Quarterly Review, published by Dropsie College for Hebrew and Cognate Learning.

"In articles by four eminent authorities, Dr. W. F. Albright, of Johns Hopkins University, and Dr. Millar Burrows, of Yale, both convinced the scrolls are authentic, are lined up against Dr. Solomon Zeitlin, professor of rabbinical literature, at Dropsie, and Dr. Ernest R. Lacheman, of Wellesley College. . . .

"Dr. Albright, one of the country's top archaeologists, said experts had established the pottery found in the cave as dating back to the first century before the Christian era. . . ."

The Scrolls were exhibited at the Library of Congress that fall; Dr. Albright was the main speaker on October 23 at the first exhibition of the three scrolls possessed by the Hebrew University. The opening was attended by about five hundred scholars and churchmen who heard Albright's lecture. After the exhibit closed in Washington on November 6 it was moved to Baltimore for several weeks, and went on to other American cities.

Finally in the October 1949 BASOR, Albright himself published on the subject, a nine-page article, "On the Date of the Scrolls from Ain Feshkha and the Nash Papyrus," including a good infra-red photograph of the Nash Papyrus for comparison of letter forms. He mentioned that "at a public meeting of the Palestine Exploration Fund, held in London July 14th, I spoke at some length about the significance of the discovery of the Scrolls, . . ." He saw at the British Museum and the London University Institute of Archaeology "many of the hundreds of fragments of sheepskin from the cave," as well as photographs of "complete or fragmentary remains of some forty cylindrical jars . . . The scrolls had been wrapped in linen and placed in the jars, which were covered by closely fitting bowls. . . . It cannot be too strongly emphasized that the bulk of the pottery . . . consists of absolutely homogeneous jars, bowls (made specifically to cover the jars), and lamps, whose pre-Herodian date in the last two centuries B.C. is beyond dispute. . . ."[2]

Albright's footnote devastatingly exposed the slipshod use by Lacheman and Zeitlin of quotations from others: "With such lack of regard for what other scholars actually write and what their latest considered opinions are, a skillful debater can easily make nonsense out of any discussion in which sequence dating plays a significant role." In concluding his article he stated, "These scrolls are original documents of revolutionary importance for biblical and related studies, and they are all from the second and first centuries B.C. (with the possible exception of the fragments of the Holiness Code, etc., which may be earlier)."[3]

If Albright had not become a fighter already in his lifetime, having to battle for acceptance of his ideas, he surely became one during this period, for he had to expose and oppose devious and even irrational arguments of Zeitlin and his progressively dwindling band of supporters who claimed the Scrolls were much later in date, or even medieval forgeries.

It finally came to a debate in person in Philadelphia with Zeitlin, who challenged Albright to it. Sam Iwry, who went along, counseled Prof. Albright, "Don't get entangled with Zeitlin in Talmudic jurisprudence because it will entrap you and you will not get out of it. Just speak in the terms and in the literature that you know best, and leave him to speak about the Talmudic evidence, and you disregard it!" As Sam recalled, Albright "always reminded me afterward that this was very good advice, because he gave a fine address and really defeated Zeitlin. The audience clapped and applauded him tremendously."

The New York *Times* for Tuesday, May 21, 1957, carried the headline, "Scholars Disagree on Date of Scrolls." The Philadelphia story of the preceding day stated: "Four specialists disagreed today on the date of origin of the Dead Sea Scrolls. The issue was debated at a symposium held in connection with the fiftieth anniversary of the Dropsie College for Hebrew and Cognate Learning.

"Dr. Solomon Zeitlin, Professor of Rabbinic Literature at Dropsie, contended that by every scholastic test the scrolls could not have been written before the Middle Ages.

"Dr. William F. Albright, . . . held that 'the relation between the contents of the scrolls and other Jewish literature of the period shows that they can date only from the period established by the material findings—the coins, the radio-carbon datings and the pottery and linen.'

"Msgr. Patrick W. Skehan of the Department of Semitics and

Egyptian Language and Literature at the Catholic University of America, and Prof. Ezekiel Kutscher of the Hebrew University, Jerusalem, said the scrolls had been written no later than the first century of the Christian era. . . ."

Excavations were carried out at Khirbet Qumran (a mile south of the first cave in which Bedouin had found scrolls in jars late in 1947) by Père Roland de Vaux and G. L. Harding, for several years beginning in 1952. They excavated buildings of the Scroll sect's headquarters near the Dead Sea's northwest shore, finding similar pottery, coins of the Roman procurators, and additional caves, some in the limestone cliff and others in the marl terrace on which the headquarters and Scrollery were constructed, until there were eleven caves in that region in which scrolls and thousands of fragments had been found. Transported to the Palestine Archaeological Museum built by a Rockefeller gift of $2,000,000 years earlier, the fragments comprised a gigantic jigsaw puzzle that teams of scholars worked on for years in humidity- and temperature-controlled rooms. Other caves were found in other wadis containing papyrus and leather scrolls and fragments with Hebrew, Greek and Aramaic writing coming down to later dates than the Qumran manuscripts, all of which were earlier than A.D. 68.

Albright announced the first exciting news from the first season of excavation at Qumran in the April 1952 BASOR, just after he returned from a long and successful lecture tour on the West Coast. On the trip he attended the reunion of the class of 1912 at UIU in Fayette, Iowa, and airmailed a letter to Sam Geiser telling him of it. While he was in the West, Ruth moved their household to a new house at 4 West 39th Street, only a few minutes' walk north from Gilman Hall. Although it was a smaller house, it was built well and was roomy enough for their needs, with four bedrooms and two baths. Albright had a study, now, with book shelves from floor to ceiling all around. In another letter to Sam Geiser he described the new house and referred again to the UIU reunion, saying it had surprised him to see how many relatives he had in Fayette County, and to see classmates and others for the first time in four decades. He now felt sympathetic with Emil Forrer's article, whose German title means "The Future—Does It Lie Before Us or Behind Us?"

On May 3 the Albrights flew to Copenhagen for his second foreign lecture tour, this time in Scandinavia and Germany. He received the Th.D. at the University of Uppsala, his eleventh honorary degree (number nine had been a D.H.L. at the College of Jewish Studies in Chicago in 1950 and number ten a Litt.D. at Yale University in 1951). After giving twenty lectures in English, French and German at the Universities of Copenhagen, Aarhus, Lund, Uppsala, Helsingfors [Helsinki], Turku (Abo), and in Lebenstedt and Hamburg universities in Germany, Dr. Albright returned to New York June 7. He would have preferred to remain several weeks longer in Europe, but had several engagements calling him back, including his twelfth honorary degree, another Litt.D., from Georgetown University.

On Albright's sixty-first birthday he wrote Sam Geiser a letter from Uppsala, which Sam published in the UIU alumni paper, telling of his trip that far and of what was ahead: "On the 30th I have a private audience with the King of Sweden, and on the 31st I receive my honorary doctorate at Uppsala, complete with cannon shot, gold ring, and doctor's hat. The ceremonies are so elaborate that there is a rehearsal beforehand, to make sure that all the candidates know exactly what to do. The other recipients of honorary degrees are all Scandinavians."

Dr. Sam replied on the 30th, saying this was the day Bill would be making memorable for the King of Sweden. (As it turned out, Albright had a severe case of laryngitis and shouted at the king, who assured him that he, the king, was not deaf!) Sam drew lasting satisfaction from his old friend's success, and asked what he was going to do with all those diplomas. "Let us hope," he wrote, "that we may in some slight degree keep our intellectual enthusiasm to the end, and have some chance of performance."

Albright wrote to his son Paul that his mother would return by June 17; they had separated on June 2 at Stockholm, met in Copenhagen for almost an hour, and then departed, he to Hamburg and she to Amsterdam. He had been very busy for four days in Germany, giving three lectures and gathering all kinds of ancient and modern data. He told Paul that it was a killing pace for five weeks, but the results were very rich and he wouldn't have missed them for anything. It was not an expensive trip, as they went tourist class and were often entertained, and his honoraria were larger than expected.

To Sam, Albright replied that he was quite sure Sam had not lost his youthful enthusiasm, and he himself certainly had not. He would hate to be young again—he preferred the middle years where they both now were, finding them much more interesting. Through life he had collected a wide variety of friends, himself not fitting into any category; he considered his life largely formed by over-compensation for the physical handicaps of his early years, without which he would, as most young men, have scattered his energies and accomplished little. His weighty collection of academic honors meant mainly greater opportunity to get across his ideas; he did not want such recognition as *Festschriften*, and would not allow a feature article to be written on him, as Sam had suggested for the Hopkins Journal, but he thanked Sam for the kind publicity he had put in the UIU paper, something he hadn't anticipated but should have, from Sam! He had missed in late years their old correspondence and was glad it was being renewed—he still had all of Sam's old letters (a large carton full of them was found after Albright's death).

In his lecturing through the rest of his life Albright would describe the Dead Sea Scrolls as "the most significant archaeological discovery of all time, as far as biblical studies are concerned." His lectures brought knowledge about them to a much wider audience than the scholarly community.

Prof. Albright was in on a cloak-and-dagger mystery story that was a fitting sequel to the saga of the Dead Sea Scrolls. That saga had begun in 1947 when a Bedouin boy looking for his lost goat in the wilderness near the Dead Sea tossed a stone through a cave opening and heard the crash of breaking pottery. On July 4, 1954, Albright received a very interesting phone call from Yigael Yadin, son of his old friend E. L. Sukenik. Yadin, after being a general in the war in 1948 at the founding of the State of Israel, had become one of the leading archaeologists of the new state, and he was in New York on a secret mission. Albright wrote to him that same afternoon, thanking him for his phone call and the wonderful news about the Dead Sea Scrolls. He was absolutely thrilled, and said he knew how thrilled Yadin's father would have been to know of this new development after his own attempts in 1948 had failed. Surely the Hebrew University ought to possess these priceless documents, along with the scrolls they already had from Qumran Cave 1. He

certainly hoped Yadin could complete the purchase, and promised to keep as quiet as the grave about it. He thought the price
mentioned on the phone was a bargain. Perhaps Zeitlin's unbelievable propaganda against the authenticity of the Scrolls had helped
concerning this favorable price! Albright remarked that Zeitlin's
colleagues were no longer taking him seriously, as one of them had
let Albright know recently.

In addition to the high value of the three main scrolls that the
St. Mark's Monastery possessed, there was the still unrolled "Book
of Lamech" (which would someday furnish quite a long Jewish-
Aramaic text dating from about 150 to 1 B.C. and would be renamed, after study of it by one of Albright's Jesuit students, Father
Joseph A. Fitzmyer, "The Genesis Apocryphon"). Albright had already studied two fragments from it and spoke enthusiastically of
it, believing it would illuminate literary Aramaic of the last couple
of centuries before the Common Era. Half a million dollars was
not too much for such unique manuscripts; years earlier, before
income tax developments, the price would have been in the millions, he estimated.

Albright said he had greatly enjoyed Yadin's visit five weeks
earlier, when his lecture had been most successful. The highlight
had been Yadin's demonstration that the text he was editing, "The
War of the Sons of Light and the Sons of Darkness," dated to the
period of Julius Caesar, between Pompey and Augustus—exactly
where Albright dated published material of the same manuscript
lot. He closed his letter wishing Yadin *bon voyage* with the expectation of meeting him in Cambridge and London in August. (Albright spent nearly two weeks in England and attended the Congress of Old Testament Scholars with over a thousand other
delegates.)

It was nearly eight months later that the sale was consummated.
By then, as Albright remarked in a letter of February 18, 1955, to
Frank Cross, he regretted that his name had been dragged into the
scene by news releases from Israel; he had done nothing more than
encourage Yadin and give him information, the same as he had
done for many others before from different institutions and faiths.
In addition, he had faithfully kept the secret as he had promised.
There had to be secrecy, because full payment could not be made
until a few weeks after the Scrolls were delivered in Israel.

Four days later he wrote to His Excellency the Israeli Ambassador, Mr. Abba Eban, saying he was very kind to let Albright assist in setting the date of the reception in honor of the man who had helped pay for the Scrolls, Mr. Gottesman. Also Albright acknowledged that he had indeed been somewhat embarrassed by inclusion of his name in newspaper accounts, clippings of which had been sent to him from various places by different people. But it didn't matter—he had no intention of making an early trip to Jordan, and he did not pay much attention to the reaction of some of his scholarly colleagues. (This was the beginning of a ban on visits by Prof. Albright to Arab countries, because of his interest in and helpfulness to Israel.)

On March 16 the reception took place. The Washington *Post* on the next day reported that "four ancient Hebrew scrolls, purchased for $250,000 by a New York banker, were formally presented to the State of Israel here last night at a ceremony at the Jewish Embassy. Wealthy Samuel Gottesman used enlarged photographs of the 2000-year-old documents in his presentation to Israeli Ambassador Abba Eban. . . .

"Guests last night included Prof. William F. Albright, Johns Hopkins University archaeologist who authenticated the scrolls before their purchase five weeks ago. He said the writings are 1000 years older than the oldest previously known work of the Hebrew Bible. . . ."

A little later Albright found out from the Israeli Consulate that when the reception took place in Washington, Abba Eban was suffering from a high fever and hardly knew what he was doing or saying. By the time he reached his bed that night his fever was 104°—and that explained everything, as Albright remarked in a letter to Dr. Harry Orlinsky, who had played a key role as go-between.

16

Autumn in Turkey

The Baltimore *Sunday Sun* for September 15, 1956, devoted a full page, six columns with large photo of Dr. Albright surrounded by statues and potsherds on shelves behind him in his office as well as some in his hands, to a feature article by Frank Henry titled "William F. Albright—Cosmopolite of Ancient Worlds." Mr. Henry said in closing, "Although Dr. Albright has now reached the official retirement age (65) at the Hopkins, he is to remain on for two more years. Then he will go to the Jewish Theological Seminary of America in New York to write a history of Israel. . . ." In a box on the page it was noted that "in 40 years of archaeological research Dr. Albright has written more than 500 books, pamphlets and lectures, in addition to making numerous translations of ancient Near and Middle East inscriptions." The items in his lifetime bibliography by then actually numbered more than 830.

Before that article appeared the Albrights had left the U.S. on August 16. ASOR President A. Henry Detweiler's notes in the October 1956 BASOR mentioned that "Vice-president Albright is in Europe attending the Congress of Old Testament scholars at Strasbourg. Word has just reached us that he has been elected President of the Congress for the next three years. This is a well deserved honor and the Schools can bask in a bit of reflected glory. He will travel later to Turkey under the auspices of the State Department Cultural Exchange program."[1]

Noel Freedman wrote to Albright in care of the U.S. Embassy, Ankara, that he had heard from some of the men who had returned from Strasbourg that "apparently it was quite a gala occasion." Albright replied (his handwriting now much larger and more difficult to read than when he was principal of the Menno high school forty-four years earlier) that Ruth and he had come on the 14th from Beirut, and on the 20th she had gone on to Rome. They had spent four days in Metz with their youngest son David (in the army in Europe), his wife and their first child, David Jr., born patriotically on July 4 at Verdun. The new father was then with his family at Cambridge, Mass., beginning his course in Harvard Law School. At Strasbourg, Albright had to go to bed because of nervous exhaustion (which in the last decades of his life periodically manifested itself in lengthy bouts of dizziness). He was able to attend more than half of the meetings of the Congress, however, and to meet everybody. Over three hundred attended. He was elected president of the organization to follow G. R. Driver. The Congress would next meet in Oxford in 1959, *Deo volente*. Albright said that his paper—on *bamah*, "high place," which Père de Vaux of the French School in Jerusalem had called "une bombe atomique," would probably appear in the Congress Proceedings; he would have to rewrite it in the next several weeks for the editor of *Vetus Testamentum*, Prof. P. A. H. de Boer of Leiden University. (It was published under the title "The High Place in Ancient Palestine" in 1957 in *Supplements to Vetus Testamentum*.)

In Ankara Albright had suffered a relapse of the nervous exhaustion and—what he said was embarrassing for an old Near Eastern hand like him—diarrhoea that persisted. He hoped to leave on the next Monday to see excavations, and would also give some lectures. Other than that, his duties were exceedingly vague, and that was perfectly fine with him. He planned to return by December 22 or 23.

In the following week he made a five-day trip driving almost 1400 kilometers visiting excavations. He met scholars and learned more about his duties, which still were vague. By then Ruth was in London and would return to Baltimore in ten days. He heard from Tom Lambdin, who then taught in the Oriental Seminary as successor to his chief professor, Frank Blake, that there were more students in the department than ever before in its history.

In mid-October Albright made a great trip to Bogazköy visiting the excavations. He learned much as well as having a change from routine matters. In November he began giving his lectures. He was researching mainly Bronze Age Hittite art chronology, after completing some writing on the same subject for the Iron Age. He found new data for the background of Genesis 14 in the seventeenth century B.C., having quietly held to his early views on that subject for many years. Saga-type literature of Babylonia, as well as Hurrian and Hittite, datable externally, bore directly on chaotic southwest Asia in that century. In addition to learning a great deal himself in Turkey, he stimulated the scholars there, who had been getting discouraged.

Nancy Renn, the first full-time woman student in Albright's department, had arrived a year before and became his first woman part-time secretary. She had stumbled through a passage in Samuel as her entrance examination in Hebrew, "hardly recognizing 'David' under the circumstances," as she recalled. "But another new student, Paul Lapp, read not only the Hebrew Bible without difficulty, but also a Latin one, and read a passage in Arabic and something in German, fluently. I could hardly believe it; I can remember going to some of the students studying in the library, with my amazement.

"Besides there being a 'Lapp' and a 'Renn' in many of Dr. Albright's classes that year, there was also a 'Mr. Gill,' and Dr. Albright was continually confusing the three names. Each time he pointed out that each of them was a one-syllable name ending in a double consonant, and his confusion was illustrating some kind of linguistic principle. Later he was to call this prophetic insight!

"What to call me was somewhat a problem to him, and many times he said he hoped I did not mind his calling me 'Nancy.' Of course I didn't! In fact, he said this made quite a change in his life, because from that time on he started calling all of his students by their first names. Up to that time they had to earn their degree first.

"During that first year as Dr. Albright's student and part-time secretary I learned to type on postcards when an answer would fit on one, never to throw away a piece of paper when the other side could be used, to save any oversized envelope for his reprint 'files,' and to make all typing erasures with a razor blade. I attempted to learn all his idiosyncrasies in letter writing, spelling of names and places totally new to me, my own form of shorthand, and acceptable typing, but my services were never up to a true secretary's level. How I shuddered as he corrected the letters I had written! [He made corrections and changes later even with experienced secretaries, however.] Along with proofreading BASOR and rewriting some of the articles that came in, I learned some valuable editing procedures.

"Probably it happened according to Dr. Albright's greatest fears of what would occur if he accepted women students. Before the first year was up, I, as well as another member of his department, had become sufficiently distracted to make it evident to 'the Old Man.' Our actual courtship was very short, and carried on outside the academic community, but when I had to break the news to Dr. Albright that I was going to get married, I hardly opened my mouth before he said, 'Is it Paul?' I gulped and was glad when his response was satisfaction. In fact, he was so pleased that he returned the next day to say that he and Mrs. Albright did not want us to announce our engagement until they could give a party for the Department in their home. That meant the secret had to be kept about a month, and by the end of the month it was hardly a secret, but it had been fun anyway."

Nancy continued, "Paul and I were married in August, and when we returned to Baltimore in September the Albrights had already left for a half year's sabbatical in Turkey. They allowed us to use their home until we found an apartment of our own. This was the kind of wonderful thing the Albrights did for many of their students through the years."

A revision of *Stone Age* was under way; Noel Freedman read galley proofs and tried to update it according to Albright's later ideas here and there, but found he needed to send the proofs and a long list of queries to Albright in Turkey. In mid-November, his health greatly improved, Albright wrote Noel that he had just learned the galleys had been in the customhouse for two weeks! He declared them of zero value and hoped to get his hands on them before leaving for Istanbul at the end of November. He appreciated Noel's comments and agreed with him, saying he would revise the galleys accordingly as soon as possible, resisting his impulses to change wording in many places. He was in the middle of his lecture series and learning much, accumulating information that would result in short and long papers as soon as he had time to write.

He proofread the Introduction as soon as he got hold of the galleys, but in Istanbul his nervous exhaustion returned and he had to spend frequent days in bed, delaying work on the rest of the galleys.

Another political-intrigue story concerned Albright's 1956 visit to Turkey. As Dr. Sam Iwry related, "At that time the Sinai War was on. England, France and Israel started it to get Nasser for the closing of the Suez Canal. The Israeli army took Sinai, and the situation was very tense. President Eisenhower and his Secretary of State, John Foster Dulles, insisted that the Israelis leave Sinai immediately and go back to their old line of demarcation. One evening President Eisenhower went on radio and TV and talked to the nation—really talking to American Jews, appealing that they persuade the Israelis to abide by what he and others thought was right, and leave the Sinai.

"Little did Eisenhower know that although the Israeli army and Ben-Gurion had already agreed to withdraw, the archaeologists, who were looking for the line of a road followed by the Israelites under Moses through the desert, had not yet finished their explorations! At the last minute in great desperation they sent a telegram to Dr. Albright, knowing that when he was in Israel he had stored up a lot of information about Sinai and the different theories on the route of the Exodus.

"In his absence, the telegram came to me," Iwry continued. "When I received this cable from Israel, I didn't know what to do. When I wrote to him I often wrote myself, but when there were official matters I asked his part-time secretary, a woman graduate student in his department, a doctoral candidate, Nancy Renn Lapp, to write. I told her, 'I can myself tell the Israelis that he is in Turkey and cannot be reached from here, but if they want to reach him they can do it themselves. Please write him a letter about other things too, but especially about this; it is urgent. Here is the cable.'

"The next day I asked her if she had written the letter. She answered, almost in tears, 'No, I didn't have carbon paper.'—Every morning a janitor would go around to the offices and give out one or two sheets of carbon paper. She was out of it and waiting for her next ration of it!

"Well, the Israelis received an airmail letter from me; they immediately got in touch with Albright in Turkey, and then he sent me a telegram telling me where I should look for some maps, charts—somewhere in his office on an upper shelf, covered with a lot of other papers. And in the meantime *the whole world was waiting for the Sinai business to be finished!* The politicians and UN people and President Eisenhower did not know that the real thing that was going on hinged on what Albright would answer the Israelis and how they would get their information about that ancient Exodus route across Sinai that they wanted to find and map before they left! As soon as they could get the information and make clear evidence of it, they would go!" (Undoubtedly this side of the story is not to be found in the Eisenhower archives; the President of the U.S. never knew that Albright's absence in Turkey was holding up the conclusion of the 1956 Sinai war!)

The months in Turkey were a great refreshment and intellectual stimulus to Prof. Albright. Moreover, he learned to use still another language to some degree.

17

Return Visits to the Holy Land

The New York *World-Telegram* and *Sun* of May 4 and the *Times* of May 5, 1953, carried stories of the special Lord and Taylor award given to Dr. Einstein and "the four regular awards of $1000 each [which] went to Dr. William F. Albright, chairman of the oriental seminary of Johns Hopkins University; Edward R. Murrow of the Columbia Broadcasting System; Dr. George S. Stevenson, medical director of the National Association for Mental Health and Dr. Theodore von Karman, chairman of the NATO advisory group for aeronautical research and development." Dr. Einstein was not present, but a photo showed the other four receiving the awards; Dr. Albright wore dark glasses.

That summer Prof. Albright spent a number of weeks teaching at Garrett Biblical Institute at Evanston. On September 5 the Albrights' third granddaughter was born—Joanne, the first child of their son Stephen, who was away in the army in Japan, and Lee, whom he had married on a short leave late in 1952. (Their first two granddaughters were children of Paul and Evelyn.) Ten days later Albright was giving lectures in Wake Forest, North Carolina, but could not visit his sister Mary because she was ill with pneumonia in Durham, where Prof. Stinespring was on the faculty at Duke University Divinity School.

When Albright had returned to Baltimore, he wrote to Elias N. Haddad, in Lebanon at the Johannes Ludwig Schneller School, for the first time in many years. Having heard from him, he expressed sympathy with the misfortunes of the Haddad family. He could see no way to find funds for a new edition of the colloquial Arabic grammar which the two of them had published in 1927. Printers in America received more pay than professors; therefore professors could hardly hire printers! There were plenty of funds to relieve those who were suffering, but none for Arabic grammar books. He told Haddad also that life had been good to him and his family; he now possessed four sons and two daughters-in-law, plus three granddaughters. His oldest son was in the Dominican Republic as branch manager for a pharmaceutical company, his second was a Christian Brother teaching math in a college in Philadelphia, his third was in Japan in the army, and his fourth was about to complete his agriculture course at Cornell. Albright was then sixty-two and enjoyed quite good health, Mrs. Albright had fair health also, and all the others were very well. He said he had not returned to Palestine since 1935. He had visited Egypt and South Arabia several times in 1947 to 1951 but could not in those years go to the Holy Land.

On the very next day after writing this letter, September 19, 1953, a Saturday morning, Prof. and Mrs. Albright flew from New York to Ireland. He was on his way to Israel! The Albrights spent several days as guests in Dublin of Prof. J. Weingreen and his wife. There William received his thirteenth honorary degree, the Litt.D., from Trinity College in the University of Dublin. Then he flew on to Israel while Ruth remained in Ireland.

Dr. Sam Iwry had paved the way for Albright's first visit back to Israel when he made his own first trip earlier in 1953, carrying a copy of a Bar Kokhba letter dating to the Second Revolt, A.D. 132-35. A copy of this Aramaic letter, found in a cave by Bedouins, had been sent to Albright in great secrecy, and he had called Sam in to help him read it and work out the problem of one word. Sam recalled, "We read this Bar Kokhba letter immediately, and I thought it would be a good thing if the Israelis could know about it. The French had it and the Jordanians didn't want the Israelis to know. Later it became clear that it must have come from a cave in Israeli territory. The Bedouins were always walking here and there across the theoretical line in the shifting sands of the desert.

"Albright told me where to go to get a very fine copy made of the letter. Then I told him I was getting ready to fly to Israel. With the help of someone in Baltimore it was possible for me to get my citizenship papers a month or two early, and I flew to Israel in June. I wrote ahead that I was bringing with me the Bar Kokhba letter, and Dr. Benjamin Mazar, president of Hebrew University, came to meet me in the limousine of his brother-in-law, the president of Israel. In the limousine we read this ancient letter—it was beautiful! They agreed immediately that Albright and I had read the difficult word correctly.

"They told me that now they were waiting for Albright to come to Israel. It had been a long time since he had been there and they had so many things to show him, so many excavations. But Albright didn't feel too well, and it wasn't advisable for him to go and stay on all those excavations. They decided that if his doctor would allow him to go, they would provide a doctor in Israel to go everywhere with him. But of course Albright wouldn't like to have a shadow, a doctor constantly with him. It was decided in my presence and after that with his family's knowledge that there would be a doctor, but Albright would not know about him.

"So Albright came to Israel in the latter part of 1953, and they took him around everywhere. They let him rest four hours every day. One time Albright came from some visit and saw that the chauffeur who was always with him was reading a book—*From the Stone Age to Christianity*. Albright asked, 'Where did you get this book?' The man said, 'Well, I knew that I was going to be the driver for Professor Albright, so I thought I had better read some of his writings.' Albright said, 'What a magnificent country! Even a chauffeur can read my book!' Little did he know that this driver was the doctor who accompanied him everywhere! I think I told him once, long afterward. He liked all these stories himself—he would not get mad; he could laugh about it after it was all past."

Josef Aviram of the Hebrew University Institute of Archaeology, secretary of the Israel Exploration Society and on the board of the *Israel Exploration Journal*, recalled that he and his associates had wanted to invite Prof. Albright for a number of years after the founding of the State in 1948. He had been unable to accept any of their invitations until late 1953; "we were glad at that time that Prof. Albright agreed and came here as the honorary guest and lecturer of this convention. We organized, besides the opening lecture in Beersheva, three more public lectures for him in Jerusalem, Tel-Aviv, and Haifa. We also took him on some excursions and trips—to sites in the Negev, and Tell Qasileh and Jaffa, and some sites in the Galilee which were excavated at that time, and Tiberias. It was very exciting for him, but he was sorry—and it was our mistake —that his wife was not with him. He said, 'My next visit I will bring my wife with me and not go by myself.' "

At the congress in Beersheba he gave his lecture in excellent but eccentric Modern Hebrew, to the admiration of the large audience. He was introduced by the prime minister, David Ben-Gurion, who was then sixty-seven, five years older than Albright. Ben-Gurion, the chairman, was a student of the Hebrew Bible and a self-taught scholar; he could not resist this opportunity. He talked at length about the contributions of Judaism to Christianity, and the fact that the idea of "grace" did not originate with Christianity, but was in the word *hesed* already in Judaism and the Old Testament—and he went on, ten, twenty minutes and more, seemingly interminably. The huge audience was impatient to hear Prof. Albright; they became really angry. "It was the first convention of the Israel Exploration Society in Beersheva," Prof. Haim Tadmor recalled, "and it was the first appearance of Albright in such a public." His wife Miriam added, "The people came from everywhere—I think there were three thousand who came from every corner of the country to Beersheva to hear Albright."

When Ben-Gurion finally introduced Albright, the latter arose and said, "Thank you, Mr. Prime Minister," in beautiful Hebrew. "I am," he said, "like that hero of an American legend, Rip Van Winkle. As you well know, Rip Van Winkle was asleep for twenty years, and when he woke up it was in a new world and nobody knew him. I am Rip Van Winkle; I come to this country after nearly eighteen years and I don't recognize it; it's all new, all transformed. I really am Rip Van Winkle. Incidentally, they tell me of a Jewish saying about one who slept for *seventy* years. But this is *much* too much for a *goy!*"

Spoken in fluent Modern Hebrew, the double-entendre delighted the audience. They applauded him for at least five minutes. It was a perfect take-off on Ben-Gurion! Then Albright said, "I don't have too much time at my disposal," and proceeded to give his lecture, stopping at the proper time, so that "instead of speaking fifty minutes, he spoke fifteen or twenty minutes only, because of Ben-Gurion," as Haim Tadmor remembered.

Shemaryahu Talmon, of Hebrew University, recalled that "most of us regretted that Albright's presentation had to be cut

short; I sensed clearly that the people didn't like it at all. But
after the lecture as I talked with him he said, 'I wouldn't have
believed, ever, that to a meeting of an archaeological society at
which I would address the audience, I would have an audience of
over 2000 listeners. This is something unheard of, unimaginable in
any other country of the world!'

"A day or two later," Prof. Talmon continued, "he led a seminar here in Jerusalem. I think that this was organized by Yohanan
Aharoni, and it was a free-for-all, not the type of seminar that we
were used to, but a little more like what other friends tell me about
the way Albright used to go about it at Johns Hopkins. We came
into the room and sat down, and he said, 'Well, in fact, we do not
have a specific topic. Why don't we ask questions?' And then I
think I discovered the full splendor and the scholarly stature of
Albright, because it was a rather variegated group; most of them
were young people who had some share in Near Eastern studies,
linguistic, historical, biblical studies, textual studies, and so forth.
And people started picking the brains of that great man, that great
scholar. I cannot compare him with any other; I have never seen
anybody so alert, so responsive, so full of pertinent knowledge, detailed, exact knowledge on so many diverse points in the study
of the ancient Near East as Albright at that time; it was an experience that those who participated in it will never forget. I have often
said, and I think it is true, that Albright must have been the last
comprehensive scholar; I could not think of anybody who had such
an intense, specialized, authoritative command of so many diverse
fields of study."

The Israeli archaeologists Moshe and Trude Dothan also remembered Ben-Gurion's over-long introduction of Prof. Albright
in Beersheva. After the Congress they and some others with Albright drove in two small Jeeps to see some of the excavation sites.
Albright was tremendously enthusiastic and excited about all the
work going on. President Mazar invited the whole university to
hear Albright's lecture in the large Ratisbonne auditorium, and
Mazar, as Trude related, became concerned because instead of
lecturing on his latest expeditions in South Arabia, Albright spent
a half hour in praise of that wonder-working marvel of an expedi-
tion-organizer, Wendell Phillips! "Mazar was getting frantic, because people didn't come to hear about Wendell Phillips, and he

started to push! Finally Prof. Albright got to the subject and gave a very interesting talk about his experiences in South Arabia."

The Tadmors had begun their studies in Hebrew University under Prof. Mazar (formerly Maisler) in 1943-44, before he became president succeeding Dr. Magnes. Mazar, who had been on Albright's excavations in the early '30's, introduced his students to Albright's books and articles immediately. "Every statement was like a source," said Prof. Tadmor. He had been finishing his Ph.D. in 1953 and was already in correspondence with Albright. For 3000 people to come to hear him in a hall which should hold about 1000 or so "was an unbelievable expression of admiration for Prof. Albright," as he described it.

Haim and Miriam Tadmor and David and Ruth Amiran were in a party that took Albright to see the tumuli at Malhah, where he had excavated a short time in the early '20's and where Ruth Amiran was now continuing. Albright also came to the Tadmor home, "a very modest apartment, and had a cup of tea and we discussed a bit of archaeology and chronology. Albright said, 'I have always wanted to be an Assyriologist but the doctors told me that I had to stop because of my poor eyesight, so I couldn't read cuneiform.' He put Assyriology at the pinnacle of scholarship, and biblical archaeology and other things came a bit lower." The Tadmors recalled that as Albright sat in a chair in their tiny living room, he said, "I'm too tired to speak Hebrew! It's too hot—the *khamsin.*" "Then he was charming, when suddenly he spoke his own language and felt at home," Miriam said. "Hebrew was not his natural language; he pronounced the *ayin* and *het* better than Israelis, and it was a kind of game."

The following year, when the Tadmors were in the U.S., they had an unforgettable visit with Prof. Albright at his home when Mrs. Albright was away. They conversed from mid-morning until lunch-time; then Albright said, "Let's have some lunch," and apologized that Mrs. Albright was not there, "but we'll manage." He led them to the kitchen, where Miriam Tadmor was to take over, and he opened the refrigerator. As she recalled, "In it was some fruit, some kind of dessert, eggs in a bowl, and a large can of ham. He looked in, then looked at us, said 'Oh!' and pushed the can quickly to the rear. He turned to me and said, 'Oh, we have nothing but eggs and fruit, but we'll manage!' He didn't want to offend us—" Her husband broke in, "The ham did not exist!" Miriam continued, "He completely disregarded it, and we made lunch of eggs and fruit, and everything was all right. This natural elegance, his way of coping with the situation, was one of the things that I always remember about him."

After the Albrights returned home in mid-October, 1953, he had to keep lecture engagements, but he wrote one of his students, Jacob J. Enz, that his trip to Israel, while extremely interesting, had so exhausted him that he had been in bed most of the time since returning. He had not been in the land for almost eighteen years and was especially thrilled that he was able to cross for seven hours into the Arab or Old City of Jerusalem and visit Père Vincent and the School. He claimed he was bursting his intellectual seams and had returned loaded down with new impressions and data. He wrote another former student, Victor Gold, that their trips to Ireland and Israel were extremely interesting but also very tiring, and mentioned as the highlight his opportunity to examine Frank Cross's material with him at the Palestine Archaeological Museum the day he was on the other side. He wrote similarly to Noel Freedman and another former student, George Mendenhall. He called his time in Israel a pressure cooker for three weeks, and mentioned losing five nights of sleep on plane flights.

Stories in Jewish newspapers in New York and Philadelphia reported his return "from Israel, where he delivered a series of lectures at the Hebrew University of Jerusalem and gave public lectures under municipal, governmental and organizational auspices. Dr. Albright, a non-Jew, delivered his talks in fluent Hebrew. The eminent scholar, who had last visited Palestine in 1935, reported 'remarkable progress,' particularly in the integration of widely diverse ethnic elements into the Jewish State. . . ."

Albright had to spend most of the month of January, 1954, in bed with dizziness and weakness, aside from attending classes and dictating a few letters. Constant vertigo continued, with inability to focus his vision, so that he canceled almost all engagements through the early spring. However, on March 23 he received a scroll from the Israel Institute at the Jewish Theological Seminary in New York, being cited for the "great contributions he has made to knowledge of the Holy Land and for his deep understanding of the purpose of the state of Israel and of its role in the historical process."

Another honor came the weekend of June 20-22 in Atlantic City, when Dr. Albright received a citation as "Man of the Year" from the Independent Order of Brith Sholom, conferred "for Dr. Albright's distinction as a world authority on ancient Palestine and Semitic languages," as the Baltimore *Sun* announced on June 17.

Sorrow had come in early March, with news of the tragic death in Iraq of his former student Roger T. O'Callaghan, S.J., in an auto accident. Albright later told Ernest Wright, "One thing I will never get over: the death of Roger O'Callaghan." Wright commented, "He thought of the great future that had been before O'Callaghan, who had been teaching for some years in Rome."

The New York *Times* for June 12, 1954, hailed an Israeli exhibit: "Fifteen hundred persons attending a preview last night of the 'From the land of the Bible' exhibition at the Metropolitan Museum of Art heard the collection described as 'a vivid illustration of the fact that the Bible is a living human document as well as Divine revelation.' The speaker, William F. Albright, Professor of Semitic Languages at Johns Hopkins University, was one of several to address the first New Yorkers to see the Holy Land antiquities of many ages that Israeli collections had sent here for a year's tour...."

An Israeli archaeologist, Prof. Shmuel Yeivin, who had known Albright in the '30's in Palestine and who was Director of the Department of Antiquities in the '50's, also spoke at the opening of the Land of the Bible exhibit, and with Albright and others attended the dinner given beforehand. He recalled later that, as Albright wrote him in his last letter, "we usually mostly disagreed; but I'm sure we learned from each other." (They disagreed over what Albright interpreted as a gate at Tell Beit Mirsim, which Yeivin was certain could not be a gate; over chronological correspondences between Mari and Egypt, and other chronological matters. Yeivin said, "We agreed on one thing—that the Chronicles has a lot of really helpful, good, correct historical material, in spite of its being late," though Yeivin thought Albright made a mistake of ten years by taking as the real truth the data in Chronicles where

Yeivin considered that a scribe had made a ten-year mistake.) Yeivin said of Albright, "He was a very good speaker; he was very clear and logical. You could see that the man knew what he was talking about."

In spite of nervous exhaustion lasting almost a year, Albright continued to keep some lecture engagements, giving twenty lectures in a nine-day trip to the universities of Iowa and Kentucky in early December, 1954. He managed to attend the year-end meetings and enjoyed especially the papers by Noel Freedman and Frank Cross. These made the SBL meetings far and away the most interesting he had ever attended, he wrote. His poor health made it necessary to withdraw, regretfully, from the Tenth International Congress of the Historical Sciences in Rome, where he had planned to present a paper. By April, 1955, he was able to give a lecture, "Archaeology in Israel," in the series of Israeli lectures at Columbia University.

Albright was in the hospital for almost a week at the beginning of July, with comforting outcome, as he wrote Noel, but he would have to plan for a vacation. He and Ruth spent a refreshing fortnight at the inn at Little Switzerland at 3,500 feet elevation in the Blue Ridge mountains of North Carolina, where he enjoyed long walks.

At the SBL meetings in late December, 1955, there was again a battle royal on the subject of the Dead Sea Scrolls. The New York *Times* reported that they were discussed in a paper by Frank Cross, Jr., and Dr. Albright, who said that "the scrolls had provided a 'wealth of evidence' as to meanings and usages of Hebrew words that might require a retranslation of parts of the Bible."

On his sixty-fifth birthday Albright gave a lecture stating: "Two —possibly more—newly discovered Dead Sea Scrolls have been stolen by Arabs and are being held for ransom," as reported on May 25, 1956 in the Washington *Post Times-Herald*. "Dr. William F. Albright, . . . said in a lecture that the discovery of these scrolls had not been previously announced. . . . The recently found sheepskin scrolls were stealthily removed from under the noses of their guards by Bedouins—nomadic desert Arabs—Albright said. . . ." The next day the Baltimore *Sun* carried an Amman, Jordan story about them: "The discovery of at least two new Dead Sea scrolls, first reported in Baltimore Wednesday by Prof. William F. Albright, of the Johns Hopkins University, today was confirmed by G. Lankester Harding, director of antiquities for the Government of Jordan. They are now in the Palestine Archaeological Museum in Arab Jerusalem, Harding said, and under study by the same scholars who have been working on the whole group of 2,000-year-old documents, the first of which were accidentally discovered by Bedouins (desert nomads) in 1947. . . . The new scrolls were being held by the Bedouins for sale at high prices, Dr. Albright was informed. Harding declined to say who found the new scrolls or how they came into the possession of the Jerusalem Museum. He also refused to discuss their number and contents. . . ."

In the spring after Prof. Albright had spent the autumn in Turkey on the Cultural Exchange program, he was supposed to fly to Israel for a convocation at which he was to receive an honorary degree from the Hebrew University. The Sinai War had disrupted travel, however. When he wrote to Freedman on March 11, 1957, his plans were still uncertain—he should leave for Israel on March 24 and return April 9. But when he phoned the Israel Embassy to find out whether civilians could visit Israel, and whether Jacob Blaustein and Maryland Governor McKeldin, who were scheduled to receive honorary degrees along with him on April 5 at Hebrew University, were able to make plans to go or whether perhaps the convocation was being postponed, he learned that the State Department's ban on travel continued. His trip was still up in the air on March 16: he had managed in Washington the previous Thursday to get permission to go, but then found difficulty with his reservations on the Rome-Jerusalem leg of the journey on El Al.

The New York *Journal-American* of April 6 headlined, "Degree Given To Ben-Gurion," with a Jerusalem dateline story: "The Hebrew University in Jerusalem yesterday awarded an honorary doctorate of philosophy to Prime Minister David Ben-Gurion for 'the exemplary devotion' with which he has served his people.

"Among other awards made in ceremonies at the university's new campus at Givat Ram [on a hill just west of Jerusalem] was an honorary degree to Prof. William F. Albright, . . ." It was Albright's fifteenth honorary degree. (The fourteenth, in 1954, had been an

LL.D. from Franklin and Marshall College, and the sixteenth would be awarded soon after his return from Israel by Pace College, a D.C.L.)

After receiving the honorary degree, Prof. Albright was taken by several Israeli archaeologists to see the excavations in progress at Hazor, conducted by Yigael Yadin. Trude Dothan remembered, "It was a terribly rainy day and it was really hard to walk on the ruins—it was very slippery. But Albright was so eager to see everything. Yigael Yadin was waiting, I think, to have an argument on the whole problem of the Conquest of Hazor, but we all had a very interesting talk. We were very excited about his coming."

Prof. Yadin had criticized Albright's view, "which was a popular view at the time, that the *glacis* and the huge enclosures were Hyksos, or rather Middle Bronze II B or C phases, in which I think he was right, but he ascribed that to the alleged fact that the Hyksos had chariots and horses, and he thought that the *glacis* were connected with chariotry. My main point was that you do not attack a city with a chariot and in any case the *glacis* had nothing to do with that. Now that was in a way contrary to a basic approach of his, but eventually I think he accepted this particular aspect of it. When fresh data was revealed or proposed, he was the first to say, 'Well, I now change my view.' I was always full of admiration at how promptly he answered queries or reacted to articles in very detailed articles of his own. I considered myself always a pupil of his although I never properly attended his courses," Yadin concluded.

As Albright wrote Freedman on April 20, 1957, he had been stuffed for nine days with all kinds of research and archaeological discoveries, until he practically had mental indigestion. In Rome he had heard a lecture on the way back, by Prof. Cullmann; in Paris he had lost a night's sleep and hadn't yet recovered from the resulting exhaustion.

By the time the Albrights returned to Israel again, he would be Emeritus Professor and unofficial Dean of Biblical Archaeologists.

18

High Tide

It is said that one of the main motivations and endeavors of a human being is to "structure time." William Albright did a good job of structuring his. Besides his earliest memberships in learned societies, already in 1930 he had become a member of the American Council of Learned Societies, of which he was elected Vice-chairman early in 1939. He had long been a member of the Linguistic Society of America and in 1941 was Vice-president; from 1936 on he was not only a member, but was on the Research Committee, of the American Philosophical Society, of which he became Vice-president in 1955-56. In 1935-36 he served as President of the American Oriental Society, which he had joined while still a doctoral student at Hopkins. In 1939 he was President of the Society of Biblical Literature. In the American Schools of Oriental Research he was for a long time a member of the Jerusalem School Committee, and a member from 1936 on of the Board of Trustees; in 1938 he became Vice-president.

In 1945 Albright became an Honorary Life Member of the Catholic Biblical Association of America and a member of the Committee on Revision of the American Standard Old Testament. By the middle 1940's he had become an honorary member of the Glasgow Oriental Society, the Société Asiatique in Paris, the Society for Old Testament Study in Great Britain, and a few years later foreign member of the Royal Danish and Royal Flemish Academies of Science and corresponding member of the Académie des Inscriptions et Belles Lettres (Institut de France) and of the Finnish Oriental Society. He served a two-year term as member of the Executive Committee of the Archaeological Institute of

America, and became Vice-president of that organization and of
the Asia Institute in 1948-49. In the early 1950's he became a member of the Honorary Committee, International Congress of Orientalists, Istanbul; a Socius Ordinarius of the German Archaeological
Institute; Honorary Member of the Royal Irish Academy; and corresponding member of the Austrian Academy of Sciences and of
the School of Oriental and African Studies, University of London.
For three years in the late '50's he was President of the International Organization of Old Testament Scholars; he also was Vice-
president of the Leeds University Oriental Society, and Honorary
Correspondent, Department of Archaeology, India.

Early in 1939 Albright wrote his father that it was an alarming
number of offices he now held in national organizations, but he had
started to turn down requests and expected to reduce the number.
Obviously he was not very successful in doing so.

His Presidential address in the 1939 meeting of the Society of
Biblical Literature, published the next year in JBL, titled "The
Ancient Near East and the Religion of Israel," was an extremely
important statement, even including his credo. He described himself as "a resolute 'positivist'—but *only in so far as positivism is the
expression of the modern rational-scientific approach to physical
and historical reality,*" and said he would not so label himself at all if
it were not that the Nazis rejected "the rational-empirical approach
to reality, calling it 'positivism.' " He said that in a sense he was even
an instrumentalist, but was opposed completely to John Dewey and
his school in their metaphysical system. He was an evolutionist in
an organismic sense, not in a mechanical or melioristic one. He
considered the most reasonable philosophy of history to be evolutionary and organismic, rather than unilateral progress, and restricted his task "as far as possible to historical description and
interpretation, leaving the higher but less rigorous forms of interpretation to others."[1]

He described his classification of mental operations, which he
adapted from the late Lévy-Bruhl, later only changing the latter's
"prelogical" thought to his own term, "proto-logical" thought,
which included most ancient mythology. Above that he placed
"empirico-logical" thought based on observation and deduction
from experience, though usually below the level of consciousness.
Most early inventions and discoveries were made in this stage which

was largely operating at the same time as the pre-(or proto-)logical stage—and both methods continue in use today, the prelogical especially among children, primitive peoples, and a surprising number of adults, especially the less educated. Logical reasoning developed in Greece in the sixth century B.C. and is used today, of course, but not at all exclusively.[2]

This major treatment of his philosophy influenced and appeared in many of Albright's works in the following decades.

Who's Who in America began listing "Albright, William Foxwell, orientalist," in the edition of 1930-31. In the mid-'50's it condensed the ever-lengthening write-up and grouped his honorary degrees by type instead of listing them in chronological order. In the 1950's he was included in the British *Who's Who* and the *International Who's Who*.

The membership that surprised and pleased him the most was his election in 1955 to the National Academy of Sciences. A few years later he mentioned it in a parenthetical aside as he expressed dissatisfaction with the appearance of politics in meetings of learned societies and behind the scenes in their affairs. His faith in the basic idealism of American intellectuals had been best preserved by his association in the American Philosophical Society with well-known natural scientists, and he remarked that because of friendships he had there developed, what was doubtless the greatest single surprise of his life had come about in 1955 when he was elected as a member of the National Academy of Sciences. He deplored the fact that nowadays young natural scientists seem more interested in position and salary than in finding truth or serving humanity's welfare. They now tended to be professionals rather than thinkers (and to Albright the word "professional" did not have a positive connotation).

These are the mature views of the young man who chose scholarship, even if it meant living in an attic.

The only other specialist in the ancient history and archaeology of the Old World who held membership in the National Academy of Sciences had been Prof. James Henry Breasted, until his death in 1935.

In addition to his teaching and work in connection with these various organizations, Prof. Albright gave the Richards lectures at the University of Virginia in 1931, the Carew Lectures at Hartford

Seminary Foundation in 1932, the Ayer Lectures at Colgate-Rochester Theological Seminary in 1941, the Strook Lectures at the Jewish Institute of Religion in 1942, the Haskell Lectures in Oberlin Graduate School of Theology in 1943, was Visiting Professor of Ancient Oriental History in 1946 at the Oriental Institute, University of Chicago, gave the Lowell Institute Lectures at King's Chapel, Boston, and the Stone Lectures at Princeton Theological Seminary, both in 1948, the Sprunt Lectures at Union Theological Seminary, Richmond, in 1949, the Messenger Lectures at Cornell University in 1951, and the Elliot Lectures at Western Seminary in 1956, aside from innumerable lectures to all kinds of audiences in between these special series.

By the 1950's Albright undoubtedly deserved every attack of nervous exhaustion that came, yet he continued his amazing output and accomplishment, while constantly promising himself to cut down on extras and refuse most invitations.

When he wrote to Noel Freedman on June 5, 1957, Albright was finally through with routine examinations, though he was still teaching two classes a week for students who were somewhat cheated by his long and frequent absences that school year (he had spent the autumn in Turkey and flown to Israel in March-April for his honorary degree at Hebrew University). It was apparent that there would be a flood of M.A. and Ph.D. candidates the next year, his last, so he would not take more than the lecture engagements to which he was already committed. As for the invitation to spend the first semester of the 1959-60 year at Noel's school, Western Theological Seminary in Pittsburgh, Ruth had advised him to accept, and he said he habitually took her advice, since it was up to her to decide whether or not to keep their home in Baltimore. He did not want to be where he could not carry on his research, but much of it could be done with such library facilities as he would find in Pittsburgh, so he accepted in principle for the term Noel expected to be on sabbatical leave, excavating in Israel.

Albright knew that Ernest Wright was editing a *Festschrift* for his seventieth birthday, and feared that his voluminous bibliography, to be included (already containing more than 860 items), would have to be subsidized at Doubleday. Noel replied that they were well briefed and "definitely committed" to publish the book

Ernest was editing, for which he already had the articles or firm promises of them by that October; "the volume should be ready for the printer by December. It promises to be a very representative group in all respects. I think it is indicative of Doubleday's regard for you that a hardheaded commercial company is willing to go out on a limb for a technical volume of this kind. I think also that they will be very surprised when this venture proves to involve no loss for them."

Albright and his wife drove to North Carolina for three weeks in late July and August, vacationing again at the inn at Little Switzerland in the Blue Ridge. Albright did a great deal of walking in the mountains, as two years before, but took along a typewriter, paper and books so that, as he wrote to Noel, it would not be entirely a vacation or become too boring.

Late in August 1957 Prof. Albright flew to Munich for two weeks to attend a scholarly congress. After his return Noel finalized plans for Albright to make a series of five TV interview programs in Pittsburgh. Noel had learned that the fee or honorarium would be at least $200 for each of the five. "I spoke to Dr. Albright about it," he recalled later, "mentioning only the programs and the plans, and the intention of preserving him on video tape for future generations. As I expected, he was very polite and completely uninterested and declined with thanks. Then I gradually got around to the two major points. One was that it would take only a weekend to do it all, and the second was that he would realize at least $1000 from the effort. As soon as he heard the magic number his defenses collapsed and he agreed forthwith, as I had known all along he would.

"The series proceeded without difficulty and came out quite well. Separate interviews were devoted to his general views about the Bible, then specific contributions that archaeology makes to the subject, the Dead Sea Scrolls and a couple of other subjects, one on the New Testament—the Gospel of John—and another on the Old Testament. Frank Cross came by plane, got deathly ill because of the turbulent weather, and could hardly make a contribution during the first two sessions." The Freedmans stuffed Frank with medicine to get him on his feet in time for the filming. "Aside from Cross's having his way paid, none of the rest of us received anything for our part in the series. So far as I am aware, Dr. Albright collected his share; he assured me the money was not really for himself but to pay for much-needed secretarial and technical assistance."

After producing the programs on a weekend and then attending his meetings in Philadelphia early in November, Albright had to stay in bed as much as possible to recuperate. He wrote thanking Noel and Neil for their hospitality and said he had received a generous check for his TV filming weekend. He had been greatly pleased at the opportunity to visit at length with Noel and Frank, and appreciated the fine support given by Paul Ward (of Carnegie Museum) and Bill Orr (of Noel's seminary) as the interviews were filmed.

The Oriental Seminary that fall had its largest enrollment—about 45 full- and half-time students plus others taking only a class or two in Albright's last year of teaching at Hopkins. Paul and Nancy Lapp were both Fellows in the School in Jerusalem, where Prof. Ovid Sellers served as Professor of Archaeology.

Ted Campbell was in his second year, and as a Fellow taught the beginning class in Accadian, in which Leona Running was one of the dozen students. Ted felt he had taught everything he knew in the first three weeks, as he expressed it later, but he really did a fine job and was always willing to check questions with Dr. Tom Lambdin, who was the other full-time teacher besides Prof. Albright.

In Albright's lectures on history and archaeology that fall, no matter what he mentioned in the ancient Near East, Leona Running felt excited, because that summer in Dr. Siegfried Horn's study tour of the Bible Lands she had *been* there; she had *seen* that! One day Albright paused in his lecturing, sitting at the head of the long table surrounded by writing-arm chairs, with the same kind of chairs lining the walls for that year's large enrollment. Albright asked a question for anybody's response: How deep is Jacob's Well near Shechem? Various students were answering "Thirty feet" and "Thirty-five feet," and Albright sat there, arms folded as usual, shaking his head. Leona was frantically trying to remember what had happened while her tour group stood around Jacob's Well the day they visited Ernest Wright's excavations at Shechem, in which Ted Campbell and Red Sinclair and Bob Boling, among that year's student group, had participated. Several of the tour members, some of whom were her Greek and Hebrew students, had tied a big key to a long rope and let it drop from the top of the well, counting the seconds with a stop-watch until they heard the splash at the bottom. She raised her hand timidly and Albright motioned to her; "Seventy-five feet?" "Right!" Professor Albright exclaimed, and Leona had a glowing feeling of having attained her first tiny success in his department. Water from that deep well had remained cold in her thermos overnight, on the trip.

But when it came to Albright's section of Hebrew Rapid Reading, that was another matter. Leona had already taught several classes of Hebrew beginners in her school and was not bad on verb forms, reading and translating, but when Albright would ask, "How would Moses' grandfather have pronounced that?" her brain froze. She was worse off than Noel Freedman had been twelve years earlier when he said he had not come late, he had come a *year* late. Leona came into Tom Lambdin's three-year cycle lectures in Hebrew Historical Grammar and Comparative Semitic Grammar *two* years late, not getting the basic Hebrew Phonology she needed until her third year, Albright's second "retirement" year. And Prof. Albright never explained what the Hebrew phonetic changes were so that one could work through them backward and figure out how Moses' grandfather would have pronounced the word!

Prof. Albright was struggling late that fall with a condition of the gall bladder; it meant following a strict diet and losing weight painlessly. He wrote Noel that he had to cut out all fat and lived mainly on prunes and whole-wheat toast.

Instead of attending the SBL meetings, which that year were in Louisville, Kentucky, Prof. Albright gave the main address at the joint convention of the American Philological Association and the Archaeological Institute of America in the Hotel Statler in Washington. The Washington *Star* of December 30 reported that "a leading archaeologist hailed modern Israel as the most fertile field for unearthing ancient civilizations," and quoted Albright as saying, "There is more attention paid to archaeology there, in proportion to the size of the country, than anywhere else in the modern world." He stated that Jordan "is very active archaeologically, thanks to the courage of young King Hussein." "He said Lebanon 'has been exposed to' European archaeologists, but added, 'In Syria, little has been done. . . .'"

Prof. Albright was picked up at his home early on the morning of January 28, 1958, by his former student, Dr. Siegfried Horn, and taken to the Seventh-day Adventist Theological Seminary, then in Takoma Park, to give a chapel talk. Other students of his on the faculty were Alger Johns and Leona Running. His talk was typical of his speeches to similar audiences in this period. It concerned recent discoveries in Israel and the Dead Sea Scrolls, especially their implications for New Testament studies. He said the Dead Sea Scrolls had caught the imagination of the world as never before—even Buddhist and Moslem groups—but that distorted interpretations of them were current. Their dates were between 200 B.C. (or earlier) and A.D. 68, the final destruction of the Essene community at Qumran and the sealing of the caves (by now he had no hesitancy in identifying the Qumran sectarians as Essenes). Thanks to nuclear physics and Dr. Libby of the University of Chicago, who discovered radio-carbon dating, these dates were established. Three laboratories, at Chicago, Carnegie Institute in Pittsburgh, and the Royal Institute of Archaeology in London, had worked with flax cloth from Cave 1. The earliest date for tearing the flax from the ground was about 100 B.C., down to A.D. 50, which well covers the period of 99 percent of the copying of all the documents found in the Qumran area (not those found in caves farther south, which from Wadi Murabba'at dated as late as A.D. 135). Prof. Zeitlin of Dropsie College had claimed a date for them of the fifteenth century A.D.! Everyone was pushing the dates back—even Zeitlin had now gone to about 500-800 A.D., which for him was a tremendous step backward. For the rest of the scholars it was a tremendous step forward! One cannot reject the evidence; coins are certain, in narrow limits. Albright said his students then in Jerusalem were making a concordance of Aramaic texts from Cave 4. "The new material is revolutionizing our understanding of the New Testament background," Prof. Albright said, using one of his favorite verbs, "and making it easier to understand better even quotations from the Old Testament. We now see they were taken from recensions that were lost and now have been recovered. Archaeology has never been as active as now. The tempo of discovery is accelerating—anything written on the subject becomes out of date soon."

February 12 was not one of Albright's best days in class; he was having dizzy spells again, as he explained so that his students would have some comprehension if he had to leave class. Leona Running sat in one of the writing-arm chairs along the wall and took notes diligently as usual. In fact, one time Albright—who in this last year was even more rambling than before in his class lectures, talking about anything that entered his head—looked over at her and said, "Don't take notes on what I am saying now! If you take notes on everything I say, you will have chaos!" And chaos was exactly what she was getting in her notebooks, but what incredibly stimulating, creative chaos!

On that February day she took notes in the class on History of the Second Millennium B.C. Albright said the students should have a map of Anatolia in their minds, and he described it as nearly the size of Texas, comparable to France and Spain; the weather was cold in winter—the ancient Hittites went into winter quarters and hibernated, snowbound, as people still do today in that area. They wore fur-lined boots with turned-up toes in Hittite times, and the peasants still do, to keep from tripping in the snow.

Albright turned aside to say, "Snow is the most extraordinary thing!" He remembered his first snowfall—when he was on furlough as a child of five in 1896 in Iowa. Where he lived, Antofagasta, Chile, there was no rainfall, much less snow; it was dry and dusty. He said he had experienced a duststorm in Ankara while in Turkey a little over a year before. When darkness enveloped Mursilis' armies, it was not the solar eclipse of 1335 B.C.—dust had the same effect. When the steppes were plowed up, the wind removed surface soil. There were tremendous deposits of loess as the result of prehistoric dust storms and dust bowls; the formations build up fast. Albright was skeptical—in 1958!—about colonizing the moon. The necessary miracles would be vastly greater than those of Genesis concerning the Flood!

He remarked that Asia Minor was a bleak but interesting region. Until two or three years before he would have said the earliest occupation sites were not before the fourth millennium. He had a different attitude in 1958—a new major phase had been discovered; pre-pottery Neolithic, he said, was his latest hobby, after Ugaritic and the Dead Sea Scrolls! Archaeology was only beginning in Asia Minor. Some classical sites had been dug in the 19th century and before World War I—Ephesus, Sardis, etc. Troy was excavated in 1887—a historic year for archaeology—the new idea was stratification. Schliemann didn't understand it well, but he understood that there were buildings on top of buildings. Professional archaeologists decades later were still convinced that Troy was a gigantic cemetery, not a mound of successive occupation. "Nobody is infallible!" Albright exclaimed. If the teacher is disconcerted, it gives the habit to his pupils! There are severe limits, though, to certainty—definite rules and principles in philology and archaeology that can't be upset.

At that point in the lecture Prof. Albright became silent and fidgety; he turned red and was obviously embarrassed. After a few mutterings he came out with it; he had just realized, at the end of the lecture, that today he had given next week's lecture on archaeology instead of the scheduled ancient history lecture! On the preceding day he had correctly lectured on archaeology, and had remained in the same train of thought for this day—and in both classes at that time he was speaking of Asia Minor. Leona Running had been so busy taking notes, with such similar subject matter in the two courses, that she had not noticed the mistake at all until Albright became embarrassed and confessed what he had done.

One time when the Albrights were talking together early in their marriage, Ruth asked William what his field really was, and he answered, "Bible lands." In explanation he said, and later included a similarly-worded statement in a publication, "They are bounded on the east by the Indus River, on the west by the Pillars of Hercules [Gibraltar, near which Phoenician remains were found on the Guadalquivir River], on the north by a line through southern Russia, which takes in the entire classical world, and on the south by Ethiopia, with special emphasis on the Fertile Crescent." He knew the archaeology, the anthropology, the languages, dialects and history, and the art and artifacts of all those countries.

With about fourteen dissertations in process, Albright was exceedingly busy in the spring of 1958, though he foresaw that about half would continue into the following fall. Still he had many oral examinations to give that spring. At the end of May he wrote Noel Freedman that Jim Irvine, who had been hired as librarian at Noel's school, had passed his orals unanimously the preceding day, and another student had done so on Monday. Now all the current candidates had passed (though he had been worried about some of them). He was relieved that he had gotten through the last of the

orals without a collapse, and looked forward to spending July with
Ruth in North Carolina again. He was sorry Noel could not be
present on June 4 for his farewell party—the plan had been given
away to him a week or two before, since they had to be sure he
would be present on that date. He had heard that some of the
committee planning it entertained great ideas of inviting Bishop
Oxnam, or the Mayor of Baltimore, or even the Governor of Maryland and other greats! They had fortunately been voted down; he
would be happier with a simpler affair.

The Albrights held open-house for the students in the department on May 3 and 11 from four to six P.M. Leona, already driving
forty miles each way twice a week for classes, was not able to attend
either time, much to her regret later when she was better acquainted with the Albrights. Neither could she attend the famous
farewell dinner. Dr. Samuel Rosenblatt and Chester L. Wickwire
(University Chaplain) sent a mimeographed letter on May 16 to
all the students in the department and Albright's far-flung circle
of former students and friends, inviting them to the farewell
banquet in Levering Hall.

On the day following it, the *Evening Sun* of June 5 carried a
story headed "Hopkins Bible scholar retires; Albright's Fans Not
'LOAFers.'" The story explained: "Since Dr. William Foxwell Albright's research has made him one of the world's greatest Biblical
and theological scholars, one of his admirers declined to form a
'Loyal Order of Albright Fans' on the occasion of Dr. Albright's
retirement last night. Dr. Albright, chairman of the Oriental Seminary at the Johns Hopkins University, is a tireless worker; hence,
said Dr. Louis Kraus, a Hopkins physician, the initials of 'Loyal
Order of Albright Fans' would be most inappropriate.

"Even if they declined the title of L.O.A.F.'ers, Dr. Albright's
fans turned out in large numbers, and those who couldn't sent telegrams, cables and letters extending warm wishes for the future.

"Dr. John Bright of Union Theological Seminary said Dr. Albright had enhanced 'the intellectual tone of theological teaching
in the United States.' 'Thousands and thousands who have never
heard of the Oriental Seminary are in its debt,' he said.

"Others who paid tribute to Dr. Albright were Dr. Samuel
Rosenblatt, a colleague; P. Stewart Macaulay, provost of the University, and Dr. Milton S. Eisenhower, the university president,

who had to cancel his personal appearance at the dinner. Mr. Macaulay read Dr. Eisenhower's tribute to Dr. Albright.

"Dr. Albright, whose research threw much light on the Dead Sea Scrolls, even received congratulations from the Sultan of Oman." (Wendell Phillips doubtless had something to do with that.)

Years later the small group of Albright students who were telling tales of their beloved teacher spoke of that occasion. Frank Cross said: "I think at this point we should tell the story of Albright's retirement party at Hopkins."

FREEDMAN: "I wasn't there. You tell it."

CROSS: "There were speeches, and Rosenblatt was the main speaker. He gave the most flowery address that I have ever heard, and most of it was accurate; he described Albright accurately, but it was in the grand manner. And here Rosenblatt as Rabbi became clear, and his power in the pulpit became clear to me—something I had never before known existed."

CAMPBELL: "When Albright retired in '58, it was Moshe Held who went into his office to bid him farewell from us all—this was after all the other folderol had gone on. Moshe had prepared a literary piece in Accadian, and presented this to Dr. Albright verbally—and made two mistakes in the vocalization of it! And he came out absolutely deflated!"

CROSS: "Albright corrected him!"

FREEDMAN: "Do you remember, one of Frank Blake's articles was on the Siloam Inscription, at the very end of which he translated it into Accadian. They were still playing those games; incredible!"

Another *Sun* story of June 5 concerned the farewell dinner and explained further about the program. "A Johns Hopkins Hospital physician last night conducted a two-hour 'clinical examination' and analysis of Dr. William Foxwell Albright, retiring chairman of the Oriental Seminary of the Hopkins, and reached the conclusion that his 42-year teaching career has left him unimpaired in scholarship and liver.

"The prognosis for Dr. Albright was excellent, Dr. Louis Kraus assured an audience of about 126 of the distinguished Orientalist's admirers who attended a farewell dinner in his honor on the Homewood campus. His retirement was lamented; but the occasion was anything but gloomy.

"Speeches, a citation, cables, telegrams and letters of eulogy, congratulations and best wishes for the future bore testimony to the influence that Dr. Albright has exerted and is expected to continue to exert, . . .

"There were some intimate impressions of Dr. Albright as he had been observed by students and colleagues. 'Have you ever seen him lap up water from the Euphrates in the palm of his hand?' Dr. Kraus asked rhetorically, suggesting that Dr. Albright really got into the spirit of the ancient places dug up by his archaeological expeditions. . . .

"Mrs. Albright, referring to a recent editorial article on Dr. Albright in *The Sun,* said: 'It's very nice to be able to read your own obit. But an evening like this gives much more satisfaction than reading of the obituaries would be. . . . It's nice to get this kind of thing while both of us are alive.' "

Writing to Prof. Albright from his island summer home, Noel Freedman said, "I made one desperate effort to make connections to Baltimore for the party on the 4th, but pressures in Pittsburgh prevented me from following through, . . . Felicitations from both of us on the party in your honor. You know how we feel." Reminding Albright of some publication deadlines, Noel added, "But I really don't have the heart to pressure you. And I'm rather overwhelmed with things to do also. . . . I won't notice if you take a couple more weeks to recuperate. I hope you do."

The *Sunday Sun* of May 25, the day after Albright's sixty-seventh birthday, carried a rather long story by Patrick Skene Catling headlined "Dr. Albright Retiring 'To Work,' " with a captivating photo of him sitting, speaking and smiling as he reached for a book from a lower bookshelf. "At the end of his Hopkins teaching career, Dr. Albright is tired of lecturing to students but not weary of scholarly labor. He has a crippled left hand, his spine is partly fused and he is acutely short-sighted, but his heart is sound, he believes, and he gives an impression of great vigor and alertness.

" 'I want to spend the rest of my life working my head off,' he said.

"His first major project will be to write the first volume of a series of books by many authors on the Jewish religion. Dr. Albright's part of the series, which is to be edited by Dr. Louis Finkelstein, chancellor of the Jewish Theological Seminary in New York, will be on the religion of ancient Israel.

"He expects to give occasional lectures, to write articles and possibly to serve as an adviser to future archaeological expeditions to countries within his broad area of special knowledge. His wife will accompany him on most of his travels; . . ."

When Noel's letter reached him at Little Switzerland in North Carolina, Albright was indeed recuperating, gathering strength so that he could "work his head off."

19

Dean of Biblical Archaeologists

It was not surprising that while the Albrights were at Little Switzerland for a good rest, Prof. Albright suffered nervous exhaustion. A card he sent to Noel on July 14, 1958, mentioned continued vertigo as well as liver trouble; he feared he would not be able to accomplish much that month. However, he read and returned proofs to Noel's office with a note saying that his being in quite bad shape was a result of nervous strain he had not fully realized; the vacation was more essential than he supposed.

Early in August Albright went to New York and arranged for his next year's work at the Jewish Theological Seminary. He would not need to move there until mid-October after the Jewish holidays; his seminar was scheduled for alternate Wednesday evenings and he looked forward to having research assistance to facilitate progress on the volume on the history of the religion of Israel which he would begin writing for Chancellor Louis Finkelstein's series.

In the middle of September his health, as he wrote to Noel, was definitely better, but a week later he admitted inability to terminate the nervous exhaustion. He anticipated his worst year yet, even worse than the last one, which he called a humdinger. However, he lectured at St. Bonaventure, south of Buffalo, and spent nine days attending meetings and lecturing at the University of North Carolina, enduring the traveling and work better than he had anticipated.

Emunah Finkelstein, daughter of the Chancellor, became Albright's research assistant and secretary for that year. In Jerusalem years later, married to Dr. Katzenstein, she recalled working with Prof. Albright, whom she had only met at SBL meetings. "On the first day of work," she remembered, "I was thinking how silly it was to call me 'Miss Finkelstein' when I worked for him. He came in and said, 'You know, I can't—there's no point in calling you 'Miss Finkelstein,' so I shall call you something else." When she responded that most people around the institution called her "Moo," Albright said, "You're too old to be called 'Moo.' I shall call you 'Emunah.'" As she said, "He just laid down the law; that was it!" Having studied shorthand as well as taken graduate work in biblical studies, Emunah was a great help. As he did with his students, Albright encouraged her to publish on her own. In checking words for a study of his she found a possible haplography in 1 Samuel 20:23. Albright was delighted with her discovery and the improved reading the correction gave, and had her write it up. When she brought to him her carefully typed final copy, on hastily looking through it Prof. Albright, with his very poor eyesight, lighted on the one misspelled word in the whole paper! (He habitually did this in opening new books or journals, also.)

"Albright said the article was fine, and 'We'll send it to the *Journal of Semitic Studies* in London, and I will write a covering letter. He was excessively generous, lavishing praise particularly for somebody who was relatively unknown. As I took down his letter I objected to something along this line and said, 'Prof. Albright, stop! I won't write this!' He said, *'I'm dictating this letter; you're typing it; write!'* So I wrote! When he didn't want any argument, there was none!"

Emunah recalled how careful he was about things during the eight months he was there. "For example, he used to wear a skull cap or black hat in the seminary [like the Jewish teachers and students, all men]. He was also careful to use c.e. or b.c.e. rather than a.d. or b.c., and always to use the Masoretic order of the books of the Old Testament. He remarked once that he had to be careful because it was done differently in Jewish and Catholic institutions."

For the reading Albright wished to do that year in Yehezkel Kaufmann's eight-volume history of Israel, Shalom Paul was assigned as his student assistant. Later Prof. Paul, now a teacher at Hebrew University, Jerusalem and Tel-Aviv, recalled reading "to him in the original Hebrew those sections of Kaufmann that pertained to the immediate area of his interest for his book on the early Israelite religion. We met for several hours two or three times a week. The amazing thing was Prof. Albright's continual sensitivity to the Hebrew language. He never once asked to have a sentence translated for him into English. He just leaned back and pensively listened and occasionally penned notes for his own use. I did occasionally interject translation when the word was a modern one with which he might not be familiar, or could be confused with a similar-sounding word. After two or three months he had received the information he needed, having obtained it in a way which very few can—from the original, unabridged version. Then he had me do something that was very helpful for me—when he had written an article he would say, 'Now tear it to pieces.' It was an exciting period for me, sitting with a great master."

Shalom Paul recalled an experience which revealed Albright the man rather than the scholar: when Albright came several hours late for an appointment, to Paul's question he replied that he had been at Grand Central Station, and explained that he had left a piece of luggage there when coming back into town. Paul said, " 'You know, you could have sent a million and one people to fetch the piece of luggage; your time is so valuable, why do *you* go down?' —it ate up half a day. Albright, with his fantastic modesty, asked how he could expect someone else to retrieve his luggage. It never entered his mind that anyone other than he should do it. This was really indicative of Albright the man, the gentleman.

"Once when Prof. Finkelstein took Prof. Albright to the early morning service in the Seminary synagogue and asked him to say a few words, Albright related that several years before when he was in Israel, as he was walking down a street with many little synagogues on it, he was repeatedly asked to become the tenth man for a *minyan*, a quorum for the service, and he would continually say, 'Ani lo Yehudi,' which many people thought was just a ploy; someone who did not want to go in and pray would say 'I'm not a Jew!' Albright had problems trying to convince them that he was really not a Jew—especially when saying it in Hebrew! (The same thing had occurred on voyages to Palestine in earlier years.)

"That year at the Seminary," continued Prof. Paul, "he gave a seminar course for five or six of us students. Whenever he ate in the cafeteria or came to the seminar he wore a skullcap out of respect for the institution. One day he forgot to put it on before coming to the seminar. In the course of his lecture he happened to scratch the top of his head and suddenly realized he was hatless. He turned a blazing red, put his hand into the side pocket of his jacket and said, as he pulled out his skullcap, 'But I brought it! See, I brought it!' And he promptly put it on his head. There were many such indications of a man who was aware of the sensitivities of his audience."

When Shalom Paul's wedding took place in Philadelphia after the close of that school year, Prof. Albright accepted his invitation and gave an entire evening, plus the train trip each way, to attend the wedding and reception. Prof. Paul remembered, "I didn't see him, out of the excitement of the day, but was told of his attendance when I received his beautiful wedding present, a gigantic bowl—I don't know from which stratum on which tell, but something from a great man. In that short year Albright-the-total-individual had a tremendous effect on me."

Mrs. Albright went up to stay with her husband a week in the apartment of Prof. and Mrs. Muilenburg at Union Theological Seminary just across the street from the Jewish Seminary. Albright had lectured just then in Chicago and had to return there for more lectures while she went on to Cambridge to spend Thanksgiving with David and his family at Harvard. In late December of 1958 the Albright couple flew to Brazil to spend several weeks with their oldest son and his family. Paul was by then located in São Paulo as president of the Brazilian branch of Squibb pharmaceutical company. The Albrights enjoyed visiting him and Evelyn and their children, and together made several trips—to Belo Horizonte and Ouro Preto, the "Williamsburg" of Brazil where the old is preserved; to Brasilia by bus to see the modernistic new capital carved out of the jungle; and some went to Rio de Janeiro, though for that trip Prof. Albright remained resting in São Paulo. There Ruth read to him a great deal again, usually detective stories to hold his attention without taxing his mind, but also a paperback translation from Dutch, *From Atomos to Atom*—a story of philosophy and natural history from Thales on which would influence his published work during his last years.

On this trip Albright met Brazilian scholars with whom he would occasionally correspond afterward. He and Ruth did not go across the Andes to Chile to visit the three cities in which he had spent his first twelve years; he felt no desire to return to them—at least not enough desire to outweigh the extra expense and time. When he wrote to Noel from New York on January 21 he spoke of his trip to South America as having been wonderful—all the more thrilling since it had been nearly fifty-six years since he left. They enjoyed the climate (and escaping from mid-winter New York); it was gratifying to see how successful and respected their son was in the half-million community in which he had many friends among both leaders and ordinary citizens.

By March 14 he could report to Noel that he was well along in Chapter VIII of his manuscript and should complete most of the first draft within the next three months. After that would come the labor of filling gaps, separating material to go into appendices, and revising in general; most of the footnote work would have to wait until the following winter in Baltimore.

During March of 1959 Albright gave more than thirty lectures in Texas, Kansas and Massachusetts. When he wrote his former student, Prof. Jacob Myers at Lutheran Theological Seminary, Gettysburg, on April 11 he spoke of his history of the religion of Israel as making steady progress and having reached the 11th century B.C., with about 150,000 words written of a projected 250,000 including appendixes and notes. He hoped to reach the 9th century by June. He thought he could send Myers a promised essay for a memorial volume for Alleman when he was in Pittsburgh in the fall (replacing Noel while he and his family were in Israel, England and Sweden), if he did not complete the essay before he left for Europe on the 15th of August. This reminded him that when at last he sent in his chapter, "Notes on Psalms 68 and 134," for the 1955 *Festschrift* honoring Prof. Sigmund Mowinckel, thinking it was probably too late, he had received a prompt note from editor Kapelrud that his contribution was the *first* to arrive in spite of the missed deadlines. (This became justification for other deadline delinquencies.)

During July when the Albrights were again at Switzerland Inn in North Carolina, Albright felt completely exhausted. As he wrote Noel, he did nothing in the two weeks but write one letter, take long walks, and lie in bed and listen as Ruth read detective stories to him. He confessed that he had continued working in New York a was worthless on his manuscript, but he had reached to 750 B.C. in] week longer than he should have, going so stale that the extra time it, though he still had to write the first two chapters and fill gaps.

The manuscript would remain in essentially that state the rest of Albright's lifetime, in spite of repeated promises and attempts to return to work on it.

The Albrights left in mid-August for England, where Dr. Albright was one of the chairmen of the International Congress of Old Testament Scholars at Oxford. Noel remembered Albright's rambling presidential speech; he had been elected to the office at Strasbourg three years earlier. Years later G. R. Driver recalled the meeting and Prof. Albright: "Although we differed strongly on many points of scholarship, we remained good friends." Albright's paper was titled "Some Remarks on the Song of Moses in Deuteronomy XXXII," and was published in *Vetus Testamentum* IX, later in 1959. Frank Cross was also in attendance; Albright was proud of Frank's paper, as he mentioned in a September 17 letter to Prof. Charles Fensham at the University of Stellenbosch, South Africa, who had been a student of Albright's last Hopkins year and who tried to bring Albright to South Africa for a lecture trip. Albright said he had also seen much of de Boer at the Congress.

Prof. P. A. H. de Boer of Leiden University, editor of *Vetus Testamentum*, recalled seeing Prof. Albright as he arrived at the Congress to register. The secretary asked for his name, and he replied "Albright." As she looked through her list she asked for his initials. Prof. de Boer remembered the look that came over Albright's face—mingled doubt and a bit of annoyance, apparently somewhat incredulous that someone did not know who he was.

After the busy time in Oxford and London, the Albrights spent two weeks in Killarney, Ireland, where they celebrated their thirty-eighth wedding anniversary—and Prof. Albright spent nine days in bed with nervous exhaustion. He dedicated his 1964 book, *History, Archaeology and Christian Humanism,* "To my wife in memory of a fortnight in Killarney (August, 1959)." At the end of his Preface he expressed gratitude to her for all her care in the difficult post-retirement period when the exhilarating effect of freedom from routine brought temptations to overwork in many ways with resulting danger of a health breakdown. He estimated that she must have read far more than a hundred books to him as he rested in bed with glaucoma drops making his eyes unusable, or suffering nervous exhaustion. His dedication of this book to her was, he said, only an inadequate token of his affection for her.

On Sunday, September 6, before leaving England Prof. Albright recorded a lecture, "What Scholars Have Learned from the Scrolls," for the British Broadcasting Corporation. Then the Albrights flew home and immediately had to move to Pittsburgh for the fall term at Western Theological Seminary. When in mid-October Albright wrote to Noel in Jerusalem, he had finished five weeks of teaching and they were comfortably and happily settled in their apartment; he had some good students, and his lecture series at the Carnegie Museum was going well.

In November and December Albright suffered a severe attack of neuritis in his right shoulder which prevented his typing but did not hinder his teaching. Mentioning it, he wrote Noel that he was enthusiastic over John Bright's *History of Israel,* just published. He recommended this "long-awaited volume" in the December 1959 BASOR, saying, "There can be no doubt that it is unrivaled in its field and that it should hold its place for many years to come. Exceedingly well documented, lucidly and often brilliantly written, it is a pleasure to read. The author has been strongly influenced both by the American archaeological approach and by the institutional and territorial approach of the Alt-Noth school. We recommend it without reservation."[1] It was a fine presentation of many of Albright's own views, and a second, revised edition would be published a few years later.

In the preceding issue of October, Editor Albright wrote concerning "two important volumes from the pen of Gerhard von Rad," "The former is the first Old Testament Theology to be published by a member of the inner circle of the great school founded by Albrecht Alt, and is closely analogous in its point of view to Martin Noth's historical approach. The reviewer differs quite widely from Alt's pupils, who have followed a course which was implicit in some of their great teacher's work, but tends to go far beyond it. (The reviewer is now two-thirds through the first draft of a 'History of the Religion of Israel,' which may be described as intermediate between history and theology, belonging properly in the former category. In many respects he has been growing more conservative in essentials since he began writing the book last

October. The importance of archaeology . . . has been impressing itself on him more and more; he has also been growing more conservative in dating various categories of literature, under the influence either of Eissfeldt or of Kaufmann.)"[2]

Ludwig R. Dewitz's oral examination took place in January of 1960, on the afternoon of a day when another student failed his orals in the morning. Albright had retired soon after Dewitz began his studies, but had guided him in the writing of his dissertation and encouraged him all the way through. "So when I presented myself to Dr. Albright just before lunch (apparently he always took those candidates out to lunch), he said that I should look cheerfully forward to the examination, since by the law of averages I could not possibly fail. To encourage me further he said, 'Let me ask you a few general questions.' All went well until he asked me, in view of the fact that my thesis dealt with the role of the afterlife in ancient Israel, whether I knew a French nineteenth-century writer who had written on the afterlife. I did not know, so he told me it was Chateaubriand; his book was entitled 'La vie d'outre-monde.' It so happened that the professor from the French Department on my examining committee asked that very question!" Dr. Dewitz remembered Albright's timely help with appreciation; probably Albright had heard the professor ask that question of previous candidates.

Prescott H. Williams, Jr., also graduated in 1960, having been Albright's student from 1951 to 1958 while pastoring nearby Presbyterian churches. Before he left Hopkins he came into possession of a typed manuscript of *From the Stone Age to Christianity*. "The reason I got it," he explained, "was that Albright had given it to Ray Cleveland to use as scratch paper because it was only typed on one side! Ray thought someone ought to have it and hold it toward the day when such materials would be collected. It is not quite complete, but most of it is there and has been kept in good shape."

The Albrights so enjoyed apartment living that fall in Pittsburgh that Ruth decided to move them into a large apartment just across Charles Street from the Hopkins campus when they returned from a strenuous five-week lecture trip to the Midwest and the West Coast. The move took place in mid-March 1960. (The former address, 4 W. 39th Street, is now part of the parking lot of a high-rise apartment building.) David's wife, Jo, their youngest daughter-in-law and the only one living in the same city, did what Mrs. Albright called a beautiful job of packing everything in boxes for the six-block move (in spite of the fact that their future youngest granddaughter was on the way).

When Albright returned on April 7 from another series of Danforth Foundation lectures he was much less exhausted than he expected to be, but had caught conjunctivitis ("pink eye") from one of his son Stephen's twin boys and could not do much work or reading. The enforced rest between lectures helped lessen the exhaustion. He began putting his reprints in order in the convenient new apartment, where his files and books were now easier to use than they had been for a long time. One wall of his bedroom was covered by shelves full of manila envelopes in alphabetic order by authors' names, full of their offprints—by the time of his death, doubtless the largest and most valuable such collection in the world.

He gave more than a hundred lectures by early May. At Wayne State University in Detroit he participated in a three-day symposium on "The Near Eastern Background of Culture." At Loyola University in Chicago he received his nineteenth honorary doctorate, a Litt.D.; the same degree had been awarded him a year earlier by Loyola College in Baltimore as his eighteenth.

Without consulting any family member or friend, that spring Albright negotiated with Southern Baptist Seminary in Louisville, Kentucky, for the purchase of his private library, settling on an amount in April and signing the agreement late in May, which gave him lifetime use of his library. When his wife and lawyer son and others heard of it, they were quite dismayed, feeling sure he could have found a better price with consultation and effort.

Again the Albrights vacationed at Little Switzerland before going to Cambridge, where Albright taught in the summer session at Harvard. He wrote Noel that almost a hundred students were taking his two classes for credit or audit, involving nine teaching hours a week; he especially enjoyed his class in epistemology, as well as exploring what was available in the Widener Library (adding he had enough material to write two more volumes if he could find the time). He enjoyed his seminar but was overwhelmed by all the paper-grading just before they flew home on August 26. However, he came through the eight-week session better than he anticipated and felt less tired after it than before. He then vowed to take Sundays off and to rest every afternoon.

On September 24 Albright confessed to Noel that he had gone to bed on Sunday the 4th and remained there until the 12th, trying once unsuccessfully to get up. A decade or two before, he was customarily laid up like that one or two times a year for about six days. In his older years the attacks seemed to come less often but to continue longer, a great nuisance preventing his accomplishing anything. (He would cheerfully say he was "dizzy as a ha'nt"!) But at nearly seventy he was thinking more of his good fortune than the bad. If Ruth could get along well for the past seven years with hardly any use of her left eye (a split retina, as well as macular degeneration), he could surely do it also! He must continue, he said, to balance research, writing and lecturing, not overuse his eyes, and not lecture so much that his nervous system rebelled.

Prof. Albright had to cancel all engagements for December. He was in the Johns Hopkins Hospital from the 9th to the 12th having an operation in the Wilmer Clinic on his left eye for glaucoma. The operation, performed on the 10th, was considered most successful. His surgeon, Dr. Naquin, told him on the 28th that vision in his left eye would improve even more when he had new lenses in his glasses and the blood had disappeared. Probably he would need to take drops for the glaucoma, but could continue working—his normal reactions would guard him against overstrain (perhaps the surgeon overestimated this guarding effect in Albright's case). Mrs. Albright much later expressed the opinion that the eye operation might have been better in its effect, but her husband wouldn't stay in the hospital long enough or behave properly, as he had done for his back operation in 1945.

It was mid-January 1961 before Prof. Albright could resume much activity. On the 21st he was one of ten professors who received tax-exempt prizes of $10,000 "for distinguished accomplishment in humanistic scholarship," the dateline New York story announced. "The presentation was made here at the closing session of the annual meeting of the American Council of Learned Societies. The council, a federation of 30 national scholarly organizations devoted to the encouragement of humanistic studies, picked the ten scholars who have contributed the most to knowledge in their fields. . . ."

Before that the Albrights went to McMaster University in Hamilton, Ontario, where he presented the Whidden lecture series. On the way back they stopped in Cincinnati and stayed in the convenient apartment they were to use for the spring term at Hebrew Union College, beginning February 1. There Albright taught two elective courses, four hours a week, in Biblical Archaeology and hoped to accomplish a great deal of editorial work and prepare for publication the lectures he had just delivered in Canada. When they finally were published in 1966 the small book was titled "New Horizons in Biblical Research." On February 5 in Cleveland, Albright gave "the Harry D. Koblitz Memorial Lecture . . . at the Temple," as the *Jewish Independent* announced.

Prof. Albright attended the spring meeting of the ASOR Trustees on April 8. In President Detweiler's report in the October 1961 BASOR he stated: "While Dr. Albright was excused from the meeting, Dr. Glueck announced that a special observance is being planned at Hebrew Union College to honor Dr. Albright on his seventieth birthday, May 24, 1961. A *Festschrift* will be presented at that time and expressions of congratulation from persons associated with the Schools will be welcome. It was voted to authorize a committee composed of Messrs. Glueck and Wright to prepare an appropriate resolution honoring Dr. Albright on this special occasion and to arrange with President Detweiler to have it produced in the form of a scroll. . . ."[3]

The Baltimore *Evening Sun* for May 28 under the heading "Dr. Albright Honored" stated: ". . . Dr. Samuel Iwry, of the Oriental Seminary and the Baltimore Hebrew College, conveyed greetings from friends and alumni in Baltimore. Several hundred congratulatory telegrams from learned societies and universities were delivered to Dr. Albright at the banquet."

Dr. Sam Iwry recalled that "this was the time when they came to celebrate his seventieth birthday. The Hebrew Union College arranged a big dinner and all the students and the faculty and invited guests really 'gave it' to him. It was a very festive occasion. At that time he gave his great speech, the Goldenson Lecture, that was afterward printed in a booklet, *Samuel and the Beginnings of the Prophetic Movement.*

"I came to represent Hopkins, and I made a little speech. I enjoyed very much seeing how happy he was there, how relaxed, as he took his walks with students always following him, and had a good library to use. Both students and faculty enjoyed him; it was one of the finest years of his retirement."

The scroll presented to Albright by the committee was a work of art, with large Gothic gilt lettering for his name, a red square behind the *W* and the rest of the lettering black Gothic, with red capitals to begin paragraphs. It was later framed and hung at the entrance to his study in the apartment across from the campus. Signed by Nelson Glueck and G. Ernest Wright for "the Committee on behalf of Colleagues, Students, Friends of Prof. William F. Albright," and printed in the April 1961 BASOR (which was late, as usual), the scroll inscription read:

"To a great scholar and gentleman, William Foxwell Albright, we pay glad tribute of admiration and affection on the occasion of his seventieth birthday.

"As archaeologist and Orientalist, he has been both pathfinder and interpreter of extraordinary importance. Through archaeological explorations and excavations, through numerous publications and students, he has contributed immeasurably to the knowledge and understanding of the ancient Near East, and thereby to a deeper appreciation of the present.

"Ever friendly and helpful, deeply religious and scientifically devoted and creative, he remains restlessly active. The years have not stayed his drive for the advancement of human enlightenment.

"For all who have had the privilege of direct association with him and for all who admire and honor him, we send our heartfelt salutations and implore God's blessing upon him and his family."[4]

A fine-print note followed in square brackets, signed by the initials of Albright's co-editor, Ray Cleveland: "On May 24, 1961, Professor Albright reached the milestone of his seventieth birthday. The occasion was celebrated at the Hebrew Union College in Cincinnati where he has been the Efroymson Memorial Visiting Professor of Biblical Archaeology during the winter and spring quarters. A dinner in his honor was attended by a large number of his colleagues, friends and former students. Later in the evening, Professor Albright delivered the Goldenson Lecture for 1961 in the College Chapel under the title 'Samuel and the Beginnings of the Prophetic Movement' . . . At the conclusion of the lecture, Professor G. Ernest Wright of Harvard University presented to him *The Bible and the Ancient Near East: Essays in Honor of William Foxwell Albright,* a volume just released by Doubleday Publishers. This book, edited by Professor Wright and remarkable in every way, contains fourteen articles designed to show the progress made during the past forty and more years in various fields in which Professor Albright himself has made substantial scholarly contributions. Ten of the fourteen contributors were Professor Albright's students; they and the other contributors are all recognized authorities on the subjects they discuss. Following Professor Albright's grateful acknowledgment of the volume, President Nelson Glueck of the Hebrew Union College presented to him a scroll inscribed with the testimonial printed above."[5]

Noel Freedman and Frank Cross were among those attending the dinner and lecture. Noel wrote to Albright on June 6 from his island summer home where he had just seen the Doubleday editor Clement Alexandre, who was "pleased to know that you were pleased with the *Festschrift,* and that the occasion at HUC was a happy one for all concerned. Needless to say I was delighted; and I may add, thoroughly impressed by your paper on Samuel. . . . The general picture of Samuel fits with everything we know and further illustrates the soundness not only historically but also conceptually (if not theologically) with respect to the OT of the Baltimore school."

At the Trustees' meeting the previous December 27, "it was reported by G. Ernest Wright that the amount of the William Foxwell Albright Fellowship Fund, including the original gift and pledges, amounts to approximately $3,600. It was voted to authorize the President to arrange for the announcement of the award of the first William Foxwell Albright Fellowship for study in the Near East for the academic year 1961-62. The amount of the Fellowship will be $2,000; it may be used anywhere in the Near East. . . ." Albright was reelected First Vice-president, but was shooed out of the Corporation meeting where the Albright Fellowship fund was discussed, as he said in writing to his old friend Dr. Paul F. Bloomhardt, whose original gift of $500 started the fund. Albright said he was a little embarrassed but appreciated deeply Paul's kindness in thinking of doing such a thing and was willing to do anything possible to help raise money for the ASOR. So soon after his eye surgery, Albright had found attending four organizations' meetings in four days quite tiring and on returning home had spent four days in bed with dizziness and lumbago.

Ted Campbell related to a few others of Albright's students when they were talking of him later, that Albright came back in 1959 for orals for those left over—himself and Boling among them —after his retirement. Frank Cross commented, "The whole system was dreadful!"

Ernest Wright said, "Maybe they've got it changed now. The real thing about it all, I think, is that we all came to realize—I suppose we all came to realize; *I* only came to realize after Albright's retirement—that he couldn't stop running. All these speeches everywhere, honorary degrees everywhere—it's as though he couldn't stop, and then he couldn't run any more. Out on these speaking tours his health gave out so much, he had to stop running and start working, and it took him the longest time to get back into the habits of working. He had done so—by the time of his death he was really producing again."

FREEDMAN: "Well, he could hardly let go of things, like the *Bulletin;* he wanted no indications that he was slipping, or that he needed to husband his energies."

WRIGHT: "But Ray Cleveland was the associate editor of the *Bulletin*, through most of these running years, when Albright was running around so much, and as you know, Ray finally went off to Jordan just to get away from this awful burden of editing the *Bulletin* when Albright was away so much."

FREEDMAN: "You're right!"

WRIGHT: "But the insecurity of Albright came out in the later years, during the 1960's, most visibly, in that he became more and more dogmatic. He was always difficult to get a point over to, at best."

CROSS: "Orally, I could never do it. In writing . . ."

WRIGHT: "You had to choose your time, choose your point, and you had to plan a campaign to get a point over to him orally, otherwise it had to be in writing. I was still O.K. in my years in the

'30's on that, but by the '60's to *me* he was a different man. He was so dogmatic! The whole business of Abraham the Hebrew and caravaneer, out of the *avar,* not the *cross-over* person, but the *dusty* one—all of this writing history by etymologies, . . ."

FREEDMAN: "He always had that weakness."

CROSS: "He was quite dogmatic."

FREEDMAN: "And he became increasingly so in theological matters."

CROSS: "My crisis thing was the *Yavneh-Yam* [ostracon found at that site with Hebrew inscription]. The Old Man wanted to write a joint article, but when I saw what he thought it meant, I told him no, I would write my piece and he could write a counter-piece to it. This scared me to death! It went on at the same time as the Cincinnati meeting where we honored him. And really to tell the Old Man I didn't want to write the piece with him, and I was greatly honored that he would propose it—it really hurt me. I didn't know what to do about it, but I could not believe what he was trying to translate from that thing. And it's interesting—he never published on it." (Albright published Cross's article on the inscription in BASOR 165 for February, 1962, without even an Additional Note.)

CAMPBELL: "He never wrote in defense of it but he did put it in ANET [James B. Pritchard's *Ancient Near Eastern Texts,* latest edition; Pritchard got his start in Albright's 1934 excavation of Bethel].

CROSS: "He finally accepted virtually all of my readings, and all of the readings he had proposed to me he dropped."

FREEDMAN: "Well, we had discovered while working on the [joint] dissertation that there were points where he could be corrected. He had made one egregious blunder in that Spatula inscription, where his whole argument turned on a certain word being singular. He insisted that because there was no *yod* for the expected first-person suffix, that showed the noun was singular, but he translated it as plural. We just tacitly corrected that, quietly corrected it in our dissertation, and it went right by; he never said a word. There were other things like that, so we knew that he wasn't totally infallible. In fact, it gave us the impression that he was always emphasizing method and systematic assembly of all the data and everything like that—and he wasn't *really* like that at all.

He had these incredible insights. They were really intuitions, but he resented that word. He was very hostile to that suggestion, but it's really true, because he could see how a new technique, like orthography, or the sequence-dating in the pottery, could provide a synthesis. He always saw that goal—that's the thing *I* learned most from him. Because I could always go through the procedures but I didn't always know what they were *for,* and he opened my eyes to these things because he was always looking for ways to get at solutions, and this was new to me. This was something which I imagine in scientific method is typical, but applying it in humanistic studies was something terrific for me. I remember he worked for years on contractions, for he thought that biblical words had been kind of smashed together, and if you could learn the secret of it you could pry them apart and read the thing correctly. But he always had that goal and often he knew what the solution was before he had the method worked out; it was incredible. Which meant that there was much that following people could do, because he didn't exhaust the subject. It was really kind of hit-and-miss with him. He never did work out the principles, for example like the orthography—he just knew."

WRIGHT: "As you say, he had this grand design, and he knew what it ought to be, somehow. I had the same impression; I always said, 'Watch out for Albright's hunches.'"

FREEDMAN: "Well, look at the Nash Papyrus—a really pivotal study at the right time. In other words, a decade before the discovery of the Dead Sea Scrolls."

CROSS: "One of the interesting things about that was that Albright changed his mind and the date of the Nash Papyrus later, and was quite wrong. That is to say, his original date was right, and if he had stuck with this date for the Isaiah Scroll which he first came out with, he would not have been some years off. He was dead right the first time, but later he tried to push it lower."

FREEDMAN: "That's what I mean. His Balaam article was another pivotal study. It reopened the whole subject of early Hebrew poetry in a way that still dominates the field."

WRIGHT: "I always had this idea that Albright knew what he wanted to prove before he could prove it. So the game was to work out the proof. Therefore there were an infinite number of linguistic games you could play to prove anything you want. That's just about the impression *I* got of all this language business," said Wright, the archaeologist and historian.

FREEDMAN: "He could turn the same argument in—"

WRIGHT: "Opposite directions."

FREEDMAN: "And did!"

CROSS: "That's too simple!"

WRIGHT: "It *is* too simple; because Albright, it seemed to me, had extraordinarily good hunches that he didn't—couldn't—work out systematically because he simply wasn't patient enough, couldn't be bothered, to assemble all the data."

CAMPBELL: "This relates to another thing that is often said about him, and many people have had the same experience, I think; that is, that if they try to oppose one of his hunches because they have succeeded in answering the points that he made in presenting the argument, they would go in and talk with him in his office about it, and he would immediately come up with about six or eight or ten other reasons than those they have answered. They always went away shattered by this, but they shouldn't have. Because the fact is that it was the question asked him that brought out the other reasons, and he might not even have used these points to support his argument, without their opposition."

CROSS: "Many people felt that when Albright said he had collected a lot of evidence to prove a point, he was merely talking; but that was not right; when he said that, he *had*."

FREEDMAN: "The thing that has appalled me is that it is literally true—that what he *didn't* publish is as much, maybe as much, as the vast amount he *did* publish! And it is all there in his notes. He wrote on everything at length, and at one point in his life he started dating everything—when he had discussed this subject with so-and-so; or he just sat down and wrote, 'On this day I have thought thus and thus.' And then he'd pile these slips up in the various envelopes and folders for these articles. There were about sixty of them sitting in his study after his death."

CAMPBELL: "Sixty articles?"

FREEDMAN: "Yes, that he intended to write, on every subject under the sun."

In a different conversation Dr. Sam Iwry also mentioned Albright's hunches and his way of working. "I think I know some of the secrets of Albright's great literary and scholarly success. I talked it over with some of our friends, and I think I'm not wrong in telling it. I never asked *him*. Albright first would get an idea by reflection and intuition. Something came to his mind after thinking or reading, and he would think, as he used to tell me about a student, 'I *think* you are on the right track!' And first of all he writes it down. After that he worries about getting support for this idea, straightening out details, filling in whatever has to be filled in. But he does not go and do it the other way, collecting first a lot of details, putting it down, and after that rounding it up. First comes the idea; he feels intuitively that he is on the right track. Once he feels he is right and on the right track, the idea continues developing, the material comes in, and as he told me, at that time 'everything falls into line.' "

Wright in the group conversation began summing up: "There's one thing: What is the mystery whereby an occasional teacher collects around him a group of students who have only one ideal in their minds, and that's to preserve *his* ideal; to preserve his identity, his ideas, his school? The other thing is the mystery of Albright always being for the poor guy—"

CAMPBELL: "The underdog."

WRIGHT: "The outcast. There was an Egyptian teacher who, according to Gordon, said in the first class of Introductory Egyptian, 'Now, the first rule in this class is, "You can't publish anything." ' This man always talked at the top of his voice, and he'd come down to see Albright every so often, and you'd hear his conversation all over the floor. Sachs and I could stand it so long, and then we'd go in and bust it up, just to save Albright. But Albright in our days just had a *string* of these people in, and you know from his correspondence what he did for all these young European scholars all through the years and through the Nazi period."

CAMPBELL: "The Nazi period is a fascinating story in itself."

WRIGHT: "Well, that's a big story in itself. But it's only those who were on the receiving end of it who can really appreciate the fact that what he said in trying to explain some of this in his autobiographical sketch was real."

FREEDMAN: "Well, he had an extraordinarily inspiring effect—I can testify to that."

WRIGHT: "As I look back on it, really, Albright is one of these geniuses from another field who comes to biblical study with something entirely fresh; but he isn't a biblical scholar, just as he isn't a philosopher, and he isn't a theologian. But he does brilliantly whatever thing he's doing."

CROSS: "He called himself in *Who's Who* an Orientalist. And that is what he was; that's an accurate description."

WRIGHT: "When you stop to think about the greatest creative figures in Palestinian archaeology, Petrie, Reisner, Albright,—they are all really outsiders from a different field, two Egyptologists and one man, an Orientalist, trained originally in Accadian studies. He was writing all those Assyriological mythological studies, and then shifted completely in the environment of the Holy Land, just as though he were a Jew being converted to the land, the Holy Land. All his childhood dreams now surface and he forgets—he just goes back on all that myth-and-ritual stuff. It was an identification with the soil as dramatic as any modern Israeli's transformation along that line."

FREEDMAN: "Which may be the reason that he ultimately became so sympathetic with Israel and the Israelis."

WRIGHT: "Whereas Haupt could never have been that. Haupt had been trained as an Assyriologist and . . ."

CROSS: "And also applied himself to the Bible . . ."

WRIGHT: "Then came and applied himself to the Bible, with disastrous results!"

But Haupt's greatest pupil, William Foxwell Albright, applied himself to the Bible with tremendous, positive results.

In mid-1961 Albright was still in what Ernest Wright called his running period. On June 27 in a letter to Noel concerning their joint editing venture (the Anchor Bible series) he said that he and Ruth needed to go to son David's law office and sign their wills before catching the jet plane to Brazil. They would return on July 21 and in the meantime he was taking along a lot of material to read critically, as well as working on the revision of *Archaeology and the Religion of Israel* for the paperback edition while in Brazil (it finally would appear in 1968).

Again the Albrights enjoyed visiting Paul and his family in São Paulo. Mrs. Albright sent Noel and Neil a postal card with color photo from Rio de Janeiro, telling of the flight of nine and a half hours from New York and another flight of forty minutes from Rio to São Paulo, with a wait of an hour and a half between.

The Portuguese language, mostly vowel sounds, seemed weird and constituted the only problem. William was usually working a few hours each day and resting a great deal.

At the end of July the Albrights went to Salt Lake City, where he was one of the lecturers in the first annual Summer Institute on World Religions. Writing to Noel just before going there, Albright mentioned that caring for his glaucoma had been excellent for his health in general; he had had only a couple of short attacks of nervous exhaustion since February. Since early June evidence had been pouring in on him that Abraham and the Apiru were really caravaneers. He would need to set the caravan trade in historical focus, as it changed in the seventeenth century B.C. and again in the twelfth to eleventh centuries.

Late in September the Albrights settled for the fall quarter at the University of Minnesota, where he was visiting professor of theology and conducted a seminar in the philosophy department as well as giving a series of eight public lectures on Tuesday evenings. Ruth already knew how to get around in Minneapolis, he wrote Noel on a rented typewriter. From there Albright went to Louisville, Kentucky for a lecture on "The Outlook for New Testament Archaeology" in mid-October at Southern Baptist Theological Seminary.

In the October 1961 BASOR Editor Albright used pages 36 to 54 for his landmark study, about which he had written to Noel and spoken for newspaper interviews: "Abram the Hebrew; A New Archaeological Interpretation." He assembled evidence substantiating the hypothesis that Abram was a donkey caravaneer, fitting into the Middle Bronze I period of deposits in the Negeb and Sinai, about 2000 to 1800 B.C. "The nineteenth century B.C. . . . seems, in fact, to have been the great period of donkey caravans, which made their way in the far north from Assur to eastern Cappadocia and back again, and in the south traversed Southwestern Asia from Babylonia to Egypt. . . .

"After the 19th century donkeys were gradually displaced by the much stronger mule . . . , but donkeys were still used in the hill country of Southwestern Asia long after the effective introduction of camel caravans in desert regions. . . .

"The writer had not succeeded in finding a satisfactory approach before this summer, but the conclusive evidence for intensive donkey caravan trade in the Negeb which we owe to Glueck and Rothenberg changes the entire picture. In the first place, we can now understand for the first time why the towns and places of residence attributed to Abraham in Genesis were key points for large-scale donkey caravans. The movement between Ur and Harran becomes easy to understand when we recall that Ur was the greatest commercial capital that the world had yet seen, . . . Harran on the Balikh was probably the northern base of operations for this trade, as well as for commerce between Assyria and Iran to the east and Syria-Egypt to the west. . . . Its meaning is 'caravan city'. . .

"Hebrew tradition makes Abraham leave the Ur-Harran axis and spend the rest of his life between Damascus and Egypt, where the fast developing caravan trade must have become exceedingly profitable. . . .

"Other towns on the main caravan route southwestward from the Euphrates which figure significantly in the Abraham stories, are Shechem, Bethel, Hebron and Gerar. . . . Beersheba may already have been a fortified town but if so was incomparably smaller and less impressive than Gerar. . . .

"But how did the traditions of Abraham survive? Hitherto there has been no answer except in the case of Gen. 14, where a verse substratum is now obvious. . . . Now we can answer the question by referring the prototypes of most, perhaps all, of the Abraham narratives to the Hebrew descendants of the caravaneers of the 19th century. These caravaneers are well known today as the *Apiru*, later *Abiraya*, Hebrew *Ibri*, who appear so often in texts from the ancient East between the 23rd and the 12th centuries B.C. The writer has collected a mass of evidence—much of it extremely obvious, once it has been pointed out—for the equation *Apiru* = 'donkeyman, donkey driver, caravaneer,' but there is no more space in this article in which to present it. Naturally the Apiru were stateless, naturally they became freebooters when they could not make a living in their trade, but they were primarily neither bandits nor *condottieri*—they were simply men who made the great donkey caravans of the nineteenth century B.C. possible."[6]

The Albrights' three-month stay in Minneapolis was very enjoyable, as he wrote to Jacob Myers at Gettysburg; in the spring they would spend three months at the University of Iowa, teaching in its School of Religion. When they returned to Baltimore on December 15, however, both needed much rest. In January they went to Houston, where he gave the Rockwell Lectures at Rice University, also visiting Philip, his youngest brother, and his family. Albright began making vows to stay at home and work on his writing and rest more, beginning in June; he knew he must restrain himself and not continue to abuse his strength as he acknowledged he had been doing since 1957. He intended to set up a sort of publication assembly line while he could still use his eyes. The $10,000 prize of eleven months earlier and the McGraw-Hill advance payments for his book in process would finance research and typing help for the next few years, he wrote Noel. He went to New York in February and signed the contract with McGraw-Hill in the office of its president, with pictures being taken on what he said was for him an historic occasion. After a conference and luncheon he returned by taxi to the Rockefeller Institute and had a wonderful time, finding the red carpet rolled out for him.

Already in mid-1950 similar plans for publication had been laid, but had not come to fruition then. On July 6 of that year Albright wrote to Freedman, saying his plans for the following two years had changed; taking for granted that the Korean War would not develop into the Third World War (which was, however, very possible), he had a new assignment resulting from luncheon the previous week with Hopkins President Detlev Bronk. He had just written to Ernest Wright about it also. He was to organize a campaign and raise a ten-year endowment for the Oriental Seminary, and change the department into an institute revolving about his ideas and research. He might center such a campaign around Rabbi Rosenblatt, or around his own Reformed Jewish students, or make it an organized attempt to interest smaller foundations, or an effort to get Protestant groups interested. It could not be a general appeal but would have to be focused on friends of friends. It would have to be done during 1950 to 1952, for he felt that after he was sixty-one there would be little point in building an institute around himself. There would have to be more publications from him and his best students, making clear what their ideas and contributions were. He enclosed a list of twelve chapters, several based on lectures not yet published, others already published since 1936, to be gathered into a proposed volume of about 250 pages titled "Archaeology and the Biblical Tradition," about which he said he had written to Ernest, and asked Noel's opinion. He would have his two lecture series in Westminster and John Knox publishing houses by the end of the year if possible—following his wife's urging that he keep them simple and clear. The former, *The Faith of Ancient Israel,* would relate to what Noel and Frank had worked on; the latter, *Exile and Restoration,* would be connected with the work of John Bright and Carl Howie.

Albright confessed to feeling a new sense of urgency, having previously disbelieved that he could gain recognition for his ideas, but now in 1950 feeling that with most religious schools and seminaries teaching such a horrifying distortion of Protestantism and Christianity, resulting in a dangerous decline in morality and faith, he simply had to bring forward his views. What was urgently needed was a solid foundation of Old and New Testament study supporting a modern theological-philosophical approach, if Protestantism was to be rescued.

The researcher was turning into a crusader in 1950. His July 24 letter to Noel said he had in mind recent doctoral students, while Ernest thought of having a larger group involved in the proposed committee to publish the volume of essays. While the idea of an institute did not work out, undoubtedly this ferment of ideas was the genesis of the 1961 *Festschrift* edited by Wright and the 1964 volume of Albright's essays, *History, Archaeology and Christian Humanism,* for which he had just signed the contract with McGraw-Hill in February of 1962 on that gala and historic occasion.

In April, 1962, Albright, then guest professor at the State University of Iowa at Iowa City, went to Dubuque to give five lectures in three Catholic institutions in two days. His health had improved after being bad for a month. While flat on his back, as he wrote Noel, he had been making progress in his thinking about Job, Ecclesiastes, and the Greek Anaximander (who followed Thales; Albright was working out ideas that would appear posthumously when Noel published Albright's article on "Neglected Factors in the Greek Intellectual Revolution"). Noel, who was then, with his wife Neil, in Ashkelon while excavating nearby ancient Ashdod with Moshe Dothan, wrote that "of course everyone around here sends hearty greetings and hopes that you will visit Israel soon. I am sure you would find the Ashdod excavation quite interesting."

Prof. Albright had last visited Upper Iowa College in February of 1952. The director of public relations wrote to him on the following May 1 that "folks are still talking about the fun some of your class had last February when you were on our campus. We only wish every member of the class could have been here. Now we're planning for your 40th anniversary . . ." However, Albright was in Scandinavia at that time. But he did attend the fiftieth anniversary celebration in 1962. After his term at the State University of Iowa ended, the Albrights spent the end of May visiting his Cornish Foxwell relatives in northeastern Iowa and attended the celebration, at which he gave the commencement address. When he had been there in 1952 his old classmate, Lula Hurd Blunt, and her husband had just left for Florida. When William and Ruth were there in 1962, Lula sat beside him at the alumni dinner. She asked him about his family. William told of their trip to Brazil to visit their eldest son. A couple across the table had a son in São Paulo also. William asked how they traveled, first class or tourist, and intimated that it was asinine to pay extra in order to sit behind a curtain and have liquor served on the plane! After the dinner Lula, as she related years later, was gushing to President Eugene E. Garbee about how great it was that she got to sit beside William Albright, and Garbee answered, "You didn't think it just happened, did you?" The Blunts were well impressed with Ruth, and Lula was surprised that William could be such a wonderful conversationalist and so poised, a contrast to his poverty-stricken student days. She remarked that he had grown tremendously in talents and polish.

William's cousin, Tom Foxwell, and other relatives attended the commencement program. An old friend spoke to Tom afterward, praising Dr. Albright's address. Tom agreed but with some reservations, mentioning that it might not have been exactly appropriate for the time and place. The old man then said, "I didn't think it was a damn bit good either!" Albright had paid his audience the compliment of not lowering the level of his discourse, though making it non-technical and suitable for a general audience.

Ruth was rather cool to Tom on their first meeting. On the phone, before he went to meet them and bring them to the college, Tom called his cousin's wife "Ruth." There was a silence; then she said, "This is Mrs. Albright." But after the families were together a little while, they all enjoyed each other so much that the Albrights decided to return the next year for the Foxwell Centennial in August.

On June 16 Albright wrote to Tom and Margaret Foxwell, thanking them for their hospitality and all their work in planning for the reunion of relatives during their recent visit. Since leaving on May 28 he and Ruth had been in Iowa City a few days, then spent two weeks traveling in the East. After a day attending the meeting of the Committee on Research in Philadelphia, they had gone the next week to Cambridge to visit their son, Stephen, and his family, and found him recovering more quickly than expected from a serious stomach operation. They were at Harvard two days, where Albright received his 22nd honorary degree (a Litt.D.; numbers 20 and 21 had been an L.H.D. at Manhattan College and an H.H.D. at Wayne State University the previous year). Now they were ready to settle down in Baltimore. His research assistant, Herbert Huffmon, had arrived and he and Albright would begin the next Monday on their publication schedule.

He wrote that Ruth had been quite impressed by the quality of his Cornish relatives whom she had met while in Iowa; both of them thought Tom and Margaret were just tops. Albright coveted their little Susan but already had five granddaughters so would resist trying to kidnap her. They hoped that Tom would persevere against all discouragements with his plan for a career in rehabilitation work, in which their New England daughter-in-law was also interested because of their twin boys, who were now making progress in school.

Albright wrote a letter to Emunah, explaining his long delay, for he and his wife had been moving about almost constantly in the three years since she had been his research assistant in New York. Her father had sent him her Jerusalem address and he was most happy to hear of her marriage to Dr. H. J. Katzenstein (librarian at the Schocken Library in Jerusalem) and thus her continued connections with biblical studies; he sent the new husband hearty congratulations for having won such a talented and beautiful wife. Dr. Malamat on a visit had told him how she met her future husband in the seminar that Malamat and Mazar had conducted at Hebrew University the previous fall. He was glad also that she was working on a doctoral dissertation. He had looked forward to seeing them both in Jerusalem, but now it seemed he would not be going there for several more years—he had just signed a contract with McGraw-Hill for several volumes. He was expanding the chapter that had appeared in her father's two-volume publication, preparing it for a Harper Torchbook edition (*The Biblical Period from Abraham to Ezra*, 1963), and would soon work on the *History of the Religion of Israel* on which she had assisted him. He needed to rewrite his chapter on Abraham and the other patriarchs; for the chapters still unwritten he had collected much material.

When he wrote an air letter to Noel he mentioned his honorary doctorate, saying that at Harvard he could not find anyone ready to accept responsibility for it, but he suspected it was an anonymous suggestion from one of his many good friends there, similar to his election to the National Academy of Sciences in 1955. He had had a good visit with Ernest Wright and Frank Cross as well as with his son, Stephen, and his family. He expressed much interest in Noel's news from the Ashdod dig, and told of help from Herbert and Mary Lou Huffmon on revising the chapter on the Biblical Period.

It was a readjustment time for the Albrights, after four years of his rather frenetic "retirement," of wandering, which, as he wrote Jacob Myers, sometimes made him feel as though he were Cain. He said he and his wife had now settled in their apartment, to which they had moved more than two years before but in which they hardly had lived at all yet. Herbert Huffmon was to receive his Ph.D. from Michigan in the fall and was turning out to be excellent help; his wife, Mary Lou, was learning to type and to use Albright's new dictation and transcribing machines. Albright considered himself fortunate to be able to use his eyes at all and to keep working on scholarly projects.

The Albrights made another western trip so that he could give the commencement address on August 24 at Brigham Young University, where he received his 23rd honorary doctorate, an H.H.D. On their return trip they visited many of Ruth's relatives in Colorado and Missouri—not so numerous as William's.

They did not go to Bonn that August in spite of their earlier plans; Noel's letter in early September after his return told of the Congress of Old Testament Scholars. Albright needed to rest a great deal in late August and early September. He had several lecture trips to make that fall, which somewhat hindered the progress of his work, but he left plenty for the Huffmons to do. He and Mrs. Albright went north for two lectures, at Boston College and Holy Cross; then he continued alone to Kankakee, Illinois, to lecture at the Nazarene school. Already he had lectured at Eastern Baptist Seminary in Philadelphia and at Asbury in Kentucky, the lectures again being sponsored by the Danforth Foundation jointly with the American Association of Colleges. Albright spoke on such subjects as biblical history, Abraham, and the Dead Sea Scrolls. As the Holy Cross paper commented, he "discussed his science with a compulsive passion as one who has discovered more than bones and shards in dead deserts." While in the Boston area he and Ruth visited Stephen and his family again, as well as meeting Noel there for a discussion of their publication projects.

After giving about fifty lectures in five weeks at ten institutions and growing very tired, Albright did not attempt to attend the meeting of the Biblical Colloquium at Thanksgiving time in Washington. Soon after it, Noel and Neil departed for Europe, where their children were in schools in England, and to Israel, where they worked on publication of the Ashdod excavation. Noel wrote Albright on February 26, 1963, "Hardly a day goes by here that someone does not ask for you, and express the hope that you will come to Israel soon." Albright replied to three long letters from Noel after giving two lectures at the end of January in Hugh's school, LaSalle College in Philadelphia, attending the American Philosophical Society's Committee on Research meeting, and having a bout with influenza.

Early in March Prof. Albright gave lectures at the university in Miami, then spent three strenuous days in meetings in Princeton. He confessed to Noel that he had talked far too much there, especially since he gave one of the two public lectures, but that he had avoided controversy with Cadbury and Enslin. He felt that a real division was being drawn on Bultmannism.

Noel's March 31 letter told of the opening, with ceremonies and awarding of an honorary degree to Yigael Yadin, of the Hebrew Union College school of archaeology in Jerusalem—two years later than the term in which Albright was originally scheduled to spend several months lecturing to inaugurate it. The

Orthodox Jews had delayed the building construction, and it was only completed by turning it into strictly an archaeological school, not a religious school of the Reform Jewish group. A couple of weeks later Noel wrote of having spent a three-day Easter holiday on the other side of Jerusalem, in the Old City. With Neil and their son David, on vacation from England, he had stayed at the American School and talked with Paul and Nancy Lapp, catching up on archaeological news of that side, also having opportunity to visit Kathleen Kenyon's trenches at Jericho. In his May 7 letter Noel reported that they and the Lapps had spent a vacation week on Cyprus while David was still with them. Noel had made useful comparative pottery studies; the dig at Ashdod would resume on June 2. He sent Albright greetings especially from the Dothans; "from time to time we have greetings to pass on from practically everyone in the Dept. of Antiquities and the University Dept. of Archaeology, also Jewish History, etc."

Albright replied rather wistfully that strange as it might seem, he had never visited more of Cyprus than its harbors and airports in transit, and probably now it was too late to think of making a visit. Noel was quite right in making comparisons with Cypriot archaeological materials; they were naturally much closer to what he would find at Ashdod than was anything to be found in the Palestinian hill country. Agreeing with Noel's comments on the state of biblical scholarship, Albright said an empirical approach was in danger of being forced out by attacks from both sides in many schools, and the left was worse than the right because of being utterly convinced of its liberality, while the right was defensive. Some things then being published could have been written decades earlier—so completely had they ignored new knowledge.

Albright met his McGraw-Hill deadline at the end of June—with much hard work by him and the Huffmons—and flew to Dubuque to teach classes in two cooperating seminaries, the students coming from various churches. He did not mention in his July letter to Noel that on June 25 he and three other persons were honored at a dinner-concert of the State of Israel Bonds Festival of the Arts, at which violinist Mischa Elman was the guest artist. Baltimore-Israel Cultural Awards were presented to Prof. Albright along with David Brinkley of NBC and Dr. Abel Wolman, professor emeritus of sanitary engineering at Hopkins.

The Albrights went from Dubuque to the Thomas Foxwell Centennial celebration which took place on August 11. Their second son, Hugh, flew out and drove them up to West Union in a rental car. As William's cousin, Tom, recalled, Hugh had a good time driving around and meeting relatives all over the area, running up the mileage on the rental car to his mother's annoyance, while Ruth and William rested in their motel at the edge of town. William's brother Paul and his wife Georgia came from California, and the cousins remembered that Paul and William got into a long, loud argument while waiting in line for dinner at the reunion. Their argument continued through the meal. Paul aggressively discussed his socialistic ideas with the relatives, many of whom he met for the first time

Thomas and Margaret Foxwell, who lived in and modernized the second house built on that homestead (the year William was born), had printed 300 copies of a brochure for the centennial containing genealogical lists, photos and stories which give helpful information about Prof. Albright's ancestors on his mother's side. The brochure was dedicated to Aunt Ella, and the woodcut of the original log cabin on the homestead, used on the cover, was made by Tom, then a teacher of art in the school system, from a sketch drawn from memory by Aunt Ella at the age of ninety-three. (Months earlier Albright had sent a check for $50 to help on expenses of the centennial.)

Ruth wrote to Margaret and Tom in mid-August telling what pleasure and joy they had experienced in the celebration, but since they were not Aunt Ella, they had needed to recuperate after the trip. They were proud of their Foxwell connection; Hugh had also had a good time, having a chance to talk about scientific things with his father and enjoy the meetings and luncheon at the Foxwell home. Ruth thought William's brother Paul enjoyed rubbing people the wrong way, but he was a good person nevertheless. William had been forced to rest at the motel during part of the visit because of the weeks of teaching in Dubuque and especially his efforts to finish his McGraw-Hill book. The next book, to be only a revision of an earlier book, should be easier on him.

When Albright finally replied to Noel on August 31, his forty-second wedding anniversary, he had good excuses; not only had he had no stenographic help during most of the summer, but he had been away some time and then ill for a couple of weeks. He was puzzled by the thirteenth-century destruction at Ashdod which Dothan had attributed to the Israelites, and suggested it could have been by the Sea Peoples.

On September 8, 1963, in the New York *Herald Tribune*, there was an article concerning the project on which Albright and Noel spent much time and wrote each other many letters. It mentioned that the Anchor Bible project was "under the direction of two Protestant scholars—David Noel Freedman, a Presbyterian, of the Pittsburgh Theological Seminary [formerly Western], and William Foxwell Albright, a Methodist, professor emeritus at Johns Hopkins University. Mr. Albright is the widely acknowledged dean of American Biblical archaeologists. . . ."

The New York *Times* for December 29 announced that the "First Encyclopaedia Judaica in 60 years Is Half Completed," and mentioned that "Prof. William F. Albright of Johns Hopkins University is chairman of the editorial council." On January 18, 1964, the Detroit *News* announced, "A Methodist Bible scholar who has won renown throughout the Judeo-Christian world was named today as the winner of the 1964 Christian Culture Award Gold Medal. Dr. William F. Albright, professor emeritus at Johns Hopkins University and one of the world's great archaeologists, will accept the award in person April 19 at the University of Windsor. He becomes the 24th to win the award. . . . Dr. Albright, a frequent lecturer on the Near East at Wayne State U., was born of Methodist missionary parents in South America. . . . He became the first scholar outside the Holy Land to verify the authenticity of the Dead Sea Scrolls, and his myriad other discoveries in excavations throughout the Near East have made him one of the world's great defenders of Biblical truth. . . . It has been said of him that he 'has expanded the Bible from the source of theological truth to a handbook of history.' " The subject of his lecture was "Is the Bible Antiquated?"

Through the fall of 1963 Prof. Albright taught a seminar course in McCoy College, the Hopkins evening school, on "How Philosophy and Logic Developed from Earlier Ways of Thinking." He gave an essay-type final examination on January 22, 1964, in three parts, with directions to try to keep each reply within 500 words,

answering five of the fifteen questions, with not less than one answer and not more than three in any one of the three sections. His
lectures in this course concerned subjects that were supposed to be
presented in his second McGraw-Hill volume, which was never
written but some of the ideas of which would appear posthumously
in the publication of an address to the American Philosophical
Society on the Greek revolution in thought.

February 22, 1964, was a special day for Prof. Albright and for
Johns Hopkins. It was the annual Commemoration Day at the
university, and on that Saturday, as President Milton S. Eisenhower
wrote to the members of the faculty, "we shall pay tribute to the
Humanities at Johns Hopkins, and honor an eminent scholar,
Dr. William F. Albright, Professor Emeritus of Semitic Languages.
He will be awarded the degree, Doctor of Laws, and will deliver the
main address." Albright had returned shortly before from three
days of lecturing at Virginia Polytechnic Institute at Blacksburg
(where Ruth's older brother Paul held a chair for many years in
industrial engineering) as "a visiting scholar in the school of arts
and sciences," the write-up on February 27 in the Richmond
Times-Dispatch stated.

The Baltimore *Evening Sun* on the 19th of February announced the celebration of the eighty-eighth anniversary of the
founding of Johns Hopkins on Saturday with Albright the featured speaker, receiving the LL.D. "It will be the twenty-fourth
honorary degree Dr. Albright has received in his 48 years of association with Johns Hopkins. He is called by fellow archaeologists
'the outstanding archaeologist of our generation,' and is known as
the dean of American archaeologists. . . ."

The most elaborate article was that written by James H. Bready,
with a photo of Albright in his study working with magnifying
glass, published in the *Sun* on February 9 in the section on Books
and Authors. Bready wrote: "William Foxwell Albright, rising
from his seat on the platform to give the occasion's principal address, a week from Saturday when the Johns Hopkins University
observes its eighty-eighth annual Commemoration Day, will be
excused any momentary uneasiness—any tugging at his glasses or
settling his academic hood. It is a rare thing for February 22's
speaker to be a Homewood faculty member, active or as in this

case emeritus. The lighting matters, also, because his eyes have always been severely myopic; he has strained them further in half a century of deciphering the hooks and loops of ancient scribes, and latterly glaucoma has set in. As for cap and gown, these will betoken the award, a moment earlier, of an honorary degree from Johns Hopkins; it is in Professor Albright's nature to feel awe regardless of the fact that this latest honorary doctorate will be his twenty-fourth. . . .

". . . To Toynbee, Albright is 'a great scholar of my generation.' To a colleague, Kathleen M. Kenyon, of Oxford, . . . Albright's work in Palestine in the 1920's and 1930's was crucial in the development of scientific archaeology. Experts now working in Israel and Jordan, on being polled last year were still more specific, rating Albright 'a genius, the outstanding archaeologist of our generation, the spiritual father of us all.' In general, to diggers and surface men, to epigraphers and find-recorders and pottery-sequence specialists, Albright is, at 72, the dean of American archaeologists.

"All this is heady stuff. Albright hastens to point out that he has done no field work in more than a decade now; . . .

"Notwithstanding, another big book is due out next week from the author of Penguin Books' *The Archaeology of Palestine* (which has been translated into Hebrew, French, German and Italian), of the major work *From the Stone Age to Christianity*, of hundreds of papers in learned journals. The new book, *History, Archaeology and Christian Humanism*, is an assemblage of scholarly and auto-biographical papers, many of them previously unpublished, as edited and revised by Albright and his research assistant, Dr. Herbert B. Huffmon.

"*History, Archaeology and Christian Humanism* will be particularly interesting for its enlargements on Albright's philosophical positions. The Bible, explicated by history and archaeology, has been his doorway to the company of the principal Western theologians. Among them, Albright is known as original systematist but even more as critical synthetist, bringing out a tenet's unseen and helpful or damaging implications. The half dozen of his honorary doctorates that are from European universities relate particularly to this work. . . .

"Of his four sons and nine grandchildren, not all will be within range on February 22. No orientalist or archaeologist among them, so far. . . . Albright would have liked to know more Sumerian, that oldest of languages with written remains. Still, if time is left— W. F. Albright's sense of adventure is as strong as ever."

The day after the event, the *Sun* headlined, "Albright Scores 'Perversion' Of Science To Spur Racism." " 'Science in the service of racism is one of our most sinister modern perversions of learning,' Dr. William F. Albright charged yesterday . . ." He had given a fiery speech.

A month later he reported to Noel that his new book was going better than his low expectation. Noel replied that he had begun reading his copy, hindered by many deadlines. "The format and appearance of the volume are splendid. Riffling through the contents, I recognize a number of familiar articles along with a good deal of revision and new material. I don't have to tell you how pleased I am to see this volume, not only as a major achievement in its own right, but as an earnest of the volumes to come."

On April 8 Albright wrote Noel that Huffmon was leaving in the summer to spend a year teaching in a Chicago seminary. He hoped to get a promising young man from England as research assistant, and was beginning to hunt for such help for the school year; he also was thinking of a new plan—looking for a trained woman who could do library study for him as well as act generally as a secretary. When Noel suggested a married scholar, Albright responded that it was too risky for a married man with a child and a career to interrupt it to become a research assistant.

After Prof. Albright received the Christian Culture Award in Windsor on the 19th of April, stories in various papers told of the event: "Rather than being antiquated, the Bible is 'astonishingly up to date,' . . . most cultural activities such as law, art and philosophy were already highly sophisticated 5,000 years ago, and . . . this is reflected in the Bible. 'No matter how technologically advanced twentieth-century man may be, he still lags far behind the equal justice for all taught by Moses, and the courageous faith of the prophets. He lags still farther behind the potential of the New Testament—a potential of divine love for mankind far exceeding the potential of self-destruction which man is now painfully realizing.'

"Albright, a Methodist, said modern science and archaeology have proved that the whole sweep of Biblical history is based on remarkably accurate oral and written transmission. . . ."

Noel wrote on the first of August, having returned from Israel to his island summer home, "I trust you have been able to forge ahead in spite of changes in your staff arrangements, . . . I was tremendously impressed by volume one . . . I lent it to Malamat to read . . ., and then we discussed it afterwards. We agreed that you have rightly been the dominant voice in Near Eastern studies for many years, and that it is your views that have proved the most fruitful and seminal in the progress of studies over the past 30 years. It was perhaps the only 'system' which fully anticipated and could accommodate the tremendous mass of data which has become available in those years. It is a frontier philosophy which will prove increasingly effective in this era of accelerating returns. So for our sake, keep it up." Noel also told of their scheduled move out to San Francisco Theological Seminary in a few weeks.

Before Albright replied on August 14, 1964, he and Ruth had attended the first and only family reunion held at the Virginia farm, August 8-11. As Mary recalled, "The whole family got together except Paul's children. Paul and Georgia came from California, and Philip and Louise and their children came from Texas. My son Forrest didn't attend, but John and his wife Cary did. How John loved the family reunion! And Cary enjoyed the Albright boys' wives and all the relatives. The little ones were all sitting down there in the dining room in a circle on the floor, chanting 'We're all cousins! We're all cousins!' It was as cute as it could be!"

Georgia had shared Paul's interest in socialism. Once when Mary remarked that she had never heard the "Internationale," Georgia sang it for her. But tragedy struck on the day following the close of the reunion in Virginia. Georgia and Paul drove up to Long Island to visit their grandchildren and daughter-in-law, widow of Donald. Paul parked the car in the sloping driveway and got out, then saw that the brake was not holding and it was starting to roll. A grandchild was behind in the driveway, and Paul, who limped, sprang to push the child out of the way. The child was saved but Paul was run over and killed. The tragedy was a real grief to Prof. Albright as well as to the other family members.

When Albright wrote Noel in mid-August he and Ruth were

soon to leave to spend a week or more in Maine on a little island in Lake Meddybemps with his old friend Dr. Paul Bloomhardt and his wife. On returning he expected to be in Baltimore most of the time until they went to England the next April to give the Jordan Lecture series in May at the University of London. Since Huffmon's departure at the end of June, Albright said, he had gone over the final typed copy of his study on the Proto-Sinaitic inscriptions, but would not send it to Frank Cross until he learned what prospects there were for its publication in the Harvard series. He had just written to a man in England who wished to come to the U.S., and asked him to be his research assistant.

The Albrights had met Stephen Mann, an Anglican monk, in Oxford in 1959 at the meeting of the Society for Old Testament Study, and found him very congenial. His views were close to Prof. Albright's. He had his D.Phil. from the University of London in New Testament and was teaching in the equivalent of high school after having left an Anglican order because his scholarly interests did not fit into their pattern. Efforts to secure a visa for him began at this time, not to succeed until a year later. The relationship would eventually turn into collaboration and co-authorship.

A further step in planning for Albright's future work took place that fall. As announced in the South Bend *Tribune* for October 25, a Biblical symposium was held at Notre Dame from Friday through Monday, October 30 to November 2, 1964. "The influence of recent findings, such as the discovery of the Dead Sea Scrolls, on contemporary biblical thinking, will be explored during the symposium by five distinguished speakers," Rev. Roland de Vaux, O.P., director of L'École Biblique in Jerusalem, on "Biblical Theology Today," Dr. Albright on "Middle East Literature and the Bible," Dr. James B. Pritchard of the University of Pennsylvania "On Gibeon," which he had dug, Dr. John Strugnell of Duke University Divinity School on "Qumran Texts," and Père de Vaux again with an illustrated lecture Monday morning on "The Holy Land." Each lecture except the last was followed in the next session by a panel discussion of the lecture topic. The fifth "distinguished speaker" was Dr. David Daube, Regius Professor of Civil Law at Oxford, who would "participate in the symposium panel discussions" as well as give a lecture in the Notre Dame Law School.

The faculty members in the Seminary (moved from Takoma Park, Maryland to Andrews University), where Leona Running taught (having finally completed her doctoral work in Albright's old department and graduated the preceding June) made plans to drive the twenty-odd miles south from Berrien Springs, Michigan, to Notre Dame and hear as many of these lectures as they could. Leona drove with student friends to the first panel discussion Friday evening, having returned home after the first lecture that afternoon. At the end of the evening she went to the high platform and reached up to shake hands with Dr. Albright. She had seen him only occasionally since sitting in his classes his last year, her first half-time year commuting from Takoma Park. She did not expect him with his poor eyesight to recognize her, but mentioned her name. He reached down to shake hands with her and said, "Yes, I've been thinking of you. I wish I could get you to be my research assistant."

Leona was completely taken off-guard and astonished, naturally unaware of what he had earlier written to Noel about finding a trained woman as assistant. All she could do was to light up like a Christmas tree and say, "Do you really want me?" Albright took a quick step forward, asking, "Are you free?" She responded, "Well, no, not really." He said, "I didn't think you would be," and stepped back resignedly. After a brief exchange she left with her friends who had been observing all this. On the drive home they tried to make her realize it was real.

After a rather excited, sleepless night, Leona came to Albright's lecture the next morning and spoke to him before and after it. His first question, "Can you type?" amused this widow who had had a detour of a dozen years of secretarial and editorial work between two teaching careers. In answer to her question, "How would I live?" Albright, once satisfied on the typing ability, answered that he would pay a salary—naming a figure that at that moment was larger than her teaching salary—and he added, for thirty hours' work a week; she could carry on a research project or take on other part-time work as well. She explained that she was being given the next summer as a sabbatical for a trip to Europe and the Middle East. Albright said, "That's all right—come to Baltimore in late September when you return."

Clarifying letters were later exchanged, the Andrews University board granted her a year's leave of absence beyond the sabbatical summer, and Albright told Noel in his December 2 letter that, though he had little time for his needed afternoon rest during the 13 days of his trips to Whitworth College at Spokane and to Notre Dame, Indiana, and therefore suffered attacks of nervous exhaustion all through November, he had found the visit with deVaux and Strugnell and the others at Notre Dame most interesting, and had obtained Dr. Running as research assistant for 1965-66—which in itself was worth a lot, he added. He was still putting forth efforts to secure Dr. Mann on a year-to-year basis, as the immigration attempt had failed.

Albright also told Noel that shortly after their return from Indiana Ruth had stomach surgery at nearby Union Memorial Hospital. They were much relieved to learn there was no trace of cancer, only peptic ulcers. She had been home since the last day of November and was making good progress.

He also bewailed the dearth of properly trained and intelligent New Testament scholars and said he felt sure that his contribution to the Trantham volume published by Baylor University, edited by Jerry Vardaman, would be considered uncritical and ignorant by almost any present-day New Testament scholar who noticed it. What he referred to was a fifteen-page article titled "Retrospect and Prospect in New Testament Archaeology," in which Albright trod on a great many scholarly toes. He traced the growth of knowledge through archaeology and linguistic studies from the ignorance of a hundred years earlier to the wealth of background knowledge for the New Testament now furnished by the Dead Sea Scrolls, with parallels for almost every new Testament book; the Coptic Gnostic discoveries at Nag Hammadi in Egypt; the highly accurate state of development of pottery chronology, including Hellenistic and Roman periods; the discovery of Koine Greek and study of Greek papyrology within those decades which set the Greek of the New Testament in its proper historical and linguistic connections, etc. He pointed out that all the important 19th and 20th century schools of New Testament criticism were pre-archaeological, and many had continued to ignore the new discoveries that were absolutely essential to proper interpretation. But he quoted approvingly Krister Stendahl and some other New Testament scholars, who were aware and competent.

For the first time since 1949, there was an exhibit of Dead Sea Scrolls in Washington and other cities, by consent of the Jordanian Government. "Virtually all the scrolls from Cave One—the best preserved of the scrolls—belong to Israel," Albright was quoted in the Washington *Post* as saying, adding that some of the most important finds were from the other ten caves which belonged to Jordan. The material, heavily insured, was flown over from Amman on December 22 and was eventually displayed also in Canada and Britain.

Noel wrote early in January about how good it was to see Albright at the SBL meetings at the end of the year. He had enjoyed being on the platform with him "during the session on Bible and Archaeology, though naturally I ought not to have been reading a paper in the field where you have made the chief contributions." Leona Running also appreciated a chat with Prof. Albright at the meetings, and took the opportunity to make a quick bus trip to Baltimore and put a deposit down on an apartment rental for the following September, two blocks south of the Albrights' apartment.

Herb Huffmon also attended the meetings and later recalled an encounter with Prof. Albright. "A group of us were talking in one of the wide hallways. Albright was standing about ten or fifteen feet away talking with H. L. Ginsberg and one or two other persons; we were all in line for the refectory. Albright looked over at us, beaming, gestured to HLG, and announced, 'Look, a solid phalanx of my (former) students!' Then he paused, hand to mouth to symbolize a goof, and added, 'Except for Mrs. (Prescott) Williams—but then, she's the prettiest.' " Huffmon added that "since that time Del Hillers and I decided that the old Hoppies (Albright did not recognize all of them as part of the solid phalanx) could have the honorary title of M.S.P. (My Solid Phalanx), subject to the above-mentioned reservation."

Huffmon also recalled a characteristic incident in Albright's last seminar at Hopkins, 1957-58. One of the students presented a paper in which he referred to some of Albright's publications: "In his article on . . . Prof. Albright revealed that . . ." At this point Albright intervened: "Mr. Brown, I may discover something, I may point to something, but I do not *reveal* anything.' " Huffmon thought it consistent with this viewpoint that Albright would never identify former students as his "disciples," whereas some other scholars have done so, even in print.

With the departure of Dr. Ray L. Cleveland for Jordan at the beginning of September 1964, the full burden of BASOR fell again on the shoulders of Prof. Albright. He added Prof. Delbert Hillers' name to the front of the December issue as having "generously assisted in the editing of this number." Later Hillers, then teaching in Albright's old department, would be editor.

In late March of 1965 Albright wrote Noel the news that Herbert Huffmon was moving back to Baltimore, to join Hillers on the regular staff of the department in Hopkins. It was apparent that Dr. Mann would not arrive from London before mid-July; Dr. Running would come by September 20. He really needed both assistants in order to accomplish the most possible before his vision deteriorated much further. He was making slow progress on his Jordan Lectures; the first would give his dating in sequence of early Hebrew poetry, with illustrations and comparisons, and he had finished the second chapter, on the question of the Apiru and the Hebrews, on which much new material had come to light as he worked on it.

20

The Anchor Bible

While the Albrights were in London for the Jordan Lecture series in May of 1965, they enjoyed a weekend in Cornwall. They were introduced to Cornish life and shown places and houses linked to William Foxwell, Prof. Albright's great-grandfather. William had never been in Cornwall before and found the visit most interesting. Cousins in Iowa have a photo of William and Ruth taken that May 16 at Land's End beside the sign showing distances to various places from that farthest-west point in England. The sign shows 3425 miles to Baltimore! Their hostess in Cornwall that weekend was not really a relative; she was the granddaughter of a sister of Thomas Foxwell's first wife, Mary, who died very young. On Thomas's return to Cornwall he had tried to court one of Mary's sisters, but in vain. He returned to America and later married beautiful young Frances Humphry. Their daughter Zephine was Dr. Albright's mother. He and Ruth referred to their Cornish hostess, Esther (Mrs. Reed) Johns, as his "almost-cousin."

In writing to Noel about this visit to Cornwall, Albright also mentioned how well his seven lectures had gone. Since they were scheduled in afternoons, he had plenty of opportunity to rest as well as time to pick up much information from friends old and new. He visited the Law Courts and the House of Lords. Though he felt he learned more than on most such trips, he realized that he was too old and his eyesight too poor to make traveling in the sense of sightseeing very rewarding. But he was sure his curiosity and his flow of ideas were as great as ever, though he could spend less of his time at work.

Noel's response of July 7 expressed delight over their Cornwall trip—Neil's father was a Cornishman, and they had visited her relatives and toured the region several years before. In his next letter he said he hoped Prof. Albright would soon have the material of his Jordan Lectures ready for publication, "as it promises to be an extremely important statement of your position on the relation between Canaan and Israel from earliest times on . . . please let nothing delay the completion of the work."

The Rev. Dr. Stephen Mann arrived from England before the end of July and began to assist Prof. Albright. Early in August Albright wrote Noel, mentioning how useful Mann was showing himself to be in criticizing manuscripts and otherwise, and how fortunate he felt to have his assistance, as he hoped, for three years. It would mean a great saving of his eyesight and an improvement in the quality of English in books and other things that were projected.

Not many days later Dr. Albright was stricken with a medical emergency. Mrs. Albright happened to be out of town; it was very fortunate that Stephen Mann was with him and took him to nearby Union Memorial Hospital. In the last week of August he underwent surgery. Noel wrote him on the 29th that he had heard indirectly he was "in the hospital to undergo a prostate operation. I . . . wanted to express my concern and best wishes for a rapid and complete recovery."

On Sept. 15, Albright was well enough to keep a speaking engagement at the Walters Art Gallery, concerning the Baltimore exhibition of the Dead Sea Scrolls. As reported in the *Sun,* "the average daily attendance for the [second] week was 1,443, the highest average daily attendance for any week in the history of the gallery. . . . Up to closing time on Labor Day, a total of 21,471 persons had seen the scrolls. With the show to close September 19, gallery officials are confident that total attendance will be close to 40,000."

Leona Running landed in New York on the Greek Line *Olympia* on September 16, after sixteen weeks in Europe, Israel, Turkey, Greece and the Aegean Islands. By the 20th, with the help of her parents and their car as well as hers, she moved from Michigan to Baltimore and into a furnished apartment. Mr. and Mrs. Glidden were able to meet Prof. Albright (dressed in his robe but up and around at home) before heading back to Michigan; Mrs. Albright was away at the time. Considerate as always, Dr. Albright attempted to give Leona a day or two to settle, but there was little to do in the

furnished apartment, and she was anxious to start helping him reduce the mountains of urgent correspondence on his desk and
attack other work as rapidly as his strength allowed. The mental
confusion which she perceived, she attributed to the effects of the
recent surgery, not yet realizing that he characteristically operated
on at least three or four mental tracks at the same time, hence constantly had to doublecheck himself, and thought everyone else operated the same way and so he doublechecked them all the time also!

On September 30 Albright dictated another letter to Noel
Freedman, saying that he had made quite a rapid recovery since
writing previously. He surely would not be able to keep all his fall
appointments, but hoped in a few weeks to be able to work quite
normally. Characteristically, Dr. Albright revised his own original
wording on the finished letter, much to the distress of his new
assistant, a dyed-in-the-wool perfectionist. She penned a marginal
note to Noel, "He did say it this way!" Later she would take his
dictation directly on his portable typewriter and let him make all
his revisions on a rough copy so that the final could look its best;
but for then she mainly used her revived shorthand. The great
problem with Dr. Albright was not any post-operative confusion
but his habit of editing himself phrase by phrase as he dictated.
With shorthand it meant constant crossing out and hoping that
when she transcribed it in her own apartment what had not been
crossed out would hang together and be complete. By taking the
dictation of letters or chapters or articles directly on the typewriter,
what she caught was his last version of each phrase, so that when he
was through dictating something, it came out of the typewriter and
before him at once, ready for his pencil editing, saving hours of
labor and delay.

Their routine of work was soon established, controlled by his
eye-drops for glaucoma. When he woke about six A.M. he put in the
first drops but his eyes were not usable for reading for several hours.
Leona would go to his office in Gilman Hall, pick up his mail, and
come down the campus hill to the apartment by 9:45 or so, signaling
with three short rings of the doorbell before using her key. They
would work until 12 or 12:15 and separate for their lunch hours.
Beginning work again about 1:15 or 1:30, they would continue until 3:00, when he had to put drops in his eyes again. Unable to read,
he would go to bed, turn on his TV, and fall asleep for a good nap.

During the late afternoon Leona was either at home transcribing what he had dictated, or up on the hill working for some of the members of the department (its name now changed from Oriental Seminary to Department of Near Eastern Studies, with Dr. Delbert Hillers as Acting Chairman). By 7:30 both Albright and Leona had eaten dinner, and if an evening of work was planned, Albright was fresh from his nap while Leona was at the end of a day's work in Baltimore autumn or summer heat, or the excessive winter heat of her apartment. After about an hour and a half of dictation to the typewriter it was enough for both. Prof. Albright, who was supposed to walk an hour every day, would change from reading to distance glasses, put on his hat, get his cane out of the hall closet, make sure his keys were in his pocket, and accompany Leona the few blocks south, going east a block to walk down St. Paul rather than Charles Street in order to be with the one-way traffic and not have oncoming car lights to dazzle his eyes. Leaving her at her corner, Albright would swing briskly and almost blindly on down a few more blocks, using his cane (or an umbrella) to detect sidewalk unevennesses, and stepping high in order not to stumble on curbs he could not see, and would return with the nearby traffic up the broad Charles Street. It was really risky; later he did his walking only in the daytime, at Mrs. Albright's insistence.

Beginning in March, 1956, much of the correspondence between Prof. Albright and Noel Freedman (often on a return-mail basis) concerned discussions, exchange of opinions and information on the progress of plans developing with Doubleday for what came to be known as the Anchor Bible project. The two of them would be co-editors of the famous series of volumes until Albright's death. The project began with Albright and Jason Epstein at the very beginning of 1956, when Albright drew Noel into the picture. On July 5 Albright signed contracts concerning the Exodus volume which he and Noel were to co-author (never written, however, but turned by them over to Frank Cross). Albright suggested that each of them begin to write an Introduction and exchange outlines and combine them later. He thought it would doubtless be—and it would have been—the most original of the Old Testament book introductions; everyone would want to see their chronology and their treatment of the historical and geographical background.

After authors were chosen for some of the volumes, time passed before manuscripts were ready for the co-editors to criticize. *Genesis* by Prof. E. A. Speiser and *Jeremiah* by Albright's former student Prof. John Bright were among the first to go through the "pipeline."

On Sunday, December 4, 1960, a feature article came out in the Baltimore *Sun* for which both Albright and Freedman had read galley proofs. Along with a photo of Albright at his desk was the caption, "Dr. W. F. Albright, . . . heads a vast project to re-translate the Bible into direct everyday English. It will appear in 32 pocket-size volumes." The three-column article began: "A new paper-backed Bible, translated into the direct, familiar style of today's English, bound in brightly illustrated covers, will take its place on the newsstands during this decade. Its 32 pocket-size volumes will be known as the Anchor Bible—named for its publishers, Anchor Books. The monumental work will be the combined product of Jewish, Protestant and Catholic scholars. It is said to be the first venture of its kind in Bible translation and publishing. . . ." (Doubleday Anchor had to try to recover its heavy investment with hard-cover books first; not all the volumes had yet appeared more than a decade later, and none were yet in the inexpensive paper-backs. Some volumes had expanded into real commentaries, different from the co-editors' original plan.) Frank Henry's article stated that "in all, about 30 distinguished scholars are, or will be, engaged in this work. The nucleus of them is a group of about a dozen former students cf Dr. Albright, especially able younger men who attended his school of Oriental languages during his nearly 30 years at the Johns Hopkins. So this unique Bible will be a product of experts in languages and in history gleaned from archaeology, and not theologians—though some of the translators are learned in theology. . . ."

Mr. Henry quoted Dr. Freedman as saying that the following factors would govern all the translators: "The translators are expected to get into the mood of the particular writer before them. If his style is elevated they will render it that way into today's English. If it is poetic they will translate it in poetic form; and straight narrative will come out that way in English—in all instances in the mood and feeling of the Biblical author."

This was one of the first articles giving publicity to the project on which the joint editors had been working hard for many months; it would turn out to be a monumental undertaking going far beyond its projected completion date in 1966 and even beyond the lifetime of its senior editor.

In June of 1961 Albright typed a letter to Noel returning the manuscript of one of the Anchor Bible authors, saying that in comparison with traditional commentaries it could be considered very good, but in view of the new knowledge of Hebrew literature against the background of Northwest-Semitic literature it was rather poor. He asked not to be quoted on that, however, as the man was only following the majority, and as Jerome had said, the majority were *bipedes aselli* (translated politely as two-legged donkeys!).

When Noel wrote to Albright on July 13, 1963, congratulating Albright on finishing the manuscript of his first volume for McGraw-Hill, he dropped a bombshell concerning the Anchor Bible project: the publishers wanted a sort of guarantee of manuscripts being written and turned in on schedule before they published the volumes already in hand.

As soon as he returned from the Ashdod dig to his island summer home, Noel visited Doubleday in New York about this development. He reported to Albright that he had found out who was raising all the opposition, and it had been overcome; he had talked things through with all their friends, who had eventually outargued and outvoted the man. At that time they were all set to bring out four volumes in September of 1964 and two every six months after that. Noel thought they could live with that schedule, keeping close track of delinquent authors. (Time would prove him far too optimistic.)

On April 8, 1964, Albright in writing to Noel suggested another European author for a volume in the Anchor Bible series. When Noel returned from Israel at the end of July, he wrote that "Speiser's *Genesis* is in press and the volume should be out by September 1, . . . Other MSS are already in the pipeline." In his reply in mid-August Albright commented on Noel's imminent move to the San Francisco area, remarking that a number of people from Baltimore were then in that area and of course Noel had family members on the West Coast. He would in any case be able to make flying trips east periodically. He and Noel exchanged suggestions for personnel for the press conference that was being set up to publicize the first volume of the Anchor Bible, Speiser's *Genesis*. The date of September 24 and the hour of 3:00 P.M. were set.

Afterward Noel wrote Albright that "the general impression was that the press conference went well, and that we can expect to see some good stories on the Anchor Bible. These in turn may help to promote sales. In any case there is nothing more to do about that, except to see to it that the books keep coming." Noel was working on a partial manuscript of Mitchell Dahood's *Psalms* and remarked, "Needless to say his work is highly original and very provocative. I am confident that many of his observations and interpretations will stand up under scrutiny, though in such a revolutionary piece of work, utilizing everything we now know about Canaanite morphology and syntax, as well as lexicography, it would be too much to expect that everything will turn out to be right. Naturally, most scholars will reject 90% of his work out of hand, but I am certain that the future is with his work, and work like it." Noel's forecast was quite accurately fulfilled when Dahood's three volumes on the *Psalms* eventually appeared one by one in the series. The editors knew they were taking risks, but knew the value of their authors' being on the cutting edge of their disciplines, even though not yet having wide acceptance among scholars for their ideas.

Stories on the Anchor Bible appeared in many newspapers and journals. One in the *Evening Sun* on Saturday, October 17, said: "Publication of an entirely new sort of Bible will begin Tuesday. Called the Anchor Bible, it employs the revolutionary archaeological and linguistic discoveries of the last 50 years to bring the meaning of the Scriptures into clear focus for modern readers. Unlike most other modern translations, the new Anchor version consists of 38 volumes, each written by a different internationally recognized Biblical scholar. Being published this week are *Genesis,* by E. A. Speiser, and *The Epistles of James, Peter and Jude,* by Bo Reicke. The other 36 volumes will be released at a rate of six each year."

The article quoted Dr. Albright as saying, "This is the first time that Catholic, Protestant and Jewish scholars have all collaborated in a series of commentaries on a religious book." And the article continued, "Accuracy of translation, not theological interpretation, has been the major concern of the editors. Dr. Albright, who has been on many archaeological expeditions, places great significance in the 'actual life and times of the people who wrote the Bible— their houses, food, customs, religious institutions and literature.'

" 'Not one scrap of this material was available even 100 years ago, and you find virtually no trace of it in any of the translations (before the Anchor version).' . . .

"The Hopkins professor estimates that while there were some '15,000 words used and understood by the Hebrews at the time of the Old Testament,' scholars were familiar with only about 3,000 until recently. These findings, Dr. Albright says, included 'thousands of inscriptions in many scripts and languages' used by Biblical peoples. Now we have added hundreds of words of known meaning to the vocabulary of ancestral Hebrew. . . .

"Work on the Anchor Bible has been in progress for eight years. . . . 'I read a tremendous amount of proofs' Dr. Albright admits, 'but not all of them in detail.' He and Dr. Freedman share the supervisory work, and 'offer suggestions and help along the way.' But he emphasizes that 'each author—and we pick our authors with great care—is responsible for his own work. We never impose our will on them. The final decision is theirs.'

"Dr. Albright maintains that 'not all the authors are believers in the divine revelation of the Bible, and some are complete agnostics.' He says that sometimes nonbelievers are 'more objective than those who have a profound interest in theology.' Dr. Albright, . . . points out that he does have a profound interest, but tries nevertheless to be objective. He feels that a good Biblical scholar should know about six modern and six ancient languages. Dr. Albright, who has been deciphering the handwriting of ancient scribes for more than 30 years, knows 25 tongues. . . .

"In the new Anchor Bible, changes of one sort or another are numerous, to the possible discomfort of some fundamentalist groups. But the Hopkins professor declares that few people 'feel that the Bible is infallible in the sense that its authors, editors and translators make no mistakes.' Dr. Albright does not believe that 'every word was written by the hand of God. The Bible was written by human beings, and is the Word of God through man.' "

Noel, in the throes of settling in his new home near San Francisco, found it impossible to return east for the Biblical Colloquium at Thanksgiving time in 1964. He asked Albright to think about Doubleday's request concerning the possibility of adding volumes on the Apocrypha to the Anchor Bible series. Albright, who had attended only the Saturday afternoon meeting of the Colloquium with Frank Cross, replied that he was advising Doubleday to defer work on the Apocrypha for a while, though they should think of possible contributors. (They were having a hard enough time finding suitable authors for all the Old and New Testament volumes.)

In Noel's letter of December 5 he described how from "quiet, peaceful Pittsburgh" he had landed in the midst of turbulence among students at Berkeley, with faculty pitted against administration, but not so much in his own seminary. With telephone and airplane connections he would soon get over his feeling of being isolated far away and out of circulation. He discussed Anchor Bible problems and bewailed having let himself be talked into a major paper for the SBL meetings on Biblical Archaeology. "You of course should be giving the paper," he wrote, "as you are the only one who can; in essence you created the subject." Albright, who was working hard with little help to meet his deadline the following week for revising his two chapters for the new *Cambridge Ancient History,* replied telling where he had a hotel reservation in New York; he would attend as many of the meetings as possible.

Early in 1965 Dr. Albright, unable to go to Israel to attend the opening of the new Israeli Museum scheduled for May, sent a tape-recorded message in Hebrew. He would be in London when the date for the dedication arrived.

Noel's letter of March 11, 1965, gave Prof. Albright a new view of their Anchor Bible project: "A Redemptorist Father here who is a student in the Graduate Theological Union, reported to me that at their house in Oakland, the lector at their communal meals has been reading the translations of Genesis and Jeremiah from the Anchor Bible. I think this is a rather remarkable development, which points to an aspect of the project and its acceptance which I would not have anticipated. After all, we have been saying emphatically that this was not a Bible for use in public worship. While meal-reading is not the same thing, it is public. And the idea of a Catholic order using translations made respectively by a Jew and a Presbyterian is intriguing."

Albright responded that this was surely a remarkable forward step. At the same time, he was bubbling over with enthusiasm for incredible but completely convincing discoveries made by Dr. Abram Spiro, of Wayne State University, concerning Samaritan and anti-Samaritan strands in the Gospels. The Dead Sea Scrolls had been the catalyst for the development, as so often happened. Albright said he had just sent Abe a long letter discussing points of agreement and warning him not to make value judgments on the material. (The scholarly stimulation between Albright and Spiro would continue for two more years, until Spiro's untimely death.)

Noel was intrigued by the comments on Spiro's research and looked forward to seeing something of it in print. "If what you say is true, it will certainly have an enormous impact on New Testament background studies, as well as the elucidation of obscure materials and references in the NT. Once again the Gospel of John will have proved to reflect very early and somewhat esoteric elements in the picture." He reported that *Job*, by Prof. Marvin Pope of Yale, was now in print in their series.

Albright had just received word, when he wrote Noel on March 23, that Prof. Johannes Munck, their author for *Acts*, who was on a lecture trip in the United States from his native Denmark, had died on February 22. His manuscript needed revision of the Danish original and completion of its translation into English. He thought that Abe Spiro might add a little material on the basis of his research, if it was not completed before the following year, when Spiro's own book was to appear. When he had told Munck of Spiro's findings, Munck had seemed greatly impressed and was even willing tentatively to write an introduction for Spiro's book. Albright took over the job of finishing the *Acts* volume.

In the fall, Noel wrote delicately urging the need for *Acts* to be made ready for publication soon, since there was a "large and growing gap" after the tenth volume was published. "It is encouraging to know that Stephen Mann will be able to devote some time to this now urgent project." Albright replied that the work on *Acts* should be done soon after his return from a lecture appointment in Miami the first week of November, and that he had canceled his West Coast trip. He added that he was almost wholly recovered from his recent operation and had regained his weight and most of his strength.

During these weeks when he was catching up on letters to his correspondents all over the world, he told all of them about his "prostatectomy," each time stumbling over the word and making Leona help him out with the pronunciation, much to his own amusement. The letters between Albright and Freedman were now crossing each other. Albright began his of October 26 by saying that the reason he wrote so quickly was that with his new secretary and research assistant, it was a temptation to move work off his desk too rapidly for his own good. Just since the previous day's letter, he said, he had realized that he might need a couple more weeks in which to work on the *Acts* manuscript (this would turn out to be the understatement of the year).

He commented on the fact that Doubleday was using for its Christmas card Dahood's Anchor Bible version of Psalm 24, with a sketch by the American artist Ben Shahn; that would help Dahood's morale. (Noel had said the card was "quite impressive and should be good publicity for the volume.") Albright also commented (concerning Abe Spiro's book on Samaritan influence in the New Testament, scheduled to be published by Harper) that unfortunately there were not too many scholars of sufficiently strong character not to join in the persecution that was likely to follow the appearance of the book. He had tried in vain to persuade Spiro to limit the size of it by warning, "mega biblion, mega kakon"—a Greek proverb, "big book—big trouble."

Noel's next letter contained a cryptic statement: "Neil and I are both well, and both waiting. I think it is more difficult for her, but I must admit it is a little nerve-wracking. But the doctors are glacially calm, which is probably a good thing." Albright ended his November 1 reply, which told of finishing the Munck manuscript except for his and Mann's notes, with a request for Noel to give Neil the Albrights' best wishes and hopes that all would go well—he also liked it better when doctors were "glacially calm." The November 4 response from Noel solved the conundrum: "We are very happy to report the birth of our fourth child and second son, whose name is Jonathan Prior. His middle name is Neil's family name. He arrived on the 29th of October, and weighed 8 lbs. 2 oz. Both mother and son are doing well, and have already returned from the hospital. . . . It has been a long time since we had an infant around the house, but it is a pleasurable experience, and we're glad to have him."

Albright sent his and Ruth's heartiest congratulations and said Ruth and Leona had read the enigmatic sentence of Noel's October 27 letter and persuaded him that Neil was expecting to give birth

very soon. Although there was a great gap in the "typological sequence"—the archaeologist couldn't resist the metaphor—and probably in fact on account of it, he was sure they were very happy
about the baby.

Work on the notes for *Acts* was in progress, and Leona had told
him, he said, that only a few pages needed retyping in the manuscript instead of the quantity he had feared. In a postscript he told
Noel of his weekend of lectures at the University of Miami and at
Barry College. For him the best part had been a visit with Cesare
Emiliani, an authentic Italian genius who was a geologist, oceanog-
rapher, physicist and chemist. It had been a most stimulating three-
hour visit, and the trip had not worn him out.

On November 11, 1965, at the meeting of the American Philosophical Society, Albright read his paper on "Neglected Factors in
the Greek Intellectual Revolution." A footnote in the posthumously published, more fully elaborated form of this topic (in
Proceedings of the APS, Vol. 116, No. 3, June, 1972) said he had
begun the research for this paper in July, 1960, at Harvard, being
stimulated by an article by his old frend, Otto Eissfeldt.

The end-of-year SBL meetings were held at Vanderbilt University, Nashville, in 1965. Stephen Mann attended from Baltimore,
Abe Spiro was there from Wayne State University, Detroit, and
Leona Running came from being with her family in Michigan for
the holidays. (Noel Freedman was in the Middle East.) Prof. Albright did not attend those meetings or the ASOR Corporation
annual meeting held there on the 29th, but he did attend the winter
meeting of the ASOR Trustees held on the 28th in New York and
"reported in behalf of the special committee which is attempting to
arrange for the publications of the excavations at Nimrud Dagh."[1]

Mrs. Albright would sometimes confidentially ask Leona what
her husband was working on; was it really productive work, something that would soon be sent off to a publisher? Or was he just following his insatiable interests in all directions (and wasting time
of paid help)? Leona was always able to assure her that what they
were working on was to meet a real deadline (often an already past
one) and that there would soon be a finished manuscript ready to
send off. They might be book reviews, encyclopedia articles, Ap-
pendix chapters for the Munck *Acts,* or something else. Leona
helped with proof-reading for the issues of BASOR periodically and

also for his monograph on the Proto-Sinaitic Inscriptions which was finally being published in the Harvard series. The Rockwell Lectures, which he had given in January, 1962 at Rice University, Houston, were rewritten and updated and brought out under the title *Archaeology, Historical Analogy and Early Biblical Traditions* from the Louisiana University Press at Baton Rouge in 1966. The Whidden Lectures he had given at McMaster University, Hamilton, Ontario in January of 1961 also appeared late in 1966 from Oxford University Press under the title *New Horizons in Biblical Research*. Between such larger projects Albright would catch up somewhat on correspondence, or acknowledge reprints from scholars in the U.S. and overseas, or even send out some of his own offprints to many scholarly colleagues. Leona sometimes accused him, however, of having no conscience when it came to meeting deadlines.

Baltimore was almost snowbound for more than a week in January. There were a few days when Leona could not get out to go and work in his study, but had plenty of work to do in her own apartment for him and other professors while Albright worked at home on manuscripts and proofs.

Occasionally in the mail that arrived daily would be a crack-pot letter, often about religion. In most cases Albright would simply write "no answer" on it and throw it on the pile to be filed. A persistent young fellow on the West Coast wrote back after Prof. Albright had sent him a kindly letter of explanation of his problem, which concerned ancient history. He questioned the validity of Albright's information and argument. When a second kind letter still brought that kind of response, Albright was at the end of his patience. He had Leona type the student's address on a postal card and begin the message side in the regular way, but instead of a message simply put the word "RUBBISH!" and make the customary place for his signature. Ordinarily Leona would have tried to talk him out of doing this, but she also was quite disgusted with the brash young student's narrow-mindedness and his complete lack of understanding of and respect for Dr. Albright's vast erudition and authoritative knowledge of the subject.

The sequel was interesting. When the Albrights were attending the Symposium on Biblical Archaeology which Noel Freedman sponsored at Berkeley and San Anselmo March 14 to 16, 1966, that student correspondent attended Albright's lecture that opened the series on Monday evening at the University of California. It was titled "The Impact of Archaeology on Biblical Research—1966." The student met Albright personally after the lecture, and they had a congenial chat!

Prof. Jonas Greenfield was then teaching in the Berkeley area and recalled Albright's lecture. "There in the audience was William A. Edgerton, or Billy Edgerton, as we called him. He was emeritus from Chicago, but he was teaching a few courses in Egyptology at Berkeley. They were old opponents and old antagonists over the reading of Egyptian and related matters, and they greeted each other cordially. Edgerton called Albright 'William,' and Albright responded with 'Billy' to William Edgerton, and a warm spark was ignited between the two old men—I suppose they were very close in age."

Drs. Yohanan Aharoni and Moshe and Trude Dothan from Israel participated in the Symposium, as did Drs. Francis I. Andersen, Frank Cross, and G. Ernest Wright. The Albrights were guests of Noel and Neil during the visit and were quite charmed with little Jonathan. Albright wrote to Noel on March 21 saying he hoped that Noel had been able to recover from all his hard work in preparing and managing the symposium, which Albright considered very successful, and that he had never seen a child of four months so alert as "Brother Jonathan." Albright mentioned that he was finalizing arrangements to spend the following year on his *History of the Religion of Israel* for Louis Finkelstein; this had priority over his second volume for McGraw-Hill.

Albright next wrote Noel that he was extremely tired when he returned from Philadelphia, where the Committee on Research had handled 150 applications. There had been many almost-fights and of course he had dived head-first into all of them, he admitted. He had signed a contract for the *History of the Religion of Israel*; but the manuscript he had worked on since 1959 (when Emunah Finkelstein helped him research and type it) would have to be completely rewritten in view of the many changes he had made in his own ideas as well as in the total approach.

Noel sent the typescript of Albright's speech at the Symposium for revision. He thought the outline was "fine, and the treatment both simple and clear. Some of the anecdotal material seems inappropriate, and here and there, of course, good speaking style does not necessarily make for good reading. I would suggest a few concentrated doses of illustrative archaeological material be applied to point up, amplify, or demonstrate certain of the major propositions you make, preferably using the most recent available material. You barely touch on a number of such items; perhaps you could limit yourself to three or four significant illustrations of the main theses, enlarge a little on these, and let the MS stand approximately on those terms."

In Albright's reply he said he was never surprised at what he might have said in giving a lecture. He marked some changes of wording in the margin of his letter as well as correcting a couple of typing mistakes, but he would never let Leona retype a letter, claiming that the penned changes let the recipient know that the one who dictated the letter had really read it before it went out. He was unaware of how this makes self-respecting secretaries gnash their teeth!

Albright and Noel were together at the AOS meeting in Philadelphia in mid-April. Noel's letter of April 29 reported that on his following visit to Doubleday he had learned that "sales of all volumes through February totalled a little less than 175,000 copies, or approximately 10,000 a month, which has been a steady rate."

On May 2 the bibliography for Munck's *Acts* volume was finally sent to New York. The next day Albright gave a lecture at Wesley Theological Seminary in Washington on "Existentialist Speculation and Biblical Reality," speaking from a pencil-written outline covering in a large hand 4½ sheets of discarded mimeographed material. He was still a careful saver of usable paper, manila envelopes and string.

In Noel's May 5 letter discussing ideas about the Apocryphal books for the Anchor Bible project, he closed with, "Since I have a birthday next week, I know you are close to one as well. Congratulations and best wishes from all of us here."

Albright responded on the 9th with congratulations for Noel's birthday and wishing him at least the same number still to come. He had just received Father Ray Brown's *John*, Vol. I, in the Anchor series; he expected it to be better treated by reviewers than the *Acts* by Munck which he and Stephen Mann had finally completed, and the Mann-Albright volume *Matthew* (which they had

decided to write together after the original author had to give up
the assignment). It was good for the series to have an irenic volume
as the first contribution from one of their Catholic authors on New
Testament books. Noel agreed; the "uniformly sympathetic" reviews "will not hurt the series at all." He had heard from Dahood
that he was "well into Vol. II of the Psalms."

Ruth's handwritten note of April 18 reached Noel inviting
him, if he could arrange to be in the East, to the birthday celebration she and her daughter-in-law Jo were planning for William's
75th birthday—a buffet supper at 5:30 on Sunday, May 22. Noel
replied, doubtful that any of the family could attend, much as they
would like to, and saying, "We all send our warmest greetings to
you both, and wish William many long years of life and health and
productive work. After all, according to the Scriptures, Abraham
embarked on his career at age 75, and Moses didn't lead the Israelites out of Egypt until he was past 80."

Albright's former students, colleages and friends flocked in from
all over the eastern seaboard on May 22, two days before his birthday. Leona helped Mrs. Albright and Josephine serve the 70 or
75 guests who milled through the rooms of the apartment. Jo had
ordered a tremendous amount of good food, already cooked and
baked, sliced and ready to serve. Dr. Albright was feeling quite
well and mingled among his guests, delighted to see his old friends
and talk with them in small groups as they crowded around him.
It was a very delightful surprise for him, one that he greatly appreciated. Noel sent a telegram: "Congratulations on the first 75
years and best wishes for the remaining 100—Genesis 12:4 and
25:7."

Another gala occasion a little earlier in the spring had been the
annual dinner for member-sponsors of the Walters Art Gallery.
The Albrights hosted David and Jo, and Prof. Albright's two research assistants for the banquet. When Stephen Mann's birthday
came in early May, Mrs. Albright prepared a birthday dinner at
home and Leona brought the cake. At other times Prof. Albright
would include his assistants in dinners at the Johns Hopkins Faculty Club for visiting Israeli archaeologists or faculty of his old
department, or other small groups. When Mrs. Albright's birthday
came on June 1, Leona took the Albrights to see "Sound of Music,"
intending to reciprocate a little, but Dr. Albright insisted on pay-

ing for the tickets. He was dubious about how his eyes would stand the wide-screen showing, but took extra pairs of dark glasses along and used two pairs together some of the time, and claimed that he really enjoyed it as much as the two women did.

A number of times when Leona arrived in the morning to work in his study, the first hour would have to be spent hunting for some document that he had mislaid, perhaps just since the previous afternoon. Sometimes it involved hunting in some of the alphabetically arranged manila envelopes of scholars' offprints on the shelves covering a wall of his bedroom; or they might need to investigate the contents of every folder in the stacks on his desk and on nearby TV tables and shelves. All the while Prof. Albright, wearing an old plaid wool jacket with frayed cuffs, and a green eye-shade, would be muttering in Arabic—bismillah, "In the name of God!" or inshallah, "If God wills!" and when the lost was finally found, al-hamdu lillah, "Praise be to God!"

The day following his birthday, Prof. Albright spoke on "The Historical Meaning of the Scrolls from the Jordan and Dead Sea Valleys" at noon in the Wheeler Auditorium of the central Enoch Pratt Free Library in Baltimore.

The Albrights made a trip in early June (while Leona Running returned to Andrews University for a convention) to Ruth Albright's *alma mater,* Lake Erie College in Painesville, Ohio. The Cleveland *Plain Dealer* for June 13 reported that the commencement speaker was "Dr. William Foxwell Albright, archaeologist and professor emeritus of Semitic languages at Johns Hopkins University. Dr. Albright described science's potential to inflict destruction or to do good. He asserted that in the rapidly changing world of today the scientist is being confronted with mass production versus mass destruction. He called on scientists to solve the problem and remove the dangers from science and technology." *Both* Drs. Albright received honorary doctorates that day as degrees were conferred on 101 graduates of the women's college and 42 candidates from the community education division. It was Prof. Albright's 25th, a Litt.D., and the first honorary degree for Dr. Ruth. Photographs of them showed two very pleased and happy people, he being especially gratified that this time she shared in the honor.

Another honor that came to Albright early in 1966 was "The

Carey-Thomas Award for the Best Example of Creative Publishing in 1965." The citation stated that this award "Has Been Given to Doubleday & Company for the Publication of The Anchor Bible Edited by William Foxwell Albright and David Noel Freedman." Mrs. Albright had her husband's copy framed in a slender black horizontal frame and hung on a narrow wall space near a window in his study.

A doctoral candidate at New York University, Stanley Eugene Hardwick, had been working on a dissertation which he completed in 1965 and then received his degree. The title was "Change and Constancy in William Foxwell Albright's Treatment of Early Old Testament History and Religion, 1918-1958." He sent Prof. Albright a copy of the dissertation; Albright was quite bemused by it and remarked to Leona that he hadn't realized he had changed his views that much, but as he looked it over he realized he had indeed. In the abstract of the dissertation Hardwick stated: "William Foxwell Albright is internationally known as perhaps the foremost Orientalist of the twentieth century. In his voluminous writings he has devoted much attention to Old Testament traditions concerning the period of Israel's history from Hebrew beginnings to the institutions of the monarchy. The span of Albright's scholarly career has coincided with the great period of advancement in scientific archaeological activity in Palestine and adjacent lands. In the light of the newly-discovered data Albright has repeatedly modified his interpretation of Biblical traditions."

After outlining his method of analyzing patterns of change and constancy, Hardwick gave the order of his presentation: "1) a delineation of problem and method [chapter 1]; 2) a biographical sketch of Albright's life [chapter 2]; 3) a survey of the treatment of early Old Testament history and religion by Albright's predecessors [chapter 3]; 4) detailed analyses of Albright's treatment of individual subjects relating to the patriarchal period, the exodus and the wilderness wanderings, the conquest of the land, and the period of the tribal confederacy [chapters 4-10]; 5) synthesis and conclusions, including discussions of constant emphases and significant changes, distended patterns of change and constancy, the validity of the main research hypothesis, and inferences and generalizations for scholarly enterprise [chapter 11]." Under the heading "Findings" Hardwick wrote:

"A few illustrative examples of numerous constant emphases are the north Mesopotamian associations of the patriarchs, the existence of Moses as a Hebrew monotheist and as the leader in the exodus from Egypt, and the omission of important early Hebrew conquests in the 'standard' Biblical descriptions of the conquest.

"Several illustrative examples of numerous subjects associated with changes are the nature of the patriarchal figures, the extent of the Israelite conquests, and the historicity of Deborah and Samson.

"The principal general finding was that throughout his career Albright becomes increasingly conservative in his treatment of early Old Testament history and religion. The greatest number and most decisive changes toward a more conservative point of view come in about the first decade of his writing career (1918-1928). But each of the other three decades involved is also marked by significant alterations toward a more conservative interpretative position.

"This does not mean that Albright becomes increasingly conservative in his *theological* views (although this is at least true of the first part of his career). Nor does it mean that he returns to the kind of Biblical interpretation characteristic of Jewish or Christian orthodoxy. Even as of 1958 he stands between right-wing conservative scholars and so-called radical scholars.

"The relationship between Albright's development, as thus delineated, and the development of Old Testament studies is not merely incidental. Substantial reasons exist for believing that Albright's development and its reflection in his writings have been influential in bringing about a more conservative outlook on many questions in Old Testament scholarship."

The modifications and changes that Prof. Albright was always willing to make on learning of new data and evidence brought on him the reproach of some of being unstable, always changing his mind, and the admiration of many for being flexible and willing to follow truth and not merely protect his ego by holding doggedly to positions that had become untenable. Thus he was able to remain at the forefront in his fields.

In mid-July 1966, Albright sent Noel a copy of a sharp letter he had sent to their Anchor Bible editor about the awful mess several copy editors using various colors of ink had made of the Munck *Acts* manuscript—especially the woman who used green ink and made, according to Stephen Mann, not one sensible change. Stephen spent three weeks of hard work over the manuscript when it was returned to them, and Albright himself put in at least a week of work, besides Leona's six full days working over the English translation comparing it with the ancient Greek text. Albright said if he had known what would happen, he would have resigned from the project and returned all monetary advances; a self-respecting scholar could not allow his name to be connected with such a project. He and Stephen had struck out all the copy editors' comments and made their own changes where there was a legitimate question, and they would write their own separate preface with their names signed (in addition to Munck's). He emphasized again the impossibility of accepting such heckling from copy editors, and in his letter to Noel explained further about the unbelievably silly questions and changes by those copy editors. He had expressed himself to the head man over the phone as well as writing the letter, and said he meant every word of it. One of his chapters for the *Cambridge Ancient History* revision had seriously suffered in a similar way, and he was a bit sore on the topic. It was true that he and Stephen had each thought the other had checked the translation and neither had, so they did that as well, after the manuscript was returned late in June. (They had thought it was off their hands when they sent it away in February.)

Noel's reply of July 19 was very sympathetic to the "account of the dreadful mishandling of the *Acts* MS, which has been bedeviled from the start with insuperable obstacles." Now he had word from the head man in question that he was resigning from Doubleday as of August 12, not because of any problems with Noel or Albright or the project, but within the company. He had been excellent for the work when he got into it; he had trained two young women to carry on as his successors. Noel agreed with Albright's fervent hope that no more of their authors would die, and thought also that "we should avoid like the plague authors who do not write in English, as the translation problem only adds to the general confusion." He had some good news to report about other parts of the project, but was disturbed over this matter and hoped that after all their hard work of the recent weeks there would be no more trouble and the volume would appear "in decent form," as they had "immeasurably improved the volume" and "worked far beyond the call of duty." (Noel showed his diplomatic abilities.)

On July 25 Albright wrote a more conciliatory letter to the resigning editor, saying both he and Noel had found him to be the best editor with whom they had worked on the project, but with a scholarship to study journalism, he had too good an opportunity to resist, and Albright wished him every success. The *Acts* manuscript was being sent that day with all their combined work on it, including all of them working over the translation. He had found the work of the copy editors more helpful than the impression given him by Dr. Mann, who was fed up with it and who had left on vacation a week before. He said that Dr. Running had seen more value in the "green" editorial contributions, but the comments had surely exceeded normal limits for copy editors. He thought the printing could now proceed; when they could read galley proofs it would be much easier to evaluate it. The month's work had almost cost him his eyesight. He itemized a bill to repay his assistants' services in making the manuscript usable. In closing he reported that he and Stephen had made good progress on *Matthew;* if it had not been for the unanticipated weeks of work on *Acts,* they would have finished the first draft of the *Matthew* introduction.

Reporting the same day to Noel, Albright said he hoped his vision would recover by the time Stephen returned in mid-August; it was nearly forfeited in working on the difficult manuscript. He also mentioned to Noel drawing up a circular letter as a guide to contributors, to avoid any more volumes swelling to such a size as a couple of recent ones, so far from the original plan of paperbacks. They might be grateful for those large ones but did not want any more like them.

Dr. Gilbert Darlington, of the American Bible Society, wrote to Prof. Albright asking for his suggestions of improving the illustrations as they reprinted their "Illustrated New Testament." Albright replied that he had asked Dr. Leona G. Running, his assistant, to take over the job, and she had in less than an hour made a number of suggestions on the basis of her previous summer's trip in Palestine and Greece. He told his old friend of working diligently with two assistants, naming also his other one; he had to be careful of his easily overworked vision, but could not complain because he had never expected to see at all when he reached 75—an opinion shared by his oculist.

A certain business man in Minneapolis regularly sent to Prof. Albright Xerox copies of articles from the London *Times* and other publications that he thought would be of interest, mainly on archaeology and ancient history. Periodically Albright wrote him a thank-you letter commenting on some of the recent items that particularly attracted his attention. On July 26 he wrote, commenting on Père de Vaux's review of a recent book by G. R. Driver, and then characterizing Driver as unable to tolerate disagreement or keep up with new findings, unaware of fields of knowledge that were essential to his work. (He never accepted the authenticity of the Dead Sea Scrolls, for instance.) Albright closed with comments on the great importance of Çatal Hüyük and discoveries made there by Mellaart, for whom he had tried in vain to get a grant against the successful opposition of a scholar who thought that no more digging should be done until all that already was done had been published—as though they could solve all problems without more digging to bring more light to bear on them!

Albright occasionally wrote also to archaeologists in India to encourage them and thank them for sending their offprints and books. In an air letter in late July he delicately indicated disagreement that the Indus Valley script, coming from about 2000 B.C., had any connection with either hieroglyphic or cuneiform scripts, or with the alphabetic script of Northwest-Semitic peoples.

Sometimes Albright wrote letters in the role of peacemaker, for example trying to explain to a colleague their mutual colleague's harsh criticism of his work as really quite reasonable—for him—because the mutual friend was practically unteachable, but extremely diligent and patient for detailed work, with a good eye for paleography.

The Albrights planned a vacation trip to visit relatives in Virginia and North Carolina during ten days in August when their son, Hugh ("Brother Alban"), could take them in a rental car; Leona was going to take a short vacation at the same time. Stephen had spent two weeks in Tennessee and was on his way to spend ten days in Quebec, getting a better idea than most English tourists about various parts of the continent of North America, including fauna, as Albright remarked in a letter to Hugh.

To his old Hopkins friend, Dr. Paul Bloomhardt, at Lake Meddybemps Albright wrote in early August with regret that he and Ruth had not been able to visit him on his Maine island in July as they had hoped. The airline strike made it difficult. On their visit to Colby College (in Waterville, Maine, where Albright had just a few weeks earlier received honorary doctorate number 26, an L.H.D.), part of their ticket had been invalid, the flight abolished, and they had spent a night at Logan Airport. But even without the strike, pressing work on a commentary whose author had died occupied him and his two assistants, and now he and Leona were feverishly working on his Jordan Lectures. He hoped in September to return to his 1959 manuscript on the *History of the Religion of Israel*. Much had been sent to publishers in the last year since his operation, though it had cost his health a price that, so far, could be paid by rest on weekends.

To a colleague who was facing possible surgery Albright wrote that in his own case, after a year he was just about in normal health again, except that he was a year older and unable to do as much. He wrote Frank Cross thanking him for having helped on publishing of his Proto-Sinaitic Inscriptions study. When his fifty copies came he looked it over in the evening and could find no printer's errors, nor even any places where he had changed his mind, since he had avoided the topic for two years; however, he should have included a few more names of scholars and other references. He gave Leona a list of twenty-five names of scholars in the U.S., France, England, Germany, Italy, Israel, Canada and India to whom she could mail presentation copies of the newly published monograph.

Leona had moved in mid-April to a row house where she had the third floor, with windows opening at east and west ends providing a bit of breeze, though it was a few blocks farther to walk. During the hot summer after the *Acts* manuscript was done, she and Prof. Albright worked hard on the final draft for Athlone Press of the Jordan Lectures he had given in May of 1965 in London. The months of steady work, including many evenings, were telling on both of them. In mid-August when they reached the end of a section of the work he kindly suggested that she leave early on vacation while they visited relatives. While she was at her school it became clear that a second year's leave of absence would be a hardship for her school and colleagues, and she felt the psychological need of returning to classroom teaching. She phoned Dr.

Albright long-distance one noon to ask him to release her from the second year, which had long before been requested and granted, promising to return and finish work on the Jordan Lectures before leaving. Dr. Albright was reluctant but graciously agreed, and later admitted it was the best thing for both, as he had to go to bed with nervous exhaustion after she moved back to Michigan.

At the end of August Prof. Albright received a cable and letter from South America inviting him to participate in a colloquium on oriental studies in Latin-American universites and research institutions, scheduled for Buenos Aires September 19-23. He suggested a title in Spanish and asked for a prompt reply as to the length of time he should speak. He would try to have it translated into Spanish before leaving, as his fluency was less than formerly. However, the Albrights did not make the trip after all. His passport did not come until Friday before the Monday they should arrive in Buenos Aires, and he was in bed every weekend with nervous exhaustion. As he wrote to Leona of this outcome, he remarked that the summer had been hard on them both. He would ever feel gratitude for the sabbatical year she had given to helping him during what was a critical year; he had sent three more chapters off to London by registered mail on September 30. (He had not let Leona actually mail the Jordan Lectures manuscript off to London before she left, wanting to reread it to catch any remaining "howlers.")

Scheduled to be published in New York as well as London, the title had been changed to *Yahweh and the Gods of Canaan*. Albright dedicated it "In Honour of the Eightieth Birthday 1 September 1967 of Otto Eissfeldt Whose Scholarly Exploration Has Made This Volume Possible."

Albright typed a note to Noel on September 28 saying his and Stephen's work on *Matthew* was progressing well; Leona's departure had left him in difficulty, although now he could get needed rest, but expected to fall more and more behind. Noel's brief and sympathetic reply ended: "It is especially true these days that a good secretary is hard to find. In fact the famous description of Proverbs 31 probably applies more to secretaries these days than to wives." When Albright had found a part-time typist, he wrote again to Leona saying they were impressed by her ninety-three elementary-Hebrew students, and it was good that she was back at her own work, or both of them would have been frustrated by his inability to do anything about all the work piling up on his desk.

Noel wrote to Albright in late December thanking him for his latest volume off the press. "I barely had time to leaf through it but have been fascinated by the numerous original and exciting points which you make. . . . Keep up the good work." A couple of weeks later—and many months later—Noel was still begging for Albright to send his revised article for their symposium volume. He thought perhaps the weekly attacks of mild nervous exhaustion were "a blessing in disguise as they will keep you from the sort of overwork and overexertion to which you are prone by inclination, training, and habit."

In an interview for the Baltimore *Sunday Sun* on January 22, 1967 the question was asked whether Prof. Albright felt religion was cracking up. " 'Of course it is,' he replied, 'but it will rise again. I'm a firm believer in God, who works with man in history.' . . . 'The New Testament was intended as a supplement to the Old and not a replacement.'. . ."

In a letter to Noel late in January about Anchor Bible matters Albright commented, as he often did orally to various people, that if only a third (sometimes he said a quarter) of Mitchell Dahood's new ideas in his *Psalms* volumes were correct (drawing on Phoenician and Ugaritic materials), it would mean more light on the text than in many hundreds of years. He confessed he was tempted constantly to work on his paper on Genesis 49, the Testament of Jacob, for the jubilee meeting of the Society for Old Testament Study in York, England, the following July (which he and Ruth planned to attend) instead of what he should be doing, but he could soon send the revised symposium article.

Albright wrote to Professors B. Mazar, Y. Yadin and J. Aviram of the Israel Exploration Society, thanking them for the honor of the proposed dedication of the next volume of *Eretz Israel* to him. He hoped they were not too optimistic in thinking that two years later he would be able to accept it in person. He spoke of a favorable report from his oculist and still being able to work six to eight hours a day at his desk unless he became overtired. For his age his health was excellent, he said, and expressed the hope that he might visit Israel one more time before his death. There were two things that had increased rather than decreased—his great interest in all phases of discovery and research, and his flow of ideas.

The December 1966 BASOR No. 184, which appeared late the following May, contained a ten-page article by Dr. Albright, "Remarks on the Chronology of Early Bronze IV-Middle Bronze IIA in Phoenicia and Syria-Palestine." (Leona had worked hard for a number of months to overcome the lag in the journal's publication, so that the October issue came out in October, right after her departure; but immediately the situation reverted to six months' arrears, though the December issue copy was almost ready for the printer in September.)

From Tokyo, where he and Neil spent three months while he was teaching there, Noel wrote to Albright on May 12 congratulating him and Mann on "a truly magnificent job of putting together a volume under very trying circumstances, and against obstacles and odds of major proportions [he had just received the published *Acts* volume]. The appendices provide a substantive contribution to the study of *Acts* far out of proportion to their modest length, and give the volume an importance which it otherwise would not have had. . . ."

Albright replied, relieved and delighted to learn that Abe Spiro was quite pleased instead of angry over what had been done in condensing his material for the appendices in *Acts* and that he had asked for reprints for his friends. Albright said he hoped Noel would enjoy his visit to Jordan that summer—that is, if first the Arabs did not attempt again to annihilate the State of Israel.

But before Noel could reply on June 9, the Six-Day War was almost over. Noel wrote, "Many thanks for your good letter of 19 May. That seems a long time ago, and a different world in the light of recent developments in the Near East. . . . In view of all this, and especially the uncertain situation regarding Jerusalem, we have decided that I should not attempt to go to the Near East at all this summer, but wait for a more favorable climate for study and research to do so. With the Israeli capture of Jordanian Jerusalem, and apparently the whole west bank of the Jordan River, all scholarly concerns are obviously up in the air. . . . I am curious to know what the status of the ASOR will be. Negotiations were far advanced, so I was advised, for the sale of the present property [the School which the Albrights had built, now too small for the needs]; but was the deal concluded before the invasion, or is everything now in confusion?" The ASOR in Jerusalem would now, as it turned out, have to be separated from a new center in Amman incorporated as "The American Center for Oriental Research."

Albright replied in mid-June, admitting he had again been a failure as a prophet, for he had not been able to think the Russians would support the Arab drive without reasonable expectation of a great victory. In the previous conflict of 1956, he said, he had been in Ankara reading Turkish newspapers in the whirlwind developments that gave nobody time for predictions. To an Israeli scholar, Prof. Anson Rainey of Tel-Aviv University, Albright wrote that the war had fortunately turned out better for Israel than ordinary scholars could possibly have predicted. He said he always considered an academically trained person very ineffective as a prophet, because he was an analyst, whereas prophecies deal with wholes in their future development. He had been rather sure the Arabs would win, in spite of the Jews' victories in 1948 and 1956. While it was said that Ben-Gurion came to believe in miracles in 1948, Albright said he already believed, but could hardly expect three in three decades.

Noel wrote from Nantucket Island that in a visit with Frank Cross he had learned that "the Qumran material has remained in the Palestine Archaeological Museum and is now under Israeli control. What will happen is still uncertain, but Frank supposes that Père de Vaux will still have the say about the study and publication of the material, and that I may still be in line to work on the Leviticus Scroll once matters have settled down. Apparently Biran is in charge" of the Museum.

In mid-July Albright wrote by hand to Noel from London. He confessed that he had been so busy finishing the galley proofs of *Yahweh and the Gods of Canaan* that he had been unable to complete his symposium article before leaving. He promised to make it first on the list when he and Ruth returned from England on July 27. They had spent most of the 12th resting after their arrival, besides his being elected to the British Academy as corresponding fellow. Later on the day he wrote, they would take a sleeper to Cornwall and after a visit there (with his "almost-cousin" again), would go on up to the meetings in York. He had declined an invitation from Mazar on behalf of several organizations for Ruth and him to continue east and visit Israel immediately—after all, they were now 75 and 76! (In writing to Mazar and Aviram that he would not be able to stand the strain of a trip to Israel at this time, he said he hoped both he and Ruth could come in a couple of years, and mentioned how thrilled he had been by the Israeli victories and the evidence that Israel's God stood by His people now just as He did in ancient times.)

This honor from the British Academy was preceded in 1967 by his honorary doctorate number 27, an L.H.D. from Dropsie College.

Albright wrote Noel after returning home from England that he had seen a great number of old acquaintances and friends in both London and York—but did not learn of any coming young scholar in biblical studies, though there were some who were good in Egyptology and cuneiform. With the negative influences of the Wellhausenists and G. R. Driver, the situation was almost hopeless. On Anchor Bible matters, he had been informed that almost 17,000 copies of *Acts* had been sold in the first month, a record for the series.

Noel responded that the news was especially good "because there was no particular publicity about this volume, and there had been a considerable gap between volumes." He thought "we may attribute the successful initial response to the Anchor Bible name and the wide publicity and even prestige which the series has achieved." He reminded Albright that he needed his up-to-date bibliography for both himself and Malamat (for the Israeli *Festschrift* that Albright had to know about in advance), and needed even more urgently the revised article for the symposium volume!

The December 1967 BASOR reported that at a special meeting of the Trustees on September 13, at which Prof. Albright was present, "it was voted that no decision be made at this time about the sale of the property of the Jerusalem School. It was voted that the Schools continue the programs of archaeological research in the immediate future as in the past."[2]

Noel's letter of October 20 could finally thank Albright for the symposium article, with which he was delighted, but in December he wrote, "I hate to keep pestering you about your bibliography for the Israeli *Festschrift* under Malamat's supervision."

On December 30 at the annual meeting of the Archaeological Institute of America held at the Statler-Hilton Hotel in Boston, "Dr. William F. Albright received the institute's Gold Medal for Distinguished Archaeological Achievement in ceremonies at the meeting," the New York *Times* article stated the next day. "The scholar, cited as the 'universal man' in archaeology, is an authority on the archaeology, religion and languages of the Near East, and author of more than 800 publications." (Prof. Albright used his various bronze medals—but not his gold ones—as paper weights in his study.)

Noel read the *Times* report while flying back west on Sunday, and sent "congratulations on a well deserved honor. I was in the East attending meetings of the ASOR and SBL. I didn't really expect to see you there though I didn't realize at the time that you would be at another meeting elsewhere." Albright responded that he had been surprised to see so many friends and former students in Boston. He mentioned that Abram Spiro had died a few weeks earlier of a massive heart hemorrhage. Noel was "sorry to hear of Abram Spiro's death, . . . I always enjoyed his company, though his enthusiasm occasionally outran coherence. It is a pity he was never able to coordinate and synthesize his investigations, as he was highly original and controlled many esoteric materials." Dr. Spiro had just spent a number of months in Greece learning modern Greek as well as refining his knowledge of Classical Greek in order to carry on further studies.

On January 9, 1968, Albright began a series of lectures at the Shaarey Zedek synagogue in Detroit. The *Jewish News* on the 12th reported him as saying, "Thanks to archaeology we have proof of the correctness of biblical traditions." He "dealt with archaeology as a science, describing to the audience of more than 900 the value of the carbon dating tests, commending the usefulness of computers for philology, declaring that the Dead Sea Scrolls and the recent discoveries by Prof. Yigael Yadin went a long way in unearthing documents and in proving biblical verities. . . .

"Paying tribute to Israel, the eminent scholar said 'there was never a time when Israelites were savages, barbarians or primitive. They were not ignorant, were ready to take advantage of opportunity and this is what made them great.' . . . he called attention to Prof. Spiro's discovery of the Samaritan origin of Stephen in Acts in the New Testament and welcomed the analysis of that discovery as it was reported in The Jewish News (May 12, 1967) review of the Doubleday Anchor Bible volume of *Acts*. He commended Dr. Spiro's research and said the late Wayne State University professor left volumes of unpublished manuscripts. . . ."

Albright wrote Noel after his return that it had been a strenuous but good trip. He had learned much about Abe Spiro's final months and death; he had been nearly paranoid at times. He reported Stephen Mann as making future plans, since his three years of part-time work with Albright would end in July; hence their work on *Matthew* was delayed, but he thought it three-quarters done—it should be ready for typing in July.

When Albright wrote Noel in early April he said he had for some weeks grown ever more sure that the original Aramaic oral tradition found in Palestine before the Christians fled northeastward prior to the war of A.D. 66-70 underlay the Syriac version of the Gospels; it would explain the surprisingly correct Aramaic forms of the Semitic personal and geographic names. The quotations of Christ's Aramaic words found in the Greek text would thus be essentially the original form, the tradition being very constant. He had used the Syriac forms of names in the New Testament ever since 1923, he said, but had not fully realized the possibilities until now. (This was the sort of addition he made to the manuscript of the *Matthew* volume, which was essentially written by Stephen Mann who read aloud to Albright for his criticism and discussion of everything as their work proceeded. Albright originally intended that Mann's name should precede his as joint authors.)

Prof. Albright learned in the spring of 1968 that he was developing cataracts in both eyes in addition to his glaucoma problem. Ruth and Stephen, Jo and David helped him celebrate his 77th birthday in a nearby restaurant, celebrating also the change of Stephen's visa to permanent immigration—he was to be assistant dean of the new Ecumenical Theological Institute organized at St. Mary's, to begin in September. Shortly before the birthday, the Albrights made a tiring trip to Chicago. They had two dinners and a tea besides visiting the great Masada exhibit that would remain at the Field Museum several months; Prof. Albright gave a lecture at the museum in connection with the exhibit. From that time on, Ruth always traveled with her husband in order to be eyes for him. After their return he had to rest in bed three days.

Leona Running wrote in July wondering whether Dr. Albright could use her help for from one to four weeks in September after the end of her summer teaching. Prof. Albright typed his reply immediately on the 11th, gratefully accepting her offer; in three weeks she could doubtless do the final typing on *Matthew*. He said his glaucoma was controlled and within a year to two one of his cataracts should become operable. He could work in his study but not travel around much any more.

Leona was fortunate to find a vacant efficiency apartment in the building where she had lived before, and spent most of September in typical Baltimore heat, happily working with Drs. Albright and Mann on final typing of the large manuscript, some of which Stephen still had to dictate to her on the typewriter. It was a long enough time to accomplish something and short enough to be a stimulating change in lieu of a vacation. Prof. Albright gave her an autographed copy of *Yahweh and the Gods of Canaan*. (Dr. Siegfried Horn remarked that it was Albright's best work so far, the ripened fruits of many earlier studies.)

The London *Times* Literary Supplement for Thursday, August 1, 1968 carried a fine review of that volume: "No more stimulating teacher in the field of Near Eastern studies can be found than Professor Albright, whose influence on the younger scholars of the United States has been quite phenomenal. The remarkable range of his learning is well illustrated in the 1965 Jordan Lectures, . . . To a wide philological equipment and a first-hand acquaintance with the ever-growing volume of literature from the whole of the ancient Near East, he adds archaeological experience and an intimate knowledge of the excavations at sites throughout the area, and also a competent knowledge of the critical study of the Old Testament which has marked the nineteenth and twentieth centuries.

"In these lectures he deals with the literary and cultural relations between Israel and her Canaanite neighbours, and . . . argues for the view that Israel exercised a religious influence on her neighbours, and credits her with having encouraged the opponents of human sacrifice in Phoenicia. This maintenance of a two-way influence is something new, which gives particular importance to this volume." The review closed with: "Not every view that is set forth in this volume will be accepted without question by all scholars, and one who has changed his view from time to time on so many questions as Professor Albright will not expect it. Yet it can be said that this volume abounds in factual information, sometimes overwhelmingly so, and that the reader who can learn nothing from it must be singularly learned. It is an outstandingly important volume, coming to its subject from the outside much more than do the usual studies which approach it far more from the biblical side."

Albright's interest in the sale of the book—better than anticipated—was detached; he received no royalties, as he had received an honorarium and the work belonged to the London institution. But in England there was a second printing, and translations into Polish and French were in process.

Wendell Phillips gave an illustrated lecture for Eastern College, Baltimore, on a Friday evening which the Albrights were able to attend, though he had to rest much the next week and cancel a trip to Philadelphia in order to be able to make an air trip to the West Coast. He and Ruth divided the days there between the University of the Pacific at Stockton and Noel's seminary at San Anselmo, having a wonderful time and especially enjoying the opportunity for long talks with Noel and Francis Andersen. At the two places Dr. Albright gave one lecture, two convocation addresses and two meetings with students and faculty.

Albright reluctantly agreed to withdraw from editing BASOR after the October issue, after thirty-eight years. He was then suffering worse dizzy spells, he wrote Noel, which his doctor described as typically like the shell shock he had seen in Korea. He and Ruth had greatly enjoyed the trip West, which she called one of her life's high points, especially enjoying the time with Neil and little Jonathan, a most precocious child.

Noel's reply quoted Neil that "you are ideal guests" and wishing "that you could have stayed longer and will return again soon." Noel thanked him for the inscribed copy of *Yahweh and the Gods of Canaan,* which he said "is a magnificent work in the creative tradition of *From the Stone Age to Christianity* and *Archaeology and the Religion of Israel.* It will provide stimulus for scholarly work for years to come."

Stephen Mann wrote a desperate note to Leona on October 28. In answer to her inquiry whether *Matthew* had gone to the publishers, he replied, "Why, the agony has only just begun! What with suggestions that the whole thing be gone over to improve the English, reduce it by half, eliminate possible theological overtones (undertones?), get the references checked again, put in a dozen or so references to literature which WFA has only just thought of, I begin to wonder. . . . On top of which there is a Bulletin galley being nursed (i.e., being re-hashed all over). All I can do at the moment is push on with the chapter on authorship and chronology, and—hope. Forgive me if I sound a little despairing. But there's no doubt to my mind that had you not been here the story would be 10,000% worse, so I'm more grateful than you can know, and the more so as both you and Hugh Albright have managed to suggest to him that it's more or less all right as it is!"

This letter helped Leona decide to spend part of her Christmas vacation in Baltimore. As Stephen wrote in early December, "nothing else will ever wrest the ms. of Matthew from WFA. As it is, for nearly two weeks he's been sitting on the galley of a short article which he and I did, and has already revised it four times. . . . My hope is to finish the final chapter of the Matthew introduction, and if I cannot get it typed, then maybe I can dictate it to you when you're here. I feel somewhat saddened by the whole thing, and WFA is certainly failing rather more rapidly than I'd thought possible."

Prof. Albright wrote to Leona on the 6th, saying he would like it very much if she could be there from December 26 to January 3. Ruth wrote in their Christmas card to Leona that she was glad they would soon see her there—she did bring a certain needed zest into their life.

Albright wrote Noel late in November that when he had recently seen his former student group at Harvard, he was especially happy that Bill Moran would help edit BASOR, for which his eyesight was no longer adequate. On that lecture tour he said a head cold made him lose his voice and affected his inner ear—he added parenthetically that he still used mustard plasters, now home-made, to cure sore throat but they had never helped a head cold unless it was moving down to the bronchial tubes. He had been in the hospital for several days, but found that the prospective operation (a follow-up of the prostate surgery of several years before) could be deferred if he had a surgical checkup every few months. He was sorry he was too busy and tired to attend the Colloquium meeting in Pittsburgh.

The December 1968 BASOR opened with a notice by ASOR President G. Ernest Wright headed "William Foxwell Albright and the *Bulletin*." He said: "With the October issue (No. 191) now in press, because of severe problems of eyesight William Foxwell Albright has resigned after thirty-eight years as Editor of the *Bulletin*. His Associate Editor in recent years and a scholar otherwise eminently qualified for the position, Professor Delbert R. Hillers of the Johns Hopkins University, has been invited by the Executive Committee and Trustees to be his successor. During the winter and spring Professor W. L. Moran of Harvard University will serve as temporary Editor [Hillers was in Jerusalem as Annual Professor of the School]." Wright told of the first issue at the end of 1919, consisting of only four pages. "Two years later Dr. Montgomery is listed as President of the newly incorporated American Schools of Oriental Research, while Dr. Albright was Director of the Jerusalem School. The content and size of the *Bulletin* changed quickly, with Dr. Montgomery as Editor of the journal's main content, which was the steady flow of exciting material written in Jerusalem by Dr. Albright. Each field trip through the country produced scholarly discussion of topographical history with many new identifications of ancient sites. . . .

"With the February issue of the *Bulletin* in 1931, Dr. Albright began his long and distinguished career as Editor. His own contributions and his editing of those of others brought the whole of the ancient Near East under critical survey. The constant reader of the *Bulletin* felt himself to be on the forefront of scholarly discovery and discussion. Scarcely an issue appeared for which Dr. Albright had not written something fresh and original. The *Bulletin* was an extension of his far-ranging scholarly activity, of his vast learning and of his enthusiastic participation in nearly every new development or new discovery. As he now retires from editing the journal that has been so much his own, an exciting chapter in American scholarship comes to a close. His students and disciples will do their best, but several of us cannot make one of him."[3]

Moran and Hillers tried to bring out several issues at once, with different printers, to catch up the publication lag, but it would not be possible for years to bring out the quarterly issues in the proper months.

Leona came by overnight bus immediately after Christmas, and the main work for several days for her, together with Prof. Albright and Dr. Mann, was completing the thick *Matthew* manuscript, which ran to somewhat more than 800 typed pages. When Albright wrote to Noel on January 6 with congratulations for his part in the SBL meetings, of the success of which he had heard from several friends, he said that the *Matthew* manuscript had been mailed to New York on the previous Friday, if he was correct. Leona had been there seven days and what she had accomplished was quite fantastic. She had made both him and Stephen work their heads off completing the manuscript, and also helped him on the new introductions he was writing for the reprinting of Burney's *Kings* and *Judges*.

The reason why Albright was not quite sure which day *Matthew* had been sent to Doubleday was that Ruth, Stephen and Leona had conspired about it while he was resting, and the deed had been done in Leona's temporary apartment after she had typed the bibliography for the volume. Stephen brought a box, paper and string for packing it up. When Leona had arrived in Baltimore she had assured Stephen that she had every intention of shipping that manuscript to New York before she caught the night bus back to South Bend; that was the only way it could ever get started through Doubleday's editorial and production pipeline.

Noel replied to Albright on January 13, delighted that "the Matthew manuscript has gone to Doubleday. Needless to say, this is a very happy occasion and it augurs well for the series and the year...."

Albright responded on February 12 that what had really happened was that with hearty support from his wife, Leona and Stephen had stolen a march on him, sending it off without his knowledge. He thought it was a good idea, though sorry he had not been able to go once more over the material of the Introduction. He agreed it would have been a mistake to delay sending it any more, and it was probably good that he had not had an opportunity to make the Introduction even more original—at a certain point that could become a vice. He and the late Abe Spiro had both learned that to be too original in New Testament studies was especially dangerous. The accepted kind of originality was in some new existentialist or form-critical idea, but his type was in history of ideas together with linguistics on one hand and archaeology and topography on the other. His problem, he said, was that his brain outran his vision and strength. New ideas came wholesale, but it was difficult to finish the older items.

Noel wrote on February 19 that he was reading a copy of the *Matthew* manuscript "with great interest and edification. I have made a few notes here and there to be incorporated in my comments which should reach Stephen Mann and you in due course."

Albright's reply was that Noel should feel free to smooth up the English, above all in the Introduction which he had wanted to go over one more time but did not have opportunity to do so—for what was a legitimate reason. (He had forgiven Stephen and Leona for sending the manuscript off, though at first he felt betrayed. Characteristically he found something good about what had at first seemed to him totally bad.) He added that he and Stephen were working on an article on *dikaios,* their joint one on *anathema* having already been sent by request to *Catholic Biblical Quarterly.*

Their work would, however, be interrupted by a trip that would be the climax of Prof. Albright's long love-affair with the Holy Land.

21

Honorary Citizen of Jerusalem

The Baltimore *Sun* for March 24, 1969, headlined, "Jerusalem Fete Honors Albright." With a Jerusalem dateline of the 23rd, the article read: "Professor William Foxwell Albright, Professor Emeritus of Semitic languages at the Johns Hopkins University, became the first non-resident today to be chosen a 'Worthy of Jerusalem.' Professor Albright, 77, was honored in a ceremony attended by a number of distinguished archaeologists, many of them his former students.

"Dr. and Mrs. Albright are in Jerusalem to attend a meeting of the consortium of American and Canadian institutions associated with the ASOR here. In honoring the professor, Mayor Teddy Kollek of Jerusalem said that since Dr. Albright first arrived in Palestine 50 years ago, 'archaeology has become a household word.'"

The New York *Times* for the 24th carried James Feron's story beginning, "Three generations of Palestinian archaeologists crowded into Jerusalem's City Hall today to honor their mentor, Prof. William Foxwell Albright of Baltimore."

The Upper Iowa College *Alumnus* for June 1969 printed the news story, by permission, with a late photograph of their famous alumnus. The story continued: "At the age of 77, Dr. Albright, ... was being made a 'Worthy of Jerusalem.' The title is awarded to those who have contributed to the city and who are past the age of 70. Professor Albright was the first non-Jerusalemite and non-Jew to be so honored. Mayor Teddy Kollek said that, in fact, there was some argument over the question whether 'worthy' was the best word since it had never been necessary to translate the Hebrew '*yekir*' [*yaqqir*] before.

374

"Whatever the term, Mayor Kollek said that Professor Albright's name had become a household word in Israel, where archaeology is easily the most popular hobby. For the scores of archaeologists who sat before him, Professor Albright's name is even more familiar. One of his former students, Professor Nachman Avigad, head of the Hebrew University department of archaeology, said in presenting the award:

" 'If today the historical accuracy of the Bible is beyond question, it is due in no small measure to the work of Professor Albright.'

"Professor Albright, the son of an American Methodist missionary to Chile, replied simply and briefly in Hebrew, recalling at one point that it was just 50 years ago that he first came to Palestine. In those 50 years, some of his colleagues noted later, he has influenced scores of younger men, many of whom now teach, and developed methods of research into the history of this area. For example, he is considered the originator of ceramic chronology, a system of dating through the identification of pottery, a major advance in the science of archaeology.

"But it has been Professor Albright's personality and his sweep of history that have most pleased his colleagues and impressed younger Israelis in the nearly two weeks he has been here.

"Professor Albright was accompanied here by his wife, Ruth, whom he met at Hopkins, where she was completing work for her doctorate. Mrs. Albright specialized in Indo-European philology. Married in 1921, they have lived in Jerusalem for 10 years, and it was here that two of their four sons were born. Dr. Albright's visit now is being sponsored by the Israel Exploration Society and by the Biblical and archaeological school of Hebrew Union College-Jewish Institute of Religion in Cincinnati. The school's director, Prof. Nelson Glueck, was one of Dr. Albright's students.

"Tall and erect, Professor Albright packed an auditorium at the Hebrew University one night last week when he discussed the Israelite conquest of Canaan. He apologized for speaking in English, saying that he had discovered that his Hebrew was 'modern archaic.' Many of the new words and expressions were unfamiliar to him, he said. He spoke at Beersheba in Hebrew a few nights later, however, and had no trouble being understood. . . .

"Dr. Albright's vibrance and immense interest in Israel have combined with his reputation to make him a great favorite here. His views have been widely sought and freely given. Asked, for instance, about the veracity of the Bible, he replied:

" 'Considering everything, the Hebrew Bible is the most extraordinarily accurate record because of the empirical attitude of the Israelites, from Moses on, to matters of fact. It's an extraordinary record of human experience.' "

Albright told something of the trip in his April 14 letter to Leona. He and Ruth had what he called a wonderful trip to Israel. They left Baltimore on March 9 and returned the 26th, both exhausted, but the information and experiences gathered had been so marvelous that he would not have wanted to miss them for anything. To Noel on the first of April he wrote that the trip, which was sponsored by the Israel Exploration Society and Nelson Glueck and therefore cost him almost nothing, was both strenuous and rewarding. He had discussed all kinds of problems with numbers of archaeologists and learned much about what was being done, visited sites and museums, and so on. He and Ruth had gone with Yigael Yadin by helicopter to Masada, which Yadin had excavated, and landed on the top, then landed at Qumran on the way back to Jerusalem. He had brought back a magnificent *Festschrift* and the award of *Yaqqir Yerushalayim* (Worthy or Nobleman of Jerusalem) as well as a great fund of information (and complete exhaustion).

The Jerusalem Post for March 24 reported that "An 'Albright evening' honouring the dean of Palestinian archaeology, Prof. William Foxwell Albright, 77, was held last night at Beit Hanassi, Jerusalem, in the presence of President Shazar and the country's leading archaeologists.

"The American scholar was ceremonially presented with the 'Albright volume' of 'Eretz Yisrael' a journal published every two years by the Israel Exploration Society. The just-published ninth volume contains articles in Hebrew, English and French, written by 40 colleagues and students of Prof. Albright, half in Israel and half abroad, and is dedicated to him. It includes the first scientific reports on the dig at the southern wall of the Temple Mount (by Prof. Binyamin Mazar), on the Qumran *tefilin* (by Prof. Yigael Yadin) and on the Arad *ostraca* (by Prof. Yohanan Aharoni). The 400-page volume was edited by Prof. Avraham Malamat of the Hebrew University.

"Speakers last night included Prof. Yadin, who presided, and Profs. Mazar and Nelson Glueck and Prof. E. G. [G. E.] Wright, head of the American Schools of Oriental Research. The presentation of the Albright volume was made by Mr. Josef Aviram, secretary of the Israel Exploration Society.

"On Wednesday evening, Prof. Albright spent a large part of a reception given in his honour absorbed in the study of a stone seal inscribed in a hitherto unknown ancient tongue which, it is believed, may be the first Philistine inscription ever found. The reception was at the home in Jerusalem of Prof. Mazar.

"The seal was shown to the guest by Dr. Moshe Dot[h]an, who found it last summer at a Philistine level (12th century B.C.E.) of the Ashdod dig. Prof. Albright immediately agreed that the script probably derived from Cypro-Minoan. . . ."

The most tremendous press coverage was the article of Sunday March 23 in the Jerusalem *Post,* covering most of two pages. It was condensed from a "press conference held at the Hebrew University last week, affording a glimpse of a wide-ranging mind and directness of vision not usually vouchsafed journalists at these occasions. Kol Yisrael [the Israeli radio network] taped his remarks." The published extracts of the spontaneous interview showed many sidelights on Albright.

Prof. Josef Aviram later recalled that Prof. Albright said to him on the way from the airport when they arrived, "This time I want to see Masada." Aviram arranged for a small helicopter from the Israeli army, and Yadin went with the Albrights. "When they came back he was so thrilled," Aviram said. "It was *all* the time Masada —that was the high peak of his life. He especially enjoyed it because Yigael Yadin, the excavator, took him and showed him everything."

Prof. Aviram also said, "His lecture in the president's house was something excellent; he spoke about everything—archaeology, of course, but also the political situation. He said, referring to Sinai and the other areas captured in the war, 'Don't give up anything, because here you are safe for the first time, and you have to occupy that territory; it is your security until peace may come.' He was so happy about the united Jerusalem! They went to church on Sunday and Mrs. Albright said, 'How nice it is that we can walk everywhere, everything is so free and secure!' Albright was very excited about the excavations in the Old City and spent about four hours there with Mazar. Nelson Glueck took him to Gezer, also. And he went to Jaffa and saw the museum and visited the excavation of Dr. Jacob Kaplan. He gave one lecture in Jerusalem as guest lecturer at the Hebrew University. He was excited about the newly discovered Temple scroll, and of course Yadin told him the whole story about it."

Prof. Yigael Yadin said concerning the Albrights' last visit together to Israel, "It was really a festival for all of us to have Mrs. Albright and Prof. Albright with us, and at that time he was so frank and open in supporting Israel politically, even in public press conferences, that I had to caution him a bit that he should perhaps be more careful on that. One of the great events was that he gave a lecture in Beersheba on a pet theory of his in the last few years about the patriarchs as donkey caravaneers. He said to me, 'I'm going to make an effort to give this lecture in Beersheva in Hebrew; that will be very difficult for me because the subject is complicated, but I *want* to present *this* lecture in Beersheva, the place associated with the Patriarch, in Hebrew.' Something very interesting happened: if suddenly he couldn't find a word in Hebrew, he substituted a German word—not an English word, but a German word, and without even explaining or thinking, he would go on for a few seconds speaking German. When I asked him afterward why he did this, he said, 'Really, I didn't even notice that! It's interesting; it's either because perhaps the German tradition and language is rather deep in me, perhaps deeper than I knew, or because both languages are foreign languages for me and therefore I passed from one to another.'

"On the trip to Masada, we flew in a little helicopter which the army put at our disposal—the army of Israel had great admiration for Albright; every soldier more or less knew his *Archaeology of Palestine* in the Penguin edition. The visit to Masada took about three hours, and he was not a youngster any more, but he didn't want to leave it. I would say, 'But you know, there is another interesting thing, but this is several hundred yards to the south; maybe we can skip it.' He said, 'No, I want to see it!' He wanted to see everything, examine it afresh. I think Albright behaved exactly the way he was behaving thirty or forty years earlier—full of zest, full of enthusiasm, not being satisfied to be told this and that but wanting to see the evidence and examine it himself as if it were his own excavations."

Recalling his first visit to the U.S. in 1954, when he was here to purchase for Israel the four scrolls that were for sale and wanted Albright's opinion, Yadin said that when he was to give a lecture at Johns Hopkins, Albright on the telephone insisted on meeting him at the train station and taking him to the lecture. "He never behaved like a great man, or as people think a great man should behave in relation to junior people. He insisted, 'I must come to meet you; I *want* to do that. But my problem is, I am not so sure I'll recognize you, and I don't know whether you will recognize me! After all, it's years since I last saw you as a child.' "

Yadin replied, "Look here, you don't have to bother to recognize me because I'll recognize you." But Albright insisted it was a big station, and Yadin must give him some clue for recognizing him. "Well, I think the only difference since the times you remember me is that I am bald now, and I have a mustache." Albright replied, "Well, that's very good; you know I am bald too; I don't have a mustache, but I am going to wear a flower on my lapel." Yadin said Albright very naively and sincerely was sure Yadin would not remember his face; "he considered himself as if *he* were the junior. This was very typical."

All the Israeli archaeologists recalled Albright's great empathy with the Israelis in the problems of their life in their State, restored to the land of their ancestors, and in the revival of the Hebrew language with its direct connection, for him, to the Hebrew Old Testament. Prof. Moshe Greenberg recalled hearing Albright when Moshe was only a young boy in Philadelphia; Albright made the correct distinction between *het* and *he* which the boy did not yet know, and stopped to explain it for his benefit; and in Albright's retirement years, "the feeling that he felt very much at home with Jews." Greenberg cited Albright's own statement, often made and published on page 288 of his *History, Archaeology and Christian Humanism*: "Until I was twenty-one, I had never met anyone whom I knew to be Jewish, but after nearly half a century of friendly association I am in some ways more at home in Jewish circles than anywhere else."

Yadin thought that, basically, Albright's "identification with the resurrection, so to say, of the State of Israel was his belief and approach to biblical history. He identified with no hesitation the modern Israel with the ancient Israel. One of the main things which really attracted him to modern Israel was the fact on which he used to speak so much, that the Hebrew language is again alive and revived. Now the Hebrew language was for him the direct connection with the Bible, with the ancient Hebrews, and he had full admiration—and criticism also, sometimes—for Ben Yehudah, who was for him a great hero who revived the language. The fact that Hebrew is the language of the new Israel, one of the real phenomena of the State of Israel that a language dead for two thousand years, so to speak, suddenly becomes a live language—this was one of the things which he admired most. That's why he admired Ben Yehudah and many others who were connected with the revival of the language.

"Amazingly enough Albright, who is not considered to be a military man, had full admiration also for another trait of the new Israeli state: that Jews had an independent army which also proved itself victorious and with fighting spirit. He was very flattered when soldiers, not only civilians, came to his lectures. I think again for him this was, perhaps subconsciously, associated with the hosts of the kings of Judah or the kings of Israel. But he expressed himself on modern political problems and showed me that he was versed in and read all the articles and statements and polemics against Israel. By then he considered himself a champion of Israel also for very practical reasons—that in this world as we are, the Jews should have a homeland. Of course he saw the problems which the creation of the State made for the Arabs; he admired the Arabs, he loved them. But *on balance,* as he always used to say, he thought that if there were two justs here, the justification for Israel to have a state was the greater one; that's why he supported Israel. I think the Bible, or his biblical interests, brought him to support Israel, but later on I think it developed and became a much deeper and more sophisticated approach to the State of Israel."

Noel's letter of March 14 came while the Albrights were in Israel on their triumphant visit, which would be his last. Albright replied on April 1, briefly describing his strenuous but very rewarding trip. Noel's reply brought Albright up to date on Anchor Bible volumes in progress; he was "beginning to feel the pressure of getting everything in order before departing in the middle of

June" (going to Israel to be Director of the School for the year 1969-70), and looked forward to seeing the Albrights on May 3 if it would be a convenient time to visit. When Albright replied, saying he had entered the appointment in his booklet, he remarked that he had expected to have to rest for a couple of weeks, but the trip had cost him more strength than he anticipated. It was fortunate that Wendell Phillips' plan for them to spend several weeks in Hawaii had fallen through; he had been apprehensive about going, himself, and did not know whether Ruth was disappointed or relieved. Writing in the same vein to Leona on the 14th, Albright said he hoped her plan to come and help him in late summer would be carried through.

In spite of needing to spend much time in bed, Prof. Albright delivered the Sylvia W. Katzner lecture at Baltimore Hebrew College the evening of May 18. On the 23rd, the day before his 78th birthday, the Detroit *Jewish News* announced that along with ten other such personages as "Israeli Minister of Religious Affairs Dr. Zerah Warhaftig, poet Uri Zvi Greenberg, and Dr. Solomon Goan, chief rabbi," "Dr. William F. Albright, orientalist, author, professor emeritus, Johns Hopkins University," would receive an honorary degree, the L.H.D., doctor of humane letters. It was his 28th honorary degree; the article was accompanied by his profile photo.

For most of the Israeli professors and archaeologists Albright's 1969 trip was their last meeting with him. Two years after his death many of them recorded reminiscences of the *goy* who was so close to them.

Prof. Shalom Paul, who had read Kaufmann to him in 1958-59, recalled that when Albright was in his late seventies, Jewish Theological Seminary "instituted a general curriculum course, the Bible in its vast panoramic setting, and invited prime scholars. No one thought Albright would come up from his hibernation. Everything was against it—the time, the trip, and by this time his eyesight was very bad. And this course was for freshman students who had probably never heard of Albright and were not majors in Bible. Albright was given one phone call, and he appeared a couple of weeks later—unable, as he mentioned, to see the people seated on the first row. And yet he delivered a lecture, standing, for an hour and a half—because this was his great love which would not allow him to do anything *but* share it with students, even though the students obviously did not understand what he was saying. He was giving his new date for the exodus and all these modern findings—it was a tribute to budding students by the greatest master of them all, and was, I think, a very fitting conclusion of my experience with Dr. Albright."

Hannah Katzenstein, administrative assistant to Dr. Avraham Biran in the Rockefeller Archaeological Museum in Jerusalem, remembered that she first met Dr. Albright on his visit in 1953, when Ruth Amiran was excavating the tumuli at Malhah which he had begun excavating thirty years before. "Ruth took him on a visit of her excavation, wanting his opinion; we could not visit the one which Albright excavated in the '20's because it was right on the borderline, but we could see it—the famous cuts. I was much impressed by his whole personality, the way he grasped immediately the special problem of these particular tumuli and the way he reacted to the questions put to him.

"I met him after that, every time he was in the country. The last time he was here his wife was with him. It was quite impressive, the meeting at the Municipality when he was made a 'Worthy of Jerusalem.' There were hundreds of people present; he was very touched, and I think he liked it. I think Jerusalem was dear to him, and therefore to be given this honor was in his line of thinking or feeling, and he liked the idea of a personal connection with the city."

Dr. Benjamin Mazar, formerly president of Hebrew University and still connected with it and still excavating, recalled the longest period of association with Albright, beginning when he arrived in Palestine at the end of 1928 still using his original name Maisler. He recalled showing Albright his dissertation, an investigation in the history of Syria and Palestine, having just completed his doctoral work in Giessen, Germany. Albright was working in his study when Maisler arrived. "He was sitting and writing, talking, doing everything all together. It was fantastic how Albright used to work. Immediately he started to speak about some problems on which he was working, and we spoke in German. He took the proofs of my dissertation and in five or ten minutes went through it! Immediately he asked me all kinds of questions and asked me to give him the proofs, so I gave them to him. I was tremendously impressed by the person who showed so much interest and devotion to science, and no less the personal interest to know about me and what I am doing or have in mind to do. Since that time we became closer and more friendly.

"The continuation was in 1930, when Albright invited me to Tell Beit Mirsim. I was unable to become a member of the staff, but I spent a lot of time there. I think I never met a personality who was more tremendously interested to involve one in his work. This experience at Tell Beit Mirsim and then at Beth-zur was for me more than an experience; my opinion was, This is archaeology! Either field work or home work makes no difference; the major point was always just to find out what the truth was."

In 1952 after Prof. Mazar was elected president of the Hebrew University, the American Friends of the Hebrew University organized an official dinner for the inauguration, to raise money to build the new campus to the west side of Jerusalem. "They invited President Truman to make the major speech, and asked me if I would like to invite somebody from the United States to deliver a speech. My answer was 'Yes, William Foxwell Albright.' The response was, 'Who is Albright? Is he a Nobel Prize Winner, or a president of a university?' I said, 'Not at all; he's just a scholar.' It was not easy to persuade them, but they had no choice! And he appeared, of course, and spoke in English and in Hebrew. He was not a great orator, but he made a tremendous good impression, at least on the intellectuals, those really interested. He was deeply impressed with the effort of the Hebrew University to build up, to renew the glory of the Scopus on the new site—it was a new vision, something with which he fell in love. He had been present at the very beginning of the Hebrew University, was made an honorary member of the Institute of Oriental Studies, and at least fifty percent of the professors still were his good friends. He knew Hebrew and the situation and understood well what a Hebrew University in Jerusalem means. It was a tremendous meeting for him—a part of his life, his thinking, his philosophy. My explanation for his attachment to the State of Israel was that he was a *re universitas* [something universal]. He was a person who had relations with all kinds of people from all over the world.

"We awarded him the honorary doctorate in philosophy in 1957. His speech was in Hebrew. I invited him several other times.

When he saw what was going on in the Negev and Galilee and all over, and was so impressed to see a conference of one thousand people coming together to study archaeology for a week—this was something which he had never seen before in his life! Masses of people in Beersheva, in Galilee and everywhere, this great interest in Bible and geography and the study of the country—this was for him a tremendous experience, both in 1957 and in 1969. He was excited with everything that happened.

"When he and Ruth arrived in 1969, the next evening we had a reception for him. He met all the people and was full of life and interest. After a short time we were sitting and he was looking at all kinds of new discoveries, photographs of them, inscriptions, and so on, and was immediately involved asking questions about what was going on.

"When I invited him to the excavations at the Western Wall, his eyesight was a problem, though he didn't say anything; it was clear he was unable to see much. I planned all kinds of politics not to take him around too much, because I knew that he was unable to see, unless we were sitting overlooking the area and I showed him some points and explained to him.

"He liked the Arabs very much," Prof. Mazar continued, "and knew Arabic. But he used to say that a Moslem is unable to become a historian. He believes in the Koran, and in the Koran, Maryam the sister of Moses, is the mother of Jesus Christ! Now if such a thing is determined as the basis of historical study, how can he be a historian? To become an historian is to escape from Islam.

"It is true that he lived very simply with his wife and children. She had become Catholic, but this was not important. I always had the feeling that he loved his family, but left the family to his wife as her business. He was involved in his studies, with his books and library and excavations, and she took care of the home.

"He had certain kinds of humor, a very sophisticated humor. He also liked to speak about persons—very much liked a little bit of gossip. He didn't like two things: if something was not morally right (like plagiarism), or was done only to show a certain result and had no basis but was only sensational. Second, he was always much concerned about people who wrote books and pamphlets and articles, zealots without basic knowledge of the subject. He would say, 'This man is ignorant, and what is he doing in the field of

Bible?' We never discussed religion, but if you look at the end of his *From the Stone Age to Christianity* or his *Archaeology and the Religion of Israel* you see it; the last sentences sum up. He was a deeply religious man, yet with the greatest respect and love, first of all, for the religion of Israel, but he was a devoted Christian. But he was not a fool, to put all kinds of things together. He was a scientist."

Prof. Haim and Miriam Tadmor recalled their last personal meeting with Albright in Jerusalem in 1969, when he could hardly see. "I said, 'Professor Albright, welcome to Jerusalem!' He looked at me and said, 'Haim, I recognize you by your voice! But you know I cannot see very much, but I still can see that you are growing bald!' To which I replied, 'It's only because you are very tall, Dr. Albright!' His humor was very touching, very personal, in a way childlike.

"Concerning the honors given him in '69, I think he was touched. Delbert Hillers was here in Jerusalem at that time, and we were sitting together in the auditorium. When Albright read papers he did not usually have a complete written text before him, and sometimes he went out of the topic into something else. That paper was all on Abraham and the ass nomadism, and Del said at the end, 'It is one of the best papers I've heard Albright give. He wrote it for months and months, prepared and read it.' When the Honorary Citizenship of Jerusalem was given to him he delivered a very nice speech in Hebrew. It was very personal and touching—we were moved by it and by talking to him and Mrs. Albright."

Prof. Tadmor continued, "I think Albright was a very religious man. In this respect he was part of the 19th-century dreamers and the continuation of the same trend that believed that Israel should be revived. Here in the land he saw what the people were doing, and biblical scholarship and biblical archaeology were done by these people as well—he suddenly saw a revival of things that go with the Bible. Another thing, he was a humanist, and he saw that people suffered and something had to be done about it. He knew the East well, and saw that the country was desolate, and he observed the difference. Here he saw a dynamic society doing something with which he could identify, being part of a dynamic society himself. All these things brought him into identification with that dynamic society rather than with a very stagnant, romantic and

beautiful East with which many British archaeologists like to identify themselves because they would like the East to stand stagnant.
He had the greatest respect for the Arabs; his Hebrew was Oriental
Hebrew, with *ayin* and *het,* and he made a point that it should be
with the Orient. He was a scholar, a humanist; he thought that
there was a place for both of the peoples in this country. The dyna-
mism and the Bible and scholarship brought all these things to the
point where he saw that his biblical archaeology is really followed
and his school and method is appreciated, followed, and applied.
If there was anywhere a strong continuation of the Albrightian
school, it is here in Israel."

Jonas Greenfield went walking with Albright once and "asked
him why he hadn't published his collected articles instead of trying
to revise them, which seemed rather a long and futile enterprise.
Albright remarked that he was on the lunatic fringe of scholarship—always willing to change his mind, always willing to assim-
ilate new material—and therefore a lot of what he said was wrong
and he couldn't stand by it today. Whereas Eissfeldt and Alt, the
two models I had given him, never changed their minds and therefore you could have their opinions even forty years after they were
written. He remarked that he thought Alt was more brilliant and
had more original ideas, whereas Eissfeldt had really gathered the
material together in a more coherent manner."

Another close Israeli friend, Prof. Avraham Malamat of Hebrew
University, who edited the 1969 *Festschrift,* recalled many memories of Albright. He had discovered Albright by himself, by coming regularly to read in the ASOR library in 1942, and then studying under Mazar. He met Albright on his first trip to America in
1951 at the SBL meeting in New York, introduced by H. L. Ginsberg. "I hadn't imagined that Albright was so tall, and he spoke to
me in Modern Hebrew—that was my second shock. He talked to me
about the high prices in America, the traveling prices that are much
more expensive than in Palestine. I was still more amazed at the way
he pronounced the *het* and the *ayin,* yet without overdoing it. I
would have classified him as a Sephardic Jew, an Oriental Jew, if I
had not known who he was.

"There are now in the world two trends, the universalism, the
global approach as Albright had it—and it is the greatest thing, in
my opinion, about Albright, that he had this integral approach; and

the other, the operating-room, taking-apart of everything, where it is true you can go deeper. I think Albright was the last man in the generation after Eduard Meyer who oversaw the whole field.

"Once I accompanied him to the railway station and I saw how modest he was in physical affairs, in food. I gave him an apple to eat, and that was enough—I think it was his whole dinner. He was so modest that he would go on foot, and later in Israel he didn't ask for a car, he only wanted a Jeep; he didn't want to live at the King David Hotel where a room was reserved for him, he wanted a cheap hotel. That was real integrity. As far as I know he was content with very little.

"Albright was generous with people who disagreed with him," Prof. Malamat continued, "but he was very strong for his own views, not easily convinced. He was generous personally but not scientifically. When in 1969 he stepped down from the airplane in Lod, his first remark was, 'And Tell Beit Mirsim is *still* Devir.' One can understand this only on the background of what was going on between 1967 and 1969, when the Israelis took over the borderland of Tell Beit Mirsim, which became attached to the Hebron region. Some Israelis rediscovered what they believe to be Devir or Kiriath-sepher, which goes back to Galling's identification of Tell Rabud. Albright was *very* angry; his first great excavation . . . He knew that now there were certain scholars who revived Galling's idea that maybe Rabud *is* really much easier to identify with Devir or Kiriath-sepher than is Tell Beit Mirsim. So his first response, like Galileo when he said, 'And the earth *still* moves,' was, 'And Tell Beit Mirsim is *still* Devir.' In these things he was very stubborn.

"In '67 he wrote us a letter after the Six-Day War, and in his cleverness saw what many politicians at that time didn't see. He wrote: 'Don't give back to the Russians any inch of Sinai.' He didn't say Egyptians, he said Russians. At this time nobody could perceive the great insight of this man, even in political affairs. In my opinion he saw the Suez Canal, not as the borderline between Israel and Egypt, but between the Western world and the Communist East, though geographically it is the opposite. He was very much for Israel because he felt that only in Israeli hands are those lands really meaningful.

"We tried several times to invite him. In '69 we could suddenly get him here, and he also had an apocalyptic feeling that this was his last visit to Israel. He mentioned this feeling several times, that he was saying goodby and before his death had really wanted to see it once more. Again we saw all those human, very generous attitudes —modesty, openness. We presented him with the volume in his honor, which was very expensive from the point of view of finances, the best volume in the series, with a Hebrew part and an English-French part, and I had the honor to be editor of it, which I accepted because of Albright. We presented it at the President's home, after Albright had earlier in the same evening in the King David Hotel given a speech in Hebrew—as disorganized as one could imagine. He spoke especially of two rival groups of Yemenites who came to settle in Israel in the '20's, whom he knew; he knew more gossip of Palestine in the '20's than anyone else present in the room, except maybe for his very close friend Mrs. Kaplan, who was midwife at the birth of his eldest son in Jerusalem and a very old friend of his.

"So he gave reminiscences of the '20's and early '30's which sounded to us like miracles, because we didn't know there were two factions of Yemenite groups, and he even sociologically explained to us what the quarrel was between them. He spoke in Hebrew. Later at the President's home he spoke in English about reminiscences of his archaeological activities in Palestine in the '20's and '30's.

"I had the great pleasure and honor to go on a private trip with Albright to Jaffa: Albright, his wife, Mr. Aviram, and myself, for an opening which was specially held for him at the Jaffa Archaeological Museum by Dr. Kaplan. I had the privilege of sitting in the rear with Albright and we had about four hours of just scholarly talk on the way from Jerusalem to Tel-Aviv and back. In the many things we discussed one could really see the flow of his ideas. If he had lived another ten or twenty years, I am sure he would have produced all these things which he gave in a nutshell, in articles, even books. For instance, we reached the area of Shoresh, where for the first time you see the Mediterranean; it's about twenty kilometers from Jerusalem. From there we had the first glimpse of the Mediterranean, and above us were clouds. He immediately developed a theory (later he told me Mendenhall already had a theory) about the cloud, what the cloud (*anan*) means in the Bible. He always had these word associations. So we spoke about *anan,* and he compared the cloud of Moses with the Assyrian *melammu.* Albright developed it beautifully, very moved by the glimpse of the Mediterranean Sea. He loved the soil of Israel; I think he loved not only the population—I think he had really a deep feeling for the soil of the Holy Land.

"He amazed me by describing the pottery which he had seen on a two- or three-day trip in northern Syria in 1935, as though he had been there only a week before instead of nearly thirty-five years before! He had a photographic memory that was really phenomenal, one of his greatest assets.

"In one of his letters he mentioned something on which he never published, though he intended to. I asked him if I might mention one of his ideas in an article. He answered me in his letter, 'A man of my age doesn't give a damn for priority—only the truth is important. You can use whatever you want to.' I think that stands for purity of soul. It means that as he grew older he became perhaps even purer. I know that some persons become much more egocentric and egotistic, but I think with Albright it worked the other way," Prof. Malamat concluded. "His generosity grew with age."

Trude Dothan recalled an incident in 1966 when she and Moshe visited Prof. Albright in Baltimore. "He showed us around the university and then took us to lunch in the Faculty Club, and that was very funny, because people forgot that I was a woman! Women were not allowed there except in a separate dining room for both men and women! We sat there, and I saw the waitresses looking not too happy, and finally one of them reminded him nicely that this is not exactly done. We went out through the back door and kitchen and finally reached the proper dining room! He was not really embarrassed, it was just very funny. He was really wonderful, so charming, and it was such an experience to be with him that day."

Moshe Dothan mentioned their trips with Albright on his visits to Israel and how he enjoyed visiting the excavations. "He never complained about anything. He was talking about the pioneers, *halutzim,* always with the highest regard, talking about how it was here in the '20's. I remember he sent us a letter of congratulations on the saving of Israel in '67."

Prof. Shemaryahu Talmon, of Hebrew University, recalled how busy Albright was in 1969—receptions, dinners, tours; "but we also met him here and there for a minute and exchanged a few words. He had established for himself a following in this country which

was not only a scholarly following; there was a very deep appreciation and almost a feeling of love for him. First, because of the appreciation one had for him as a scholar, as a man, as a gentleman;
and second, here was a great man of the profession, the great, grand
Old Man of the profession, who steadfastly and without reservation
endorsed the State of Israel—for the fact that now Israeli scholars,
whom I think he appreciated very much, had free access to science,
could work out their own systems, approaches, and methods. So
when he came here he was flooded with requests to visit this and
that and another site; it was almost impossible to catch up. He almost flew from one to another. I think all this brought about a very
interesting, very heartening combination that resulted in the attitude of a deep appreciation of—I think one could say identification with—Israel as he saw it."

This visit was probably the crowning peak of Albright's life in
relation to the Holy Land, but gentle slopes and another peak still
lay before him.

22

Celebration

After returning from Israel, Albright had too many speaking engagements already promised, for which he paid with bed rest most of the summer. He confessed this in a letter to Edmund Wilson thanking him for *The Dead Sea Scrolls 1947-1969,* which he had reviewed favorably in the *Sun* on July 27.

Leona Running drove to Baltimore on schedule in mid-August and worked with Prof. Albright and Stephen Mann for several very full weeks. Much was accomplished; many letters went out as Albright tried to catch up on his correspondence while she was there —it had piled up while he lacked secretarial help and was bedfast. To Prof. Shmuel Yeivin at Tel-Aviv University he wrote recommending promotion of one of his associates, and said he was sorry Yeivin was away from Israel when he visited in March. His cataracts, he said, were growing, but any date for operating seemed to be receding; he would keep on working as long as he could. (He sometimes told Leona his fantasy of what he would do after he went blind and couldn't work at scholarly things: he would spin fanciful tales for children, similar to those he had created in his earliest years.) A letter to Prof. Malamat accepted an assignment to write an introductory chapter for a book, with an overly optimistic hope of doing so before Dr. Running would leave. Albright sent his good wishes to all his acquaintances and friends in Israel.

A manuscript he should have corrected and sent off months before was promised that summer, with explanation that he was improved in health and had the help of a good typist for three weeks. Permission to quote from his works was granted an editor; to an old friend he confided his irritation with certain journals which had accepted from him contributions for which they had contracted and paid, but which they ruined by rewriting and expanding, or else rejected completely and buried in their files. What kind of material did they really wish? Couldn't one be allowed to translate the text for himself? One editor by phone had told him so many things to include that Albright warned him it would sound like an encyclopedia article; when the editor received it, he complained that it sounded like an encyclopedia article! He asked Albright just to speculate instead. Albright related the incident with disdain, horror, and incredulity.

To an Israeli scholar he wrote that he had been really disappointed on his trip to Israel not to be able to see the early Arad pottery. By September 3 he was writing friends that he was bearing the pace quite well and he and Dr. Running were accomplishing much that otherwise might have been postponed months or years. They were just completing final work on an article of a paper he had read in the fall of 1965 at the American Philosophical Society meeting, the research for which dated back to 1960, "Neglected Factors in the Greek Intellectual Revolution."

On September 22 Albright dictated to his part-time typist, who had returned after Leona's departure, an air letter to Noel Freedman, who was in Israel for a year as Director of the ASOR in Jerusalem. Sam Iwry, who had returned from a visit to Israel, had told Albright of visiting Noel at the School and being pleased by the cordial reception he received. Albright declared that without Sam he would feel lost; they were lucky still to have him in Baltimore.

Noel's reply told of visits not only by Sam but by Nelson Glueck. "I earnestly hope that in time the School really will be equally accessible to all people, and especially scholars of every background and conviction. . . . gradually I think we can restore the days, with changes, which prevailed in the '20's and '30's under your direction. Incidentally, speaking of echoes from the past, we had dinner the other night with the Vesters of the American Colony Hotel. We had never met them before, and enjoyed the conversation with them immensely—mostly about the past."

The Albrights' third son, Stephen, and his family had moved from Connecticut to Virginia, and the Albrights visited them on a Sunday early in August. Their oldest son, Paul, and his family had moved to New York after many years in business in Brazil. In

November Paul's daughter Nancy was married. The proud grandparents were there for this first wedding in which they belonged to the bride's family, the wedding of their oldest grandchild.

When Albright wrote Noel in December, he and Stephen had the *Matthew* manuscript back with Noel's and the copy editor's notes and queries. Albright blamed part of the state of the Introduction on the fact that it had been sent in before he had gone over it again as he intended.

On January 7, 1970, Dr. Albright slipped on an icy sidewalk on the campus and suffered a concussion as he fell backward and struck his head. Two men acted the part of the Good Samaritan and took him to nearby Union Memorial Hospital; at the moment he did not even know where he lived. They stayed with him there almost an hour and then, when he could think more clearly and remember where he lived, they took him home. When he tried to get up from his bed after resting a couple of hours, he found he was, as he always used to say, "dizzy as a ha'nt." By the time he dictated his January 19 letter to Leona telling her of this accident, which had disrupted his plans for work, he had recovered his balance quite largely but still had some dizziness. He still planned to teach a seminar course at Yeshiva University, going up to New York for it on the first Wednesday of each month, February through May, involving two or three days each trip. No other trips were planned except those for the Research Committee in Philadelphia on the first Friday of February, April, and June. He hoped his concussion would be healed long before Leona's planned spring quarter to be spent helping him before her summer trip in Europe and the Middle East.

In the interesting two-page mimeographed annual letter Mrs. Albright sent to their friends on January 17, telling of their year's highlights, she added a note to Leona telling of his fall on ice and that after ten days he was still shaky but of course refused to rest enough. And her letter told of their delightful trip to Israel and the good care everyone had taken to spare their strength and eyesight. The climactic news was that the American School in Jerusalem had been renamed the W. F. Albright Institute of Archaeological Research. It was a tribute to their many years of service, and made them very happy. (Mrs. Albright could not know that almost exactly three years later as a widow she would have her picture taken before the gate with this new name on it in large white letters, in front of the building they had built forty-five years before. Noel Freedman had helped work out the change of name early in his year as director.)

Nearly five weeks after his fall Albright still felt the effects, as he wrote to Noel. He now had neuralgic pains running down his back, first on one side, then on the other. When he wrote Noel again it was to say on April 6 that his health was much better and he had been in New York and Philadelphia the previous week, the first time away from Baltimore since his fall. He had given his lectures and visited his family members with no bad effects. Not much work had been done on *Matthew*, but he and Stephen had collected some important new ideas, and that day Leona had returned, ready to work for two months. Noel responded from Jerusalem, "delighted with your report of progress in your physical condition, . . . also pleased to know that Leona Running is back with you for a while anyway, since that will mean obligatory progress on *Matthew*." On May 11 Noel responded to news of further progress that "it is good to know that you are moving along to the completion of the work, . . . The book will be both provocative and stimulating."

The spring AOS meeting in April had been planned for Baltimore in hopes that Dr. Albright might be able to attend if it was there. In his last years, while he was unable to believe he was slowing down mentally at all, his deteriorating eyesight made it most difficult to attend meetings, especially at night or in strange places. With Leona there to take him in her car to the Lord Baltimore Hotel, park in an underground garage, and walk in with him until he was safely located with old friends who would take him to lunch and be with him until he was ready to return home in mid-afternoon for his eye-drops and rest, it was possible to manage. He greatly enjoyed several days of meetings through the morning and early afternoon, not attempting to go in the evening. He wrote an old friend afterward that Dr. Leona Running had shepherded him to the meetings and watched that he did not go astray to some unknown part of town. (However, in the car they did make a wrong turn and get lost twice, once ending up on the south side of the harbor with a view of the city new to Leona and not seen in years by Prof. Albright!) He added that his cataracts continued to grow slowly but steadily, but were not yet operable and might never become so. He felt blessed in being able to keep on working at his desk.

Dr. Albright's seventy-ninth birthday passed quietly, with a card and new wallet from Leona and similar remembrances from others of his immediate circle. Two days before, he had written Noel that, unbelievable as it might seem, Dr. Running had just registered and mailed several sections of the *Matthew* manuscript to Doubleday (this time with his knowledge and blessing). Stephen Mann had been able to put some time on it since the end of his teaching term. The joint authors were looking forward to the horrified, or shocked, or puzzled reactions from their future reviewers for their historical orientation, dating all the gospels rather early, with excellent lines of supporting evidence. He said Stephen was going to amuse himself during a short break by composing insulting reviews in the style of certain scholars. Fortunately they both possessed tough hides. (In late May of 1969 Albright had written Prof. F. C. Fensham, his former student at the University of Stellenbosch, South Africa, that the majority of biblical scholars do not accept new approaches or points of view different from what they were exposed to in their days as students. As an example he cited G. R. Driver in England and his students. He added that he was accumulating a growing mass of material not yet published, which would not be accepted by many people for some decades. He and his assistant, Dr. Mann, were collaborating on it, aware that it would be infuriating to most New Testament scholars. One nice thing about growing older was that one need no longer worry about the effect on one's students and their careers produced by one's "heretical" ideas!)

Albright added a postscript to Noel's letter, saying that the photo just sent of the new name on the entrance of the former ASOR in Jerusalem, now the AIAR, had greatly pleased Ruth (it pleased him also!); he himself had been captivated by the beauty of the new front approach to the building. (The 1967 plan to sell the property had been abandoned.)

Noel's reply told of preparations to leave Jerusalem, their year almost ended. "We are well into the round of farewell parties, and give and receive greetings from and for you all the time. You have innumerable friends and admirers in the country, but that is no secret. It has been a particular pleasure and honor for me to have ordered the new gates with the new name for the old School." Another honor had come that spring also, when Dr. Albright was elected honorary fellow of the Royal Asiatic Society.

The front page of the April 1970 BASOR carried a photo of Albert Henry Detweiler, Oct. 4, 1906—Jan. 30, 1970. The "In Memoriam" was written by Prof. Albright and was immediately followed by his belated obituary for Carl Herman Kraeling, whose photo appeared on page 5 with his dates, Mar. 10, 1897—Nov. 14, 1966.

In the first half of 1970 another sorrow came to Prof. Albright in the death of a former student: "On Sunday, April 26, word reached friends and colleagues in America that Paul Lapp had drowned while swimming off Cyprus," Prof. Delbert Hillers wrote in the October 1970 BASOR. "With his death at the tragically early age of thirty-nine, the American Schools and American scholarship in general lost the outstanding Palestinian archaeologist of his generation, one who excelled all his contemporaries in mastery of pottery typology and in field experience. . . ."[1] Nancy Renn Lapp was left with five children, and after burying her husband near Bethlehem, returned to the U.S. to continue his work of teaching at Pittsburgh Seminary. She recalled later that after their wedding, "in the next twelve years our contacts with Dr. Albright were mainly by correspondence, usually between Jerusalem and Baltimore. The support and encouragement we needed were always there. Just glancing through our files I found evidence of the many comments Dr. Albright had on a find or the stratification of one of Paul's digs, and several letters were extracted so I could use his comments in the current work of publication. There are also several letters with more fatherly advice, as he often wrote concerning some more personal problem. Most of all to be remembered is the note I got from him May 1, 1970, after my husband's death. He did not fail to mention his subconscious pre-marital confusion of 'Miss Lapp' and 'Mr. Renn,' but he also remembered our five young children, the career Paul had had, and the task before me. Up to his death, Dr. Albright encouraged me in the continuation of Paul's work."

On July 6 (after Leona had spent a month on her trip overseas) Prof. Albright typed a letter to Margaret, wife of his cousin Tom Foxwell in Iowa. He told of his fall early in January and resulting mild concussion, from which he recovered only in the latter part of

March. Then a "demon typist" who had assisted him occasionally for several years came for a two-month stay and had him working hard to finish things while she was there. The pace would be too much for both if it were all the time, but he found the arrangement very useful periodically in getting his writing done, dictating to her on the typewriter. He had spent a month recovering after her departure; a tonic prescribed by his physician helped. He said Ruth spoke of their making a trip to see Aunt Ella, but he was doubtful that it would be possible with his deteriorating eyesight. Ruth had fair distance vision but not close (they complemented each other); his cataracts were not ready for surgery. He mentioned the possibility of their going in August to visit Shirley and Finley at the farm in Virginia if Hugh could take them.

Prof. Moshe Goshen-Gottstein of Hebrew University had contacts by correspondence with Prof. Albright from the mid-forties when he was just finishing his doctoral work. When he met Albright in person at Strasbourg in the Old Testament Congress of 1956, he had the first real long discussion with him over lunch together with Julius Lewy. Goshen-Gottstein was not in Israel when Albright made his last visit in '69, but in America, and heard the reports from the American side. He recalled, "I had the feeling that he was always trying to find new things, new evidence—he wasn't somebody who goes in for a rounded-out work which needs 80% rehash and 20% new things. What he was really after was constantly to break new ground, to see new vistas, to take up a single point and from it develop all kinds of rays in all directions, but not in a way which forced him to put this into an over-all statement of a grammar or a dictionary or a history or an exegetic endeavor. Somewhere in him he felt that actually this was what he *should* do, and so he played with the idea, but he pushed it off and off and always made something else more acute or more novel come in his way as an excuse to say, 'Well, as long as I haven't done this, how can I really write something all-embracing?' "

Noel Freedman, to whom Goshen-Gottstein was speaking, cited *From the Stone Age to Christianity* as "an excellent example of an outline of such a major comprehensive work, and his last one, *Yahweh and the Gods of Canaan*, is the same kind of thing," these being "almost entirely programmatic in character." When Noel had asked Albright about the *History of the Religion of Israel* which remained unfinished, Albright said, "Well, with all the new ideas I have, with all the new things that have happened, it's not yet time to write the definitive history."

Prof. Goshen-Gottstein remarked of Albright, "He's not reproducible. Each of his students takes up a particular part of Albright and follows on. And that's part of what present-day specialization really is."

A Hopkins colleague in Gilman Hall, Dr. John Walton, Professor of Education, recalled that when he first met Dr. Albright in 1947, the library stacks and reading room on that floor were shared by the Education Department and the Oriental Seminary. "From the very beginning," he said, "I was impressed with Dr. Albright, I think for three reasons: (1) One of the most outstanding things about him was his tremendous interest in what he was doing, his energy, his vivacity. He sort of radiated energy and interest in his work. He was an alive and extremely energetic man. (2) I think the thing that most people were most impressed by when they got to know him, was the tremendous erudition. He just knew *an awful lot*. And I use the word 'awful' in the literal sense—it was awe-inspiring, the knowledge he had about so many different things. (3) Something that I learned to appreciate over the years, because my association with him continued until he died, was his friendliness, his interest in people.

He was not the remote, reserved scholar that people think about when they think of a man of his erudition and his intellectual contributions, but he was a very humble person. We served together on several committees, many oral examinations, and I found out how perceptive he was about practical matters, how practical he was in his decisions about college programs—how much he knew about even professional education. He had wide-ranging interests and one could not classify him as a man who had scholarly esoteric interest only; he had a great deal of practical sense.

"I walked home with him many times over these many years, and the conversation was always very interesting, but did not have to be about esoteric matters—it could be about everyday affairs. It was quite obvious that Dr. Albright supported individual rights, freedom, and equal opportunity; never once was he on what might be termed a conservative side on those things. No self-styled 'liberal' had any greater humanity about him than Albright, who had a generally conservative bent about political matters. There was never any question about where he stood; he said perfectly frankly where he stood. But he was not fanatical about it, one way or the other.

"We used to have meetings here in the area of his general interest—religious history, theology, philosophy, and so forth—and I was always amazed at how much more he knew about some of these matters being discussed by the so-called experts from the outside, than *they* knew. He had much more background. In a few instances the visiting speakers were immediately and obviously awe-stricken by the idea that Dr. Albright was there to listen to them! They constantly looked at him and referred to him to see how well *they* were doing, rather than his watching them!

"Dr. Albright had no patience with intellectual arrogance, because he knew how much there was to know. I've been on the orals boards of some of his students. A student who was having some difficulty, Dr. Albright would try to help; he was very considerate. If a student thought he knew everything, Dr. Albright would 'throw the book' at him. Albright was the last that I would call the really greats at Hopkins. He seemed to tower out of another age, above the present age, at all times. He specialized in many things. He was one of the last of the universals."

On August 17, 1970, Dr. Albright dictated a letter to Mrs. Ruth Amiran, thanking her for the copy he had received of her fine volume, *Ancient Pottery of the Holy Land,* and for dedicating it to him.

Ruth Amiran first began learning from Prof. Albright in 1934-35, when she met him at the School and joined him and two of his students in a car for a trip to Megiddo. She said, "There isn't one problem in Palestinian archaeology, perhaps even farther afield, Near Eastern archaeology, that he didn't touch. If I do now some things around Arad, on every bit he touched already! Nobody would dream to say that he *solved* all the problems; who does? He was so terribly curious to know—that certainly was one of his main characteristics. The most important information is still in his notes; they were taken into consideration by the excavators, and are by now reflected in all the general results in the various books; but these are *his*." She had taken her archaeological training mainly under Prof. Sukenik, and in her first year studied Albright's

Archaeology of Palestine and the Bible. "At the time as a student you never think how big is the man, how enormous is his head! The scope of his writings is tremendous. Every day, once, at least, I go to something of his writings—at least once a day! I don't think we have today anybody of that general capacity and strength, and, I think, honesty in scholarship. His interest was always progressing on the *front* line."

Soon after her return from overseas Leona drove to Baltimore, for Dr. Albright had typed a note to her saying he would be glad for her help for at least the second half of September; his part-time secretary's husband had had an accident and this had taken her away for some weeks. Noel soon wrote, reporting to Albright on his year at the School and in Israel and concerning Anchor Bible business. A number of manuscripts were then in process with Noel or at Doubleday. He added, "News from the Near East is very disquieting these days, but I fear that things will get worse before they improve." There was war in Jordan between Jordanian troops and Arab guerilla fighters.

In late September Albright signed the last annual Hopkins Roll Call letter he would send out, adding greetings for Noel and Leona on their copies. When he wrote Leona in late October he admitted that he had had to spend much of the month in bed after attending the meeting of the first weekend in Philadelphia following her departure. Since he had suffered most of the summer from nervous exhaustion, he said he could not blame this on her two weeks there; in fact, the urgent work produced during those weeks had helped him to feel better.

In November, as a member of an accreditation team evaluating two Jewish institutions in New Jersey, Dr. Albright and his wife traveled and he gave lectures in addition to the committee work. They wrote asking Leona to come for a week before Christmas. Albright spent the first part of December in bed, and was unable to attend meetings in New York and Philadelphia.

Leona arrived by overnight bus and phoned, and Dr. Albright suggested she come right out by taxi to the apartment and stay there this time. The major task was to clear up systematically all of Noel's and the Anchor Bible editor's marginal queries and notes on the *Matthew* manuscript. Stephen Mann and Dr. Albright also worked on the manuscript, singly, with each other, or with Leona, as needed. After several grueling days it was all cleaned up, necessary typing was done, and this time it was given up to Doubleday with Albright's blessing for the final time, two years after its surreptitious send-off. A new Anchor Bible editor, Sallie Waterman, made a quick train trip down from New York to pick up the bulky manuscript and take it back the same day, not trusting it to holiday mail delivery.

Mrs. Albright's year-end letter to family and friends told of events beginning with his fall on the ice and his concussion, and work produced with help from Dr. Leona Running at different times in the year. The eyesight of both the Albrights was declining, and she could no longer do needlework, but they complemented each other's vision for traveling.

Delbert R. Hillers as editor wrote the first article, "Fifty Years of the Bulletin of the American Schools of Oriental Research," for the December 1970 BASOR which was, as proclaimed on the front page, an "Anniversary Issue In Honor of William F. Albright." With added paragraphs, this represented in printed form the speech Delbert had given at the annual luncheon of the Alumni Association of the American Schools at the October 1969 meeting in Toronto in connection with the SBL meeting (which from then on was scheduled in the fall rather than during Christmas vacation). Hillers sketched through the issues of BASOR from the first one on, tracing "how much it has changed from its inception, on the one hand, and secondly, how accurately it mirrors the character, the personality one might almost say, of the American Schools, . . . As if a leit-motif for a symphony were being announced, the name W. F. Albright appears in Bulletin No. 1. . . .

"One of the most momentous stages in the Bulletin's development is marked under the heading 'Change of Editorship' in Bulletin No. 41. W. F. Albright paid grateful tribute to the long labors of President Montgomery and expressed his intention to continue the Bulletin's work of: '. . . popularizing the results of research without cheapening them.' Prof. Albright continued to edit the Bulletin actively through number 192 of December, 1968, that is, through 152 issues, through 38 years . . . one may fairly say that over these long years, the Bulletin became very much Dr. Albright's own, a reflection of his interests and his judgment. At the same time it continued to serve the interests of the Schools because in an extraordinary way Prof. Albright's interests matched those of the collective membership of the Schools. Those were years of great expansion of the Schools' activities, and Prof. Albright, and through him the Bulletin, kept pace and often a stride ahead. . . .

"A new genre was created in those days: the Additional Note. . . . The impartial reader, the membership of the American Schools, rather enjoyed the lively tempo which this practice imparted to scholarly discussions, and valued it as a symbol of the intense personal concern which the Bulletin editor felt for the content of the journal.

"Already by the late 1930's the Bulletin was becoming ever more technical, faithfully reflecting what was happening in the field of studies it reported. It was not totally austere, since it could still carry the report of the Director of the Jerusalem School, Dr. Nelson Glueck, that 'A letter from Dr. Mackay announces the death of Lady Petrie's cat. The interesting feud between the cat and our dog thus takes an untimely end.' Nevertheless, the issue for February, 1938, announced the first issue of the *Biblical Archaeologist*, intended to make the results of original research available to the public in a readable form. Since this had not so long before been the stated purpose of the Bulletin, it was already then evident that the Bulletin, like any vital organ, had changed in the course of its life. There has been a unifying theme, however, which unites the first issue to the last, the theme of service. The Bulletin has existed to serve the interests of the American Schools and of American scholarship. It is fitting that we who have been so well served should take occasion to pay tribute to Fifty Years of the Bulletin, and to the long editorship of Prof. Albright, whose service has been beyond our power to calculate or to repay."[2]

Dr. Hillers added, "As the Bulletin approached milestone No. 200 in its history, it seemed altogether appropriate that such an anniversary issue be dedicated to William F. Albright. Limitations of space dictated by the Schools' budget made it impossible to think of producing a volume large enough to reflect all of Dr. Albright's many scholarly interests, or to include contributions from all scholars who would wish to pay their respects to him on such an occasion. Instead it was decided to put out in Dr. Albright's honor an issue of more-or-less ordinary size and scope. Each of the current editors has contributed in some way, and a few other scholars associated with the Schools have been invited to submit articles, in order to achieve variety in the topics treated. Trustee Robert L. Crowell has generously arranged for the preparation of specially slip-covered copies for presentation to the Albrights."[3]

Before the eleven articles and notes by former students and colleagues, a four-page article by Frank Moore Cross, Jr., was placed: "William Foxwell Albright: Orientalist" (remarks made at the Alumni Luncheon in Toronto). He began: "The student who attempts to write a tribute to William Foxwell Albright undertakes a dangerous task. I know of no student of Albright's who does not hold him in great affection, and love may impede objective evaluation. The reverse also may be true; we may be too close to him to perceive his real stature. One thing is certainly true: no student of William Albright has the scholarly scope to evaluate all his contributions. . . .

"Albright has listed his profession as 'Orientalist.' The whole of the ancient Near East has been his bailiwick, its geography and archaeology, its languages and literature, its history and religion. I suspect that he is the last such orientalist: a generalist with the specialist's precision in designated areas of Egyptian, Mesopotamian, Anatolian, and Syro-Palestinian studies. . . . Each of the great discoveries in the Near East has galvanized Albright with excitement, and he has been found regularly in the forefront of those who endeavored to interpret the new data and to build new syntheses comprehending the new evidence. . . .

I have heard the complaint that Albright is forever changing his mind. Those who make such criticisms should note that his changes of mind regularly follow the introduction of new data or new arguments. Such changeableness is marvelous, a mark of genius. . . .

". . . Perhaps Albright was never in worse form than when he consciously undertook to be a pedagogue. At the same time he was the greatest teacher I have ever known. He led the student immediately to the leading edge of research in a given field, usually faster than the student could go. I am not at all sure why all first-year men at Johns Hopkins did not simply abandon the field and go home. Somehow, however, he instilled in the student his own excitement, his own delight in solving a crux, something of his devotion to scholarship. . . .

"I wish to speak finally of one of the central unifying elements in the scholarship of W. F. Albright. Albright is a master of typological method. In his programmatic studies and in his large syntheses of historical data, he is normally found to be imposing on unclassified and chaotic bits of evidence the discipline of typological analysis. This is most evident in his magnum opus, the three volumes of *The Excavation of Tell Beit Mirsim*. In this work Albright established the fundamental chronology of Palestinian archaeology. He accomplished this by removing sequence dating of ceramic forms from the realm of intuition and guess, placing it upon a systematic footing. . . . Albright became the father of Palestinian archaeology with his minute and precise observations of typological features of pottery, and the grand synthesis of ceramic chronology in the Bronze and Iron Ages. . . . His model of historical development draws heavily on the analogy of the typological sciences. He perceives continuity in history and the emergence of novelty in an orderly set of relationships following the patterns of typological change. As in typological series, the past is intelligible; its changes irreversible. Yet the future is unpredictable owing to elements of freedom and spontaneity. Albright stands thus on the side of empirical and positivistic philosophers. . . ."[4]

Dr. Delbert Hillers later recalled his acquaintance with Prof. Albright during his last fifteen years. Sent from Concordia Seminary in St. Louis in an internship to start a Lutheran missionary congregation in a Baltimore suburb, he "immediately thought of what a wonderful chance it was to study at Johns Hopkins." One of his "older professors, Dr. George Victor Schick, had been one of the earliest Ph.D.'s at Johns Hopkins under Paul Haupt and had the experience at Hopkins of serving as an instructor or teaching fellow, and was one of Dr. Albright's teachers. I can remember Dr. Schick observing with a chuckle, 'Yes, Albright was a good student!' I had friends who were studying with Dr. Albright, particularly Paul Lapp. On the day that classes were to begin in 1955, I showed up in considerable fear and awe of Dr. Albright, to ask if I might take some courses on a part-time basis. I had no letters to recommend me, I didn't even have the university application forms. But Dr. Albright simply asked me who I was, and when I told him I was from Concordia Seminary, he asked whether I had studied with George Victor Schick. Then he sent me off to get the proper forms. Of course I had no transcripts yet. Dr. Albright signed, as it were, a blank check, putting his name at the bottom of this rather odd application, and sent me back to the admissions director, whose comment was, 'That's Dr. Albright! He lets everyone in!'

"I know from my student days and also from being on the faculty later and from hearing people talk about Dr. Albright, that in a way this came very close to being the literal truth! He was quick to believe that there was some good, some promise, and that almost everyone had something to contribute. I remember his observing in later years that he had discovered it wasn't always the most gifted people who had done the most, but the people who were most industrious.

"I had Albright that year for Ugaritic class, chosen partly at his suggestion and partly because it fitted my pastoral schedule. But this was an utterly baffling experience. I had the impression that very interesting things were going on in the class and that Dr. Albright was saying important things, but I didn't understand them at all! Father Joseph Fitzmyer was kind enough to take me aside in the hall once in a while and explain what was going on in this mysterious class.

"I returned to my seminary to finish my final year and came back, in more proper order, for the year 1957-58, which was Albright's last year of teaching before retirement. It was an unusually large crowd of students gathered to get in on this last year of instruction by Dr. Albright. After he retired they went their several ways and things immediately shrank back to normal size or even less. It was perhaps not a typical year with Dr. Albright, because he was even less than usual under any constraint to do things in a normal, straightforward manner. He would open his mail in class, and I seem to remember his remarking one time that after a man was 65 years old he should be permitted to ramble a little! He felt very free to hold forth on what was uppermost in his mind at the time, and to let you make the connections if you were able, to what was said in the books. He was not going to tell you what was already written down in the books. So I remember a great deal of time was spent on the chronology of Alalakh, where he was engaged in a controversy with Woolley, but if you weren't completely up to date on this, you were not deriving much sustenance from the history lectures.

"It was indeed a rich experience. Occasionally if one can think

back and recall memories out of this chaos, they are surprisingly coherent; you begin to put some of the pieces together; you realize
what Albright was after in his extremely rambling, indirect
approach to things. After that year I took a Master's degree at
Hopkins—it seemed to be the thing to do, because I was going to
teach Hebrew at Concordia Senior College in Fort Wayne, Indiana.
A number of us gathered to write exams; about fifteen, for both
Ph.D. and M.A. exams gathered in a room, and Dr. Albright went
around the room and had each of us suggest a question for the
examination. Then he added a question or two of his own, and we
were supposed to choose half of all these. We wrote madly for days.
I don't think Albright ever looked at one word of what was written
on those exams—I can only hope not! We got our degrees and left.

"After teaching Hebrew two years," Dr. Hillers continued, "I
returned to Hopkins to find things much changed, as was inevitable.
When he was in Baltimore Albright conducted himself with complete and I think remarkable courtesy and understanding toward
the new people who came into the department and who naturally
had different approaches and ways of doing things. He was always
ready to talk to a student or the new faculty people—when asked—
but I honestly do not recall any incident where he could be thought
to be meddling or interfering or even being a bit aggressive in giving advice and sharing his experience.

"Even before I started on my dissertation in 1962-63 (and it was
a great encouragement to discuss my topic with Albright and find
him enthusiastic and encouraging about it), I was fortunate enough
to be invited to join the faculty of the department. When I received the degree I came in as an assistant professor, and continued
to see Dr. Albright from time to time. The association became
much closer and more regular when the chairman, Professor Wil-
fred G. Lambert, left quite suddenly one summer to take a position
in the University of Birmingham, England, and I was to serve for a
time as acting chairman. It was worked out that Dr. Albright would
continue to occupy his office, with me in there also. He used it only
as a place where he received mail and BASOR proofs. He would
come over nearly every day when he was in town, and if I was there
he would often open his mail and talk either about what he found
in or heard through his correspondence, or about his work. He went
on in a kind of high-level 'stream of consciousness' talk, not much of

a 'conversation' in the sense of give-and-take. The next time he came in he would pick up the topic again, often repeating some of the things he had said before and going on to add new material. This permitted a kind of insight into how he was working on these things which eventually would find publication. Obviously it wasn't a lot of working out of drafts on paper, but he was constantly working and revising it in his own mind. From my own point of view it was very educational, in a way. I still felt very much as I did as a student in relation to him. He seemed to appreciate someone just listening, acting as a sounding board for his ideas.

"He was quite receptive to other people's ideas, though he could be quite abrupt and almost curt if an idea didn't seem to him to have any promise at all. When I got halfway through presenting an idea one time, he said, 'Yes, of course,' anticipating what I was about to tell him—not that he had thought of it before, but he saw the direction I was going in, and jumped in before the words were out of my mouth. He could be very quick. You didn't have to waste words with him.

"However, I found that in his later years it became more and more difficult simply to get him to listen and understand what you were trying to tell him. He would sometimes jump to conclusions and be very rigid in a way that he wouldn't have been if he had stopped and listened to what was being said. He became, it seemed to me, locked up in his own thoughts and more difficult to communicate with.

"I had an experience," Dr. Hillers continued, "of attempting a collaboration with Dr. Albright on one of his typical papers read in 1955 at an SBL meeting, on *edut* in the Scriptures. I still have his paper, which was one sheet, typed on one side—simply an outline with the essential facts. I wasn't present, but I assume he spoke his allotted twenty minutes and did so with perfect coherence and polish. He kept working on the topic for years and years, even past his retirement; contributions that were offered him by H. L. Ginsberg and others were written on pieces of paper and dropped into the file on this subject. People who knew about this and heard him speak on it, especially his students, were eager for it to appear. I discovered, when Dr. Albright readily agreed to it, that collaboration with him was something I was not prepared for. The more I waded through this material and the suggestions he had amassed, the more it seemed problematical and bogged down; if Albright had been doing it on his own, it was the kind of thing he could cut through and deal with very quickly, in a magisterial way; he would not have fussed with all the small problems which were bothering me about this. It dragged along. I learned that his ways of working were not like mine. Time rather overtook this project; other people who had his earlier notes, scattered through his publications, on the subject, picked it up and published on it, spelled out the implications of it—but not in as good a way as he would have done. I think that what is there in Albright's amassed material is really now available; what he might have done with it himself we won't ever know.

"The editorship of the *Bulletin* was very much the same kind of situation. Ray Cleveland worked with Dr. Albright for years as what Albright would call 'junior editor.' When he went overseas to work in Amman on Arabian materials sent there by Wendell Phillips, he was no longer going to be able to continue as co-editor, and I was right at Johns Hopkins. Again I had the idea that perhaps Dr. Albright would appreciate someone who was able to do the detail work, take over the dull side of things—copy editing, proof-reading and the like—and spare his eyes, spare him for deciding about the content of the journal and the real editorial work. But it never worked out that way. It remained in his hands, and on the other hand he was very generous about asking my opinion on matters where one didn't always care to have an opinion! Materials would show up on my desk when he saw fit; proofs would be kept in his hands long after they should have been returned to the printer, and I soon realized how little experience I had to contribute, even in the mechanical things. All the years Dr. Albright edited the *Bulletin,* he really did it all by himself. He just ran it, wrote much of the content of it. It wasn't his only outlet, because he was publishing things all over elsewhere, but it was a way he had of reviewing what was going on in the field for the benefit of the readership of the American Schools. It was a unique way of running such a thing on a shoestring, which was also highly characteristic of Albright; economy was always dominant in his mind.

"No matter how chaotic it might seem from the viewpoint of anyone outside, you always had the feeling it was really pretty clear in his own mind—right down to the end. I think the problems became more severe, with his failing health and eyesight, and increased problems with the printers, and the usual problems of lack of cooperation on the part of contributors, and so on. It became farther and farther behind the publication dates. But especially in the good earlier days it was an amazing achievement which he did single-handedly and on the side.

"Often if you learned anything from Albright it was just along the way, when he didn't have any intention of teaching you at all, but you were just observing the tendency of his mind, his habits of work—not that you would imitate them directly, but that the sort of ideals he aimed for were extremely good.

"He had a very pronounced shyness, so when I describe my own relations with Dr. Albright it is necessary to say that they were always rather formal. He only began to call me by my first name after I had finished my dissertation. I knew Dr. Albright really only as an old man. His older students from previous years often nicknamed him 'the Old Man.' I never picked that up, but I knew him literally as an old man, and it was sometimes astonishing to continue to discover how nearly blind the man was. I saw him day in and day out for years, yet at one dinner party at Hans Goedicke's house, when my wife and I arrived and found the Albrights already there, we simply went into the living room, not introducing ourselves because we knew everyone; but Dr. Albright did not know who I was. When he saw me in the familiar surroundings of Gilman Hall, Room 126, of course he knew who I was, but seeing me at a distance of five or six feet in somebody's living room he quite honestly did not know who I was. It revealed how seriously impaired his vision was and how much he got by with guessing in the ordinary affairs of life.

"This fact of his nearsightedness and increasing glaucoma and finally cataracts was very much on his mind in his latter years, and it affected his attitude toward attending professional meetings. In early years he frequently attended and took an active part. He seemed to know everyone in the world and everyone knew him. In latter years he would either refuse or show great reluctance to go into crowds of people in an unfamiliar setting where he feared he would not recognize those he knew.

"I had one memorable train trip back from New York with

Dr. Albright. It was no great feat unless one realizes that I am very poor at finding my way around strange cities and did not know New York at all, and was with Albright, who was nearly blind. It was a case of his telling me from memory how to find the way in a newly refurbished train station. When we finally boarded the train, he had been so stimulated by the people with whom he had talked, that he insisted on talking all the way to Baltimore—a four-hour ride—serious talk about scholarly subjects, when I was totally exhausted!

"When I returned from my first season of excavation at Balatah, Ernest Wright's dig, Albright walked into the library in Gilman Hall on a quiet afternoon and found me; he was fairly dancing up and down with curiosity, wanting to know what had happened. I, having been working in one hole all summer, was prepared to wait and read the report and find out what had really gone on. I felt very inadequate for the task of trying to tell him what had been learned from this season's excavation, but he was like a child —he had much more enthusiasm about it than I did. He was keen to know everything.

"Albright's telephone manner I always found rather disconcerting. When he was finished he would simply hang up, without even a goodby. This was not in pique or anger—it was simply that the conversation was finished. [It might have been partly due to his growing deafness in later years.]

"Albright took an almost monastic view of the scholarly life. A scholar was not a professional. When some on the faculty after the second World War were pressing for increases in salary, Albright opposed the very idea of a scholar being concerned with salary and agitating for more money.

"It must be a matter of some regret that with Albright and Glueck gone a good many stories of the really old days have been lost. We had one unforgettable evening at the American School in '69, on Albright's last trip to the Holy Land. Prof. and Mrs. Albright and Nelson Glueck were invited to the Director's house for dinner, plus all of us who were School appointees that year. Glueck and Albright got into a kind of story-telling match, each topping the other. They both had many Petrie stories—Flinders Petrie had been very eccentric all his life, and more so in his old age, when he lived in the School. Albright always told how Petrie took levels and did surveying by the brim of his hat, aiming at the particular object on which he wanted the level, and then estimating the angle from the horizon. Albright in his own operations rose a little, in apparatus, above what Sir Flinders Petrie used, but still by the standards of many other excavators, who insist on comfort—there's enough hardship about excavation without making extra hardships!—Albright observed a pretty parsimonious level of operation.

"Albright once said when some question came up of the stratigraphy of Megiddo, which has been under discussion in recent years, and he had just read one of the more recent treatments and became very excited about it, 'But I was there, you see, and I *saw* this and that. The trouble with these people is, they don't know the tradition!' That was one of the things Albright had, in addition to knowledge of the publication: what could be called the oral tradition—having through many years seen many things with his own eyes. His experience in Palestinian archaeology was one that few people until now, when the Israelis who can live with it a long time can do this work, could have; he had the experience in the early times of being there personally and seeing everything.

"When Dr. Albright made his well-known final farewell visit to the Holy Land, he was of course taken all about the country. Dr. Bill Dever took Albright to the newly cleared, so-called High Place at Gezer, which Macalister dug and which the new Gezer expedition cleared away again in beautiful shape to show Albright. Dr. Dever took Albright around there with a tape recorder, recording his observations.

"I was present also," Del Hillers related, "at some of the festivities in the house of the president of Israel, and at the party at Professor Mazar's home. That was perhaps the high point for me, to see Albright among old friends and acquaintances, and busy of course with new things. They were picking his brains! Dever had some new inscriptional material not yet published and brought it to Albright for his opinion. He sat down right in the midst of the party with a reading-glass to look at these photographs. This is what everyone was doing—coming to Albright with their offerings, so to speak, and wanting to know his opinion."

When Dr. Albright dictated his January 11, 1971 letter to Noel Freedman about Anchor Bible concerns, he reported that Ruth had had one of the pictures Noel sent of Jonathan framed—the one of him standing in front of the new gate at the Albright Institute in Jerusalem. Dr. Albright wrote Leona asking if she could help in late April and May with the proof-reading of *Matthew* galleys. Responding to her suggestion for working in late August and September, Albright said he had always been happy to accept when she offered to help him, and thought he would have an abundance of work. (This was not to be, however.) He reported that Ruth's hearing was now deteriorating, as well as her eyesight. He himself had just learned from the German Oriental Society that the International Congress of Orientalists had awarded to him the Mark Lidzbarski Gold Medal for Excellence in Semitic Studies at their latest meeting, which was held in Australia.

Albright wrote Noel on March 1 about Anchor Bible business and hoped Noel and his family were looking forward to living in Ann Arbor; Noel had written the preceding fall about finding a house to buy, with large grounds, near the University of Michigan, to which he would move in the fall of 1971. Noel responded that they were "definitely looking forward to the journey to Ann Arbor although we will miss the still glorious scenery and unsurpassed weather of the Bay Area. I am sure that it doesn't compare with the even more spectacular scene which must have greeted you on your first visit in pre-earthquake days."

Albright typed a letter to Noel reporting that he and Stephen would read galley proofs on *Matthew* also, but Stephen was very busy and Albright's eyes were so bad that the two of them could not do it without Leona's help. He did want the reviewers in their panning of it not to be able to cite misprints and careless errors, at least. He also told Noel of the Lidzbarski medal that had been awarded to him at the Australian meeting of the International Congress of Orientalists. The medal had been produced and was to be sent, probably by way of the German Embassy in Washington. (In the preceding year Albright had mentioned to Leona that he had been invited to attend the Congress in Australia, give a lecture and receive a gold medal; but he and Ruth were physically unable to make the trip, and he indicated that if they wanted to give him a medal, they could just mail it to him. He seemed then not to care much about it, having received so many awards and medals, including one from the American Philosophical Society the third year it was awarded. But when he had been formally notified of it and knew it was on its way to him, he appeared to be gratified by the honor.)

Noel's reply of March 31 brought his "congratulations on the Lidzbarski award. You should have received it long ago, but better late than never."

The galley proofs for *Matthew* did not reach Leona until the first of May. On the fifth she sent the first seventy to Albright so that he and Stephen could start their reading of the preliminaries and the Introduction while she continued working on the remaining 109 galleys. By no more than meeting her classes that week she put 35½ hours on the galleys and sent the last of them to Baltimore. Dr. Albright wrote notes on May 11 and 12 acknowledging receipt of the two batches of proofs and remarking that with all the experiences in the past he should not have been astonished at her speed; he hoped she was not totally exhausted by this extra effort just before the close of her school year. In writing to Sallie Waterman at Doubleday, Leona remarked, "It is a rich experience to work through such meaty material in a concentrated way, in a short time. I think they have some wonderful material here—of course you won't be surprised that some critics go at it with hammer and tongs, nevertheless!" Sallie's reply expressed appreciation of Leona's work and wished she could share her comments with others about its being a rich experience . . .

On May 13 Dr. Albright typed his last letter to Margaret Foxwell in Iowa in reply to hers of May 9, which told that Aunt Ella had fallen and broken her hip and was hospitalized. Albright recalled that Aunt Katie had broken her hip when seven years younger than Aunt Ella now was—Aunt Katie had died at ninety-nine. (Aunt Ella would die later that summer in her 103rd year.) Albright remarked that since his 79th birthday he felt he had aged more than in any other year since 1963. It had recently become more difficult for them to travel around, as Ruth was becoming deaf as well as having worsening eyesight, high-blood pressure and arthritis, though she was still quite active. Albright was still able to work, though he made more typing mistakes, he said; his flow of ideas was, if anything, more rapid, though he could not rely on his memory as before. With the help of several magnifying glasses he could still do much work at his desk. He sent love to all the relatives.

Dr. Hans Goedicke, the Egyptologist who was by then chairman of the Department of Near Eastern Studies at Johns Hopkins, recalled that when he arrived in 1960, "Dr. Albright had already been retired two years, and especially during those years he had very little contact with the department. It was only considerably later, after his 70th and 75th birthdays, that the fences were mended again and that he took more interest in the department. He came over daily, first of all to pick up his life-line, consisting of innumerable letters, an endless correspondence. On these occasions there was possibility for chatting and comments on recent developments. What came out most strongly during these discussions was Prof. Albright's fantastic memory, which he retained until almost the end of his days; a memory which made it possible for him to quote details which some younger people would not be able to do. His connections with Egyptology were very personal; I have the impression that ancient Egyptian was a special kind of love-affair for him, and that might be one of the reasons why he came back to it again and again.

"It was to his credit in his late years that the contact grew closer with his old department. For administrative reasons as well as others, I had the occasion repeatedly to ask him for advice, which he always offered most graciously and which always proved very useful." (In the first few years after his retirement, Albright purposely kept aloof from the department in order not to seem to meddle and to try to continue to influence it. Besides, he was out of town most of the time then.)

Goedicke continued, "There are some very amusing little stories in his latest years, especially in connection with his eightieth birthday. Prof. Albright had a habit of referring to his age by saying that the current year was actually his year of age. So when he was past his 78th birthday he referred to himself as being 79." In one of the conversations it suddenly hit me that something ought to be done for his 80th birthday; I ought to set up and prepare for a *Festschrift* of some kind. So I went to work, and after I had everything set up and the invitations for contributions were out, I finally checked his biographies and discovered that I was a year ahead of time! I was in a rather awkward situation, trying to keep the horses at a slow pace; people wondered why the proofs came in so slowly, and why the project didn't progress as fast as it was indicated at first!

"However, despite the fact that the book was in press for almost two years, I succeeded in keeping it secret until *one week* before Prof. Albright's eightieth birthday, and it was by one of those unforeseeable coincidences that he learned of this project at that time. What happened was amusing: one of my colleagues had applied for a grant-in-aid from the American Philosophical Society, and of course this application came to Dr. Albright for review, among others. It happened to be the first one on the pile, and very much to his astonishment Albright found a reference to a book called *Studies Presented to William F. Albright on His 80th Birthday,* and that birthday was still a week away! However, he made no remark about it, and it was only at the official presentation of the book that he revealed the fact that he had already known about this project for a little time. Nevertheless he was very grateful, and I think he thoroughly enjoyed this celebration of his eightieth birthday, at which time many of his students and friends gathered, and it was a great occasion which I am very glad we were able to celebrate for him."

Mrs. Albright told the story on him at the party, after he had confessed that it wasn't exactly a surprise. She said he had come out into the kitchen, where she was trying to give instructions to the weekly maid, waving a paper in his hand and asking, "What is this? What is this?" She answered, "Well, read it to me and I'll *tell* you what it is." And so he had read to her this application for a grant for something to be contributed to the Albright 80th birthday *Festschrift.* She had to keep her promise and tell him, "Yes, you're to receive it at a party on May 24. So, since you found this out by accident, you are to act as though you didn't know."

Albright had already written on the May 24 page in his small 1971 diary or appointment schedule booklet, a note to himself to hold this date free for his family. After he and Stephen received the *Matthew* galleys from Leona by May 12 and worked through them, finishing them for Doubleday twelve days later, Albright was as usual exhausted and his eyes were in very bad shape.

Such outstanding scholars and good friends of Dr. Albright as Johannes Pedersen of Copenhagen, who was 85 and not well, H. H. Rowley of England, who already had cancer, W. Baumgartner of Basel, who was elderly and had commitments, Gerhard von Rad of Heidelberg, also elderly and committed to prior assignments, and Father Albert Jamme, off in Saudi Arabia excavating, had to decline with regret Dr. Goedicke's invitation to contribute an article to the Albright *Festschift*. James B. Pritchard of the University Museum in Philadelphia, John L. McKenzie, S.J., of Notre Dame University, and D. Winton Thomas of Cambridge, England, found the time allotted too short to be able to accept, and also declined with regrets. Prof. Edward Ullendorff, of the School of Oriental and African Studies, University of London, in accepting the invitation and the 1969 deadline, pointed out in a postscript that in reference works in which he had looked up Albright's birth date, it was uniformly listed as May 24 of 1891, so the eightieth birthday would not be one year but two years after the deadline that was given. By the time Dr. Goedicke received this letter written in November of 1968 and heard also from Noel Freedman with the same information, thus becoming aware of his one-year error, he doubtless had received enough acceptances so that he could not reset the deadline and reinvite those who had declined on account of the shortness of time for preparing a contribution.

Francis I. Andersen, of Church Divinity School of the Pacific, in accepting suggested that any general tribute prepared should include "something about a side of Dr. Albright's life that has not been noticed in public. I mean his work as a teacher, in personal relations with his students. I can recall arriving at Hopkins [from Australia], raw and innocent, with all the culture shock that hits a foreigner, and to find acceptance and encouragement, and not to be put off when I made a fool of myself. As long as you were willing to learn, Dr. Albright did not seem to mind how ignorant you were. And I appreciated that."

Leona decided to make the day-long drive to attend the birthday party, going to Washington on Friday and spending the weekend with a friend, then driving to Baltimore on Monday a few hours before the celebration. But she deliberately mailed a birthday card to Prof. Albright on Friday morning before leaving Michigan. As she later learned, when it arrived at the Albright apartment on Monday morning, May 24, Prof. Albright rather disappointedly said to his wife, "Well, then, Leona won't be coming." A photographer taking photos of Albright as he greeted each guest at his reception in Evergreen House, caught an expression of very surprised delight on Albright's face as his eyes focused on Leona and he realized that she *was* there!

People came from the entire East Coast of the United States for this last birthday celebration of their beloved teacher and colleague. His old colleague Prof. Ovid R. Sellers came the farthest, from Santa Fe, New Mexico. They all chatted and walked around through the stately rooms of the mansion, filled with artistic and valuable collections and rare books, until the Albrights arrived with their sons and their families. When Albright had delightedly met all who had come to honor him, Dr. Goedicke read telegrams and letters of greeting from many who were unable to come, and then presented the specially leather-bound *Festschrift* volume.

After the visits were over and the guests had departed, the Albrights with their sons and the three daughters-in-law, plus Stephen Mann and Leona Running and one or two others, gathered at the Hopkins Faculty Club for a family dinner. Prof. Albright looked terribly tired, hardly able to sit up and enjoy the excellent meal, and was quite obviously unable to see much. Leona at one point caught his attention and mentioned that she would be free to come and help in mid-August. Prof. Albright replied in a very tired voice, "We'll just have to wait and see."

In the Baltimore *Sunday Sun* for May 30, James H. Bready published another of his feature articles, "At 80, a Festschrift for Professor Albright." He began, "What will do as birthday present for a man of learning who already has 29 honorary doctorates? A man who began receiving academic gold medals years ago and whose inclusions in the acknowledgments, footnotes and bibliographies of scholarly works are beyond anybody's counting. Well, you hold a party for him at Evergreen House. Then when his numerous and noisy friends are assembled and quiet, you have the current chairman of his old Johns Hopkins department present him with still another book. And this book prints his name in the biggest type yet—not as cited authority, not even as author, but as title: 'Near Eastern Studies in Honor of William Foxwell Albright.'

"This book is a Festschrift, or literary compilation in honor of a great man. What with the upward leap of publishing costs lately, the Festschrift has grown rare. And this one is on the grand scale: a Johns Hopkins Press book, printed in England, in three modern languages plus side trips into ancient Semitic forms, with chapters contributed from a dozen nations by 35 of his most eminent colleagues in Biblical, archaeological and allied endeavors. Retail, the book is $15 and that low a price is possible only because Wendell Phillips has generously underwritten it.

"The Festschrift must be, of course, a surprise. Professor Albright must have no inkling. Yet the procedure is familiar to him— something of this sort went on when he turned 50, a festival volume also commemorated his 70th birthday, there was that fuss over him in Israel two years ago, and his now being 80 is no help because his awareness of whatever goes on in Near East studies remains, as always, instant. As a matter of joyous fact, when Hans Goedicke, Egyptologist and chairman of the Department of Near Eastern Studies at Johns Hopkins (the name for it was Oriental Seminary, during the years 1929 to 1958 when Professor Albright headed it) handed the book to the new octogenarian, at the party the other afternoon, the look on Professor Albright's face conveyed pleasure, shyness, gratitude—but no startlement. A grant application, proudly listing an Albright Festschrift article and sent to him to screen, gave it away.

"There were no speeches, and no one tried to wrest Professor Albright's copy of the book—in its special, full-leather binding— from him, for a quick peek at what Francis I. Andersen of the Church Divinity School of the Pacific had to say about 'Passive and Ergative in Hebrew,' or at the Old Israelitish *Erweckungsbewegungen* set forth by Hans Bardtke of Karl Marx University in Leipzig.

"But a stream of well-wishers wrung Professor Albright's hand and congratulated Mrs. Albright beside him and said hello to their sons, all on hand for the ceremony—Paul and Stephen from New York and business; Hugh, the Christian Brother from LaSalle College in Philadelphia, where he is academic dean; David, the Baltimore lawyer. Admirably behaved, two Albright grandchildren were there, David's girls. President Milton S. Eisenhower was detained by a finance meeting, but the flower of Homewood intellect bloomed there in John W. Garrett's old parlor and art gallery. Federal judges came by; the chairman of the University of Maryland regents; the editor of the 70th birthday Festschrift, down from Harvard [George Ernest Wright]; Anchor Bible colleagues; members of what is spoken of about the learned world as the Albright school of Palestinian digging and study.

"Mayor D'Alessandro came, and stayed late. Baltimoreans were largely unaware, last year, when the first and so far only City of Baltimore Medal for Distinguished Contributions to Scholarship, Research and Teaching was awarded, by this mayor, to William Foxwell Albright. Other titans of academe will doubtless receive it in their turn—but Mr. D'Alessandro has an unpublicized layman's interest in Holy Land research.

"Then, the telegrams, 'Happy Birthday!' was the chorus from Sumer, as Noah Kramer put it; from Beirut, from Jerusalem, signed Malamat, Yadin, Aharoni, Orlinsky; from Edinburgh, with 'our unstinted admiration for your vast erudition'; from Noel Freedman, Professor Albright's Anchor Bible co-editor; from Wendell Phillips, in Honolulu to give a commencement speech. Mr. Phillips is the young admirer confined to Marine Hospital here with poliomyelitis, in 1946, whom Professor Albright used to visit. It was Mr. Phillips who raised the money for the 1950-1951 South Arabia expeditions that rounded out Professor Albright's field work. Mr. Phillips, now an oil industrialist, recalls these times in a preface to 'Near Eastern Studies in Honor of William Foxwell Albright.'

"One non-guest was a New York book editor who, not expecting to know people at a Baltimore party, that same hour took a northbound Metroliner—Sallie Waterman, with a finished book in *her* hands. Miss Waterman's book was *Matthew*, the galley proofs bearing final corrections by its translators and commentators, W. F. Albright and C. S. Mann. Come October, *Matthew* will be the seventeenth volume, and first synoptic Gospel, in the Doubleday project launched in 1956 as the first interfaith Bible, and the first modern revision in which full explanation accompanies every new wording. Overseeing the Anchor Bible has been the major preoccupation of Professor Albright's retirement years. Then in 1968 he decided to do *Matthew* himself, in tandem with Father Mann, who heads the Ecumenical Institute of Theology at St. Mary's Seminary on Roland avenue.

"All this from a man still vigorous—an aunt of his is alive at 102 —yet whose eyesight is so precarious that, allowed to read a few hours daily, he must sometimes rig up three magnifying glasses in series. W. F. Albright devotes no time and no energy to complaining. Mrs. Albright explains this resoluteness partly as lineage —the Pennsylvania German (Albrecht) father, a Protestant missionary in Catholic Chile, married to a Cornishwoman—'they're the really stubborn ones.' That leaves the amiability to account for, in a fresh-water Iowa college undergraduate and Johns Hopkins Ph.D. who, across decades of personal accomplishment and international turmoil, has been friends equally with Jews and with Arabs.

"The party over, life is now tranquil again in the Albright household: until August 31, when Mr. and Mrs. Albright will have been married an even and harmonious 50 years."

It was an outstanding journalistic tribute from one who had often written of Prof. Albright during the later years of his long career. Soon the Albright apartment would be upset—rugs taken up and sent out for cleaning, walls of dining room and living room painted, getting ready for the fiftieth wedding anniversary, which would never be celebrated.

23

Ebb Tide

The eightieth birthday party was a very gratifying occasion for Prof. and Mrs. Albright, even if it did turn out not to be a surprise. The guests who had come from far and near scattered, the sons and their families returned home, and the exhausted couple took to their beds for some days of extra rest. On June 1 Ruth Norton Albright turned seventy-nine.

On May 27 Stephen Mann wrote to Leona Running that it had been good to see her again, and "especially that you were able to attend the jamboree. When I look back on the travail of *Matthew,* I'm sure that only your own determination to mail the original ms. off finally broke the nexus! Otherwise, I'm sure that it would still be sitting on the desk of WFA somewhere..."

The front page of the April 1971 BASOR carried a photo of Nelson Glueck with dates, June 4, 1900—Feb. 12, 1971. Prof. Albright wrote the "In Memoriam" for his old student-colleague-friend; little did he know that by the time this issue reached subscribers he himself would be unconscious with eventually fatal strokes. (Leona's copy reached her July 12.) Among other things Albright said of Glueck: "Nelson Glueck was the first of my students to master the then obscure art of dating Palestinian pottery by use of its many typological differences as well as by careful analysis of changes of form in each type from first introduction to vestigial remains—which often last through several cultural phases.... While he learned the principles of archaeological stratigraphy it was as a typologist that he distinguished himself....

"Both of us, as well as other well-known scholars, have proved to be wrong in considering Tell el-Kheleife as essentially a series of

421

copper refineries inside a protective fortress wall. We were also wrong in dating the typical pottery of the refinery sites in the Wadi Arabah, between the Dead Sea and the northern end of the Gulf of Aqabah in the tenth century B.C. or even several centuries later. Actually, most of this pottery must be dated in the late 13th and 12th centuries B.C.; instead of being Solomonic or later Edomite it turns out to have been imitated largely from Egyptian models of the Ramesside period. It was thus characteristic of Midian as well as Edom . . . It was also contemporary with the Philistine ware of the 12th-11th centuries B.C. It must, however, be remembered that scarcely any of this material had previously been found outside of Edom, so intrinsic probability was almost our only guide. This is, however, an unsafe approach in an empirical science like archaeology!

"In my firm opinion Nelson Glueck's greatest single discovery bearing on biblical history was his identification of the period of the early Patriarchal narratives of Genesis featuring Abraham with M.B.I. (late 20th and 19th centuries B.C.). This he pointed out long before I reached the same conclusion in 1961 (*Bulletin* No. 163, pp. 36-54). During the past decade, new material supporting Glueck's discovery has been pouring in at such a rate that any contrary view becomes extremely difficult—if not impossible. [At about the time Albright was writing this, he wrote on April 5 to Dr. F. C. Fensham at Stellenbosch, South Africa, that his approach to Israel's early history had become more conservative, owing to the inundation of new data on early tribal traditions and direct support from material outside the Bible. Most of the new sources were still unpublished and he predicted some decades would pass before biblical scholars in general were persuaded that the new conservative approach was sound. He was amused to find warnings against his publications, some considering them too radical and others too fundamentalist!]

"Glueck's most important contribution to general history is almost certainly his work on the history of the Nabataeans and especially the economy and ecology of the most famous North-Arab nation of pre-Islamic times. . . ."

Prof. Albright mentioned as "the most important event of his life—marriage to Helen Ransohoff Iglauer on March 26, 1931. The summer before he had solemnly sworn at Tell Beit Mirsim to marry the first girl he met after returning to Cincinnati. The immediate reason for this oath was his fear of becoming as crusty a character as an old bachelor who was well known to both of us [undoubtedly Dr. Aage Schmidt]. Later he claimed that he had married the first girl to whom he telephoned after returning to Cincinnati. Helen Glueck herself is a most extraordinary person, . . . it is scarcely surprising that she and their only son, Dr. Charles Jonathan Glueck, are also outstanding physicians. . . .

"Nelson himself was always a person of singular charm and extraordinary integrity. He was an indefatigable worker and a man of rare vision. . . . He always cherished warm friendship toward the Arabs. Successive wars between Arabs and Jews hurt him deeply but as a patriotic American he remained politically neutral, though as a loyal Jew he sympathized deeply with the predicament in which Jewish refugees from all over the Old World found themselves after the Holocaust and during new persecutions throughout the Moslem world and in many Christian and pagan lands."[1]

William F. Albright's signature at the end of this eloquent tribute to his long-time friend and colleague was the last he would sign to any obituary, of which he had written so many during his own long career.

At the bottom of the front page of the October BASOR was a note headed "One generation passeth away . . ." which read: "With the death of Nelson Glueck still fresh in the minds of members of the American Schools, we are now saddened further by the passing, as this goes to press, of three great scholars: Albrecht Goetze, Roland de Vaux, and William F. Albright. . . ."[2]

In Dr. Albright's fiftieth annual appointment-schedule booklet there were no entries after the May 24 notation to hold that day free for the family, until June 3, when a trip to Philadelphia was scheduled. The next day the painters were to come to paint the dining room while the Albrights were away; they would continue traveling to New York and spend the weekend with Paul and his family. Then there were no more entries until June 23, when Harry Orlinsky was to come at 11:00 A.M. Monday, July 5, was noted as a holiday. On Tuesday the booklet showed an appointment Dr. Albright had made with Dr. Wolfe, his oculist. On Sunday July 11 a notation read that Dr. Ossman might come to the apartment and examine him in mid-afternoon. Then the booklet was blank until

Friday, November 5, when Albright had noted another check-up with Dr. Ossman at 9:00 A.M. and that he should eat nothing but unbuttered toast and tea beforehand.

However, the July 11 appointment with Dr. Ossman was already too late. On the ninth of July Mrs. Albright heard her husband call out and found him sitting in his bathroom, rigid, gripping the nearby bowl edge to keep from falling. He was taken to the hospital in an ambulance and put under intensive care for the cerebral stroke he had suffered. Word went out to family members and close friends by phone; Stephen Mann phoned Leona Running in Michigan soon after the weekend. For a couple of days there seemed to be some hope in the situation, but further strokes followed. A speech therapist tried to work with him; he was able to express—in many of the languages he could speak, all mixed up together—an incomprehensible mixture of words that no one could untangle to understand him. Apparently all incoming information was blocked. He could call and call for Ruth and apparently not know that she was right there, answering him and touching him. For a while his physical strength made it necessary to restrain him to keep him in bed and quiet. Then he became able to walk about the hospital, with help, but still was not in contact with anyone mentally.

Leona phoned Mrs. Albright daily as soon as she learned of the illness, but the situation continued the same. On August 18 Stephen Mann wrote to Leona, replying to her letter concerning the possibility of finding in Albright's study some articles that were almost ready to be sent to publishers: "There is no additional news of any more hopeful kind about Dr. Albright, who has now been moved to the Armacost Nursing Home and is still in a semi-conscious state. He is capable only of talking endlessly to himself in French and Hebrew, seems to be only vaguely aware of his surroundings, and his prognosis is not in the least bit hopeful so far as I can judge. Doctors are saying nothing, and Mrs. Albright is herself desperately tired. I would suppose that it is possible, sometime in the future, to go through some of Albright's material in order to discover what can—or cannot—be salvaged from the wreckage. . . . I think that I shall leave any such exploration or a rescue operation until sometime in September." (Noel and Leona would conduct the operation in his study in October on their way to learned societies' meetings in Atlanta, Noel publishing posthumously Albright's monograph on "Neglected Factors in the Greek Intellectual Revolution" and other materials.)

A year later Stephen Mann recorded with Leona Running his memories of and association with Prof. Albright. "I first came in touch with Prof. Albright in 1959 when he was in England for an Old Testament international conference, and in fact met him through his wife. I came to the United States in 1965 on an invitation from Prof. Albright which had been conducted by correspondence in 1963 and 1964. It wasn't clear to either of us at that time exactly what this would entail or involve, but Prof. Albright was at that time committed to publishing three or four volumes for McGraw-Hill, only one of which was published, his famous *confessio fidei* on Christian Humanism. Whatever his own thoughts may have been about areas of cooperation or ways in which I could assist him in his academic work in his retirement, they were all thrown overboard by the untimely death of Johannes Munck, author of *Acts of the Apostles* in the Anchor Bible series.

"Our work to salvage this volume was interesting in that it gave me some insight into Prof. Albright as he then was, and as indeed he later became. It was quite clear from the amount of unpublished material that he already had accumulated—mainly lecture series— that William Albright had been, was, and remained to the end a perfectionist. He obviously had a photographic memory, something very few other people possess, and could remember precisely where his footnotes were to be found, and his supporting evidence, and where to look in order to expand points which were outlined only roughly on pieces of scratch paper.

"I gained also an insight into Dr. Albright's religious development. At the time when I arrived and we began cooperating on Munck's *Acts* commentary, Albright was still worshiping regularly in the Methodist Church, at Wilson Memorial church not far from his apartment. I think that the alliance of political conservatism plus the strongly Puritan upbringing of his youth caused him to begin to look with very grave doubts, and in the end extreme disfavor, upon what was happening to American Methodism in the last ten years of his life. He found statements from the Methodist headquarters quite deeply disturbing. To him there were far too many obvious inputs of a biblical and historical liberalism from which he always deeply revolted. To find this at the very core of the confession in which he had been raised in the end caused him to talk quite seriously to me on several occasions about transferring his allegiance from Methodism elsewhere.

"On several occasions I talked with him about some questions which had been raised in his own mind about becoming a Roman Catholic. I told him, and indeed his son Hugh was of the same mind, that any such shift in confessional allegiance would almost certainly give an edge to his critics to say, in response, 'Well, we thought all the time that there was nothing very academically detached about Prof. Albright's biblical conservatism.' But a combination of political conservatism and a religious conservatism which found him more and more unhappy in Methodism wrought other quite subtle shifts in his thinking. There was never any question in Prof. Albright's mind about the historical veracity of the gospels in essence, nor was there ever any doubt, so far as I could discover, in Prof. Albright's mind about the unique relationship of Jesus to the Father, and certainly no question in his mind about the daily possibility of miracle and certainly no doubt about the resurrection of Jesus. There was, however, a very noticeable change in the last five or six years of his life, as I was associated with him; doubts arose in his mind about the response which Christian history had made to the person of Jesus, notably in creedal definitions such as those of Nicaea and Chalcedon. It was quite plain in the latter years of his life that he was growing closer and closer to Judaism, and on several occasions he confessed to me that he found himself far more happy with Jews than he did with his co-confessional Methodists. He had a consuming impatience with what has been called 'liberal Christianity' as eroding the Gospel. He was far too well educated to minimize the contribution which Hellenism had made to the Gospel, far too well educated to minimize the importance of Hellenism as it impinged upon the New Testament. But his own *credo* as it is contained in the chapters on historical approaches in *History, Archaeology and Christian Humanism* spells out, I think, very clearly indeed his own attitude towards what he saw as the anti-historical bias of scholars like Bultmann. I think that book came as close as anything will ever do to explaining Albright's interest in, concern for, devotion to and examination of New Testament documents. It was the result of a questing mind, a mind severely disciplined by historical inquiry, but Albright never had any doubt whatsoever that the all-pervasiveness of original sin had to be taken seriously as a contribution of Christian thinking to the human scene. It was no accident and certainly grew out of Albright's integrity as an individual that, for example, he would prefer Reinhold Niebuhr universes ahead of a modern scholar like Tillich. This impatience with liberal Christianity could occasionally lead him into seeking a uniqueness for the books of the Old Testament as historical documents which contemporary scholars regard with rather more caution. Nevertheless, it does have to be said that for all Albright's passionate attachment to Judaism as a vehicle of the revelation of God, he was far too detached and far too perceptive a scholar to allow any kind of attachment to cloud his judgment over historical sources.

"In my view," Dr. Mann continued, "it was no accident that some of Prof. Albright's most respected colleagues and friends on the Johns Hopkins campus were men of like mind with himself, inquiring, pragmatic, disciplined intellectuals, unswayed by the moods of the moment, and taking a calmly detached view of the human scene. One thinks, for example, of Albright's very deep respect for Prof. John Walton, head of the Department of Education at Johns Hopkins. At the same time Albright's friends on the Hopkins campus were drawn from a very wide circle of acquaintances and friends. There was never any precise line at which one could say, 'Oh, Prof. Albright would not be interested in that.' He was, perhaps, the last example we shall see in this century in the United States of a Renaissance man. He would have found himself completely and thoroughly at home with some of the founding fathers of this Republic.

"I had never supposed that Dr. Albright would ever contemplate, after the Munck volume, having any more to do on an extended scale with New Testament material. However, when a certain author withdrew from writing the Anchor Bible *Matthew* commentary, Albright suggested to me that we collaborate in taking his place and writing it. By this time Albright's formal attachment to Methodism in terms of regularly attending Sunday worship had ended. It was therefore interesting in doing this commentary to watch the detached scholar dealing with the plain meaning of Greek words, the plain meaning of the Christian Gospel as it was first proclaimed and first understood by an Evangelist, and perhaps the puzzle which is still left in my mind is how it was possible for anyone so deeply attached to the proclamation of Jesus in the pages of the New Testament to sever apparently so easily formal worshiping connections with the allegiance of his forebears. Perhaps the answer lies in the impatience of the scholar with the kind of thing which has been constantly fed to us in recent years from pulpits and the utterances of ecclesiastical ministries. Prof. Albright was at one time deeply interested in the emergence of what have been called 'underground churches,' or what are known as 'cell groups' or even 'house churches.' I do not feel that Prof. Albright would ever have been very happy in such circumstances; nevertheless, his own humility as a man, as a scholar, remained with him to the very end, whatever kind of impatience he may often have expressed about what he often described as 'intolerable nonsense.'

"Perhaps there is some significance attaching to the fact that the vast majority of Roman Catholic Biblical scholars of eminence in the United States have, in fact, been through Albright's hands. Several of them have achieved world-wide distinction. One thinks, for example, of Joseph Fitzmyer and Raymond E. Brown.

"Albright told me, 'This has always been one of the great sorrows of my life—my eyesight has always prevented me from looking into another man's eyes, because there I think I might have found answers on occasions, and there too I might have saved myself some considerable mistakes and embarrassments.' It is possible that Albright's lament about his eyes sprang from a realization that he was far too easily used by various people on various occasions. Probably his greatest scorn was reserved for those who have tried to ride the crest of total and immediate relevance.

"The process of collaboration in the actual process of producing *Matthew* was not quite as orderly as sometimes one could wish it to have been. We determined that the text of Matthew should be allowed to stand and to make its own explanations, whether those were religious, theological, sociological, etc. We therefore agreed to begin by translating the Greek and dealing with the problems of translation as they came along, to see what light possible difficulties of translation threw upon the whole scene of the first half-century of the Christian Era. The translation took a very considerable period of time, because it was while doing the translation that a great many historical and theological ideas were thrown to and fro between us, and it was not until the translation was almost halfway through that I began to discuss with Prof. Albright the way in which I thought the introductory material, as distinct from the commentary, should be approached. It was quite clear to both of us that Matthew's gospel would demand a whole section on the attitude of Jesus to the law. It was quite equally clear that any approach to Matthew's gospel was worthless unless it had something to say about the Synoptic Problem and the ways in which that problem has been dealt with by previous scholars. In the end, the Introduction was very largely my own work, written in rough draft and discussed exhaustively with Albright, often producing three, four, and five drafts of the material before both of us were satisfied with the final product. It was in many ways a difficult enterprise, because we had to start almost in a vacuum, with no particular guidelines from any other Synoptic material yet in the series; on the customary view Mark's gospel is the foundation of the Synoptic relationship, but both of us were convinced that the priority of Mark as what has been called 'an assured result of modern criticism' was vastly exaggerated and would not bear examination. Albright periodically would half-humorously say that we could sit down and write the reviews for the *Matthew* commentary! I certainly shared Dr. Albright's feeling that most of the reviews would be either extremely condescending or violently critical."

In fact, for example, the *Catholic Biblical Quarterly* a year after Albright's death published a critical review of this work by William G. Thompson, S.J., who concluded: "It is especially difficult to express my disappointment with this commentary on Mt when its senior author has been one of the great figures in American biblical scholarship. William Foxwell Albright has been and remains a giant in the fields of Palestinian archeology and Semitic languages . . . His work has covered such a broad terrain that the fields which have profited from his talent and erudition have now been divided and subdivided into several highly specialized disciplines. No one man can any longer control the vast amount of historical and linguistic materials which he has helped to uncover. He will not be remembered for this commentary on Mt. But I hope that his final contribution to the world of biblical scholarship will not tarnish the significant work he did."[3]

Dr. Mann continued, "Nevertheless we felt after three years or

more of constant discussion of the gospel itself, of its presupposi-
tions, of its theological emphases, that we were dealing with a tradition which stood alone, a tradition which was firmly based on oral
reminiscence, early hardened into fixed form, and bearing little, if
any, precisely determined relationship either with Luke or with
Mark. I think that Albright would have been more than a little
fascinated if he had lived long enough to have heard of the researches going on in Jerusalem between Robert Lindsay and David
Flusser, attempting to establish the priority of Luke! He approved
the efforts of scholars who believed that the old solutions to the
Synoptic Problem were altogether too simplistic—one thinks here,
for example, of W. R. Farmer, who had Albright's unmitigated
admiration.

"It will be interesting to see how far Albright's fear is well-
grounded that critics will regret that Albright did not, in the words
of the old proverb, 'stick to his last' and remain with Old Testament studies. More and more it was borne in upon us as we dealt
with the *Matthew* commentary that above everything else it was
necessary to take very seriously indeed two facets of the inquiry:
first of all, the social, historical, and political background of the
first century, insofar as that kind of background could be accurately
ascertained, and secondly, that we should take very seriously indeed
the now much better known disciplines of oral tradition, particularly as those disciplines are exemplified in the rabbinic literature.
The collaboration was, I think, for both of us a very invigorating
experience, even if at times it could be equally frustrating for both
of us. A remark of Albright's to his wife with respect to this collaboration left both his wife and me a little puzzled. When the
manuscript was nearly completed, Albright remarked to his wife
that he was very glad that this collaboration had taken place because 'It is quite clear that my theology is very much like that of
Stephen.' To this day I do not know what, precisely, that judgment
implied, but I do not think of any area in the whole of the *Matthew*
commentary where he and I had any serious disagreement in that
commentary and the Introduction as it now stands. To much of it
Albright brought his own particular and peculiar disciplines—his
passionate devotion to the elucidation of place names; his concern
for historical minutiae as those applied to personal names, and
those kinds of issues. It was inevitable that anyone who collaborated

with Albright would bow to his superior knowledge. I do not believe that there was any single theological issue in the *Matthew* commentary upon which Albright and I found ourselves in serious disagreement.

"Looking back on it, I very much doubt whether, the way things were going, the manuscript would *ever* have found its way to the printer in final form, had it not been for the intervention and determination of Dr. Leona Running. I have called attention to Albright's perfectionism, and this was only too manifest in the final stages of the preparation of *Matthew*. Dr. Running probably remembers far better than I how many times the manuscript had been typed and retyped. But *always* there was a suspicion in Albright's mind that by going through the manuscript once again with his failing eyesight he would be able to find something which had been overlooked in the whole process. Having gone through it once more and having been questioned closely by Dr. Albright as to whether we had or had not incorporated suggested changes, one afternoon when Prof. Albright had gone to take his rest, with Mrs. Albright's connivance and encouragement, we parceled the *Matthew* commentary and mailed it by insured mail to Doubleday. I am *wholly* certain that if this step had not been taken—a step, incidentally, which provoked a feeling of betrayal and shock—this manuscript would never have left the Albright apartment until the day Albright died! Even so, when the manuscript began to be returned in galley form, it took all the powers of persuasion on my part and on the part of other people for Prof. Albright to trust anyone else to look at the galley proofs. But mercifully, by this time, he had begun to realize that his eyesight had finally called a halt. Looking back, I think it is probably true that had he not had those final weeks of working with consuming anxiety over the exhausting minute detail of galleys, quite likely the stroke would not have happened.

"I think that the reception in Evergreen House was probably the highlight of his life, that in some very strange fashion this was a peak summit in Albright's life, and that he could now begin to say his *Nunc dimittis*. And the change between Albright as he was that afternoon and as he was later on at the dinner party was very marked indeed.

"I once or twice broached with Albright the possibility of picking up loose ends of things which he and I had started and put on

one side during the past six years. Albright was momentarily enthusiastic about taking up where we had left off, but then it was
quite obvious to me that he was not only very, very tired, but had
also lost track of the discussion. In that respect I am inclined to
wonder whether, before his fatal stroke and last illness, Albright
had not in fact had one or two minor strokes which had begun to
take their toll by cumulative effect."

Mrs. Albright indeed remarked that in those last few weeks after
the galleys had been sent off and the birthday celebration was over,
he would come out to the kitchen to tell her something and would
have to stop and grope for words. She said that was not habitual
with him as she claims it has always been for her.

Mrs. Albright and her sons told the doctors attending Prof.
Albright after his strokes that in view of their being absolutely certain that no restoration was possible, they were not to make heroic
efforts to maintain pulse and breathing in Albright's body from
which the wonderful mind, one of the finest of the twentieth century, had irrevocably departed. In September in the nursing home
pneumonia developed in his lungs. Another doctor was on duty for
the weekend, and made special inquiry as to bringing him back to
the hospital for intensive care. Mrs. Albright and David repeated
their instructions given to the chief physician. It must have been
from the depths of a bottomless pit of isolation that Dr. Albright's
cry, "Ruth! Ruth!" came, if he was conscious but unable to receive
any information during those long weeks from July 9 to September
19, unable to know that she was right there with him, hour after
hour, day after day. It was an equal agony and heartbreak for his
wife of half a century—the August 31 golden anniversary date
passed unheeded—to watch, helpless and unable to exchange any
word or information or make any plans or arrangements together
with him or get any counsel from him, as that marvelous mind
stopped functioning but the strong body fought so long to retain
the breath of life.

On a Sunday morning, September 19, the struggle ended, and
word went out by phone and telegram to those waiting to hear,
good or bad.

By Wednesday, September 22, friends and colleagues came
again from far and near, this time to pay their last tribute. Of the
plans, Stephen Mann recalled: "It was quite clear to Mrs. Albright

that, maintaining her own sense of humor as always, as she put it, 'William would revolve in his coffin if he thought that the funeral service was going to be held in Wilson Memorial Church.' This was obviously a sensitive issue, and when Albright became ill and was still at the hospital, unconscious so far as anyone knew, I suggested to Mrs. Albright that some arrangements be made to deal with possible contingencies. To begin with, I went with Mrs. Albright one morning to Union Memorial Hospital and said the prayers for the dying from the Episcopal Prayer Book (incidentally, to the great shock of a nurse who was in attendance with Prof. Albright). I then began to discuss with Mrs. Albright possible ways of dealing with the funeral, if indeed we had to face that contingency. I suggested to her that I could get in touch with my own bishop and ask if we could have an ecumenical funeral in the Episcopal Cathedral. I explained the circumstances of my request to the bishop, and he immediately agreed that this was the best thing we could possibly do—to have Albright buried from the Cathedral and involve two persons from Wesley Theological Seminary, one of whom had been a pupil of Albright's and a very dear friend, Dewey Beegle. Therefore, before Albright's death it was arranged that the funeral should take place in the Episcopal Cathedral of the Incarnation in Baltimore, that we should use the Revised Episcopal Funeral Rite with the lessons read by Dewey Beegle and James Logan, two Methodist ministers; that the homily should be preached by me as the one person last associated with him, and that the funeral service itself should be conducted by the Dean of the Cathedral, Dean Peabody. This was done, and the commendation of the body was made by Dr. Dewey Beegle; the interment prayers at the committal were read by me," Stephen Mann concluded.

Dr. Albright's sister Mary and her husband, Dr. William F. Stinespring, came from Durham, North Carolina; his sister Shirley and brother Finley came from the farm in Virginia. Leona Running drove again from Michigan; Nancy Renn Lapp came from Pittsburgh Seminary; Sallie Waterman made one more one-day trip by train from Doubleday in New York. Ernest Wright, Frank Cross and William Moran flew down from Harvard and Noel Freedman from Michigan University; Joseph Fitzmyer and many other former students and colleagues were there, including the faculty of Albright's old department, Dr. Milton Eisenhower, and many old colleagues from other Hopkins departments. Albright's grandson, David Jr., in cassock, carried the cross and led the procession of clergy and honorary pallbearers. The long casket was covered in purple with gold bands forming a cross.

Afterward Mrs. Albright served a buffet lunch in her apartment, with Jo's help, to those who had come from a distance. She remarked that William would hardly have *believed* it if he could have known the names of all who came to honor him for the last time; he would have been surprised and gratified. While it was not a large group in the beautiful church, it was a choice and concentrated gathering of outstanding intellects, she thought.

From all over the world, telegrams and letters poured in upon Mrs. Albright, from those who had been associated in some way with her husband and from those in high positions in church and state in many lands. A few days after his coffin had been lowered into the grave in Baltimore, a service of commemoration and eulogy was held in Jerusalem, attended by his host of friends in Israel who were unable to come to the Baltimore funeral. Uncounted columns in innumerable newspapers and journals told his life story and recounted his contributions to and influence upon biblical studies and other disciplines. Fortunately he had received equal honors and recognition in his lifetime, when he could appreciate them.

William Albright's was a lifelong pursuit of truth, as Ruth Albright put it—the truth about the background of the Bible. Because he was not working for his own honor but only to find the truth, and served only that one mistress, truth, he could afford to change his mind when more evidence came to light. With that singleminded devotion, and with a life companion who, while she could not have made him what he was, undoubtedly prevented him from failing to become the great scholar and famous authority that he could and should become, William Foxwell Albright was truly one of the greatest minds of the twentieth century.

Noel Freedman's "In Memoriam" for Prof. Albright in the February 1972 BASOR would occupy ten pages eloquently and close with: "It is very difficult for me, who studied and worked under him for the past twenty-five years, to believe that he is gone, that the voice of the thunderer has been stilled, that the infinitely creative mind will make no new discoveries, formulate no new hypotheses, construct no new syntheses. In spite of his long and active career and the profusion of his writings, he always seemed to be in mid-course, on the verge of a more definitive pronouncement, a more comprehensive summation of everything that had gone before. Nothing seemed beyond his grasp and capability, and it was only a matter of time before he fully expounded the truth for which we had been searching. We would wait with confidence for the leader to light the way and guide us to the goal. But now we see him no more and his mantle has fallen on the ground;" and Noel quoted II Kings 2:12 in Hebrew, "My father, my father! The chariots of Israel and its horsemen!"[4]

Notes

PREFACE

1. Leon Edel, *Henry James*, Vol. 3, *The Middle Years*, p. 275.
2. Ibid., p. 17.

CHAPTER SEVEN

1. BASOR 4, p. 4.
2. BASOR 4, pp. 4, 5.
3. BASOR 4, pp. 6, 7.
4. BASOR 4, p. 7.
5. BASOR 4, p. 12.
6. BASOR 4, p. 15.

CHAPTER EIGHT

1. BASOR 5, p. 22.
2. BASOR 5, p. 5.
3. BASOR 8, p. 16.
4. BASOR 12, p. 17.
5. BASOR 12, p. 14.
6. BASOR 10, pp. 2, 3.
7. BASOR 10, p. 3.
8. BASOR 10, p. 5.
9. BASOR 14, p. 3.
10. Melvin Grove Kyle, *Explorations at Sodom* (Revell, 1928), p. 47.
11. Ibid., p. 70.
12. BASOR 14, pp. 4-7.
13. BASOR 14, p. 10.
14. BASOR 14, p. 13.
15. BASOR 15, p. 5.
16. BASOR 17, p. 9.
17. BASOR 19, pp. 5, 19.
18. BASOR 21, p. 11.

CHAPTER NINE

1. BASOR 25, p. 15.

2. BASOR 25, p. 16.
3. BASOR 25, p. 17.
4. JAOS 47, p. 346.
5. BASOR 26, p. 11.

CHAPTER TEN

1. Melvin Grove Kyle, *Excavating Kirjath-Sepher's Ten Cities* (Eerdmans, 1934), p. 25.
2. BASOR 23, p. 3.
3. BASOR 23, p. 14.
4. BASOR 23, pp. 3-6.
5. BASOR 29, pp. 1, 2.
6. BASOR 29, pp. 3, 4.
7. BASOR 31, pp. 4, 5.
8. BASOR 31, p. 6.
9. BASOR 31, pp. 8, 9.
10. BASOR 31, pp. 10, 11.
11. BASOR 31, p. 11.
12. Kyle, *Excavating Kirjath-Sepher's Ten Cities*, p. 81.
13. BASOR 39, p. 3.
14. BASOR 39, p. 7.
15. BASOR 39, p. 10.
16. BASOR 47, pp. 6, 16, 17.
17. BASOR 51, pp. 5, 6, and 7.

CHAPTER ELEVEN

1. BASOR 30, p. 10.
2. BASOR 32, p. 8.
3. BASOR 35, p. 2.
4. BASOR 34, p. 9.
5. BASOR 35, p. 14.
6. BASOR 36, p. 8.
7. BASOR 36, p. 15.
8. BASOR 38, p. 21.
9. BASOR 41, p. 31.

10. BASOR 43, pp. 3, 4.
11. BASOR 43, pp. 9, 10, 12.
12. BASOR 43, p. 31.
13. BASOR 45, pp. 34, 35.
14. BASOR 46, pp. 19, 20.
15. *The Archaeology of Palestine and the Bible*, pp. 7, 8.
16. *Journal of Biblical Literature* 51, p. 382.
17. BASOR 49, p. 25.
18. BASOR 55, p. 24.
19. BASOR 56, pp. 3, 11.
20. BASOR 57, p. 30.
21. BASOR 57, p. 31.
22. BASOR 60, p. 9.
23. BASOR 60, p. 16.
24. BASOR 61, p. 20.
25. BASOR 60, p. 25.

CHAPTER TWELVE

1. BASOR 63, p. 12.
2. BASOR 62, p. 26.

CHAPTER THIRTEEN

1. BASOR 66, p. 36.
2. BASOR 69, p. 30.
3. BASOR 79, p. 37.
4. *Journal of Biblical Literature,* 60, pp. 187-189.
5. *Journal of Cuneiform Studies* 2 (1957), p. 427.
6. *Studies in the History of Culture* (Menasha, Wisconsin, the George Banta Publishing Company, 1942), p. 50.
7. *The Biblical Period from Abraham to Ezra*, p. vii.
8. *History, Archaeology and Christian Humanism*, pp. 200-204.
9. *Ibid.,* p. 316.

CHAPTER FOURTEEN

1. *Near Eastern Studies in Honor of William Foxwell Albright*, ed. Hans Goedicke (The Johns Hopkins Press), p. xix.
2. BASOR 109, pp. 5, 6, 9, 10.
3. BASOR 109, pp. 11, 13.
4. BASOR 109, pp. 13-15.
5. BASOR 109, pp. 16-18.

6. BASOR 109, p. 20.
7. *Qataban and Sheba* (Harcourt, Brace and Company, 1955), pp. 22, 28.
8. *Ibid.,* pp. 29, 43, 48.
9. *Ibid.,* p. 72.
10. *Ibid.,* p. 120.
11. BASOR 123, p. 8.

CHAPTER FIFTEEN

1. BASOR 110, pp. 2, 3.
2. BASOR 115, pp. 13, 14.
3. BASOR 115, p. 15.

CHAPTER SIXTEEN

1. BASOR 143, p. 2.

CHAPTER EIGHTEEN

1. JBL 59 (1940), pp. 96-98.
2. *Ibid.,* pp. 98-99.

CHAPTER NINETEEN

1. BASOR 156, p. 41.
2. BASOR 155, p. 35.
3. BASOR 163, p. 5.
4. BASOR 162, pp. 1, 2.
5. BASOR 162, p. 2.
6. BASOR 163, pp. 40, 43-48, 52-54.

CHAPTER TWENTY

1. BASOR 181, p. 4.
2. BASOR 188, p. 7.
3. BASOR 192, p. 2.

CHAPTER TWENTY-TWO

1. BASOR 199, p. 2.
2. BASOR 200, pp. 3-6.
3. BASOR 200, pp. 6, 7.
4. BASOR 200, pp. 7-11.

CHAPTER TWENTY-THREE

1. BASOR 202, pp. 3-5.
2. BASOR 203, p. 1.
3. *Catholic Biblical Quarterly* 34 (1972), 485.
4. BASOR 205, pp. 12, 13.

Index